THIS BOOK IS PRESENTED
TO RHODES HOUSE LIBRARY
BY

The Publ. libr. of S. Australia.

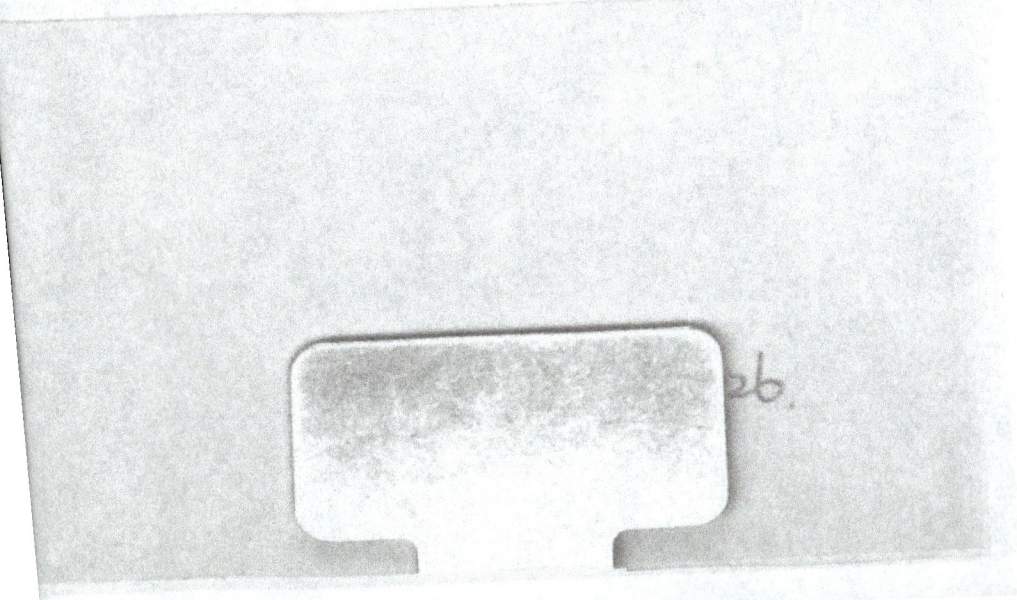

History of the First Bushmen's Club in the Australian Colonies, Established at Adelaide, South Australia
by William Marks Hugo

Copyright © 2019 by HardPress

Address:
HardPress
8345 NW 66TH ST #2561
MIAMI FL 33166-2626
USA
Email: info@hardpress.net

HISTORY

OF THE

FIRST BUSHMEN'S CLUB

IN THE

AUSTRALIAN COLONIES,

ESTABLISHED AT

ADELAIDE, SOUTH AUSTRALIA.

COMPILED FROM VARIOUS SOURCES, AND FURNISHING IN DETAIL ITS ORIGIN
AND PROGRESS UP TO THE PRESENT YEAR, 1872; ALSO
MISCELLANEOUS READINGS, LETTERS, ETC.

WITH A

PREFACE BY THE COMPILER.

The whole of the Profits by the Sale of this Work will be devoted to the interests of the Club.

ADELAIDE:
PUBLISHED BY SUPERINTENDENT OF CLUB,
AND SOLD BY BOOKSELLERS.

1872.

WILLIAM KYFFIN THOMAS, PRINTER,
GRENFELL-STREET, ADELAIDE.

PREFACE.

DEAR FRIEND—You have in your hand "The History of the Bushmen's Club of South Australia;" a book intended to do good, compiled by an humble man, of very humble pretensions, in a very plain style, so that it may be understood by all.

The subject discussed has now become familiar to most persons in South Australia; still it is not so well understood as it ought to be, and this book is published in the hope that the facts it contains may be generally instructive and interesting.

Many erroneous impressions are prevalent with regard to the Club, which have hitherto deterred many bushmen from joining it; but a desire is now apparent in this colony and elsewhere for a more accurate acquaintance with its general characteristics than a few scattered letters and newspaper articles are able to furnish. A perusal of this volume may possibly meet this reasonable wish, and will satisfy all of the importance of the movement on the Bushmen's behalf.

The reader is requested to view this institution as what it will be (D.V.) rather than what it now is, and to treat its importance rather as regards its prospect in the future than as a fact of the present.

Much of the subject-matter was published in the newspapers, but as it appeared at different times it would involve much labour to hunt it up; and then very few persons get their papers bound or even filed : in this volume they are collected together and put in a permanent form for preservation.

Great pains have been taken to render its contents accurate and interesting. The newspaper reports, the general, annual, and monthly reports, extracts from correspondence, and other documents, have been examined and copied with great care: the design being principally to trace the progress and remarkable prosperity of the Club, and to give exact information upon points likely to interest colonists generally. It will be found to contain simple and valuable information about the actual operations of the promoters and Committee, and will be interesting to all classes of the community, but especially to the bushmen of Australasia and their best friends.

It is not too much to say that a large circulation is anticipated (to which end the first edition is published at an unusually low rate), especially as the profits arising from the sale of the work are to be devoted to the extension of the Club and its objects; and in this simple way a number of adherents and fellow-helpers may be raised.

The compiler's principal task has consisted in selecting and arranging the materials, letters, newspaper articles, extracts from correspondence, &c., &c., liberally placed at his disposal by friends who are for the most part personally acquainted with the contents of them, and but for whose assistance the work could not have been compiled.

In a few more years the information which has thus been secured and is here placed on record would probably (in the ordinary course of things) pass into oblivion. As it is, the compiler feels that there are many gaps yet to be filled up; but the field of history is a wide one, and is open to all who will labour in it.

The amount of time employed and the pains taken to

render this work worthy of the approbation of the bush people and their friends it is perhaps prudent to conceal, until it is known whether that approbation will ever be bestowed upon it.

The reader will find some subjects treated of in this work about which there has been much controversy in the Bush; but nothing has been introduced that is not most conscientiously believed to be true, nor has anything been omitted that is believed to be true for the purpose of adding popularity to the work. If the reader finds sentiments here that are new to him or that are contrary to his former views on this subject, he should weigh them well before he either receives or rejects them.

The compiler writes from long and familiar acquaintance with the bush and bushmen and the different phases of bush life, having visited nearly all the colonies and enjoyed special advantages for arriving at a just estimate of it. He does not, however, pretend to infallibility, though he claims to have spared no pains in his investigation of facts, and to have aimed at impartiality in his judgment.

There is a heroism of skill and toil belonging to bushmen worthy of a grateful record. Their lot in life is indeed often a dull and solitary one, and it is doing a public service to endeavour to cheer it by a record of their struggles and triumphs in the cause of human advancement. The compiler has learnt much from others, and feels grateful for many important thoughts and suggestions herein; yet he has done his work as the *Lord's freeman;* hence no one is accountable for the thoughts and principles set forth in the following pages but himself. Being confined by his duties to the Club in Adelaide, and still feeling anxious to labour as far as he can in the cause of Christ and humanity, he resolved to prepare and publish this volume, desiring it to supply in part the place of his personal appearance; believing that if any person is benefited by hearing a discourse on any topic he may also be benefited by reading the same, and if one person be thus benefited others may be. His object is to do good (the Lord knows his heart) to the full extent of his power; he has spent the best days of his life in the service of his Lord and Master and the bushmen; and although he has been a very weak instrument he has some reason to believe that his labours have not been in vain in the Lord. He loves the cause of Christ as truly and sincerely as ever he did, and feels as deeply concerned for the elevation of man, peace, harmony, and purity as ever he did; he is as willing to labour for his Divine Master as ever he was; but time is short, our days are swiftly passing away, his time of active service in the cause of Christ will soon close, and he wishes therefore to leave this record in a permanent form. While expressing gratitude that he is permitted to tell the history of the first Bushmen's Club in Australia, he humbly, thankfully, and joyfully attributes all ability therein to the Divine Author of all things. May He be pleased to extend still further the usefulness of this labour of love on behalf of the bushmen, and to Him alone be all the glory!

It remains for the compiler to acknowledge his many obligations to beloved friends, whose advice and instructions he counts among not the least of the blessings his God in wisdom and goodness has given him. He therefore embraces this public opportunity afforded him of paying a lasting tribute of thanks to all those who were mainly instrumental in establishing the Bushmen's Club. Among them he is happy to rank one, the soundness of whose judgment and the disinterestedness of whose motives, as well as zeal to do good among men throughout a long and useful life, have not failed in his declining days to secure the highest veneration and respect of men of almost every shade of thought and opinion in this colony. The gentleman alluded to is the venerable, faithful, Christian philanthropist, George Fife Angas, Esq., who from nearly the commencement of the labours of the compiler in the cause of Christ in this colony, has to this day, directly and indirectly, taken him by the hand as a Christian, manifesting the most generous confidence; and (under God) has benevolently supported the cause of the Great Master through him (the compiler). The name of that gentleman will descend to the remotest posterity as that of a promoter of any really good thing—who has been the untiring advocate of measures in the world calculated to promote social, moral, and religious advancement. To Mr. Angas the compiler owes no small portion of that consolation which for many years formed his support in his trying and (humanly speaking) hazardous missionary journeys in the wilderness of Australia. Had it not been for the disinterested countenance thus afforded him for Christ's sake by men above reproach the work must have sunk prematurely.

To another friend, J. H. Angas, Esq., son of the gentleman alluded to above, the compiler is also equally indebted, not only for some of the original documents respecting the formation of the Club, but for kind Christian courtesy, countenance, and support when needed in his labours. He feels in his conscience that any thanks emanating from him cannot repay these gentlemen for their kindness to the bushmen as a class, as well as to himself as an individual.

To His Excellency the Governor* and the late Lady Edith Fergusson, and the gentlemen forming the preliminary Committee, its Secretary, and its Treasurer; to the Trustees—Messrs. J. H. Angas, D. Murray, W. K. Thomas; and Board of Management—Messrs. C. B. Young, Neville Blyth, and H. Giles—as well as others high in authority and public estimation, he has also been indebted. They will, he trusts, never escape his memory or his gratitude; the approval of a good conscience will he feels sure be a sufficient reward for them.

---

* Sir James Fergusson.

Last, but not least, to the Press of South Australia he is very much indebted for the success of the movement so far; especially to the Editors of the *Register* and *Advertiser*. He is glad to be their debtor, for he feels that wherever it can be shown that we are not altogether original, so much the better : our desire should be to enter the circle of the great dependence of all things on God.

In a succeeding portion of the work (should his God spare him to see its completion), the compiler trusts to render additional service to his adopted country by an attempt to deduce from past experience of bush life the best means of educating the children of shepherds, bushmen, &c., and also the best means of improving the social and moral condition of the Australian bush people generally. Should even the attempt to do this be the means of awakening public attention on those two very important points, affecting as it does the best interests of the colony, he will feel well rewarded for all his labours. The gratification will (D.V.) then be his, when he lies down to die, of having left no unworthy legacy to the bushmen of Australia.

And now, O Lord, to Thee is this work commended. It is nothing with Thee to help with few or many. Man's feebleness cannot hinder if Thou wilt work. Work Thou, O Lord, to Thine own Glory.

Adelaide, 1872.

HISTORY

OF

THE BUSHMEN'S CLUB.

In the month of June, 1866, the Bush Missionary "William" wrote a note to a friend of his (Mr. G. S. Allsebrook, of Willowie Station, belonging to J. H. Angas, Esq., and situated near Mount Remarkable, South Australia), representing to him the desirability of establishing an institution of a social nature as a home for bushmen, somewhat after the pattern of the Seamen's Homes, and requesting his sympathy and help. Mr. Allsebrook rather discountenanced the proposition, considering it at that time impracticable. "William," however, continuing his Evangelical labours throughout the bush, still collected more information on the subject, until about the middle of June, 1868, when a combination of circumstances brought the matter to an issue in the following manner :—" William" was resting for a short time at Willowie, as was usual for him to do occasionally in his peregrinations, through the kindness of Mr. Angas. That gentleman happened to be staying there also with his family for the winter. "William" felt driven by his conscience to make another effort on behalf of his long-cherished scheme, and made personal application to Mr. Angas for advice in the matter and support for the movement, stating that a number of bushmen were in favour of it, and would subscribe towards the same providing a responsible person was appointed to receive the money. Mr.

Angas at once entered heartily into the matter, and the first practical step was taken. He presented a book to "William" to get the signatures of all bushmen in favour of the home throughout his journeys in the Gawler Ranges, Port Lincoln, and Fowler's Bay districts, on the first page of which was written the following address :—"It has been suggested that the establishment of a Bushman's Home at the Burra or some suitable locality (on the same principles as a first-class Sailors' Home), together with a savings bank and labour office, would be of great benefit to the labouring classes of this colony. The object of the present application is to ascertain the views of all parties interested in such an undertaking, who are requested to enter their names in this book, with any suggestions they may think proper to make, so that, should the general feeling be favourable, measures may be taken for founding the institution; no subscriptions to be collected for this purpose on any pretence whatever until the affair is properly organized and made public and duly authorized agents appointed. Persons desirous of making further communications on this subject are requested to address to 'William,' Post-Office, Angaston. *Note*—The column for 'Remarks' to include opinions as to the locality suitable for the home, its desirability or necessity, amount of annual subscriptions to constitute membership, and other suggestions." Almost simultaneously with the latter movement the following article appeared in the *Advertiser* bearing upon the manner in which bushmen were treated in the city by loose characters :—

"BUSHMEN IN TOWN.

"A correspondent informs us that in going along King William-street a few days ago he accidentally heard one of the fallen sisterhood address her female companion thus—'I must try to get hold of a bushman, and clean him out.' Of course, this was a confidential communication—a revelation of private plans and purposes intended for the ears of a bosom friend, and not for the public. It indicated an industrial scheme not very original in its conception, but intended to be profitable in its results. Our correspondent thinks something should be done by the authorities to protect as far as possible those silly fellows who are preyed upon, maltreated, and robbed when they visit town by conscienceless harpies who lie in wait to 'clean them out;' and he calls upon the Press to direct public attention to the question.

"Now, we need hardly say the subject is one which it is not easy to deal with; and the evil is one which it is not easy to remove. No newspaper pretending to respectability could discuss the subject in *all* its bearings without calling forth a howl of indignation from a large portion of its readers. By tacit consent society has agreed to taboo any except the most indirect reference to an evil which is eating into its heart like a cancer and polluting the streams of healthy existence; and, perhaps, from one point of view society is right. Pitch cannot be touched, however gingerly, without defilement. The open discussion of some questions of social economy would do more harm than good; but, in the case to which our correspondent refers, there is a systematic course of action suggested with which both the Press and the authorities can deal without offending the nice proprieties of the most fastidious. Here it is clearly indicated that there is a class of our population who deliberately lay schemes to rob the unwary and simple. The thing looks almost like a business. Just as a young man might say 'I will look out for a Government billet which will provide for me for life,' the person to whom our correspondent refers said 'I must try to get hold of a bushman and clean him out.'

"Unhappily, we all know how this is done. The records of our Police Courts afford too many illustrations of the easy process of 'cleaning out a bushman.' A man goes shepherding in the bush for a few years, living a hard and solitary life, seeing but few of his fellow-creatures, and in many cases deteriorating morally and intellectually—not necessarily, we are glad to say.

"There are some shepherds who, by books and the study of nature, manage to keep their minds in a healthy and living state; but a large proportion of shepherds in the far bush get degraded and brutish by their solitary life. Having no mental resources of their own, they sink lower and lower until they live only an animal life. Now the great ambition and desire of these men's lives is to 'pile up' a cheque for wages which they may have the pleasure of 'knocking down' in a few days of drunken dissipation and debauchery.

"We have been told by squatters that there are men who will live month after month on their stations as shepherds, spending nothing but what is absolutely necessary, in order that they may have the satisfaction of knowing that their wages are accumulating to a given amount which will enable them to purchase a 'glorious spree,' as they call it, and to spend their all in a few days in those fancied delights which their imaginations have pictured. When these men have saved eighty or a hundred pounds they start for town, bent on stupid, drunken indulgence. The first thing done is to get drunk, and then they become the prey of those harpies who prowl about the streets 'like roaring lions seeking whom they may devour.' In a week or two they have 'knocked down' their cheque; they have been plundered on all sides and at all hands. Publicans of low character have got their share, 'ladies' like the one to whom our correspondent refers take them under their gentle shepherding, bullies and loafers get them to 'shout,' and very soon the money is gone, and the poor stupid creatures, weakened by dissipation, on the verge of incipient *delirium tremens* by excess, are cast out and left to find their way as best they can to the bush again.

"Now, the question which arises in view of this state of things which is going on under our eyes is, can the authorities do nothing to prevent it? Of course, if a man is coarsely robbed, and can identify the robber, the police will hunt him or her up and bring the guilty person before the Magistrate; but can nothing be done in the way of prevention? A bushman 'on the loose' is as easily recognized as a sailor ashore; and in every instance where he is attended by suspicious-looking harpies of either sex the police ought to keep an eye upon him and warn him of the dangers to which he is exposed. A hint to the harpy, too, might not be amiss. Some time ago a suggestion was thrown out for the establishment of a Bushmen's Home something on the principle of a Sailors' Home, where men from the country could be received into comfortable lodgings and respectably boarded on moderate terms, where their hard earnings might be taken care of, and their material and moral interests watched over. Such an institution might be made of very great use to the more respectable class of bushmen by preserving them from temptation and guarding them against robbery. It would, of course, miss its aim with a certain section of them, who would neither submit to the restraints nor be satisfied with the quiet comforts of a respectable institution—who come to town purposely for dissipation, and cannot rest content while a shilling remains in their pockets. Such men must go to the bad, and it would appear as if nothing could save them.

"Still, for a large class of men now living on stations, an institution of this kind would be of great service. Perhaps, when pastoral matters begin to look up again, our wealthy squatters will turn their attention to the question of a Bushmen's Home."—July 29, 1868.

"William" desires to give publicity to this part of the proceedings to put the origin of the Club beyond dispute. He feels that he has no right to absorb all credit of the undertaking, and desires to give honour to whom it is due, believing this explanation will supply the missing link (about which there has been some little controversy among bushmen) in the history of the Bushmen's Club. Having now discharged his conscience in this matter, the rest of the proceedings for establishing the Club will be introduced in their regular order as far as practicable.

It may not be out of place to mention here that "William" returned to Collingrove from a six months' journey through the western parts of the colony, bearing with him the signatures of 174 proprietors and managers of stations and 651 bushmen who heartily approved of the movement. On the strength of this Mr. Angas gave him letters of introduction to several leading gentlemen in the city, and furnished him with the names of others, who were considered favourable to the bushmen, and it was thought prudent to enlist the services of Mr. H. Hussey in the matter. The first resolve was to get up a preliminary meeting, and to do this the following advertisement was published in the *Advertiser* and *Register* of the 23rd December, 1868 :—" BUSHMEN'S HOME.—A preliminary meeting of persons interested in the erection of a Home for Bushmen will be held (D.V.) at White's Arbitration Room, King William-street, on Wednesday, December 30th, at half-past 2 p.m., to adopt measures for the attainment of that object." Immediately after this advertisement the following leading articles appeared in the daily papers:—

[From the *Advertiser* of December 25, 1868.]

"Some few months ago we called public attention to the importance of establishing a Bushmen's Home, in order to keep poor fellows who come down from the country out of the hands of harpies who prey upon them on their occasional visits to Adelaide. We are glad to find that a movement is about to be made to carry out this desirable object. An advertisement in our business columns announces a preliminary meeting to be held on the 30th instant with a view to the establishment of a Home. We believe the matter is in good hands, several gentlemen personally interested in the northern sheep-runs having taken it up. We understand that a somewhat extensive scheme will be suggested, which will include important provisions both for bushmen and their families. The idea is to have a Home in one of the northern townships large enough to accommodate some 200 or 250 men and a certain proportion of married women. Such a home would form a rendezvous for unemployed bushmen, and a place to which they could always resort with the certainty of finding comfortable board and lodging on reasonable terms, where they would be out of the way of those who at the present time so often rob them of their property and then cast them out of doors, and where their money could be taken care of for them. It would be an easy matter to have a branch savings bank connected with the institution for this purpose. A friendly society might also be established for the assistance of the afflicted. It is also suggested to have a boarding school for the children of shepherds living in the bush, where on reasonable terms they would have the comforts of an ordinary home with the advantages of an elementary education. We are not sure whether such a branch of the establishment is feasible. We are afraid that the limited means of shepherds would prevent their paying for their children's board and education, however much the charges might be cut down; still, if by outside assistance this could be accomplished, it would be a great advantage. We are afraid, from what we hear, that many of the children in the far bush are growing up little better than heathens, and for them such an institution as is proposed would be an incalculable blessing. Then we believe it is proposed to have a coffee-room, with library and news-room, in connection with the Home. It must be admitted that the scheme is an ambitious one, and will probably require years before it could be carried out in all its parts; but something would be gained if a beginning were made, and we trust the meeting to be held on Wednesday will at least lead to this result."

[From the *Register* of December 26, 1868.]

"From the very infancy of squatting there have been apprehensions entertained by the thoughtful as to its moral effects on labour. It places men (masters as well as servants) at a very great social disadvantage, and demands of them sacrifices which human nature cannot undergo with impunity. The similar experience of sailors had established this fact long before bushmen were recognized as a special class. Their few months' isolation on board ship exhibited a demoralizing effect upon them which few could resist. Their absolute withdrawal from social enjoyments excited their passions, weakened their self-command, and at the end of a voyage returned them to society in a half-brute, half-childish state. They became the easiest victims of temptation, and the most unmanageable offenders against the public peace. Jack was always popular with landsmen, but rather as an inferior animal than as a fellow-citizen. Sailors' Homes presented themselves, not as a merely philanthropic idea, but as a moral and economical necessity. Their success has been an incalculable benefit both to Jack himself and to his employers; he has become a new man through their influence, and he can now maintain on shore the high character he has long possessed at sea. The tone of the English mercantile marine has been refined and elevated through these simple institutions—Sailors' Homes. The bushman's case is exactly analogous to the sailor's, and if there be any difference it is stronger. The longest sea voyage now-a-days does not exceed six months, and very few sailors indeed are not able to spend some part of every year ashore; but men sometimes live in the bush for years together, and their longest spell only allows them time to rush down to Adelaide and squander their accumulated savings in a few weeks' debauchery. Bush life is also more lonely than life at sea, and has more numerous disadvantages. Bush society (where there is any at all) is very scanty, very widely scattered, and its intercourse very limited; the routine altogether more monotonous than that of the forecastle—the breaks in it are fewer, and the opportunities of utilizing them are more difficult. The sailor is discharged at a port teeming with life and bustle—the bushman at his station, which may be hundreds of miles away from any settled district. We, living in the gay cities which adorn this pleasant fertile seaboard of Australia, cannot possibly realize the dull existence which thousands of our fellow-countrymen are dragging on in the interior. Surrounded as we are with every form of civilization, we cannot conceive the semi-heathenism, or the dismal, often maddening solitude that prevails in the bush. The more the white race spreads and the further its offshoots are separated from the main body, the lower it must sink toward the level of the inferior race which it has supplanted. The only civilizing influence that can be exercised on white men in the bush is their connection with centres of population along the coast. Where that is weak, as in the remote districts of Riverina, not only the ties of civilization, but the higher ties of morality and religion, are invariably relaxed. Crime assumes a savage, brutal type, as in bushranging. The process of degradation is very manifest in the older settlements; its results render it undeniable. Time after time we have warned the squatters of the demoralizing tendency of bush life, and of the still worse reaction which drives the bushman back into town bent on debauchery. Frequently we have alluded to his humiliating appearances in the Police Court, fleeced, fooled, penniless, and friendless. The occasional contact with civilization which ought to refine him is perverted into the means of his ruin. 'Great fool, not able to take care of himself,' is the self-complaisant reflection of those who know neither his temptations nor his weaknesses. Society has rendered it practically impossible for him to take care of himself. Thirty years' experience in our colony, and eighty years' experience in New South Wales, have proved that he cannot take care of himself. He must be helped and encouraged, as the sailor was in a former generation. His employers must take him by the hand, as the English shipowners set them an example many years ago. The Press may advise and counsel, but theory is fruitless until it can be brought under practical influence. This, which has been so long wanting in any movement on behalf of bushmen, appears to be at last attained. The squatters themselves have begun to stir in the matter. A well-devised and comprehensive scheme has been submitted to them individually, and it is about to be considered by them in a collective form. A meeting is advertised to be held on Wednesday next (30th inst.), at which we believe full particulars will come before the public. A prospectus has been prepared, the leading principles of which have received the approval of many hundreds of persons in the squatting districts—not only employers, but bushmen of all grades and classes. Numerous promises of subscriptions have been obtained, and the general desire to see such a useful object realized has been so strong that success is almost a positive certainty. The originators of the scheme (Mr. G. F. Angas and others) are sufficient guarantee for the sagacity and prudence of its execution. They are not men who will ask others to help without doing their own share; nor will their example in such a work be without stimulating effect. The scheme has also other zealous promoters in a humble sphere. The well-known bush missionary 'William' has during the past year been advocating it from station to station through the Far North and Port Lincoln districts; he has explained it to the various settlers and their employès, consulted them about the most convenient site, and obtained from them a long array of signatures in its favour. Some, not satisfied with verbal approval, have entered themselves as subscribers in anticipation. The attitude of the pastoral community in general is exceedingly favourable; and nothing remains to be done but to secure a good central direction and to test the liberality of the public. A detailed description of the scheme ought to come from its authors rather than from us, but its main features may be indicated without forestalling any of the proper business of Wednesday's meeting. The institution will be made a home in the fullest sense of the word, with every attainable requisite for enjoyment as well as for business. Attached to the boarding-house there will be a coffee-room and library. The commercial department will consist of a labour office, and possibly also a savings bank. The men will be encouraged to form a friendly society for themselves, and no doubt some of the existing orders will be very willing to relieve the management of any trouble on that score. There will further be kept in view as an ultimate object the establishment of a cheap boarding-school for bush children. Putting all these together, they form a total which may probably deserve the character which has been applied to it of being ambitious. It should be remembered, however, that the institution is intended to be progressive. Its promoters will have sufficient common sense to restrain them from attempting to realize their ideal all at once. A sufficient beginning may be made with a boarding-house and a labour office; then, as the self-supporting principle is carried out, the more applicants who present themselves the faster will be the growth of the institution. It is reckoned that accommodation will ultimately be required for two or three hundred single men and a dozen or so of married couples. The masters will have an apartment to themselves, suitably fitted up, and conducted on the model of a club. The first point likely to cause any difference of opinion is the site, there being two rival claimants—the Burra and Port Augusta. Practically, that is a much less important question than it seems; for, whichever town has the honour of possessing the first Bushmen's Home should it prove successful, the other will very soon after obtain one of its own. We hope, as a result of this movement, soon to see comfortable bush hotels both at Port Augusta and the Burra; there would then be fewer bushmen to be seen rampant among the drunken orgies of the back slums of Adelaide or penitent in the stern presence of Mr. Beddome."

The before-mentioned advertisement having appeared in the daily papers, and slips of same having been sent to several gentlemen in the colony, a preliminary meeting was held on Wednesday, December 30, 1868, in White's Arbitration Room, of which the subjoined is a full report, copied from the *South Australian Register* of the 31st December, 1868:—

"A preliminary meeting of persons interested in the establishment of a home for bushmen was held on Wednesday afternoon, December 30. There were present the Hon. T. Elder (in the chair), the Hon. W. Morgan, the Revs. G. Stonehouse, S. Mead, and J. C. Woods, and Messrs. J. H. Angas, H. Scott, F. W. Stokes, H. Giles, M. Goode, W. K. Thomas, C. Sabine, W. A. E. West, H. Hussey, and several others. The Chairman remarked that the object of the present meeting was to consider whether something could not be done to ameliorate the condition of the pastoral population, and to endeavour to initiate an arrangement of a domestic nature for their social comfort and improvement. The idea suggested was to establish a Bushmen's Home in one of the northern townships, where comfortable board and lodging could be obtained on reasonable terms, and where the inmates would be removed from the snares and temptations which beset them on coming into town. The object was a praiseworthy one, for the evils which the proposed undertaking was intended to cure were patent to every one who gave the subject the slightest reflection. It was not in the power of the employers alone to carry out this desirable improvement; they must be supported by the men themselves, and assisted and encouraged by the public at large, otherwise their scheme would not succeed. Individual exertions could be of little avail in such a case, but an earnest and combined effort would in all probability result in a real and permanent advantage to all. The working men engaged in their pastoral districts might be divided into three classes. First, those who worked regularly and laid up their savings remaining frequently for years in one employ, or removing to a neighbouring station for the sake of a change. These, he was sorry to say, were comparatively few in number. Second, the men who, forming a large majority of the whole, worked regularly for a time, but as regularly left the station to spend their earnings in a few days' 'spree,' and then returned to their work. It was for the benefit of this class more particularly that the Bushmen's Home was designed. The third denomination were the loafers—a set of lazy, useless vagabonds, who prowled about the country like wolves in sheep's clothing, and were a positive nuisance instead of being any benefit to the settlers. He feared a Bushmen's Home would be of little service to them. The men belonging to the second class, as a general rule, drew the whole of their wages once or twice a year, left the station, went to some public-house, drank till their money was all gone, and then returned or else travelled in search of new employment. It might be said in palliation that much of the drinking habits of these men might be attributed to the solitary existence they lead for months together, visited by no one for weeks at a time, and also to the fact that living upon meat and damper without vegetables created an ungovernable craving for stimulants which rendered them an easy prey to artful and designing knaves. When they went to a public-house in this state of mind and body, it was no wonder that they should give way to drink, foolishly spending their money and recklessly injuring their constitutions in riot and debauchery. It was, as he said, to rescue these unfortunate persons from such contaminating influences, which led to misery and degradation, that the present movement had been set on foot; and he knew of nothing that would contribute more to this desirable consummation than the establishment of a well-conducted Bushmen's Home, where cheerful society, respectability, and all the advantages of social and domestic life could be secured. He might here mention, as a melancholy proof of the necessity that existed for such an institution, that one of their leading medical gentlemen told him not long ago that the Lunatic Asylum was largely supplied from their northern sheep stations; and really it was not to be wondered at if the poor shepherds, living in seclusion, and afterwards giving way to intemperance—in some cases drugged by the publicans, who fleeced them of their hard-earned wages—should become insane. This was another terrible aggravation of the evils complained of. What a fine field for the exercise of Christian philanthropy, if they only knew the right way to go about it! He trusted their meeting that afternoon would stir them up to their duty in this matter, and that, with the blessing of the Almighty, their efforts to assist their fellow-creatures would be crowned with success. Mr. C. Sabine consented to undertake the duties of Secretary *pro tem.* in conjunction with Mr. H. Hussey. Mr. Angas moved—'That this meeting hereby affirms the desirability of establishing a Bushmen's Home, and pledges itself to use its best endeavours for the attainment of that object.' There was no doubt as to the necessity of this institution. It was estimated that there were about 7,000 persons connected with pastoral pursuits occupying the north, north-east, and western districts of the colony; a great proportion were single men having literally no home, and destitute of friends or connections resident in the colony, their possessions consisting mainly of a pair of blankets and a few articles of clothing. Their time was occupied when not at work in travelling from station to station; and when those who were at work drew their wages they spent them in drink, which was worse than throwing away their hard earnings. It was natural to suppose that the employers had very little sympathy with such men, and objected to accommodate them when travelling sometimes for months during the year. To meet the wants of callers, eating-houses had been opened in various places, but they did not meet the case of the bushman, who required a place where he could enjoy the intercourse natural to human beings, and where he would be protected from those who followed him in town, knowing he had money, and relieving him of it, left him to beg his way back to the place where he could get employment. The money expended annually by bushmen would be sufficient, he believed, to erect homes in many of the principal country towns. The mode of life pursued by many bushmen was most injurious. It unfitted them for earning their livelihood, and ultimately consigned them to the Hospital, Destitute or Lunatic Asylum; while many perished in the bush. The promoters were of the opinion that the Home should be a commodious building in a healthy situation near some large and central town in the northern district, within easy access of Adelaide by rail, and having facilities for telegraphic and postal communication. The institution should be under the control of a Board of Management, with suitable officers, and should provide accommodation at least for 200 or 300 single men when travelling or out of employment, also for a dozen families, and a section of the building to be appropriated and fitted up for the use of employers when required. It was also considered very desirable that there should be connected with the Home a savings bank, labour office, reading and coffee rooms, and a friendly society; and, if sufficient funds were obtained, that a boarding-school should be opened for the children of shepherds and others residing near the institution, also an evening school for the instruction of adults. A little land would be required for purposes of recreation, and to afford paddocking for horses. It might be asked how many men would patronize such an institution; and he might mention that 'William,' the well-known indefatigable and benevolent bush missionary, had obtained the names of 174 sheep-farmers and overseers and 651 men engaged in the bush who heartily approved of the scheme, and had informed him that had time permitted hundreds of other names would have been collected. The cost of such an establishment would necessarily be very considerable; but he was fully persuaded that if the sheepfarmers and others interested came forward and assisted, the least difficult part of the work would be the raising of funds. If such an institution was not established, they might look forward to a very bad state of things for the social condition of the bushmen; New South Wales afforded an index of what they might expect. Mr. Sabine (for Mr. Scott) seconded the motion, expressing his opinion that it would be found desirable to erect more than one Home, as an institution which would benefit the northern people would not be convenient for those in the neighborhood of Port Lincoln. These institutions must to a great extent be supported by the bushmen themselves, who would thus provide themselves with a home when old and incapacitated for work. He suggested that it would be a good plan for the masters to give the men certificates of character when leaving their service, so that they would not find difficulty in getting other employment. The motion was carried. Mr. William Kyffin Thomas briefly moved—'That the following gentlemen form a Provisional Committee for making the necessary preliminary arrangements :— Hon. Captain Bagot, Hon. Thomas Elder, Dr. Brown, Messrs. S. Davenport, J. H. Angas, Thomas Giles, C. Sabine, H. Scott, R. B. Smith, James Smith, H. W. Stokes, C. Smedley, Saml. Tomkinson, W. Kyffin Thomas, John Williams, C. B. Young, H. Hussey, and "William," Bush Missionary, with power to add to their number.' Mr. Giles seconded, and the resolution was carried. Mr. Stokes moved—'That in the opinion of this meeting the neighbourhood of the Burra is the most suitable locality for a Bushmen's Home.' Mr. West seconded, expressing his concurrence in the object of the meeting and the selection of the Burra as being the most suitable place for a starting-point, as that place was the centre for the transfer of stock, and was now very prominent in consequence of the general use of the Barrier route. Mr. Angas supported the resolution, pointing out that the buildings at the Bon Accord Mine there might do for the purpose, since they possessed also the advantage of having a good supply of water. There were 200 or 300 acres of land connected with the property, and it was probable that this could be rented or purchased. One of the fundamental principles of the institution must be that it should be self-supporting, and another that it should be conducted on temperance principles, otherwise the object of the promoters would be frustrated. The resolution was carried. The Rev. J. C. Woods moved—'That the Committee draw up a prospectus, obtain the names of persons willing to act as officers for the institution, and arrange for collecting subscriptions.' He thoroughly agreed with the object, and promised his hearty support. The Rev. G. Stonehouse briefly seconded, and the motion was carried.

Mr. Hussey proposed—'That a public meeting be called of all persons interested in the establishment of the proposed institution so soon as the Committee have completed the preliminary arrangements.' He mentioned that he had been commissioned by Mr. G. F. Angas to say that he was unavoidably prevented from being present ; but he took a deep interest in the movement, and though he could not take an active part in it he would feel a pleasure in giving it his liberal support. Mr. D. Murray seconded the motion, which was carried. Mr. Angas thought the matter only required to be put before the men in a proper light, and they would cheerfully subscribe to it. He suggested that the subscription-list should be published from week to week in one of the papers, so that the subscribers would see that their donations were received and acknowledged ; also that the sheepfarmers might subscribe a small sum, say a halfpenny or a penny, per head on their sheep ; and as there were about a million and a-half of sheep in the north, they could easily see what a fund would thus be available. The resolution was carried. Mr. Thomas moved—'That the Secretary put himself in communication with the members of the Provisional Committee and ascertain if they are willing to act ; if so, to ask them to attend a meeting to be held on Monday next.' Carried. The meeting then closed with a vote of thanks to the Chairman."

Agreeably to the resolution moved by Mr. Thomas at this meeting, the following Circular was at once sent to the gentlemen nominated to form a Provisional Committee :—

"Bushmen's Home.
"Adelaide, December 30, 1868.

" Sir—At a preliminary meeting held this day to consider the best steps to adopt for the speedy establishment of a Bushmen's Home, it was resolved to apply to you for your concurrence in forming one of a Committee to carry out the object.

" The first meeting of the Committee will be held at White's Arbitration Room on Monday, January 4, at half-past 2 p.m., when I shall be glad if you can make it convenient to attend.

"The favour of a reply will oblige,
"Yours faithfully,
"CLEMENT SABINE, Temporary Hon. Sec.
"To ——————."

In due course the first meeting of the Committee of the Bushmen's Home was held at White's Arbitration Room on the 4th January, 1869. Present—Hon. T. Elder (in the chair), Messrs. D. Murray, J. H. Angas, W. K. Thomas, C. B. Young, H. Hussey, C. Sabine, H. Giles, and "William," Bush Missionary. The minutes of the meeting held 30th December, 1868, were read and confirmed.

Mr. C. Sabine proposed, and Mr. J. H. Angas seconded—"That the Hon. T. Elder, M.L.C., be the permanent Chairman of Committee." Carried.

It was resolved that the Bank of Australasia be the bank at which the Bushmen's Home account be kept, and the most favourable terms applied for as to deposits in the first instance.

It was resolved that Mr. C. Sabine be Honorary Treasurer in addition to his appointment as Honorary Secretary.

Letters were read from Messrs. S. Tomkinson, H. Scott, and J. H. Browne, consenting to act on the Committee.

Letters were read from Messrs. S. Davenport, C. Smedley, and M. Goode, declining to act on the Committee.

A draft prospectus was read, altered, added to, amended, and finally adopted as follows:—

"*Committee.*—Chairman, Hon. T. Elder, M.L.C.; Honorary Secretary and Treasurer, Mr. C. Sabine. Members—Messrs. J. H. Angas, J. H. Browne, S. Cornish, H. Giles, H. Hussey, D. Murray, H. Scott, W. K. Thomas, S. Tomkinson, C. B. Young, and 'William,' Bush Missionary.

"*Bank*—Bank of Australasia.

"It is proposed to erect a Home for Bushmen at the Burra or some other northern township, with a view to promote the social and moral improvement of that class of persons whose occupation deprives them of many of the advantages and comforts of civilized life. The institution, whilst furnishing a temporary home for the unemployed, is likely to become a favourite place of resort for others living in the bush when occasionally visiting the settled districts. It is intended at first to provide victualling and sleeping accommodation for from 50 to 100 persons, the place being so arranged as to admit of enlargement. There will also be a reading-room and library supplied with newspapers and periodicals, baths, smoking and refreshment rooms, cricket and skittle grounds, and stables and paddocks for horses. The Home will be under the direct management of a superintendent, who will be under the control of the Committee. The utmost freedom of action consistent with the proper working of the establishment will of course be afforded to the inmates; but it will be necessary to adhere to fixed regulations for the preservation of order, decorum, and cleanliness. Contributions received in the first instance will be devoted to the purchase or lease of a site and erection of buildings. The amount of annual subscriptions will be fixed when the place is built. Annual subscribers will enjoy all the advantages of the institution, and be charged a reasonable amount for board and lodging. Non-subscribers frequenting the Home will be supplied merely with board and lodging at the usual rates. No bushman who is orderly will be refused accommodation and meals for at least one day if he require them, even if he has no money; but in such case he must give an order for the amount due to be presented to his next employer. There will be facilities afforded to masters and men in one part of the Home for the engagement of labour. There will be a branch post-office and a savings bank in connection with the Home. No intoxicating drinks will be permitted to be used or introduced into any part of the building. Any measures taken to organize such an institution must receive the large and hearty support of bushmen, for whose benefit as a class it will be established; but the Committee also appeal confidently to the public of South Australia for assistance, it being understood that when once the establishment shall have been put in working order it must be self-supporting, and its continued existence must depend on bushmen themselves, who are earnestly requested to subscribe. 'William,' the Bush Missionary, will supply forms which can also be obtained at the various stations in the country, or from the Honorary Secretary in Adelaide. Subscriptions will be duly acknowledged once in every month in the *Observer* and *Chronicle*. It is not proposed to commence operations until a sufficient sum has been subscribed.

"Adelaide, January 4, 1869."

It was arranged that Messrs. C. B. Young and C. Sabine be a Sub-Committee to revise the same and put it in proper order for being printed, with the names of all those who consent to act on Committee.

It was resolved that the prospectus be advertised in the *Observer* on the 9th and 23rd of January, and in the *Chronicle* on the 9th and 30th January, and in the two daily papers on the 1st February.

It was resolved that 2,000 prospectuses, 300 circulars, 300 subscription-lists, and 300 envelopes be printed, and that the distribution take place as early as practicable.

The following brief articles bearing upon this subject are taken from the *Register* and *Express* of January 5th and 8th, 1869 :—

"THE PROPOSED BUSHMEN'S HOME.

"A meeting of the Committee of the Bushmen's Home movement was held in White's Arbitration Room on Monday, January 4. The Hon. T. Elder presided, and there were also present Messrs. J. H. Angas, W. K. Thomas, C. Sabine, C. B. Young, D. Murray, H. Hussey, and the Bush Missionary 'William.' The Honorary Secretary (Mr. Sabine) laid before the Committee a draft prospectus, which provides for the erection of a Home for Bushmen at the Burra or some other northern township with a view of promoting the social and moral improvement of that class, and which would also be a place which is likely to become a favorite place of resort for others living in the bush when occasionally visiting the settled districts. It is intended at first to provide victualling and sleeping accommodation for from 50 to 100 persons. There will also be a reading-room and library supplied with newspapers and periodicals, baths, smoking and refreshment rooms, cricket and skittle grounds, and stables and paddocks for horses. The Home is to be under the management of a superintendent, under the control of a Committee ; and whilst freedom of action consistent with the proper working of the establishment will be allowed, fixed regulations will be framed for the preservation of order, decorum, and cleanliness. Further provision is made for a labour office, savings bank, and branch post-office ; and an appeal is made to the bushmen and the the public for assistance, as the institution is designed to be self-supporting. The Chairman produced a plan of the buildings on the Bon Accord mining property at Kooringa, referred to at the previous meeting as being suitable for the purpose of a Home, and the plan was approved of by the Committee. Other matters of detail, such as arranging terms of subscriptions and providing for the distribution of prospectuses and printed subscription-lists on the stations and elsewhere, were considered and settled, and the meeting then closed."

[From the *Express* and *Telegraph* of January 8, 1869.]

"BUSHMEN'S HOME.

"The prospectus of the proposed Bushmen's Home has been issued by the Committee. The idea for which we have long contended is now likely, with the generous assistance of the public and the help of bushmen themselves, to become an accomplished fact. It is intended to commence operations at the Burra or some other northern township. The object of the Home is to promote the social and moral improvement of that large class of persons who are employed on the sheep stations in the northern part of the colony, and who are now on their visits to the settled districts exposed to great temptations. Though the scheme in all its parts contains a good many praiseworthy objects, it is intended at first to start with provision for boarding and lodging from 50 to 100 persons, arrangements being made for future enlargement. We are glad to find that the necessary elements of health and amusement are not forgotten by the promoters. There are to be a reading-room and library supplied with newspapers and periodicals, baths, smoking and refreshment rooms, cricket and skittle grounds, and stables and paddocks for horses. No intoxicating drink will be allowed in the establishment. The whole arrangements will be under the management of a superintendent, who will be responsible to the Committee, as every effort will be made to preserve good order, decorum, and cleanliness. As it is intended to make the Home entirely self-supporting when the buildings are erected and got into working order, annual subscribers will enjoy all the advantages provided and will be charged a reasonable amount for board and lodging, while non-subscribers frequenting the institution will be supplied only with board and lodging at the usual rates. Travelling bushmen, too, if orderly, will be supplied with one day's accommodation and meals, even if they have no money, on giving an order on their next employer for the cost. The Home will also afford the advantages of a labour office for masters, and in connection with it there will be a post-office and savings bank. We have already intimated that the institution is intended to be self-supporting; but the preliminary expenses for the purchase of land and the erection of the necessary buildings will be considerable, and to meet these an appeal is made to the general public, especially to those interested in pastoral pursuits. We heartily wish success to this benevolent scheme. Its advantages, if fairly started, will be very great to the persons whom it wishes to serve, and who at the present time too often fall a prey to the designing and unprincipled. Influential and energetic gentlemen are at the head of the movement, and if they are well supported by the public success is pretty certain."

Agreeably to the resolution passed at the Committee meeting, 267 subscription-lists, accompanied by the following Circular, were sent to the managers and overseers of the different stations throughout the colony :—

"Committee-room, Adelaide, January 4, 1869.

"Sir—The Committee of the Bushmen's Home have requested me to forward to you a subscription-list, and hope that you will use your best endeavours in canvassing your run and obtaining the subscriptions, and trust every facility will be given to the men in your employ for this purpose.

"Will you kindly return the list to me when completed, taking care that under no circumstances shall it be sent later than by the last mail in March.

"I am, Sir, yours, &c.,
"CLEMENT SABINE, Temporary Hon. Sec."

At this stage of the proceedings considerable agitation was occasioned by self-interested parties who sought to infuse prejudice into the minds of the bushmen and raise opposition to the institution, as the following extract taken from one of the daily papers will show:—

"PROPOSED BUSHMEN'S HOME.

"'An Old Bushman' writes in strong terms against the establishment of the above institution, believing that the promoters hope through its agency to keep down the rate of wages. He warns his mates against suffering themselves to become objects of charity, and urges them to help themselves by always having a 'friend,' and 'let that friend be a good horse and a pound or two to carry you in search of the highest wages and the best station. Support none but the best inns and respectable landlords, and then you require no "home" save what your own good honest character will provide you with, and which may be had anywhere in the colony by all respectable men.'

"We quite agree with the writer in recommending every bushman to lay up a little money and to keep where he can a good horse; but he is scandalously cynical, and does gross injustice to the motives of those who are endeavouring to provide for the bushmen's further comfort. He appears to forget the number of those who now come into the settled districts with money, and perhaps horses too, but who leave them on foot and with empty pockets."

About the same time another letter of a similar character was published as follows:—

"TO THE EDITOR.

"Sir—A swagsman, and not ashamed to own it. I have done the 'wallaby' for years past in search of a billet. I don't suppose that a tenth part of the time I have been in the country has been spent in idleness, yet I am one of those unfortunates called 'knave and vagabond.'

"Well, all I can say is that if an earnest desire on the part of at least nine-tenths of the bush working men—who prefer their own legs as the means to carry them in search of work to the more expensive one of riding in Cobb & Co.'s coaches—is to be considered a proper qualification to entitle them to the abusive epithets heaped upon them, then so much the worse for squatters, as it is well known that a majority of us swagsmen are the very ones from whom they derive their principal supply of hands.

"The true state of the case is that certain large sheep-owners (there are only two or three) are extremely unpopular with swagsmen in consequence of their harsh treatment of the hands in their employ, and are only too happy in taking every opportunity to vent their spleen on those of us who want neither their 'tucker,' work, or money; and now, in order to save themselves the expense of getting hands up from Adelaide, think of starting a depôt or home in order to have us in their power. Depend upon it, it won't do; we prefer to sail upon our own bottom. I don't deny there are several good men and true connected with the movement whose good wishes are sincere, but they are being misled in thinking a Home is wanted. A decent home can be had anywhere in the country if a man is not a loafer and unwilling to work. We are not of the 'social evil' class, or tramps on the look-out for plunder, and therefore require no home or reformatory. We are a respectable, hard-working class of men—not 'knaves' or 'vagabonds.' I have not been a swagsman all my life, but, like other colonists, had to do in the colonies the very opposite of my calling in the old country. 'Knaves and vagabonds,' as is well known, sometimes sit in high places. Let those who do so look to their own conduct before venturing to cast the first stone.

"I rely on your medium for the publication of this injustice to a maligned class of men, and the working men will thank you.

"I am, Sir, &c.,

"A Swagsman."

[We publish this letter, omitting the name of a person specially mentioned, as we can see no reason to doubt the good intentions of all parties concerned in promoting the Bushmen's Home. Of course, no swagsman or other person need go to the "Home" unless he thinks fit; and we have no fear of so independent a class as South Australian bushmen being coerced in any way whatever.—ED.]

The following refutations, written by anonymous friends of the cause, need no comment from the compiler, as they will speak for themselves :—

"TO THE EDITOR.

"Sir—Your correspondent 'A Swagsman' is quite in error when stating that 'certain large sheepowners, to save themselves the expense of getting hands up from Adelaide, think of starting a home or depôt to have the men in their power.'

"The idea of the Bushmen's Home was, I believe, first publicly suggested by the *Express* nearly twelve months since. The active origination of the present scheme is entirely due to the Bush Missionary 'William,' the working man's best friend, who, as stated by Mr. J. H. Angas at a meeting recently reported in the papers, has since last June, during a journey on foot through the west and parts of the north, obtained the names of '651 bushmen who heartily approved of the scheme.'

"The plan is being taken up by and on behalf of bushmen, without whose contributions in the first instance and support afterwards it must fall to the ground. You will, therefore, pardon my saying that the Editorial foot-note appended to 'Swagman's' letter about coercion, &c., hardly meets the case.

"The practical test about to be thrown out in the way of prospectuses and subscription-lists will in a few weeks prove whether the 651 who have in some parts of the colony already promised co-operation do or do not represent the feeling of the main body of bushmen in South Australia.

"I am, Sir, &c.,
"JASON."

"TO THE EDITOR.

"Sir—I was surprised the other day on reading in your paper a letter signed 'Swagsman,' on the subject of the proposed Bushmen's Home, to find how far his statements are from being correct. He indignantly scouts the idea of bushmen wanting a Home, and says they are quite capable when in town of taking proper care of themselves, and that they do so. I have not the paper before me, and therefore cannot quote his exact words, but the foregoing is the import of them.

"Now, how often we read in the police reports of the way that bushmen get rid of their money in town! They meet with some questionable characters who, beguiling them into getting drunk, or by other means, get hold of their victims' money, which of course they don't intend to return. The unfortunate man sometimes tries to recover the money in the Police Court, but very often, in absence of sufficient proof, the guilty ones get off free. Such cases are not rare in the papers; and almost every day we may see in the streets men, unmistakable bushmen, 'knocking down' their cheques in various excesses, drinking or in other ways spending or wasting their hard-earned wages.

"'Swagsman' says bushmen, as a class, are intelligent and sensible. If so, their intelligence and sense certainly lies latent when they indulge in the excesses I have mentioned. Of course, I don't deny that many are so. I have known in the bush well-educated men, classical scholars, shepherding or bullock-driving. 'Swagsman' himself (to judge from the style of his letter) probably uses his good sense and keeps within prudent bounds in town; but why does he affirm that all or even the majority do so? He must know it is otherwise.

"I think that the gentlemen who have started the matter of a Bushmen's Home deserve credit for their endeavours to benefit a hard-working portion of the community; and I disagree altogether with 'Swagsman' when he says it is done with an eye to the benefit and convenience of the squatters.

"If the promoters of the Home can induce bushmen, instead of coming to town, spending their cheques in 'spreeing,' to lay it by in the branch savings bank (which I suppose will be established in connection with the Home), in that way much good may be done, besides the fact of men being away from the temptations of Adelaide, to which, if exposed, they would probably yield. Of course the promoters of the Home will not attempt to coerce bushmen into living there, as 'Swagsman' thinks; nor will the institution be for the benefit of any other than bushmen.

"Hoping that bushmen will give it the support it deserves,

"I am, Sir, &c.,

"An Ex-Bushman."

[We think this letter may properly close the discussion. It is absurd for any one actively to oppose the establishment of a bushmen's lodging-house. No one need go there who does not like it, and no one need stay there an hour longer than he pleases; it is purely voluntary throughout.—Ed.]

About this time the subject began to press itself upon the attention of persons in the sister colony of Victoria, as will be seen from the following extract, which is taken from the *Australasian* of January, 1869. The writer of the article begins thus :—"A movement has been commenced at Adelaide towards a much-needed reform. A public meeting has resolved to establish a home for bushmen upon the same principle as a Sailors' Home. The constant tendency in bush labourers to waste in reckless and insensate extravagance the hard earnings of many months or even years, and the wild orgies in which they indulge, are too notorious. This tendency arises mainly if not altogether from the peculiarity of their employment. They are withdrawn for a lengthened period from every form of social enjoyment. They lose from disuse the power of, so to speak, measuring their wants, and those habits of self-control which even the worst of those who live among their fellow-men insensibly acquire. They have no opportunity of spending their wages, and therefore never draw them. At length the time comes for a spell. An ignorant, simple man, with plenty of money, with the higher wants of his nature undeveloped or repressed, eager for enjoyment, yet not knowing what enjoyment is, and unversed in the practices of social life, sets out upon his travels. What he does when he reaches town, and what becomes of his money and who profit by it, the police reports sufficiently record. Very frequently, however, he is not allowed to proceed so far. The local grog-shop is on the look-out, and the poor fellow finds that he can have the pleasure of being hocussed, drugged, and robbed without going to Melbourne or Adelaide for these enjoyments. It has been well observed that the conditions of bush labour resemble in many respects those of seafaring life; and that, as experience has shown that the sailor needs peculiar care, a similar experience points to a similar result for the poor bushmen. The success, too, of Sailors' Homes has encouraged the philanthropic gentlemen who have inaugurated this movement in Adelaide to try in the present case the effect of a corresponding remedy. We learn with pleasure that the plan has received the warm support both of employers and of bushmen. It is time that some measures should be taken not only to improve the condition of a useful body of men, but to check the encouragement which their weakness gives to thieves and prostitutes, and, worse still, the keepers of low public-houses. We shall effectually prune the luxuriance of these vicious parasites of the great social tree by depriving them of one large source of their present nutriment."

The foregoing article was reprinted in the *Register*, and proved the means of stirring up the bitterest feelings and animosity of the opponents of the scheme, who, finding that prejudice failed to do their work, commenced a system of ridicule of which the following is a specimen, taken from the *Licensed Victualler* :—

" The Bushmen's Home—A visionary scene.
"Outside the 'Home,' 12 o'clock at night—A bushman slightly affected by colonial ale—A policeman, mild, but dignified.
" Policeman—'Come; you can't be kicking up a row here.'
" Bushman—'You shut up, guv'ner; this is my home. I want 'er get in; I wan'r go bed.'

"Policeman—'Come along with me. You see you can't get in. I won't have you disturbing "William." This is a quiet house.'

"Bushman—'Not a bit on it. I am one ov the prop—rop—rioters. O, blow "William."' (Kicks at door.)

"Policeman—'None of that, I say; you come with me.'

"Bushman—'You jus' keep y'own company. Whar right you stop a man going his home?'

"Policeman—'You should have gone home earlier. What right has a bushman to be in the streets this time o' night?'

"Bushman—'Been Theater. I am Warraby Jack. Jack all right. Got in the Jolly Boy—respectable hotel. Why shouldn't I get my home? Paid for it. "William" got cheque an' swag.'

"Policeman—'You've been drinking, old man.'

"Bushman—'Whar o' that? you didn't pay my drinks. (Shouts out) I say, Bill Chiffles, let a feller in, will yer?'

"Bushman No. 2 (puts his head out of window)—'Is that you, Joe?'

"Bushman No. 1—'Yes. Here's a bobby says can ger in. Jus' come down help punch his head.'

"Bushman No. 2—'We're all locked in here since 9 o'clock, and "William's" out at a prayer meeting, or I'd do it willing.'

"Policeman (indignantly)—'Punch my head! would you, my man? Come along.' (Claps twitches on him, and violently escorts him to Police Station.)"

In the early part of the month of January, 1869, "William" (in addition to his Evangelizing work in the bush) took in hand actively to distribute prospectuses and gain information as to the amount of support likely to be given to the Home. To further the work and interest bushmen, as well as to give them an idea of the internal working of the Club when formed, he prepared an address of his own to read at the different stations, which he did after placing the following notice on the door of the kitchen or shed:—

"BUSHMEN'S CLUB.—SPECIAL NOTICE.

"An explanatory address will be read (D.V.) after supper in favour of the Bushmen's Home or Club.

"All objections will be answered, if possible.

"All hands upon the station are respectfully invited to attend, as a great work is in progress, which, if completed, will, it is believed, do good to all.

"WILLIAM."

The following is a copy of the address :—

"To the Bushmen and Public of South Australia.

"All of you who are in the habit of reading the newspapers must have observed that a movement was set on foot (first in the country, and afterwards in Adelaide) by persons deeply interested in the welfare of the bush population and of the colony generally for the establishment of an institution of this kind. The result of this movement was a meeting, called by advertisement, of all parties interested in such an undertaking, and held at White's Arbitration Rooms, in Adelaide, on the last day of the year 1868. The following are the names of some of the gentlemen present at that meeting :—Hon. T. Elder, M.L.C. (in the chair), Hon. W. Morgan ; Revs. G. Stonehouse, S. Mead, and J. C. Woods ; Messrs. J. H. Angas, H. Scott, F. W. Stokes, H. Giles, H. Hussey, C. Sabine, S. Tomkinson, C. B. Young, W. K. Thomas, and 'William.' In the first instance the Burra was considered the most desirable spot, but it has been since decided (in accordance with the wishes of the majority of the bushmen, &c.) to have the first Home in the neighbourhood of Adelaide. The result of a second meeting was the framing of a prospectus (since published), arranging for the collection of subscriptions, and the distribution of prospectuses and printed subscription-lists on the stations and elsewhere. The work of collecting is now going on throughout the country, and, as far as I can yet learn, favourably.

"I will now proceed to give an idea (as I have been present at all the meetings) of what the Home is likely to be if funds can be raised.

"First, let me remark that I never did think a Bushmen's Home or any other good thing would please all men or could be established without opposition, nor is it possible while there are conflicting opinions in this world.

"I remember that the seamen—or, I should say, the low

publicans, brothel-keepers, crimps, spongers, and others—strongly opposed (professedly on the seamen's behalf) the establishment of Seamen's Homes by raising a hue and cry about bondage, wages, &c. It was not the benefit of the poor sailors they cared for, but their own loss, for Satan never gives up his prey without a struggle. The result of many years' experience in the working of these institutions in various parts of the world has shown that those self-interested alarmists and supposed friends were entirely in the wrong, for the Homes have proved themselves to seamen one of the greatest blessings of our day and generation. In a good work we must expect slander, misrepresentation, and opposition, as it is impossible that all men will see what is for their good. We do not expect reproach from good men or right-minded men, neither shall we get it ; but from the classes I have referred to we do expect it. For myself, I am much surprised at the Bushmen's Home sailing on so calmly, and I thank my God for it.

" Respecting the temperance principles of the place, there are many more bush people in favour of its being a quiet, sober retreat than otherwise—a retreat from the before-mentioned undesirable characters. I have issued myself the greater part of 500 abstinence pledges in the bush, and these people (or as many as kept it), I have no doubt, appreciate and will avail themselves of the advantages which the Home will hold out. These pledged men are, or ought to be, according to their promise, influencing others to follow their example ; and we cannot say to what an extent temperance principles may eventually reach throughout the bush.

" From my own intimate knowledge of this Home business, I can assure the men in the bush and the public at large that it is purely philanthropic, and not, as it has been infamously asserted, to the dishonour of all parties concerned in it a squatters' affair, designed to bring down wages or the men into bondage. I, for one, scout such an infamous, base insinuation ; and I believe it to be the invention of those who have kept the bushman in bondage to drink long enough, and to be designed, if they can accomplish their purpose, to overthrow the work by prejudice and stop its progress. But it will not do, depend upon it. Bushmen and others, I dare say, can give a guess where such insinuations come from. When they remember and reflect on the many cheques which have enured to their benefit, these individuals may well be enraged and indignant, for in the establishment of a Bushmen's Home they see an end of their ill-gotten gains through the knocking-down cheque system. I assure the bushmen that the squatters will have no more to do with fixing the rates of wages than at present, or with the disposal of the members of the Home, and that every person would be as free in the place as out of it. All that squatters, in conjunction with other gentlemen, have to do with it is simply as trustees for its establishment; and I think they are the most fitting and proper persons to look after the comfort and interest of a class which is so valuable to them —viz., good men. Remember, most of the bush labour is employed by the squatters.

"I ask you one question—Will those who set at variance employers and their men, and make them dissatisfied and discontented, give the men and their families bread to eat when they are out of employ, without means to pay for it? You know very well they will not. There is very little sympathy between bushmen and any other class of people in the country. Few will tolerate a bushman at all but for what they can get from him whilst he has the money. After his money is gone he wanders about like a stranger in a strange land, and is often driven by sheer necessity back to the bush even for a meal of food (old bushmen know that this is true), for in the thickly-settled districts he is shunned and ofttimes almost despised.

"My friends, allow me to observe that there is more time, talent, and interest required to establish an institution of this kind than at first sight appears, or than many are disposed to think necessary; and what labouring man—or, I may say men—have the time, even if they had the means, to do it? I think it extremely kind, considerate, and creditable to the gentlemen of the Committee and others who have devoted so much valuable time and taken so much interest (to which I can testify) for the welfare of this class of colonists.

"The Home, to commence with, will probably contain

apartments as follows :—Dining-room, restaurant and coffee-room, dormitory, reading-room, library, kitchen, store-room, labour office, branch savings bank and post-office, wash and bath house, smoking place, stables, sheds, kennels for shepherds' dogs, &c. This will be increased when needful as funds permit and as it becomes patronized.

"I propose that the funds raised be appropriated as follows :—First, for building, purchasing, or leasing a Home ; second, furnishing and fitting up ditto ; third, to pay wages, debts, and incidental expenses ; fourth, a fund for keeping the Home in repair and in general good order inside and outside ; fifth, a benefit fund for relieving cases of necessity amongst bushmen. If built, it should be in such a way that it can if necessary be extended in every department.

"The complete establishment must be built as funds can be raised ; but there can be no objection to begin, in the first instance, on a small scale. Let the main building be erected and extended as funds permit, and opened as built. This is the best plan for progressive institutions of this kind. It will not only by its profits materially assist in extending the building, but will also be a great present benefit and blessing to the long-neglected homeless and wandering bushmen. The Home can be built and subscriptions collected at the same time, always keeping the latter in advance of the former.

"I now come to the more pleasing part of my address— viz., as to what the Home will probably be if funds can be raised to carry it out. You must be well aware that no institution can prosper, or its inmates be comfortable, without proper and explicit rules and regulations. The following suggestions, subject to such alterations and modifications as times and circumstances necessitate, I now make, with a view to give an idea of the working of the proposed Bushmen's Home.

"In an establishment of this kind care should be taken that a portion of Scripture be read, with prayer, daily ; but it must be left to the consciences of the inmates whether they like to attend such morning devotions or not—all should be advised and kindly invited to do so. There are many pious bushmen who will gladly avail themselves of such a privilege. The Lord's Day must be strictly observed according to law; none but absolutely necessary work can be permitted or tolerated on this day. Men will after a little while begin to respect the Sunday, and feel that they are really at home. There should not be permitted at any time brawling or disturbance or any scandalous actions derogatory to the honour of God, the corruption of good morals, or the discredit of the institute (such as obscene songs, filthy talking or jesting), as these things are not only insulting to right-minded persons, but unbecoming the character of decent men.

"Such rules, at first sight, may appear a little strict; but they are certainly very necessary, considering the careless way in which many at present live in the bush.

"For all this the greatest liberty should be permitted consistent with reason and the proper working of the institute. Working men themselves (even the most vicious) know that order is necessary; and when the advantages of the institution become generally known the rules will commend themselves to every thoughtful mind. There is, I think, little fear that it will suffer by its strictness in these things from any lack of patronage.

"Inmates should be advised and encouraged to conduct themselves in a fraternal, clean, quiet, and orderly manner for the sake of peace, comfort, and happiness.

"If any one is dissatisfied with the rules, regulations, servants, victuals, attendance, or on any other just or reasonable grounds, he should quietly make it known to the superintendent, that a remedy may be applied if it can be had. This would prevent grumbling or murmuring about the place, and also keep other inmates from becoming dissatisfied and miserable.

"In the event of any just cause of complaint against the superintendent, it should be made in writing (signed by the complaining party) to the Committee (three forming a quorum), or no notice should be taken of such complaint. It would then be the duty of the Committee to investigate the matter and set it right.

"The daily routine should be somewhat as follows:—First bell at 7 a.m., to awaken the inmates; second bell at 7.30

a.m., morning reading and prayers (to all who like to attend); third bell at 8 a.m., breakfast (grace always before meals by superintendent or other); fourth bell at noon, dinner—the tables to be cleared by 2 o'clock; fifth bell at 5 p.m., tea. I would suggest that for the instruction and amusement of the inmates, to fill up the space of time between tea and supper, there should be lectures, a debating club, preaching or reading, scientific amusements, adult schooling, music and singing classes, a notice of which should be posted up in some conspicuous place after breakfast, so that the people may know what will be going on in the evening. Sixth bell at 9 p.m., supper.

"The labour office, savings bank, and post-office should be open every working day at specified times, subject to such rules as may be found necessary.

"Notice-boards and printed forms should be provided, and every application for hands or work (whether contract or otherwise) from the country, &c., should be posted up daily, with, if possible, the wages to be given or price of such contract, in a public place inside the Home, that the men may choose their own situations or work, and not, as the enemies to the Bushmen's Home movement have wrongly and slanderously asserted in the papers, be compelled to accept any kind of work or place contrary to their inclination or judgment.

"Bushmen should be advised and encouraged to transmit their wages or savings periodically to the Home savings bank, that their interest may be going on, and receive their bank-books, or, perhaps better, a receipt, for their money, and have their books kept at the bank to prevent fraud or loss, without leaving their places or stations at such short intervals and continually shifting about as some do. Nothing is ever gained by this line of conduct; and when a man knows that he has an account at the bank it makes him feel that he is really living for something, and will, in nineteen cases out of twenty, induce him to try to add to his little stock of savings.

"Every boarder should be requested (though not compelled) to deposit what money he does not want for immediate use on his arrival at the Home bank (instead, as has too often been the case, in the publican's till) for safe keeping, and any other valuables he may possess in the store, for which he should get a store receipt. He should be able to draw out daily, at the proper office hours, what money he may need, as long as it lasts, if it is deposited for safe keeping only.

"The reading-room and library should be open daily for the sale and exchange of good books, &c. A supply should be selected by the Committee and kept at the Home for disposal at a low charge. The reading-room should be well supplied with newspapers and approved periodicals.

"Refreshment-room.—No intoxicating drinks of any kind or description to be kept or drunk upon the Home premises. The following should be permitted :—Tea, coffee, chocolate, milk, syrups, currant and raspberry vinegar, kali, lemonade, sodawater, gingerbeer, or any other harmless, sober drinks; fruit, confectionary, &c., &c.; and these to be sold at the lowest possible charge—in fact, a kind of restaurant for the men to sit down and to enjoy themselves as rational beings.

"Besides the regular holidays there should be two annual entertainments at the Home; for if unemployed men are not found some innocent amusements, they will probably find some vicious ones themselves. Let there be one at the anniversary of the founding of the Home, and another after shearing—these to be duly advertised. There should also be occasionally excursions, picnics, tea parties, cricket matches, or any innocent amusements or recreations that can be devised to keep up a lively feeling amongst the people.

"The pious and grave should also be able to spend their time at the Home in a way congenial to their peculiar habits of life, and with profit to their minds.

"Such a state of things would be found much better for bushmen than being plundered on almost every side, hocussed, robbed, locked up, brought before magistrates, heavily fined, getting diseased, lying about in public-houses, sometimes drunk and delirious for days and even weeks at a time, wasting their hard earnings, wandering about the stations and huts sometimes almost starving, losing their self-respect, and ofttimes dying in the bush.

Of course, I know that this does not apply to all (God forbid!); but I know also that this is the case with far too many, who after their debauch return again to their work (if they can get it) in a depressed, shattered, and debilitated condition, neither wiser nor better men. Some bushmen do this repeatedly to the end of their lives, and not only do no good in their day, but show an evil example to the rising generation—acting more like the brutes that perish than responsible and accountable beings. Any careful single man might, if he chose, reside comfortably in the Home three months in every year of his labours in the bush.

"I apprehend some arrangements will be made by which any boarder may invite an old mate or friend (travelling or otherwise) to stay at the Home with him by paying his expenses whilst there. This would enable bushmen to assist a companion, as they readily do under such circumstances, when he is out of work.

"A provision should be made for distressed bushmen by the establishment of a club or friendly society, something like that of the Masons, Oddfellows, or Rechabites. They will be able to arrange this matter when they get together at the Home, and make proper arrangements for raising a fund for assisting the unemployed.

"I would remark here that men cannot expect to be admitted to the privileges and benefits arising from this institution if they squander away and waste their means in riotous living, drunkenness, debauchery, &c., and then think to fall back on the sober, steady working men to support them. This would not only be unwise, but decidedly unfair to the honest, industrious man, and would also be giving countenance and encouragement to profligacy and vice, which it will be the chief aim of this institute to counteract and suppress.

"By a little wise management and prudent common sense the working man who is sober and has his health need not want in this country. Remember that it is wages well spent that will effect good. A fund should be established for the support of aged members unable to work, instead of sending them to the Destitute Asylum. Consider, youth is the sowing-time for old age.

"There should also be a fund for widows and orphans, who are sometimes left in a deplorable state in the bush, if means could be obtained. To the married people I would say—The most of you have families, and there is a suggestion recorded for a free boarding-school for bush children, if funds can be raised. This should be borne in mind, and is a matter of great importance to the future generation. Your forefathers did good for you, and you must do the same for your offspring. Your families will probably grow up and reap the advantage of your present generosity ; therefore, if you get no benefit from it, your children will.

"The working staff, to commence with, should be as follows :—First, a permanent standing committee of trustees ; second, a committee of bushmen (being members of the Home) to act in concert and co-operate with the trustees for working the institution, to be called the 'Bushmen's Own Committee.' These should be chosen by ballot or otherwise from none but working men. Only annual subscribers should be permitted to nominate, vote, or sit as members of the said committee or as representatives thereof, and no person should be entitled to more than one vote. I think this is a very fair arrangement for all parties, and no bushman or labouring man can find fault with it. Third, superintendent to act as accountant of Home, &c., and clerk of labour office, until the work grows sufficiently to admit of assistance ; fourth, caterer or steward ; fifth, good cook ; sixth, under-steward or voluntary help from distressed bushmen. The services of a medical man should also be obtained if possible.

"No hired servant of the establishment should be permitted to receive from any member, boarder, or other person visiting or staying at the Home any present or money without the consent of the committee ; and notices should be posted up conspicuously to this effect.

"Members of the Home should have, when the proper time arrives, a card of introduction to agencies or Homes of similar character that may be established in other places that they may require to visit, in order that they may secure comfortable and respectable accommodation when away from the parent Home, so as not to fall into the hands of designing persons.

"All annual subscriptions (when arranged) and weekly board must be paid and kept paid in advance.

"The Home should be open to all comers who choose to submit to its rules and regulations, the charge being as low as possible, compatibly with the current prices of provisions, good attention, cleanliness, and comfort. All profits, however made, to go to the benefit of the Home, and all officials to be paid by salary as the committee may decide.

"Any communications addressed by subscribers or others in the country to the superintendent should be carefully and punctually attended to, and everything done to promote the welfare, comfort, and happiness of the people belonging to this institute.

"Members going into the country to their work should have the privilege of storing any of their effects, which should be taken all possible care of; also of corresponding with the Home, which would be a kind of agency for obtaining and sending necessary letters, books, &c., to any bushmen or others on the stations, and for transacting any needful business for them, and, if possible, without extra charge or expense.

"A cabinet or museum should be placed in a conspicuous part of the Home for the reception of bush curiosities, specimens, or works of art.

"It is impossible to over-estimate the importance of such an institution as this to bushmen and labouring men, physically, socially, morally, and religiously, and these are the cardinal points aimed at in the formation of this one. It will centralize the men if conducted on sound, broad, liberal principles, with a consideration to their comfort and happiness, and provide for them the great desideratum of an uncorrupt labour office. It would cement in proper bonds the employers and the employed, and would prevent many differences which at present exist. It should not be a cramped affair, but be made as attractive as possible in all its relations; for (under God) its vitality depends upon this, and scrupulously keeping all kinds of intoxicating drinks (even colonial wine or hop beer) out of it. Most bushmen are easily led to drink to excess—sometimes the smell of liquor will do it; and a single glass of wine or beer has led many men of this class, to my certain knowledge, to ruin. It must be excluded, however hard the case may be, in every shape and form (except under the hands of a medical man or for religious ordinances), or it will not only kill the men, but will be the death of the institute. Through these means the long-neglected bushman will feel that he is a brother-man and member of society, and treated like one. This very fact realized will tend to keep him (under God) from those vices and besetting sins which have been the ruin of thousands temporally and spiritually, and may, by the favour of God, bring him yet to feel that he is a Christian also. Of course, if any person cannot place himself under the rules of the Home, both for his own good and the good of others, he cannot be admitted to the benefits and privileges arising out of it, which may be many.

"The rules and regulations (when framed) should be printed and hung up about the premises, so that all persons may have access to them at any time.

"Now, my friends, I want you to view with unprejudiced minds the usefulness of such an institution as this. I ask— Is there not something noble in it? We are placed here in this world to do good one to another, and we cannot do so without it costing us something. It now remains with you to say whether you will help us or not. I pray God, for Christ's sake, to give you both the will and the power to do so. Let us hope there is a better time coming, not only for bushmen, but for all classes; but you must each and all of you individually put your shoulders to the wheel and add your share of the contribution (one good effort does it all), and then we shall, by the blessing of God on our joint efforts, succeed in this great and benevolent undertaking.

"I must now strongly urge upon the holders of subscription-lists or collectors the necessity of at once opening their lists and soliciting subscriptions, which should lie open until the expiration of the extended time—viz., after shearing, if they are not filled before; if filled up previously, let them be forwarded to the Secretary. This will agitate the matter, bring in advocates for the cause, and keep the claims of the institution before the public. Contributors can give any amount they please; and where there are no regular subscription-lists they can send a donation or post-office order direct to the Treasurer and Secretary of the Bushmen's Home (Mr. C. Sabine, Adelaide), who will return a receipt for the amount or advertise it in the usual way.

"After the first or parent Home has been set going in good order it would be well to erect branches or receiving homes in the outlying districts, if found needful, and provided funds can be raised under the same organization.

"The first year or two will be the most trying time, probably, for the Home, until its practical advantages become known and appreciated.

"If the money collected is not applied to the purpose for which it has been received, it should be returned back to the subscribers, less the expenses. All contributors should give their names in full, and place of residence, that they may be found if needful.

"Friends, I must now leave the matter with you, feeling that I have not done the subject half the justice it deserves. I should be glad to see an abler person take the matter up on behalf of the bushmen. There are, or soon will be, subscription-lists lying at every head station in the colony (as per resolution passed at the last meeting); and I cannot close my address in a better way than by asking you to cast aside all prejudice, to go forward generously, add your names to the list of contributors, and show the colony at large that you are not only able but willing to do good for yourselves when you see the way clear to do it. Many say that the bushmen never will make an effort to establish themselves and gain a footing as a class. Now, bushmen, it remains with you to answer this practically and show them they are mistaken.

"Many thanks to those kind and zealous friends who have already contributed to so noble a cause.

"I now ask your kindly feelings and generous donations towards the proposed Bushmen's Home. Mind, I do not not receive money for it myself; but I will (D.V.), in conjunction with my evangelizing work, do all I can to open the lists, and to induce others to do so, by visiting all the stations I possibly can on foot during the coming shearing season.

"If any person has any objections to make to this address or any part of it, they are respectfully requested to make such objections verbally known now, or they can do it by letter; or if any one has an amendment to suggest, I shall not only be glad but very thankful to hear it.

"Any communication addressed to Mr. H. Hussey, care of Mr. Sabine, during my absence from Adelaide, will receive careful attention.

"I will now conclude by saying the more I think on this subject the more I feel constrained to say God bless the work, for Jesus Christ's sake. Amen.

"WILLIAM.

"Adelaide, May 6, 1869."

We will now endeavour to follow "William" in his arduous journeyings on behalf of the Home through the country. The first letter received from him after his departure by the Hon. Secretary respecting this movement was written from Canowie, and dated January 29, in which he spoke of the Home as everywhere popular, excepting in the north-east, where considerable opposition was manifested, as the following advertisement emanating from the Committee in Adelaide will show:—

"ADVERTISEMENT.

"It has been represented to the Committee that a report has been circulated in the north-east that certain employers are interesting themselves in this movement against the benefit of the working men, and that on this account some bushmen are declining to co-operate.

"The Committee take this opportunity of informing bushmen thereof, so that they may take steps to counteract any effect such a report may have on the progress of the institution. "CLEMENT SABINE, Hon. Sec.

"Adelaide, February 19, 1869."

After this it was also thought expedient to issue the following explanatory address in consequence of the prospectus being considered rather obscure, viz.:—

"BUSHMEN'S HOME.

"What advantages will bushmen derive from subscribing to erect a Home?

"*Notice to Bushmen.*

"The Committee have been requested, on the ground that the published prospectus is obscure on the point, to state what benefits are likely to accrue to bushmen by establishing Homes in the colony.

"To this question the Committee can only reply that, having at first taken action at the instance of some 600 residents on stations who personally represented to 'William' the necessity for a Home, their work at present is only initiative.

"The bushmen who subscribe will have a voice in the election of a working committee and local committee, which, when the thing is ready to start, must be appointed; and it will rest with themselves to develop at a future time various plans for their own comfort and the general improvement of their condition in the same way as do clubs and societies of a more pretending nature. The success of the institution will depend on the manner bushmen themselves support it.

"It is for bushmen to come forward and represent to the Committee their views on a subject in which they have somuch interest. This can be done by letter or otherwise.

"The Committee would point out that 'William,' the Missionary, is now traversing the north and north-east, &c., giving addresses to the men on this very subject; and he is conferring with the subscribers and inducing others to subscribe by pointing out the advantages of the Home, and, having learnt the opinions of bushmen, he will report to the Committee the result of his labours.

"South-eastern subscribers will, of course, expect, when the trial Home shall have been erected at the Burra and found to answer, that another shall be erected at or near Adelaide; and it is expected that other homes under the same organization will afterwards speedily be erected elsewhere.

"*Wages Question.*—The Committee distinctly affirm that they do not intend to deal with the question of wages in any shape or form. Of course, there will be a labour office— merely a department in every Home where men can meet with masters, and each party suit themselves on their own terms to the best mutual advantage.

"General Agency.—Members of the Home will be able to avail themselves of the services of the superintendent in transacting matters of business or money affecting themselves.

"Place of Abode.—One object aimed at by this institution is that bushmen may know that whenever they are travelling from one employ to another, or are taking a holiday or looking for work, they may (if members) have one or two fixed places which they have a right to make use of as their own (subject merely to ordinary regulations) where they can stay as short or as long a time as they please at moderate charges, and feel in every sense of the word 'at home,' where they may keep themselves respectable, meet their fellow-bushmen, indulge in rational amusement, and be as independent though more comfortable than if stopping at any ordinary boarding-house or inn, enjoying also the privileges named in clause 2 of the prospectus.

"Representation and Protection.—The working men may rest satisfied that when the affair is in working order subscribing members will have their fair share of voting-papers, so that their interests will be protected to the utmost, as the Committee are taking the matter up solely on the bushmen's behalf to accomplish for their comfort and improvement that which bushmen, without any present organization of their own, would by themselves be unable to accomplish.

"CLEMENT SABINE, Hon. Sec.

"Adelaide, February 24, 1869."

After the publication of this address the following remarks appeared in the *Observer* of the 27th February, 1869 :—

"In another column the Committee of the Bushmen's Home have adopted a wise and politic course by striving —and we doubt not the result will prove successful—to set before those who must be most immediately concerned the advantages anticipated from the establishment of this institution. They at the same time meet in a fair spirit and courageous tone the objections which have found their way into print; whilst they have not hesitated to grapple with those which may have not been so prominently urged, but are rather being quietly insinuated, or which, again, are merely lurking unseen, unspoken, in the breasts of men who, from long-enforced isolation in the distant bush, far from friendly counsel and companionship, may cherish doubts as to a project for their benefit begun amidst the busy hum of the metropolis. Bushmen, however, must not forget that, although the meeting at which the project was broached was held in Adelaide, information had been collected long before by those whose hearts were set upon ameliorating the condition of a class the appearance of members of which in any centre of population with a cheque representing the labour of twelve months, and requiring to be 'melted,' was the signal for 'crimps' and 'spongers'—words not to be found in Webster, but wofully significant—to be on the alert. Who that has travelled in pastoral districts in the Far North, South-East, Western Plains, Yorke's Peninsula, or other directions, has not enjoyed the rough but hearty hospitaliy of shepherds and stockmen without being able to fill his note-book, if so disposed, with stories but too true of the visit to town, no friend there, the apparently kind attentions of one who by some means catches sight of the order on a mercantile firm, notes, or draft, and sets himself gradually to lead the victim step by step, till some morning, with blanket and billy, the tramp has to be resumed back from some classic part of Adelaide, where casinos and worse are plentiful, to the flock of sheep on a wide brush-bordered plain or bare hillside?

"It would be a fatal mistake for the public, however, to suppose that the objectors are many, or the arguments urged and difficulties raised are cogent. The bush apostle 'William,' who before the city meeting was held had travelled nearly to Eucla in one direction and far away in others, brought 600 proofs in signatures of as many men that the Home was desired (longed for); and all who know aught of shepherdom can tell that the feeling is very general. A letter from 'William,' dated Arkaba, Feb. 22, lies before us, in which there is abundant evidence that in the north and north-east, while on foot he journeys like a Peter the Hermit, on a more prosaic but far more noble crusade, he, not forgetful of his main work, from which nothing turns him aside, is ever receiving fresh proof of the popularity of the Bushmen's Home movement, whilst personal appeal and explanation clears away the bulk of any remaining prejudice or difficulty.

"The second prospectus, for such it may be termed, deals with the advantages to be secured, the wages question, general agency, representation, and protection; and we cannot do better than invite attention to it. Meantime we may add that the subscription-lists are rapidly filling up, the number of adherents increasing, and many are expressing that species of gratitude which is described as thankfulness for favours about to be received.

"From Paralana, on Feb. 6, one of the gentler sex sends us the following welcome acknowledgment in return for our advocacy of the movement:—'May you succeed with the Bushmen's Home. All men on this station will subscribe to it willingly, and many thanks you have received from them.'"

The *Chronicle*, also of the same date, published the following remarks on the aforementioned explanatory address:—

"The Bushmen's Home seems now in a fair way of being established. It is making its own way in an unpretending manner in the country districts. The Committee has not thought it desirable to call the attention of the Adelaide public, nor to solicit help from residents in town, until after an expression of opinion from those outlying runs, and the test of the amount of subscriptions received show a guarantee to the public that bushmen are interested in this great work of self-improvement. We would especially direct the attention of bushmen to an advertisement addressed to themselves from the Committee of the Bushmen's Home, which seems to imply that the Home is making itself known and its privileges felt outside the settled districts, although little or no stir is made as yet near town."

At this stage of the Club's progress "William" thought it prudent and necessary to publish the following address to the bushmen of South Australia, with a view to stir them up to action and awaken their sympathies on behalf of the movement. It was written at the Blinman Mine, and sent to the Hon. Secretary (C. Sabine, Esq.), who kindly undertook to get it inserted in the *Observer* of January 23, 1869, as will be seen by the following note :—

"TO THE EDITOR.

"Sir—Enclosed I beg to hand you an address from the Bush Missionary 'William' which has been forwarded to me, and I shall feel obliged by your permitting it to be inserted in your columns.

"I am, Sir, &c.,
"CLEMENT SABINE, Hon. Sec. Bushmen's Home."

[ADDRESS, per favour of the *Observer*.]
"To the Bushmen of South Australia, from 'William.'

"Dear Christian Friends and Brother Bushmen—I venture to make this appeal, knowing that there are a great many persons in the bush desirous of leading a steady life, saving their hard earnings, and doing good for themselves; also that the number of sober men is largely increasing in the colony. As the greater part of these have no home or friends in this country, and no place to resort to, I think the Bushmen's Home just the needed thing for them. I am constrained to make this urgent appeal on behalf of the institution (I know full well its necessity), having travelled for years amongst the bush people and seen all the phases of bush life. I remember that our Lord Jesus Christ went about doing good to the bodies as well as the souls of men, and commanded His disciples to follow Him as an example. If any class of people in this world want a Home (like the one proposed), it is the bush people.

"Bushmen, I beseech you all, for your own good, to come forward cheerfully, zealously, and prayerfully, not only to assist in the building of this thrice-blessed institution, but to support it by patronizing it when it is built. Many leave the stations with good intentions, but are unable to carry them out through so many temptations being thrown in their way (for all have not Christian power) by undesirable characters who are ever seeking to entrap and prey upon the unwary. Bushmen generally are honest, open-hearted men. (I do not say they are all Christians—far from it; nevertheless, God has many of His people in the bush.) Their open and frank demeanour is the cause, I fear, of their being so easily duped and imposed upon by sharpers and others.

"And now, brother bushmen of South Australia, I make my appeal especially to you. Many of you know well that you have offered me on different occasions generous and valuable presents (many thanks for them, just as much as if I had received them); but, like the Apostle Paul, I take no man's money (as pay) in the Lord's work, that I may make the Gospel of the free grace of God without charge, and I do this that I may stop the mouths of the enemies of the Cross of Jesus, the Christ. You have, almost without exception, been kind and considerate towards me for the Lord's sake. You have fed and in a measure clothed me, and that is all I can or do expect; and I ask you now to be as kind to yourselves, now you have the opportunity, as you have been to me. Cast aside all prejudice and pride, and as one man come forward and contribute generously to build yourselves a home and a name. Surely, if a man would expend money, it should be in such a good cause as this.

"I feel sure that much greater good will grow out of this undertaking than has yet been anticipated in the shape of school instruction, provision for the aged, infirm, and destitute, and general improvement of your social position; and when you have a central place of resort you will be able of your own selves to devise means and ways of benefit which are at present hidden from your sight.

"Awake and begin now to take care of yourselves; and I pray God, for Christ's sake, to give you the desire, the will, and the power to help us.

"I am, your servant, for Christ's sake,
"January 14, 1869."   "WILLIAM.

Immediately after this the following letter appeared in the *Chronicle* of February 20, 1869:—

"BUSHMEN'S HOME.
"TO THE EDITOR.

"Sir—In an address I formerly published I expressed a wish to see a Home, so much needed, built for the comfort of bushmen, so as to preserve them from being preyed upon by some of the publicans and a few lodging-house keepers, and I am very proud to see that it is likely to be carried into effect; but my object now in addressing you is to point out where I consider this scheme is likely to lack support.

"In the first place, then, it is proposed to establish the Homes in central situations, such as the Burra. Now this, I think, will be found eventually to be an error, as the bushman, on leaving a station, does so to see a little recreation and amusement, so as to enliven him after a long stay and the monotony in a bush life. This he cannot, of course, see in a little township; there is nothing but the public-house to resort to—no amusement whatever.

"I may be met with the argument that he will not feel this, as he will have everything comfortable, and a library, &c., provided. This is all very good; but how many are there who cannot read or do not give their minds to it?

"I will give you a slight sketch of the manner I adopted on the Melbourne side. First then in settling up; I drew my money in two cheques—a smaller one for the road, and the remainder in another. This I enclosed, addressed to myself, to the care of my news-agent, to be left till called for; so that if I spent or lost the smaller one on the road, I was forced to go to Melbourne or elsewhere to get the other. On reaching town, I first sought a respectable lodging-house; then went out and bought whatever I might require in the way of clothing, bedding, &c.; then I put £2 into a party's hands, to give me when I had my swag on my back, ready to leave town. After this I knew what money I had to spend. In the morning then I arose (bush fashion) early, went and had a walk before breakfast, and my glass of ale on the road. I then returned, and cleaned myself, and again went out to see anything worth seeing, and calling in anywhere for a glass when I felt dry. Thus I passed the day, taking care, whilst enjoying myself, to keep sober. Then in the evening, if I felt inclined, I went to the theatre or other place of amusement. This, Mr. Editor, is what I think will be found needful to get the Home supported--to build it where amusements can be found.

"The second objection relates to the labour office. If

the squatters imagine that the whole management of regulating wages is to lie with them (that is to say, that they are to offer such wages only as they think fit, and the bushmen bound to accept them), then, I think, few bushmen will be found subscribers; that is, if they are not for their subscriptions to be entitled to a voice in its rules and regulations before they are put in force.

"As regards myself, I shall be willing to subscribe annually if the Home is built in Adelaide, and I do trust it may be raised, as I feel assured in time it will do much to elevate a class so much secluded from the enjoyments of most other classes.

"I am, Sir, &c.,
"Now or Never.

"February 20, 1869."

To show that the Home was at this time gaining popularity in the pastoral districts, the following is copied from the *Chronicle*:—

"Blinman, March 6, 1869.

"A meeting was held in Blinman Chapel on Saturday evening last, R. G. Lawrence, Esq., in the chair, to hear the missionary 'William' explain the advantages of the proposed Bushmen's Home, at the Burra.

"Mr. Lawrence, having briefly opened the meeting, introduced 'William,' who proceeded to explain in a most elaborate manner the objects of the institution, and entered most fully into the minutiæ of its proposed every-day life. The meeting, which was a crowded one, listened in a very attentive manner to his address. A subscription-list was presented by the temporary hon. secretary, Mr. Morley. It was most generously responded to by the parties assembled, no less a sum than £24 10s. being subscribed in the room. The prospectus of the scheme being fully before the public, it would be needless to describe more particularly the address, which is, of course, an elaboration of the prospectus. All listened attentively to the speaker; and after the usual votes of thanks to the lecturer, chairman, and hon. secretary, the meeting was closed by singing a hymn, accompanied on the harmonium by Mr. Thorn. Immediately after the close, a fresh meeting was announced, to give 'William' an opportunity of canvassing the total abstinence cause. This he did in a somewhat lengthy address, and succeeded in gaining four disciples."

The *Wallaroo Times* furnishes the subjoined interesting references to "William," the Bush Missionary.

After referring to the Bushmen's Home movement, the writer says :—

"About 'William' there hangs a tale. We believe no one in the colony knows his surname, or much more of his history than that he has been for years engaged in the noble work of traversing the vast Australian continent, visiting the outlying stations and shepherd's huts, distributing tracts and other small books. All the journeys he accomplishes on foot, and to him distance appears to be a matter of not the slightest consideration. He will start on a walk of fifty, sixty, or even a hundred miles to visit one shepherd's hut. The tracts and other religious books he distributes are, we believe, supplied principally by Mr. G. F. Angas, of Angas Park, who keeps 'William's' depôt in town always supplied. After a journey, 'William' occasionally rests a day or two at Angas Park, although, we believe, Mr. Angas knows not much more of him than there is contained in this paragraph. It may easily be imagined that in some of his journeys, which extend from south-east to north of the Burra into Queensland, 'William' has sustained hardships of no ordinary description ; but from his own account of himself, he almost rivals the camel in his power of endurance under a scarcity of water. From the natives he has learnt that by various ways life may be sustained in the absence of better food, and armed with his staff and package of books, he will make his way over districts that would beat a well-appointed caravan.

"Sometimes 'William' quaintly observes, 'This old body likes to give in ;' but I say, "No! No! You must come on" —and come on it has hitherto done—so much so, that 'William' sees no fear on undertaking any journey. More than once he has talked of walking across the centre of the continent to Western Australia, but from this he has up to the present time refrained. What will probably be the finale of such a career, it is easy to say. Under some gum-tree in the lone bush, the dust of the Bush Missionary will probably return to dust, and the spirit to God that gave it.

"Such are a few of the particulars we have been able at times to glean respecting this remarkable man, of whom our contemporary, the *Register*, in its issue of the 1st inst., remarks :—' On foot he journeys like a Peter the Hermit on a more prosaic but far more noble crusade, and from which nothing turns him aside.'

"We believe there is reason for supposing that 'William' has travelled over a large portion of the globe, and he has been heard to refer to the Crimean war. Could his history be published, it would undoubtedly surpass in interest a work of fiction. We have at times almost been tempted to regret that, through the reticence of the chief actor in the scenes, particulars of a life almost apostolic in its simplicity and in the devotion exhibited to a work little known of his fellows should be lost ; but they are the well-earned property of the man, and as such, although we confess to a wish to know more, we shall regret if we have infringed in this notice upon a right that we can but respect."

Still keeping pace with the march of events connected with the Institution, it will be necessary now to introduce the following correspondence from the *Register* :—

"TO THE EDITOR.

"Sir—If not troubling you too much, the insertion of the following lines may throw some light on the reasons why the Bushmen's Home is so unpopular on many stations in the northern districts. I may here remark that my avocations having taken me up north not long since, and being brought into direct communication with that much, but undeservedly, abused class—the bushmen, I have gathered the following objections in course of conversation from worthy fellows :— First—That the squatting interest being opposed to the independence of the hands, it is evident to them that the large squatters on the Committee are combined for a purpose of their own. Second—The great unpopularity of the Chairman and Secretary among bushmen is a death-blow to the movement in any form. Third—That, as in this country all men are of one rank in life, respectability and industry of individuals being accepted as a fact, bushmen do not like being singled out as a class requiring reform ; and that such an establishment as a Home is likely to stamp independent men with an inferiority, which they do not feel, supposing they were to resort to such a practice. Fourth—That many of them have noticed that, while one or two comments favourable to the movement, from persons not bushmen, have been prominently inserted in the newspapers, many letters from bushmen themselves, strongly condemning the Home, have—if not altogether suppressed—not had justice done to the writers, as the letters, instead of being inserted in the open column, only an extract or two has been given in the notice to correspondents; therefore it looks as if the same freedom granted to the squatters to discuss the matter is not being extended to the men, all of which has a tendency to create distrust in the minds of such men as bushmen, who lead a solitary life, and are generally deep thinkers. Fifth—That with the cessation of immigration, the new chum was merged into the ranks of the colonists, and, therefore, a patronising condescension on the part of some would-be aristocrats is insufferably out of place in these days of progress.

"Such, Sir, are the objections urged against the Home ; and I may here add that there is also a powerful opposition to be found in the ranks of the respectable northern storekeepers and innkeepers, who regard the attempt to supply any portion of the public with stores and accommodation by the squatters (as it will be doing if the Home is started) as an unwarrantable competition with the private enterprise of respectable tradesmen.

"I have now fulfilled my promise to some of those bushmen, who conversed with me on the subject of the Home, in writing to your paper. It now remains for me to rely on your kindness to insert it.

I am, Sir, &c.,

"HAWKER.

"March 13, 1869."

[The writer, of course, takes a hawker's view of the question, and perhaps a publican's view also; but we have not the least objection to publishing his letter, as it is temperately written, and expresses his reasons for what he advances. The letters we refused were intemperate, and dealt only in assertion, or rather insinuation. Their publication could have done no sort of good.—ED.]

This captious or querulous letter was not left long unanswered, a kind anonymous friend undertaking a reply of which the following is a copy :—

"TO THE EDITOR.

"Sir—In your impression of yesterday, a letter appeared signed 'Hawker,' and I was in hopes that this day's *Register* would have published an answer to the very illogical reasonings of 'Hawker.' I will take his letter *seriatim*.

"His first objection to the formation of a Bushmen's Home is, that 'squatting interest being opposed to the independence of hands, it is evident to them that the large squatters on the Committee are combined for a purpose of their own.' Now, Sir, if the squatters had any designs against the bushmen, instead of endeavouring to protect them from imposition and extortion, and, I may say, their own imprudence, they would rather encourage the present practice of squandering their wages, as it cannot be doubted that the sooner a bushman's money is spent, the more he will be at the mercy of the squatters.

"Secondly, 'Hawker' says, that 'the great unpopularity of the Chairman and Secretary among bushmen is a death-blow to the movement in any form.' This may be a valid objection to these gentlemen personally, but it does not touch the merits of the question. Besides, it does not follow that either of these gentlemen would retain their positions after the formation of a Bushmen's Home ; indeed, unless they were ubiquitous, I do not see how they could act as Chairman and Secretary to the many Homes that would most probably be established.

"Thirdly, 'Hawker' makes a most astounding assertion even in this democratic colony. He says, 'that as all men in this country are of one rank in life, respectability and industry of individuals being an accepted fact (whatever that may mean), bushmen do not like to be singled out as a class requiring reform, and that such an establishment as a Home is likely to stamp independent men with inferiority, which they do not feel, supposing they were to resort to such a practice.' I will not go into the question of the grammatical construction of the latter part of the above, as 'Hawker' may not have Lindley Murray quite at his finger ends, but I would point out the absurdity, not to say arrogance, of saying, that all men are of the same rank in this country. In no civilized country in the world are all men of the same rank ; there are and ever will be distinctions, and the low, ignorant, brutalized bushman (and there are such) does not and cannot hold the same rank as the well educated moral man holds. That every man should be equal before the law is perfectly just ; but equality before the law can never be supposed to place all men upon a level. Whenever 'Hawker' himself shall have a fortune sufficiently large to enable him to retire from business, he will, no doubt, discard his present opinion with something like a glow of indignation at such an absurdity. It is a well known fact that bushmen, as a rule, are—like sailors—the most careless and improvident of men. They say this themselves ; and to establish Homes for their comfort and security is a laudable undertaking. There are no doubt many exceptions, but it is too true that bushmen of the lower class are improvident, drunken, and immoral. It is well known that after receiving wages—sometimes a considerable sum—they will go to a public-house, and give the owner their money, on the understanding that they drink it out ; and it is no less true that these unfortunate men are fleeced in the most shameful manner. No wonder that publicans and storekeepers oppose the movement ; it would deprive them of their large ill-gotten gains. In all changes there are some whose interests must clash with the new order of things. When first the idea of the 'Sailor's Homes' was broached, the low lodging-house-keepers were all in arms, and a great deal of trash was said and promulgated on the subject ; but the plan has succeeded. The sailors are men like bushmen, and, according to 'Hawker,' are of the same rank as all others, and yet nobody says they are degraded by frequenting the Homes. On the contrary, as they are not exposed to gross and immoral temptations, they must be improved, and might perhaps become better men hereafter. Surely the same influence acting upon the bushman could not tend to make him more dependent than he is now; indeed, far less so, as his money would be better taken care of for him, and he would not have the temptation of indulging in the gross sensuality so dreadfully prevalent at present. Any one conversant with the low-class bushmen knows how shocking is the life led by them. 'Hawker' truly says that the bushmen lead a solitary life; but if he made a slight alteration in the word 'thinkers,' he would be nearer the mark.

"You have answered the fourth objection; I therefore leave it unnoticed. And the fifth is really too absurd to require any answer. Englishmen are often very republican while they work for their daily bread; when they become employers of labour, it is astonishing how conservative they become. I am not a squatter, nor am I in any way connected with that class, but I cannot resist my desire to refute such arguments as 'Hawker's,' based as they are on such erroneous notions and one-sided views. I should be glad to see an abler pen than mine take up the cause, not of the squatter, but of the bushman, whose elevation and improvement should be an object with every right-thinking person.

"In conclusion, I would observe that a Home is much more wanted in Adelaide than at the Burra, where not half-a dozen bushmen would ever think of spending their holidays. It is chiefly to the capital that the bushman looks for what he calls his 'spree,' and it is there that he requires care and protection more than anywhere.

"I am, Sir, &c.,

"A FRIEND TO THE BUSHMEN.

"Adelaide, March 10, 1869."

A clipping from the *Australasian*, inserted here, will show that in our sister colony, Victoria, they clung to the hope of a successful progress for this undertaking of ours; and trusted that, in spite of the prejudice thrown out against it in this colony, we would not let any obstacle hinder us in giving at least a fair trial to our projected scheme. The Editor of that paper remarks :—

"We regret to observe that the project of the Bushmen's Home in South Australia, from which so much was not unreasonably expected, seems to be less popular among the class it was intended to benefit, than the friends of that class could have anticipated. So far as we can understand, the objections raised against it are the results, some of mere prejudice, and others of personal interest. It is said that the chairman and secretary are unpopular, that the bushmen do not like to be patronized, that a Home implies something humiliating, and that 'the northern storekeepers and innkeepers regard the attempt to supply any portion of the public with stores and accommodation by the squatters as an unwarrantable competition with the private enterprise of respectable tradesmen.' Here, we suspect, lies the sting. The publicans will not without a struggle loose their best customers. We trust that the promoters of this truly good undertaking will not be disheartened by any such interested opposition. We observe that it has been urged that the place where such an institution is really wanted, is in Adelaide, and not at the Burra. It is to the capital that the bushman goes for his 'spree,' and it is there that he particularly requires protection and advice. These considerations appear to us to have great weight. The truth probably is, that there ought to be a Home in each place. We trust, however, that no care will be withheld, and no effort spared to give this project a fair trial under fair conditions of success."—*Australasian*, March 27, 1869.

The next letter is a voice from Port Lincoln in favour of the Club, written by a rather eccentric, but well known bushman :—

"TO THE EDITOR OF THE 'ADVERTISER.'

"Sir—Several months ago, long before the idea of a Bushmen's Home had been thought of, or steps taken to initiate the same, you, Sir, first drew attention to the subject by an article written in the *Advertiser*, entitled "Cleaning a Bushman out." This rose from your hearing one of the frail sisterhood of Adelaide lamenting the hardness of the times, their own impecuniosity, and the desirability of catching a bushman and cleaning him out.

"The idea of Bushmen's Homes, then started, has now become developed, and bids fair to be an accomplished fact and one of the institutions of the colony. But, like all other philanthropic efforts for the amelioration of humanity, it has been met at the outset with feelings of antagonism, and letters have been written to the Press decrying the movement, and even assailing the motives of those who have come forward so liberally, giving their exertions, time, and money, in order to accomplish so desirable an object. These letters, I believe, have not generally emanated from *bona fide* bushmen, but have been written at the inducement of those whose sources of livelihood are not the most unexceptional, and who now begin to see that their craft is in danger, if a consummation so devoutly to be wished, as the establishment of Bushmen's Homes, is arrived at. A great number of shepherds, hutkeepers, knock-about hands, and other bushmen in this locality fully appreciate the desirability of having a Bushmen's Home, are ready to become subscribers, support it to the utmost of their ability, and hope soon to see a branch Home established in this isolated and far away part of the colony. Search the English language through, and scarcely can you find one word more desolate or terrible than the one 'homeless.'

"To fully understand the loneliness of the bush in the far away settlements, it must be felt; it cannot faithfully be described. It has been compared to a sailor's life at sea; but what is the monotony of a few months spent at sea, where there is always something to vary the scene and attract the attention, compared to the complete isolation, the years of utter weariness spent in the far away wilderness? There the solitary bushman casts his watchful eyes around, gazes from earth to sky, but finds no relief to cheer him; his flock of sheep, his dog, himself, are all that break the vacancy.

> All hushed above, beneath, around,
> No stirring form, no human sound.
> This is a loneliness that falls
> Upon the spirit and appals;
> It is a silence makes one shrink
> As from a precipice's brink.
> And you will rarely meet it, save
> In the far bush, or the cold grave.

"Patience, which is said to be a virtue, is here taxed to the utmost powers of endurance, and it requires the concentrated spirit of a dozen Mark Tapleys, amalgamated with the same number of Robinson Crusoes, to be at all jolly under such circumstances.

"So depressing, so almost maddening are the influences of this solitude, that men lapse sometimes into almost imbecility, and occasionally show symptons of incipient idiotcy, become shy if spoken to, and nervously afraid of the society of their fellows; or else nature seeks a reaction, and the cheques for arrears of wages are drawn, the solitaire rushes into Adelaide, and in the novelty of the exciting change, feels lost and bewildered. Then he is marked out and spotted by the crimps, the keepers of low, dirty, vermin-haunted lodging-houses, the emissaries of the inferior public-houses, or the bullies of the houses of ill-fame, and, helpless as one of his own sheep when rushed by wild dogs, he soon falls an easy prey.

"First flattered and 'cleaned out,' then bullied and 'turned out,' he re-shoulders his swag (if that by a fortunate chance has been left to him), and returns to the bush, a sadder, but not often a wiser man. It is the same old tale so often told; and who is to apply the remedy, who is to be his brother's keeper? Are not the efforts of those who have now come forward so nobly, in aiding and succouring those now erring and suffering at their own doors, as worthy of as much commendation as if they had encompassed the uttermost parts of the earth and seas in ameliorating the condition of the benighted heathen abroad?

"And look at the different class of men that compose bushmen now, to what it was a quarter of a century ago; the old overlander and the Vandemonian element, then all prevalent, has disappeared, and among the ranks of shepherdom are now to be found men of all classes—artists, architects, clerks, doctors, tutors, ex-military men, clergymen's sons, literary men, university men, &c., and what is the cause of this? Because Adelaide, like Melbourne, Sydney, and other large towns, is overstocked with men of education and talents; they meet you in every corner of the street, jostle one in the highways and byways, can be known by their broken boots and seedy apparel, and their anxious faces looking helplessly, and too often hopelessly, for that employment to give them bread, which they never find. If a situation is advertised, a hundred applicants rush to fill it, and many of the disappointed ninety-nine try the bush as a *dernier ressort*. A contemporary of yours lately waxed merry at their expense, and recommended the unsuccessful candidates to follow the profitable occupation of rag and bone collecting for the home markets. Boccacio wrote his love tales whilst Florence was desolated with the plague. Nero played the fiddle while Rome was burning. And this same facetious writer, like a new but petty Democritus, can see nought but joke and merriment in the sorrows and misfortunes of his fellow-colonists.

"One gigantic evil felt in this remote part of the colony is, there is no school to be found for the children of bushmen. You may travel for hundreds of miles and find the rising generation growing up altogether uneducated. The parents keenly feel this, and would most gladly give a moiety of their earnings to see their children taught. The proposed school in the Bushmen's Home would meet this want.

"Bushmen, as a class, are a very hospitable race—generous in their sympathies, fond of practising the virtue of xenodochy, entertain strangers with a rough but ready welcome ; and it is a pity to see men of this stamp tossed about as they are. In the north of this province, for instance, there are, to my own knowledge, from time to time, men to be met travelling for months together, with a heavy swag on their backs, on the wallaby track, seeking work, sleeping in draughty old woolsheds or deserted huts, their garments in tatters, their money all gone—'cleaned out'—and they themselves enduring with manly resignation hardships and privations that would fill the soul of a London workhouse casual with supreme disgust.

"As the cold and wet of winter are now fast approaching, a renewal of this state of things is sure to happen ; and wise and happy is he who has the foresight to perceive the coming evil and make provision against it, qualifying himself to become an inmate of the Bushmen's Home, so that, should necessity require, that may be open when all other homes will be shut against him.

"I am, Sir, &c.,
"J. BOND PHIPSON.
"Lake Hamilton, Port Lincoln, March 27, 1869."

We now turn our attention to the work which "William" undertook to do in the bush on behalf of the Club. Some of his operations will be gathered by the perusal of the following public reports :—

[From the *Observer* of March 20, 1869.]

"'WILLIAM,' THE BUSH MISSIONARY, AND THE BUSHMEN'S HOME.

"We extract the following from a letter written to a friend by a gentleman in charge of a considerable station in the far north :—

"'"William," the Bush Missionary, stayed here a few nights since, and has been resting himself for a day or two at a neighbouring station. He intends returning to Adelaide, going down the eastern side for the purpose of explaining at the different stations the object of the Bushmen's Home. I think (as all must who give it due consideration) that this a grand and laudable work; but I have great doubts of its immediate success. It will require time to convince the class it is intended to benefit of the great amount of good it will unquestionably do them if they avail themselves of its advantages. "William" is extremely zealous in the cause, and feels sure of its success. Wherever he goes he reads a long address of his own which enters into minute details connected with the Home; and though he will not himself take a sixpence by way of contribution towards it, he makes most anxious enquiries as to whether a subscription-list has been sent by the Honorary Secretary, and in the event of overseers (as in my own case) not having received one, he writes to town requesting that one may be forwarded at once. You know that I am not a very strong admirer of irregular clergymen; but I can respect a person of "William's" evident sincerity and earnestness.'"

[From the *Register* of April 2, 1869.]

"We hear that a large number of subscription-lists have been returned to the Hon. Secretary of this institution, and that they represent in the aggregate a considerable amount. The list from the Blinman Mine contributed the sum of £30, and several others are not far behind; but as we understand the entire amount of contributions from the bush will shortly be published, it is unnecessary to give any details on the present occasion. The lists already received show that the bushmen are in earnest about their Home, and that they are determined to have one or more of these places of resort, in spite of the attempts of some few captious persons who have endeavoured to raise an opposition to the movement. So soon as the bush has been thoroughly canvassed, we understand a public meeting will be held in Adelaide for the purpose of bringing the claims of the proposed institution before the notice of the colonists generally in town or country. It appears that 'William,' the missionary, may be expected in town in the course of two or three weeks, the chief object of his visit being to represent the bushmen and furnish such information as his extensive knowledge will enable him to do as to the situation and management of the Home."

A Burra correspondent, writing to the *Chronicle* of April 10, states that general sympathy is expressed there with the proposed Bushmen's Home movement. He says—"Doubtless a branch establishment at the Burra would be productive of most beneficial results, and be the means of providing comfort and good accommodation to bushmen arriving from stations situated in the north and north-eastern districts, without presenting the usual temptations inseparable from the ordinary means generally available. It must be highly complimentary to bushmen to think that at last some earnest and influential persons are endeavouring by their exertions to do something to alleviate the vicissitudes and hardships attendant upon the isolated nature of bush life by providing institutions of this description."

The Treasurer, being desirous of ascertaining the exact state of the finances prior to a public meeting being held in Adelaide, issued the following advertisement :—

"The time for returning the subscription-lists in aid of the above institution is extended to 28th April, by which date it is hoped they will all be sent in, whether filled up or otherwise."

Matters having now been brought to an issue, steps were taken to make arrangements for a public meeting. The following Circular was sent to each member of the Committee on April 23, 1869:—

"BUSHMEN'S HOME.

"Adelaide, April 23, 1869.

"Sir—You are respectfully requested to attend a meeting of the Committee of the above, on Thursday next, at my office, Grenfell-street, at 2.30 p.m.

"CLEMENT SABINE, Hon. Sec."

In response to the aforesaid Circular, a meeting of the Committee was held on Thursday, April 29, at 3 p.m. Present—Messrs. H. Scott (Chairman), J. H. Angas, H. Hussey, R. B. Smith, C. Sabine, and "William."

The minutes of the preceding meeting, held on January 4, were read and confirmed.

The Honorary Secretary stated that, besides the subscription-lists handed to each member of the Committee, 267 lists had been sent to stations in the bush, of which number 45 had been returned with £316 6s. 6d., eight had been sent back from the dead-letter office, and seven had been returned without subscriptions; leaving 207 lists besides those in the hands of the Committee still to be sent in.

"William" said he had visited 37 stations since the Committee last met, and that he had read at each an address to the men prepared by himself entering fully into the design and objects of the Home, and that the address had been well received, and the men had no objections to make. The speaker then read his address to the Committee for comment.

It was resolved—

"1. That in consequence of so many subscription-lists being still out, the Committee considers it inexpedient to hold a public meeting at present."

"2. That the Secretary communicate with parties still holding subscription-lists, requesting them to return the same without delay, in order that the result of all the applications may be ascertained."

" 3. That, with a view to meet the wishes of the majority of the subscribers and others interested in the proposed institution, it is desirable to establish a Home, in the first instance, in or near Adelaide ; and that any subscribers objecting to this be requested to communicate with the Committee."

" 4. That the address read by ' William' be revised by a Sub-Committee and printed, and copies thereof be forwarded to the various stations and parties interested in the Home."

" 5. That all subscription-lists in future be advertised weekly as received."

" 6. That supplementary subscription-lists be issued, returnable after shearing."

"William" intimated his intention to make another long tour through the stations advocating the cause of the Home in addition to his mission work.

Mr. Sabine (Hon. Sec.) stated that having fulfilled the duties of temporary Secretary for the time he had undertaken to do so, he should be unable, from press of engagements to act much longer, but would continue nominally to act until a Secretary could be found willing to undertake the work. At the same time he acknowledged the valuable assistance rendered him by Mr. Hussey.

A vote of thanks to the Chairman closed the proceedings.

In accordance with the resolution passed at that meeting of the Committee, "William's" address to bushmen was revised, and 2,000 copies were printed, the greater part of which were circulated in the bush. The address was also inserted in the leading daily and weekly newspapers gratuitously in May, 1869. Pursuant to resolution, supplementary subscription-lists were prepared, of which 441 were sent out, addressed to managers and overseers of stations, small sheep-farmers, and others, with the following Circular accompanying them :—

" BUSHMEN'S HOME OR CLUB.

" Sir—On behalf of the Committee of the above institution, I enclose you a subscription-list and address, respectfully soliciting your contribution towards its erection, and

also that you will use your influence to obtain subscriptions from others favourable to the movement.

"Please return the subscription-list (blank or otherwise) not later than the end of October, together with a cheque or money order for the amount subscribed, to C. Sabine, Esq., as addressed, to prevent unnecessary expense in collecting, and to enable the Committee to make the necessary arrangements for effecting the object contemplated.

"Yours truly,

"H. HUSSEY, *pro* Hon. Secretary."

Circular to Sheep Station :—

"BURHMEN'S HOME OR CLUB.

"Committee-room, Adelaide, May, 1869.

"Dear Sir—The Committee of the above desire that you will kindly read or give the enclosed address to the people in your employ, or nail it up in a conspicuous place; and also that you will set before them the advantages to be derived from the establishment of such an institution.

"Please use your best endeavours to induce the people to subscribe to this desirable object. A subscription-list will be forwarded herewith; and if you have previously received one, have the kindness to return it at once, blank or otherwise, and open the one now forwarded. (See heading to subscription-list.)

"The cheque for the amount contributed should be sent in with each list to C. Sabine, Esq., to prevent unnecessary expense in collecting, and to enable the Committee to make the necessary arrangements for effecting the object contemplated. "Yours truly,

"H. HUSSEY, *pro* Hon. Secretary."

Form of subscription-list sent with Circulars in May, 1869 :—

"BUSHMEN'S HOME OR CLUB.

"Subscription-List No. —.

"To Bushmen, Shearers, and Others.

"[Care should be taken that subscribers' names are given in full, for purposes of registry and acknowledgment. All subscriptions will be advertised, and should subscribers not see their names they had better at once communicate with the Secretary.]

"The size and comfort of this establishment will depend mainly on the amount of subscriptions received from the bush.

"This list should be returned to C. Sabine, Esq., Treasurer, Adelaide, not later than by the last mail in October, 1869.

"South Australia, May, 1869."

Date.	Christian Name and Surname.	Residence.	Amount.

"William" also, as previously intimated to the Committee, started on another long tour through the bush, advocating the cause of the Home, during the shearing season of 1869.

To prove that much interest began to be manifested by the bushmen themselves in this movement, the following letter from Melrose, dated April 25, 1869, and signed "A Subscriber," was addressed to one of the leading daily papers. It is here introduced for perusal:—

"TO THE EDITOR.

"Sir—In reference to the Bushmen's Home, the which has been the principal topic of conversation lately amongst the so-called class, allow me, as a bushman, to offer a suggestion that, I think, will prove beneficial to its progress. I see in the prospectus that it is proposed to erect a Home at the Burra, or some other northern township. Allow me to give my opinion, and also the opinion of the generality of bushmen, whom I have conversed with on the subject, that, if so, it will without a doubt prove a complete failure; and if in Adelaide, or within an hour's walk, I firmly believe it will answer, and become a useful institution.

"My opinions are drawn from an experience of twenty-four years' bush life, and some of that as far as inhabited; and previous to that, an apprenticeship to the sea; so I think I may be allowed to give an opinion of the wants of such a class of people. I ask, for example, if after two or three years, or say a twelvemonth's living in the far north on hard fare, you will feel the want of a change, and a bit of a spell—'as all do at stated times'—who would choose such a hole as the Bon Accord Mine, or the Burra, to enjoy themselves? I am sure I would not; and I am also sure that a very few will. What enjoyments will a man get in such a place? whereas in town he will be able to see the little that is to be seen. Allow me to state that the generality of bushmen are a shade above the natives, some of them being well educated and intelligent men, and know full well the enjoyments of a civilized life, and at intervals will have them, cost what it will. It is all very well for 'William'—not that I wish to speak disparagingly of such a man, as I believe him to be a true Christian, though rather an eccentric character—to go about with his ideas, but it is contrary to human nature to find many like him. Sailors' Homes have proved a success for the very reason that they have been situated in or close to the principal city, so that the inmates could go out and enjoy themselves according to their different inclinations. You might as well try to form a Sailor's Home in such an island as St. Paul's, or some such lonely spot, as to form a Home for bushmen in the bush, where they cannot get their desires. Bushmen are not all drunkards (far from it), and at the same time are not water-drinkers; but can sit and enjoy themselves as well as some of our leading men in Adelaide, and their doing so does not lower them any more than the Member of Parliament. It would be a pity after so much being done, if the Home, as proposed, be started at the Burra or anywhere in the bush, and then prove a failure, as it is bound to do, as it would also at once damp the undertaking. First form it where it is bound to be a success, and then at some future time, if thought expedient, try a branch elsewhere.

"To conclude, I consider the Home a most splendid proposition, and should like to see it prove a success. Hoping that I have not taken up too much space in your valuable columns,

"I am, Sir, &c.,

"A Subscriber.

"Melrose, April 25, 1869."

"The Bushmen's Home.
"To the Editor.

"Sir—In reference to the above subject, your correspondent, 'A Subscriber,' gives us a few would-be apparent logical and sentimental statements. Now, Sir, I concur with him in part of his letter. He very properly asks who would choose such a hole as the Bon Accord Mine, or the Burra, to enjoy themselves? but further on he says, "whereas in town he will be able to see the little that is to be seen." Now, what is there in town to be seen, I should like to ask him? For my own part, I know nothing of Adelaide town, nor do I want to; but if the newspaper reports of the Police Courts be true, it is a place abounding in rogues and prostitutes— a fine place to encourage bushmen or any who, according to your correspondent's own acknowledgment, are a weak-minded lot of individuals, only a shade better than the natives.

"Now, Sir, I have seen a good deal of the bushman, and I know of none of that class to which your correspondents belong, except 'A Subscriber' and 'A Friend to the Bushmen,' who have covered themselves with animosity, and are ashamed to see their own names in print. But this I will be bold to say, Mr. Editor, that there are amongst the bushmen many more intelligent and better-educated men than some of the South Australian M.L.C.'s, M.P.'s, and J.P.'s. But to return, however, to the subject of the Bushmen's Home. Has either the Committee or 'A Subscriber' advanced any reason to induce bushmen or any one else to subscribe to the funds? I presume not. The Committee in their reports say, that even if a bushman has no money, he will receive one day's accommodation, and that they must have an order upon his next employer; but they forget to state that he must take whatever employment they like to offer him, and that at any price they think proper. It is this that has induced so many of the greatest opponents of the bushmen (we omit the names, ED.), who are their acknowledged enemies, to support the establishment. They imagine that by these means they will be able to get their work done for little or nothing; that when the bushman's money is gone, he will be glad to seek the Home for the sake of one day's accommodation, and to get employment, say two hard days' work for half a day's wages. They likewise forgot to state that certain squatters had issued orders to their employed, informing each of them, that if they did not give something towards the Bushmen's Home, their assistance would be no longer needed.

"Bushmen, in general, are open-hearted people, in fact too much so, after the treatment they have received at the hands of some of the squatters. But, of course, there are exceptions amongst squatters as well as any other class.

"In concluding, Mr. Editor, I can say without hesitation that the Bushmen's Home movement is one of the most trivial and malicious ever put in motion.

"I am, Sir, &c.,
"AMBROSE EDWARDES.

"Western Plains, May 4, 1869.

[This is the first letter we have received in which the objections of certain bushmen to the proposed Home have been put in any tangible form, and therefore, though not agreeing with the writer's statements or inferences, we suffer him, upon the simple principle of fair play, to speak for himself.—ED.]

It is needless to say that the friends of the bushmen could not allow such a letter to pass without correcting the many misstatements made therein.

The following is a copy of the reply to the letter which Ambrose Edwardes wrote in opposition to this movement on the bushmen's behalf.

"TO THE EDITOR.

"Sir—In a recent issue of your paper, I observed a letter signed 'Ambrose Edwardes,' in relation to the above institution, which calls for a few words of explanation. The writer is evidently labouring under a total misapprehension as to the objects contemplated in establishing a Bushmen's Home, and also as to the motives which have prompted its promoters in setting it on foot. He appears to think that the squatters are the prime movers in the matter, and also that it is intended to make the question of wages a leading feature of the proposed Home. Having carefully watched the proceedings from the first, and having attended all the meetings which have been held relative thereto, I can confidently affirm that the question of wages on no occasion formed any part of the deliberations of the Committee; and that, so far from the squatters seeking to make it an engine of oppression to the men in their employ, they have hitherto rather held themselves aloof from the movement; but if they see, after a thorough canvass of the bush, that the men are really desirous of having a comfortable Home for themselves in town, many who have not subscribed will, no doubt, contribute liberally towards the institution.

"Mr. Edwardes will see from the prospectus, and from the recently-published address of 'William,' that the labour office in connection with the proposed Home is calculated to afford reciprocal advantages, both to employers and to those seeking employment. Your correspondent seems to think that men will be coerced to take any kind of employment at any rate of wages which may be offered; but he may rest assured that men will be as free to act in these respects in the proposed Home as they are at the present time. So much for the labour question.

"As to the movement for the establishing of a Bushmen's Home being a 'trivial and malicious' one, as characterized by your correspondent, I am inclined to think that he is either ignorant of the import and meaning of these words or else has grossly misapplied them. If he had used the words 'important and philanthropic,' he would, I conceive, have been much nearer the mark, unless he regards the comfort and welfare of his brother bushmen as a 'trivial' affair, and any effort tending to ameliorate their condition a 'malicious' undertaking.

"Mr. Ambrose Edwardes winds up his letter on the Bushmen's Home with a statement which certainly is not borne out by facts—viz., that some squatters have threatened to dismiss those in their employ who refused to contribute to the Home. Such a report as this, if unfounded, should be severely reprobated; and if true, which is very improbable, the parties concerned cannot but be regarded by the friends of the Home as its greatest enemies.

"Much might be said here as to the advantages of the

proposed Home; but as they are fully set forth in the recently-published address of 'William' previously referred to, I shall not occupy any more of your valuable space on this subject at present.

"Hoping that your correspondent will allow his mind to be divested of all prejudice against the proposed Home, and that he may live to enjoy some of its comforts and advantages when established,

"I am, Sir, &c.,

"H. HUSSEY.

"May 20, 1869."

Ambrose Edwardes, not being satisfied with this reply, again rushes into print:—

"TO THE EDITOR.

"Sir—In the *Observer* of the 22nd of May there appeared a letter of Mr. Hussey, in which he writes in rather a warm spirit, and puts a heavy stress upon the words 'trivial' and 'malicious,' and says the words 'important' and 'philanthropic' should have been used. It may be important, as far as the squatters are concerned, but no further; and as far as squatters' goodwill goes on behalf of the bushmen, it is most trivial. The word 'philanthropic' cannot be justly used, and as far as the squatters are concerned it is a most malicious movement is the Bushmen's Home movement.

"Mr. Hussey says the question of wages has never been mooted at any of the Committee meetings. Perhaps not; nevertheless it is not likely that any member of the Bushmen's Home Committee would publicly own it if ever it had been, because they know it would be a death-blow to the movement.

"Mr. Hussey's remarks about the address of 'William' gives me an opportunity to reply thereto. 'William' has carefully selected his cards. He has pointed out the popularity of the Bushmen's Home amongst some of the bushmen, but he carefully avoided or utterly neglected to state that it was so amongst the minority, and that the majority scorn with disgust the very name of a Home. 'William' likewise accuses all who oppose the Home of being an infamous lot of low publicans. I can confidently assure him that there are a great many who oppose the Home, and who are not nor ever were in any way connected with nor do they sympathize with that class; therefore that fact of the address is as unjust as it is untrue. And what reliance can be put upon the other portion of the address, whilst one part thereof is so utterly false?

"As Mr. Hussey puts so much reliance on 'William's' address, allow me to refer him to the said address. It says these pledged men are or ought to be, according to their promise, influencing others to follow their example. Assuming that these men are squatters, and that they subscribe toward the funds of the proposed Home, are they to influence others to follow their example? If so, can Mr. Hussey inform me of any greater influence that could be brought to bear on some of the bushmen than that mentioned in my last?—although I am happy to say that it is not all the bushmen who would be so bamboozled.

"Furthermore, Mr. Hussey says the squatters have hitherto held themselves aloof from the movement, which, to use his own words, is certainly not borne out by facts. Does Mr. Hussey mean to say that there are no squatters on the Committee?—that the position of Chairman or that of Secretary to the said Committee is not filled by persons interested in squatting?—that a meeting held some few few months since, at which the Bushmen's Home movement was first mooted, the mover and seconder of the resolution to the effect that the establishment was necessary are in no way connected with squatting?

"When Mr. Hussey can assure me that the above has been done without the assistance of squatters, he may rest assured that the opposition which is now held out against the Home will be withdrawn, and that those who now oppose the Home will exclaim—'Behold a paradise on the earth in the shape of a Bushmen's Home!'

"I am, Sir, &c.,
"AMBROSE EDWARDES.
"Western Plains, May 25, 1869."

[We have now given ample space to writers on both sides of the question, and are compelled to say that any further letters on the subject of the Bushmen's Home can only appear as advertisements.—ED.]

To expedite the return of the subscription-lists and to give notice of the determination to change the site of the Home from the Burra to Adelaide, the following advertisements were inserted:—

"BUSHMEN'S HOME OR CLUB.—Persons to whom subscription-lists have been sent who have not returned them are requested to send back such lists without delay, together with the amounts collected, so that the result of all the applications may be ascertained.

"CLEMENT SABINE, Hon. Sec. *pro tem.*

"May 1, 1869."

"BUSHMEN'S HOME OR CLUB TO BE ERECTED IN ADELAIDE.—Notice is hereby given that, in deference to the wishes of many contributors, and to meet the views of those who declined contributing but promised to do so were the site changed, the Committee, at its meeting on the 28th April, unanimously resolved to establish the first Home or Club in Adelaide; steps will therefore be taken accordingly, and a fresh canvass made.

"Any contributors who may be dissatisfied with this alteration will please communicate such objection at once to the Committee.

"CLEMENT SABINE, Hon. Sec. *pro tem.*

"May 5, 1869."

A BUSH CHILDREN'S HOME.

To the Editor of the *Register.*

Sir—I see a number of good and benevolent gentlemen have attempted to set on foot a Bushmen's Home—a most worthy object; though how far it will be responded to by the class it is intended to benefit yet remains to be proved. As a bushman, I value the intentions of the projectors of the scheme, but at the same time doubt its proving a success. However, if it fails we shall be no worse off than before. Many of us have passed the best years of our lives in the bush, and have done without such an institution; but there are those to come after us now growing up in the bush in ignorance.

Sir, can nothing be done for them? We who came from home had a small amount of learning; they, poor things, start worse in the race of life than their fathers. However anxious a shepherd may be to educate his children, it is quite out of his power to do so. I have known anxious parents leave the bush and settle down and try to get work in the neighbourhood of a school for the sole object of having their children taught; but their necessities have driven them back to the bush, and to the sorrow of seeing their children reared to misery.

For the credit of the colony and for its well-being it is most desirable some steps should be taken to prevent the evils that must be expected to result from an ignorant population.

Sir, I think something might be done to save our little children from becoming a disgrace to South Australia. Why could we not have a Children's Home, where they might be taught and boarded at a low rate? With the little their parents could afford and the subscriptions of the benevolent, subsidized by the Government (the same as other schools), I think much could be done for the rising generation.

If some good Christian gentlemen would take the matter up, the whole of the bushmen, masters and men, would alike heartily join in the movement. It is a want we daily see and feel. It is sorrowful to reflect on the position of these poor children. The Scriptures are a closed book to them; they know not their Creator; the tracts "William," the good, leaves are but as waste paper. With such a state of things, what can we hope for?—what may we not expect?

To some more able advocate (but not more zealous) I leave the glory of working out this great Christian charity to a successful issue. Such a man will be a benefactor to his race, and will have the blessings of generations yet unborn.

That this question of the education of our bush children may be taken up in the manner it deserves is the earnest wish of

A Subscriber.

North, May 31, 1869.

The Bushmen's Home.

To the Editor of the *Register*.

Sir—In your impression of the 5th inst. a letter appeared headed " Bush Children's Home," and signed by " A Subscriber."

If the writer of that letter carefully read through my address to the bushmen and public of South Australia which was published 6th May last, he would have observed a reference in it relative to the same subject, which has been a source of very serious consideration and apprehension with me. If the writer will join heart and hand with other married people in the bush to raise the much-needed and long-desired Home or Club in the first place, he will move a step in the right direction to consummate his own wishes for the said home and school for bush children.

The school, no doubt, will grow out of the proposed institution, and our plan must still be to establish that first. Looking to the parties he has mentioned in his letter for support is very precarious, and good in theory only, I fear.

If a free boarding-school does not grow out of the proposed Home, I cannot at present see where it is to come from. We must begin at the beginning, and in the right way, especially now that steps have been taken, and kind and Christian friends have given us a start to establish a Home in the first place. There will then be an organization, but at present there is none whatever amongst bushmen. When this is done it will, like a goodly tree, produce good fruits, and a school for children will no doubt be one of the fruits thereof.

What we want to get is a central place or head-quarters; and I believe we shall then not only have a school, but, I trust, a fund also for assisting bushmen's widows and orphans, as well as the sick and destitute. But we cannot have fruit and flowers without the root. The Home I look upon as the root.

The result of the canvass to be made throughout the bush during the coming shearing season will demonstrate whether there is to be a Bushmen's Home in South Australia or not.

I can assure you, Sir, that the sister colonies are watching the result of this movement almost as anxiously as ourselves.

A very small proportion of married bush people, so far, have come forward to help the Home. They seem to forget that their children are growing up, and will probably need an institution of this kind, if they themselves do not, in the future, as well as school now.

Truly both establishments are very much needed; but they must come in their regular order if they are to be permanent. The school will, I apprehend, work better under the eye of the bushmen's own committee, for I fear there are many parents here in the bush who would positively not suffer their children to leave them without having their confidence strengthened.

Depend upon it, they will work best connected in the way I have shown. The Home or Club is not intended to benefit single men only, as many of the married people suppose; but all bush people, married and single, will reap reciprocal benefits from it. Children, also, who are growing up will need homes of this description when they leave their parents to gain a living in the world.

I can assure your correspondent that if he had travelled the bush as I have done, and in the work I have been engaged, that he would not have found that unity amongst bushmen of which he speaks even to establish a school under the present circumstances, let alone supporting and working it for any length of time. There is, I regret to say, a shyness—I may say a backwardness—amongst some bushmen to subscribe for building their own very needful and much-to-be-desired Home. Theory is one thing, and practice another; and your correspondent would admit this if his mind had been exercised as mine has been of late. He says "the whole of bushmen, masters and men, would join in the movement." How does he know this? I can and will indulge the hope that we should have the sympathy of a great many. That would be something, and we should probably at first get a few contributions from Christians and kindly-disposed persons. I must say I rather doubt that they would all come forward; there would be no difficulty in doing it if they would. As I said before, theory is one thing, practice is another. The desirability of the thing no one can doubt—so far, so good; but can it be put into practice in any better way than I have already several times suggested?

If your correspondent will take to himself a share of the work, and the glory of establishing the much needed Home or Club for the bush people generally, he will not only be conferring a benefit on the rising generations, but will also be indirectly helping to raise the school he needs.

Did space permit, I might show how the Home will probably maintain the school with the help of the bush people; but more anon, as I fear I have already encroached on your valuable space. However, this shearing season will no doubt decide whether there is to be a Home and school, or no Home and no school for bushmen and their families.

I pray God, if it is His will, to favour the work we have in hand, for it is a great work, for Jesus Christ's sake. Amen.

I am, Sir, &c.,

"WILLIAM."

Willowie, June 22, 1869.

THE BUSHMEN'S HOME.
To the Editor of the *Register*.

Sir—A "Bushman's" letter in your paper of Monday last, pointing out the harsh treatment the working classes in the bush receive at the hands of some squatters, in the shape of filthy flour, sugar, and other rations, totally unfit for human food, is, I grieve to say, to our cost too well known to us bushmen. And, Sir, these are not the only impositious which are practised on us on some stations. There is a man in town with his family at the present time, who has been charged as high as £2 5s. per bag for seconds flour in the Port Lincoln district, when the rate payable for first quality flour in Adelaide, according to the papers, was only £1 per bag.

Now, Sir, I ask, are we not justified in strongly opposing a bushmen's so-called Home, when we are impudently asked to trust our interests and liberty in the hands of such men as these? When I was last up North, I met men on several stations who told me that they were compelled to subscribe to lists for the Bushmen's Home, as they knew if they refused to do so they would get the " sack." One poor father of a large family told me, with tears in his eyes, that he had given ten shillings, after being pressed by the overseer, as he knew he dared not refuse to subscribe, for fear of having to take the " wallaby" with his wife and five children. At the very time the ten shillings were forced from him, his children were in want of boots.

The whole affair of the Home is a squatters' movement for their own benefit, which is proved by the fact that it originated in the private office of the largest squatting firm in the colony, and the officers are all connected with squatting. Are we bushmen weak enough to be blinded by the pretence that it is for our benefit ? Time will prove that those bushmen who, like myself, have warned their brothers against this affair, are the truest and best friends in the colony.

I shall now conclude by enclosing my real name and address, so that if any disinterested person (not a squatter) requires proof of my statements, he can communicate with me, through you, when I and others will produce such evidence to satisfy any reasonable man that the pretended good intentions of the promoters of the Home are nothing but a sham, and it is all being done to get bushmen under the thumbs of a certain clique of the squatters.

I trust, as you have expressed a desire to admit the working man at all times to a free discussion in your paper, on any question of importance to his class, that this poor attempt of mine, to open the eyes of the public to a real state of the case, will appear in Monday's *Register* and next week's *Observer*.

I am, Sir, &c.,

A BUSHMAN OF TEN YEARS.

[The publication of the above letter—one among many that has been sent to us—will afford the speakers at this evening's meeting an opportunity of answering the objections, which, however unjustly, are very prevalent among bushmen.—ED.]

TO THE EDITOR.

Sir—I wish to say a few words in reply to a letter in to-day's *Register*, signed "A Bushman of Ten Years," in which he complains of "the harsh treatment which the working classes receive at the hands of some squatters, in the shape of filthy rations, totally unfit for human food," and also insinuates that the proposed establishment of the Bushmen's Home has originated with the squatters, whose interest, he says, it is to play into their own hands by keeping down the rate of wages. Now, Sir, I am a bushman of fourteen years' experience in station-work in the north, and have found good and bad masters during that time. The same remark will also apply to the working men themselves; but, except in a very few instances, I have never had to complain of rations.

This is the experience of others also, and therefore "Bushman's" reflection, which he evidently intends to refer to the majority of the stations, is utterly unfounded. I should like to ask him upon what station he has been employed, and where he earned his money, in order that he may substantiate the statement he has made, and the reflections he has cast upon the employers.

With regard to his second objection, my opinion of the proposed Bushmen's Home is, that it must be supported principally by bushmen themselves, assisted by the contributions of the masters. Bushmen do not want charity. What they require is to have a comfortable home provided for them—at their own expense—as a refuge from destitution, and where they may associate with the respectable of their own class, and have their money taken care of—a great desideratum. They require to be treated as if they were not an isolated class of beings, whom nobody cares for; to be regarded as men possessing the same intelligence and gifts as those who move in a more civilized state of society, and the Bushmen's Home is to be established on this principle. From the very nature of their occupation, bushmen are subjected to great temptations when they come within the bounds of civilization; and it is my opinion, as one of that class, that the Home will counteract the evils to which they are there exposed. When established, the institution will at once show the difference between the real hard-working conscientious bushman and the loafer, whose only interest it is to get a living by the easiest means, and whose object has been to cast reflections upon those of the employers who are working in this good cause.

I am, Sir, &c.

HENRY STEPHENS (of Oladdie).

Adelaide, December 20, 1869.

An attempt has recently been made in New South Wales to establish a Bushmen's Home, in accordance with the efforts with which our readers are familiar, as having attracted much attention in South Australia. We regret to learn that the attempt has been unsuccessful. The promoter of the good work was Captain Scott, a police magistrate. But, after all his exertions, he found that at his first public meeting only five persons attended, of whom three were officers of his own department; and at his adjourned meeting the attendance was reduced to one. He sent applications to the various banks, but received only one donation, and his subscription-list only showed a sum total of £4 10s. In these circumstances nothing remained but that Captain Scott should return the money he had received, pay the preliminary expenses out of his own pocket, and abandon the project. Such a termination to such an undertaking is indeed melancholy. It is notorious that bushmen, from the nature of their occupation, are subject to peculiar temptations, and are liable to peculiar incapacities to resist temptations. Even if the best and kindliest endeavours to assist such persons are often received in a spirit very different from that in which they are made, those who have entered upon the good work ought not to be cast down. In this case perseverance brings with it its direct and material reward. It is to the direct pecuniary interest of all employers of labour, and of stockowners among the rest, that their workpeople shall be sober, honest, respectable men. It is their interest, therefore, and it is their duty, to do all that is in their power to put an end to that lamentable waste and drunken riot that too often, under crafty guidance, takes the place of innocent and cheap recreation.—*Chronicle*, August 21, 1869.

The Bushmen's Home movement is very quiet, but let us hope that this promises good rather than evil. It would be a sorry affair if it should not succeed as well as the Sailors' Home, which now bids fair to be a substantial institution, with good buildings and excellent promoters. — *Observer*, August 21, 1869.

Homes for Bushmen.
To the Editor of the *Australasian*.

Sir—It was with a feeling of regret I read lately in your paper, that a movement, initiated by Captain Scott in New South Wales, to found a Bushmen's Home, had signally failed to enlist the sympathies of labour employers. Institutions of this kind throughout the bush would confer a great boon on the labouring classes, and relieve employers, who are tormented by the present system of feeding travellers At first a small outlay would be incurred in the building and maintaining of each Home, and surely no settler or farmer would object to contribute a little for this purpose, seeing that by this means a stop would be put to the vagrant system—at any rate there would be no excuse for it.

Eventually, I am confident they could be made to be self-supporting, and whatever abuses might creep in at the first go-off would speedily disappear as the advantage of Homes came to be recognised by the men themselves.

All honour to such men as Captain Scott, or those in South Australia who have attempted, however unsuccessfully, to arouse the sluggish sympathies of the squatters, and to make them understand that what is good for the labouring man in this instance, as in most others, would be most beneficial to themselves.

In the hope that you, Sir, may help to ventilate this vexed question, and as you nearly always do aid a good cause by honest writing,

Yours, &c.,

A Spectator.

[ADVERTISEMENT.]

Bushmen's Home or Club.—*Notice to Holders of Subscription-Lists.*—The time having expired for returning the subscription-lists on behalf of the Bushmen's Home, you are respectfully requested to forward as soon as possible the list which was sent you last May, with whatever amount has been subscribed, to the Hon. Treasurer, Mr. C. Sabine, Adelaide, as the Committee wish to ascertain the total amount contributed.

In cases where lists may be still blank, it is requested that such also will be returned immediately to the Hon. Treasurer, or if the list has been lost or mislaid, that a statement to that effect may be forwarded, as each list sent out has been numbered and registered, and until all the lists have been returned, the Committee cannot give a complete statement of the result of their appeal to the bushmen at the public meeting, which it is intended to hold in Adelaide as soon as arrangements can be made.

H. HUSSEY, Hon. Secretary.
C. SABINE, Hon. Treasurer.

November 18, 1869.

"William" having returned from his journey from canvassing the shearing sheds, the Committee thought it judicious to hold a meeting on the 2nd December, 1869, to receive a report of progress. The meeting was held in Grenfell-street at half-past 2 p.m.

Present—J. H. Angas, Esq. (Chairman), S. Cornish, H. Giles, D. Murray, C. Sabine, C. B. Young, H. Hussey, and "William."

The minutes of the last meeting were read and confirmed. The Secretary read the following report:—

" 185 subscription-lists have been returned; 48 with subscriptions amounting to £268, and 137 blank, leaving 256 still out. In order to secure the return of as many of the outstanding lists as possible, a circular has been sent to each station, requesting the same to be returned immediately, filled up or otherwise.

" Several short letters have been received with the returned lists, but there is scarcely any reference in them to the principles of working the institution, leaving it probably to 'William' (who has visited many of the stations and afforded a large amount of information) to state the views of the bush people generally on the above subjects so far as he was able to ascertain.

"No steps have been taken to raise funds for the Home from any other source than from the bushmen since the last meeting of the Committee, it being understood that an appeal should not be made to the public generally until after a public meeting had been held in Adelaide."

The Hon. Treasurer (Mr. Sabine) read a financial statement, from which it appeared that the total amount received on behalf of the institution was £590 11s., and the expenditure had been £59 1s. 5d. The past appeal to bushmen resulted in 464 subscribers, the amount of whose contributions averaged 12s. 3d. each. The second appeal was responded to by 520 subscribers, with an average amount of 9s. 5d. each. Total, 984 subscribers; average subscriptions, 10s. 10d. each.

"William," the Bush Missionary, read a statement detailing his labours in the bush on behalf of the Home since last Committee meeting, as follows:—

"Mr. Chairman and Gentlemen—I beg to state that since our last Committee meeting, held on 29th April, thanks be unto God, I have, in conjunction with my evangelizing work in the bush, travelled on foot about 1,600 miles on behalf of the Bushmen's Home or Club, and visited about 160 different places or stations in the north, north-east, and western plains of this colony. Whilst the shearing season lasted I visited 37 woolsheds, and opened the subscription lists lying there. I have also read 56 times an address compiled by myself from what has from time to time appeared in the papers what I know to be the desire of the promoters of the scheme, the operations of the Bushmen's Home Committee, and my own experience of bush life (which address I am prepared to read before the Committee if they desire it). It sets forth the many disadvantages that the bush people (at this time) labour under—many of them by their own improvident way of living—as well as showing to them the advantages and benefits to be derived by the establishment of such an institution as the one proposed. I have also distributed throughout the colony between 1,500 and 1,600 printed addresses (authorized by your Committee at its last meeting) entering into detail of the proposed rules, regulations, management, general working, and other matters connected with the Home. To show with what success this has been done I must refer you to the Treasurer's and likewise to the Secretary's reports. The total sum of £590 11s. given there is not so great as was probably anticipated at the outset; but there is much cause for thankfulness and gratitude to God. We must remember, gentlemen, that the most of this amount of money has been gathered from amongst a hardworking, self-denying class of men, many with numerous families and rather low wages at present. If we look at the large number (984) who have subscribed this sum, and then add to these the names of 500 more who signed my book in favour of the movement—making a total of 1,484—it will, I doubt not, be a sufficient evidence of the necessity of some such place, as well as a kind of guarantee for its future support when its benefits and advantages become practically known to the bush people. There would have been, no doubt, twice this number in favour of it but for the pernicious effects of prejudice which has been excited in the minds of large numbers of bush people through slander, misstatements, and misrepresentations by those who are its secret or avowed enemies, and who see that their questionable craft is in danger. This prejudice I have had (in some places) to stem like a torrent, and to counteract it has cost me much labour and anxiety; but I think I have, by the grace of God, succeeded in placing the Home in the minds of the bush people on a firmer basis through it than it was before. Many bushmen have said to me, after the meetings I have held at the stations had been closed, 'When we see the Home going on as you say, and that it is the intention to really conduct it on the principles you have just laid down, we will gladly help it all we can.' Some who would subscribe said, 'Well, I will give 10s. now, and if it goes on all right I will give some more another time when I see what the Home is like;' and I believe that eventually they will add much more to the general fund. It is purely a question of time to disarm their prejudice. They have so seldom had anything of a philanthropic nature done for them, and so little interest taken in their affairs, that many of them are shy and very suspicious about this movement on their behalf; but by conceding to their wishes as far as practicable, and by judicious management, we may succeed in raising the requisite amount. My opinion as to the best way of accomplishing this is to call a meeting as soon as convenient and solicit help from a generous public, and to start a model Home on a small scale commensurate with the amount contributed. Looking at this undertaking in a pecuniary point of view, the Adelaide public should be interested in a movement of this nature, especially all parties whose business is in any way connected with the pastoral interest; and, indeed, all branches of trade, more or less, will be benefited by the first or parent home being in the neighbourhood of Adelaide, for it will probably centralize a great portion of the bush people (at any rate, occasionally) in Adelaide, and people must be fed and clothed somehow. This will increase trade in some degree, and, moreover, it will probably (after a little time) bring a great part of the £150,000 or £200,000 paid in wages annually into the city, not to mention the social, moral, and other good results which must accrue to society at large and the men themselves; for it will certainly take out of the hands of undesirable characters the major part of this large sum, and set it going in its proper and legitimate channels, and this will do good to trade, to society, and to the bush people as well, and not (as it is now) to just a few individuals only, who monopolize a great part of this large sum for a worse purpose really than throwing it into the River Torrens. I have not the slightest doubt (nor ever had) as to the success of the undertaking when once it is organized and started—that is, if the bushmen themselves are consulted and properly represented, and each one has his fair share of the internal management of the place either by a committee or directors of their own. To carry this out, I would suggest that a few bushmen (say about ten) from different parts of the colony be nominated to act with the committee of management that may be chosen at the public meeting to be held in Adelaide. They should have the privilege of doing this whether they avail themselves of it personally or by letter, or not at all. I also suggest, on behalf of the bush subscribers, that when the property is ready to be conveyed there should be six trustees in all—viz., two settlers, two citizens, and two bush people appointed, if possible. I now come to another stage in the proceedings—viz., when the Home is ready (D.V.) for launching, the directors and superintendent will probably be selected and appointed; and I suggest that before these steps are taken an appeal should be made by advertisement (in consequence of the bush people being so scattered and migrating) to all subscribers for their approval, and all who do not answer the said advertisement after a sufficient time has been given for that purpose to be considered as approving and acting in favour of the parties so nominated and appointed. I mention this, because the bush subscribers, being so unsettled as they are, many see a difficulty here. But we can and we must reach them through the usual medium, the newspapers, or circulars, for any purpose that may be wanted of them, until they have an organization of their own, which it will be desirable to form as soon as possible, for the better working of their society. I also suggest that the bush people, as many as choose, become members of the Home or Club, by the payment of an annual Club-fee, as members of other Clubs do, to defray the necessary working expenses, this fee to be fixed when the Home is lawfully established, but in no case to be above one guinea per annum. The benefit and privileges of being a member should be set forth in due time in a proper prospectus, to be prepared for that purpose, and a copy sent to all bushmen likely to become members thereof, soliciting their membership. The prospectus should be advertised for a season in the principal papers, and I think it but fair to the present subscribers, that all future non-subscribers, wishing to become members of the Club—not boarders of the Home remember—should pay an entrance-fee, to make up for their non-subscribing to build the place, the amount of this fee to be decided hereafter, and to go to the building or extension fund; this does not apply to the boarders at the Home, but only to those who wish to become members of the Bushmen's Society, and be entitled to certain privileges, to be yet set forth at the proper time in the proposed prospectus. I suggest also that the members make their own by-laws for the working of their own Club, or Bushmen's Friendly Society which will probably grow out of it—such by-laws and such rules subject, of course, to the approval of the trustees, and according with the trust deed. Their Directors *may* be chosen from among themselves, at any rate they should have the privilege of choosing them if they wish it; this will also give them something for their membership; or else let the trustees or directors frame the rules and by-laws, agreeably to the trust deed, and subject them to the approval of the annual members. Perhaps from all sources, after a public meeting, we may realize about £1,200; this will probably be supplemented by a little more yet from the country, as there are still some stations to be canvassed. I have hope also that we shall get part, if not all, of a piece of land given to us by a few generous philanthropic friends, to build the Home upon. There is, I believe, a gentleman of the Committee in communication with parties about this matter. With these prospects the Committee would, I think, be fully justified in beginning to build a Model Home on a small scale. There is one great benefit connected with such arrangement, that if it is small it will be free; that will be far better than a large fine building encumbered with debt; indeed, it must be untrammelled to succeed on a paying self-working principle, and to give it a fair trial on its own merits and profits. If found necessary after a while, it can be easily extended, and if not found practicable as a bushmen's Home or Club, it may make a good 'home for aged bushmen,' a 'free school for bush children,' or be disposed of in any way a legally authorized meeting may think fit. To prove a success, it should be started at once with the means at the disposal of the Committee. A sufficient beginning may be made with well-arranged boarding apartments and a labour office; then, as the self-supporting principle is carried out, the more applicants who present themselves the faster will be the growth of the institution. When opened, if there are only five men in the place, there will only be that number to provide for; or if there are 50 or 500 it will be the same, for the boarders will clear their own way as they go, as there will be no rent or interest to pay, and the membership will probably after a little while pay all the working expenses, except actual victualling, and leave something over. The object in the undertaking is not so much to make it an extraordinarily profitable institution, as to benefit labouring men; consequently the charges for board, &c., should be made as low as possible. I suggest that three-quarters of the amount already subscribed, after all preliminary expenses are paid, be expended in land and building, the remaining one-fourth in furnishing and fitting up the Home, and giving it a fair start, keeping a small reserve fund in hand. I desire now to make a few remarks with reference to the management of the proposed Home in the first instance. In deference to the wishes of many of the subscribers, and in consideration of the somewhat small amount of funds at present collected, and having no money contribution to offer myself towards this grand and good work (for I possess none), I have (D.V.) resolved, after much thought and mature consideration, to offer my services for this purpose without pay, and try to give the Home a start and get it in good working order. This I (D.V.) will do if the Committee think it desirable, and request it of me, and will put this resolution to the vote of all the subscribers for an expression of their opinion in the matter. This can be done by advertising for all objectors to this arrangement. I especially desire this, as I have informed the bushmen in my address on my rounds through the country, that all subscribers will have a voice in the selection of their superintendent, and in making their own by-laws, &c., and faith must be kept with them. It must be taken for granted that those who do not reply to the advertisement, after a sufficient time allowed for that purpose, are in favour of this offer. This decision which I have come to, though it will, if my offer is accepted, occasion a great loss of personal liberty to me, I do not conscientiously consider a sacrifice of principle, as I believe it to be the Lord's work to do any kind of good in a lawful way; and in this case it is peculiarly justifiable, considering all the circumstances, for I am persuaded that the establishment of such an institution will not only add to the comfort of the men, but to the social and moral improvement and elevation of the bush people generally, to whom I owe a large debt of gratitude, having been for years at the *Lord's charges* amongst them in these colonies. Since I have been in South Australia, I have been sustained in my labours by Christian friends, without whose kindness I should have been unable to prosecute so well the trying work given me to do, or accomplish so much for the salvation of souls, the glory of God, and the good of my brother-men. May it please the Lord to reward them all for their disinterested kindness to me for Christ's sake. Under these circumstances, and to carry out this proposition, it will be necessary for me to be provided with an apartment entirely to myself, as also the means and ways to carry out the business of the institution in a proper manner. This arrangement will probably save the infant Home two or three hundred pounds at starting, which will be a great consideration, and will, by the blessing of God upon the work, in a great measure give confidence, I think, to the minds of many of the bush people, and will be as good a contribution as I can under my present circumstances possibly give. If the course I have mapped out is pursued, I firmly believe the thing will work. The bushmen will probably enter into the matter with more zeal, and a better spirit will, I trust, prevail. Let them experience the benefits to be derived from it. This will be the best argument that can be used, and the most successful advertisement which can be put forth, as the bushmen will listen to their own mates before they will to anyone else. It will also prove to them the falseness of the misrepresentations that have been made, and so freely circulated among them, and that the movement made in their behalf is truly a philanthropic and praiseworthy one ; and all that is really wanted by their best friends is their social and moral comfort and elevation. It will also prove the Committee's earnest desire to carry out the wishes of the subscribers and bush people (if they can understand them) in this matter to the fullest extent of their power and ability. I cannot conclude without reference to the goodness and lovingkindness of the the Lord my God, and to the hospitality and valuable assistance I have almost everywhere met with from managers, overseers, and old bush friends, high and low, throughout the pastoral districts, in behalf of my work. This has considerably lightened my labours, made my yoke easy, and my burden light. I wish more especially to refer to the kind considerate Christian gentlemanly courtesy displayed by friends, who are my fellow-labourers in this great and good work, who have devoted so much valuable time gratuitously, and taken so much interest for the bushmen's greatest good and welfare, and this through much misrepresentation, prejudice, and opposition. Many, many thanks to the press of South Australia for their invaluable assistance on all occasions, which, I trust, they will still continue towards this truly benevolent work. I doubt not but they will reap their fruits in due season. I have often had to confer with members of the Bushmen's Home Committee, and also personal friends, and am much indebted to them all on the bushmen's behalf as well as my own, for their very valuable assistance, counsel, and advice, on all occasions, early and late, in season and out of season, wherever it was needed.

"May it please our Heavenly Father to bless the work of our hands, and establish it upon us, for our Lord Jesus Christ's sake.—Amen.

"God save the Queen!

"WILLIAM.

"Adelaide, South Australia, December 2, 1869."

On the motion of Mr. D. Murray, seconded by Mr. C. B. Young, it was resolved that the report read by "William" be adopted and embodied in the minutes.

On the motion of Mr. Young, seconded by Mr. Murray, it was resolved that a public meeting be held in Adelaide on behalf of the Home; that the Chairman (J. H. Angas, Esq.) and Mr. Young communicate with His Excellency the Governor, to ascertain if he would consent to preside at a meeting any evening during the week after next; and also that Mr. Sabine see the Mayor of Adelaide and solicit the use of the Town Hall for the said meeting.

On the motion of Mr. Sabine, seconded by Mr. Young, it was resolved that the following gentlemen be applied to in order to ascertain if they would consent to take part in the proceedings of the public meeting:—Dr. Short (Bishop of Adelaide) or Dean Russell; Revs. Binks, Cox, Lyall, and Parsons; Captain Bagot; Messrs. J. H. Angas, N. Blyth,

J. H. Barrow, J. H. Clark, S. Davenport, S. Tomkinson, J. M. Solomon (Mayor), and "William."

On the motion of Mr. Murray, seconded by Mr. H. Giles, it was resolved that Mr. H. Hussey continue to act as Honorary Secretary.

The Secretary was requested to write to Mr. Thos. Elder, to ascertain whether the lady having an interest in the piece of land near the Company's Bridge, North Adelaide, would consent to give up her interest; also whether, in the event of Captain Hart not being disposed to surrender his share, the other two-thirds—viz., that of Mr. Elder and of the lady referred to—could and would be made over for the purpose of the Bushmen's Home.

A vote of thanks to the Chairman concluded the meeting.

A gentleman deeply interested in the movement, writing to the *Wallaroo Times*, makes the following pithy remarks respecting the intentions of the Committee to change the site of the proposed Bushmen's Home :—" I perceived that a proposition was agreed to that, instead of the Home being in the bush (where it would probably be as much frequented as might be reasonably anticipated in such a locality, and no more), it should be established in Adelaide. The project of making the Home in the bush was about as sensible a one as it would be to make a Sailors' Home on board ship. When Jack has his holiday he likes to be ashore, and when the bushman has his holiday it may be taken for granted that he does not want it in the bush—that he requires some change, and that he will make his way into the streets of a town, if possible."

Matters having now arrived at a culminating point, it was resolved at the seventh Committee meeting, held on the 8th December, 1869, to hold a public meeting on the 20th December, 1869; and pulpit notices as follows were sent to the ministers of the various denominations, and also advertised in the daily papers :—

"BUSHMEN'S HOME.—A public meeting on behalf of the abovenamed institution will be held (D.V.) in White's Room, Adelaide, on Monday evening, December 20, 1869, at half-past 7 p.m.

"His Worship the Mayor of Adelaide will preside.

"'William,' the Bush Missionary, will state the result of his visit to the bush on behalf of the Home ; and a statement of what has already been done towards establishing the institution will be made on the occasion.

"Addresses will be delivered by the Lord Bishop of Adelaide, Dr. Short ; Revs. J. G. Millard, F. W. Cox, J. Lyall, and J. L. Parsons ; Hon. J. H. Barrow, M.L.C. ; Messrs. N. Blyth, M.P., S. Davenport, J. H. Angas, and other gentlemen.

"The public generally and bushmen especially are invited to attend.

"There will be no collection."

A Committee meeting was held on 8th December, 1869, to report progress. Present—Messrs. C. B. Young (Chairman), C. Sabine, J. H. Angas, "William," and H. Hussey.

Mr. Young reported that Mr. J. H. Angas and himself had waited upon His Excellency the Governor, to invite him to take the chair at the proposed public meeting. His Excellency stated that as he was at present residing in the country he could not promise to preside at an evening meeting, but would do so if it were held in the afternoon.

The fact of His Excellency declining to attend an evening meeting rendered it necessary to call the Committee together at the earliest opportunity, which was done accordingly.

Mr. Sabine reported that he had waited upon the Mayor, who had agreed to waive the usual preliminaries for obtaining the gratuitous use of the Town Hall for such a laudable object as the establishment of a Home for bushmen.

On the motion of Mr. Sabine, seconded by "William," it was resolved that the Mayor (Judah Moss Solomon, Esq.) be requested to preside.

The following resolutions to be initiated at the forthcoming public meeting were adopted, and the movers and seconders arranged as follows :—

BUSHMEN'S HOME OR CLUB.

Order of Business, Resolutions, &c., for Public Meeting to be held in White's Rooms on Monday evening, December 20, at 7.30 p.m.

1. Chairman's (the Mayor of Adelaide) address.

2. Hon. Secretary (Mr. H. Hussey)—Report of proceedings to present time.

3. Resolution. Mover, Lord Bishop of Adelaide; seconder, S. Davenport, Esq.; supporter, Rev. J. G. Millard—

"This meeting, recognizing the fact that the bushmen of South Australia occupy an important position in the community, regrets that hitherto sufficient consideration has not been paid to their requirements, particularly when absent from their employment."

4. "William" will give a statement relative to the proposed institution.

5. Hon. Treasurer's (Mr. C. Sabine) financial statement.

6. Resolution. Mover, J. H. Barrow, M.L.C.; seconder, Rev. J. L. Parsons—

"That, considering the success which has attended the efforts already made for establishing a Bushmen's Home, this meeting is of the opinion that the time has now come when it is expedient to provide such an institution in or near Adelaide."

7. Resolution. Mover, Rev. F. W. Cox; seconder, J. H. Angas, Esq., J.P.—

"That this meeting, being of opinion that the establishment of a Home should not be left to the unaided efforts of bushmen, earnestly solicits the aid of the citizens and residents of the settled districts generally to assist in providing a Home in or near the city."

8. Resolution. Mover, N. Blyth, Esq., M.P.; seconder, Rev. Jas. Lyall—

"That the following names be added to the existing Committee :—Hon. J. H. Barrow, M.L.C., N. Blyth, Esq., M.P., S. Davenport, Esq., T. Magarey, Esq.; and to represent the bushmen—Messrs. Evan McKay, Wm. Coleman, Wm. Roberts, John Canham, John Quayle, Wm. Bradbury, John Gilles, Samuel Lovering, T. Lillywhite, and — Pelton."

9. Resolution. Mover, Rev. C. Manthorpe; seconder, C. B. Young, Esq.—

"That the thanks of this meeting be given to His Worship the Mayor of Adelaide for presiding on this occasion."

Bushmen's Home.

[From the *South Australian Advertiser*, December 21, 1869.]

A public meeting to further the movement for the establishment of a Bushmen's Home was held in White's Room on Monday, December 20. The attendance was large, and the Mayor of Adelaide (Mr. J. M. Solomon) occupied the chair.

His Worship commenced the proceedings by remarking that they must all be aware that in a colony like this—one of the main interests of which was sheepfarming—there was a considerable number of men, known as bushmen, who required that some persons should take an interest in their welfare when they visited large centres of population, and that this should be done they would all admit was both necessary and proper. The Home should be established on much the same principles as the Sailors' Homes which had been erected in various places and found to confer so many benefits. Taking into consideration the heat of the weather, and the fact that the object of the movement was one that needed nothing, he was sure, to recommend it, he hoped the gentlemen who had to address them would curtail their speeches as much as possible. (Hear, hear.)

Mr. H. Hussey (Hon. Secretary) then read the following report :—

"In stating what has been done towards the establishment of a Bushmen's Home, I have to report that at a preliminary meeting held in White's Arbitration Room on the 30th December, 1868, the desirability of founding such an institution was unanimously affirmed, and the gentlemen present on that occasion resolved to use their best endeavours for the attainment of the object. A Committee was appointed to make the necessary arrangements, consisting of the following gentlemen :—Chairman, Hon. Thos. Elder, M.L.C. ; Honorary Secretary and Treasurer, Mr. C. Sabine ; Messrs. J. H. Angas, J. H. Browne, S. Cornish, H. Giles, H. Hussey, D. Murray, H. Scott, W. K. Thomas, S. Tomkinson, C. B. Young, and 'William,' the Bush Missionary.

"Mr. Elder having left the colony, the Committee have been deprived of his valuable services. I may also state that as Mr. Sabine could not conveniently continue to act both as Treasurer and Secretary, he consented to fill the former office, and at the request of the Committee the duties of the latter office devolved upon me.

"One of the first steps taken by the Committee was the issue of a prospectus, briefly setting forth the kind of institution it was thought desirable to establish. This, accompanied with circulars and subscription-lists, was forwarded to the various stations throughout the colony, as well as to small sheepfarmers and others. Seven hundred lists in all have been sent out; of these 318 have been returned, —204 blank, and 114 with subscriptions—leaving 382 still out. The Treasurer's statement will show the monetary result of this appeal to the bush people.

"The Committee having decided to canvass the bush for subscriptions in the first instance, in order to test the feelings of bushmen themselves towards the proposed institution, no systematic efforts have been made as yet to obtain contributions from the citizens of Adelaide, and from residents in the settled districts.

"At the preliminary meeting above referred to, it was proposed to erect the first Home at the Burra, or some other northern township; but at a subsequent meeting of the Committee, it was resolved, in deference to the wishes of a majority of the subscribers and others interested in the institution, to establish the first Home in or near Adelaide.

"A large number of addresses prepared by 'William,' the Bush Missionary, have been circulated throughout the colony, setting forth the principles upon which it is proposed to conduct the Home, and the comforts and advantages bushmen are likely to derive from the establishment of such an institution. 'William' has also undertaken long and arduous journeys in the bush, for the purpose of presenting its claims to those it is intended more particularly to benefit, and as he will furnish all needful information as to his proceedings, it is unnecessary to say more on this subject."

Mr. Clement Sabine (Hon. Treasurer) read the financial statement, from which it appeared that the receipts amounted to £646 11s. 8d., made up as follows:—To subscriptions from 1067 persons on 117 stations, £567 11s. 6d.; to contributions from overseers or owners, £4 9s. 3d.; to subscription-list at Bank of Australasia, £12 ; to interest from Bank received, £6 ; and to balance due to Treasurer, £2 17s. 2d. The expenditure amounted to £59 18s. 5d. The number of bushmen who had contributed towards the erection of a Home was, he remarked, a test of the extent to which the movement was appreciated. Although the contributions were insignificant, and the total amount small, still the number who had contributed had altogether exceeded the expectation of the Committee; and he could say that those who had subscribed might be expected to give the institution their support. At first he entertained doubt as to the success of the Home ; but from what he had since ascertained, he was satisfied that it would succeed. The difficulty would be raising the first funds. They would require £3,000 before they could do anything in the way of erecting or renting a place suitable for a Home, and it was not intended to borrow. The present then was the time to place the matter before the public, and invite their assistance. He had been given to understand that the bushmen would have subscribed more liberally, had they believed the Home would be erected. Now that the matter had gone forward, they would receive additional subscriptions from the men. He had every confidence in the Home being built, and, moreover, that it would be well patronized. When once erected, it would be its own advertisement ; men living in the institution would attract others there. (Applause).

His Lordship Bishop Short moved—" This meeting, recognising the fact that the bushmen of South Australia occupy an important position in the community, regrets that hitherto sufficient consideration has not been paid to their requirements, particularly when absent from their employment." He observed that when they considered that 700 circulars had been issued, and over 1000 bushmen had subscribed, and further how the property and interests of the proprietors of runs were united with the well-being of the men who went there to labour, the class was certainly an important one on whose behalf they had met on that occasion. (Hear, hear.) The question arose—Did these men form a class who deserved the assistance of the public in the manner proposed ? Assuredly they did. (Hear, hear.)

Some time since he used annually to take a journey into the bush, and he had never ministered with more pleasure or satisfaction to himself than he had to bushmen—fine honest and hearty fellows—in the woolshed, or in the kitchen. He felt a great interest in the class; and there was, he thought, something in their life that should evoke sympathy. Think of men following silly sheep for a long period of time, deprived of communion with their fellow-creatures. He felt that if these men came to town at the end of the year, and were tempted to break out and knock down their drafts, it was not surprising they were made a prey of, and in many instances they went back ruined and beggared to labour for another year. What wonder then if they became what were called archangels ruined. (Applause.) Sailors, it was said, earned their money like horses and spent it like asses; and, in his opinion, much the same might be said of bushmen. He believed if there was a Home where their earnings would be taken care of, and their comfort looked after, many of them would be saved from that prodigality and waste of life and substance of which they had seen numerous instances. He had no doubt as to the propriety of establishing the Home. Hitherto, to his mind, the men for whom it was intended had not been sufficiently considered by the public. Having pointed out that some years ago certain squatters established schools, and otherwise endeavoured to educate and improve the children of their employès, he remarked that these arrangements had ceased to exist by reason of the drought, which, like a flood of ruin, or like a tidal wave, had passed over the pastoral interest. In conclusion he stated that it was to the advantage of the community generally to help forward the movement to save this important class from further deterioration, further poverty, further loss of everything that rendered life valuable. (Applause.)

Mr. S. Davenport seconded the motion. He had had, he said, the pleasure of meeting His Lordship in the bush for the period of twenty-one years, and from his zeal and devotion to his sacred duties, there were few better qualified to speak on this subject as he had done. Referring to the recognition by the resolution, that the bushmen were an important part of the community, he said, this was repeating a simple proverb, because it was bushmen who started the colony—bushmen with capital, and bushmen with labour. If there was anything striking in the establishment of that city and colony, it was during the first five years of their history—nothing was exported, save what had been raised by bushmen. There was no produce exported in the first year. In the second, £770 worth of produce reared by bushmen, was exported. In the third year it decreased to £321. Next year the produce amounted to £8,480, and the next year it reached £35,485 17s. This showed the benefit of the bushmen, who gave life-blood to the community. It was natural to conclude, that to those who had done so much for them they owed a great debt of gratitude. Sociably it was very desirable that the interests of the bushmen should be attended to. Last year bushmen produced a million's worth of produce; but why should not a million or half a million more have been raised during that time? He might be pointed to the drought for an answer, but he demurred to this, and said sufficient inducement had not been given to the bushmen to encourage the settlement of the country. It had not been properly recognised that the bushmen were a clear profit to the country, for they occupied land beyond the settled districts, and there were many hundreds of miles of country in the colony still unoccupied and unknown. If they treated their public property as they would their private estates, they would know the colony more familiarly than they did. Socially this movement for the benefit of bushmen was important, because he saw no reason why in a few years these bushmen could not purchase small properties in various parts of the colony, and he was pleased to see that a Savings Bank was to be established in connection with the Home. (Cheers.) This was not an act of charity, for the bushmen did not want their charity, and they would be sorry to offer charity to them. He was glad to see that the management was to be carried on by a Committee of the bushmen themselves, because this was very wise and proper. He spoke of the advantages of Clubs, and as professional and mercantile men could have their Clubs, why should not bushmen have a Club. Bushmen, however, were so scattered as not to have that strength which followed from unions. He spoke of the analogy between bushmen and sailors. Bushmen spent a life of solitude, monotony, and hardship, and on these grounds they claimed their sympathy. The effect of these circumstances on the bushmen's minds made them easy victims when they came into the settled districts, and were met by people who, in a sneaking underhand manner, sought to take their money from them. He concluded by referring to the benefits of a Bushmen's Home, and wishing it every success. (Applause.)

The Rev. J. G. Millard supported the resolution. He thought the previous speakers had thoroughly exhausted the subject, but as a minister and a citizen he felt it his duty to respond to the call of the Committee. Anything which benefited man deserved their warmest sympathy and support. He expressed sorrow that there was anything like opposition or antagonism to this movement in the community, but after considering the arguments used against it he had come to the conclusion that the persons who had written on the subject were either very ill-informed or else that they were interested parties who looked on the movement with prejudice. It had been asked why they should select a particular class of people for their social, moral, and religious care—why not take care also of the shoemakers, tailors, smiths, masons, and others when they came into town? Well, much as he should like to see a movement made for each of these classes, they could not compass everything at once, and they had better begin with the most pressing cause—that of the bushmen. He referred to the special peculiarities of bushmen, and the proportionate need there was to meet these peculiarities. He spoke of his experience in the bush of New South Wales and Queensland when he commenced his ministry twenty or twenty-one years ago, and then said he sincerely hoped this Home would be a great success, as it would be a great discredit to the whole community if it did not prove so. It had been said this was a squatters' affair, and let them look to it! No doubt they had the largest interest in it, but it was a matter in which the entire community was interested also. (Cheers.) He congratulated the promoters of the movement on the success which had followed their efforts.

He was sure there were better times in store for the Home. He said "God speed these better times, and God bless the men who sought to advance them." (Applause.)

The motion was then put and carried unanimously.

"William," the Bush Missionary, then gave the following statement of his personal experience among bushmen and others with reference to the Home, including portions of his report to the Committee on his return to Adelaide, which said report was not at that time published, and it was necessary to repeat it for the information of the public :—

"Your Worship, Ladies, and Gentlemen—Being fully sensible of what may reasonably be expected from me by an audience such as the one I have now the honour to address, I thought it better to prepare a statement, which, with your kind permission, I will now read. I beg to state that for several years I have, by the grace of God, been travelling through the bush in these colonies, doing the work of an evangelist among the stations, huts, and bush people, and whilst doing so I have had opportunities of making myself acquainted with their habits and have been enabled to study their peculiar characteristics, which persons accustomed to the comforts of a city life can hardly understand.

"The scattered population in the bush have a strong claim upon the sympathy of those residing in more highly-favoured localities. Bushmen (as a correspondent of the Press observed) often endured hardships and privations of no ordinary kind and with a resignation deserving a better cause, sleeping about in draughty old woolsheds or dilapidated huts, travelling at times hundreds of miles on foot seeking for employment sometimes four or five months, often carrying a heavy swag under a scorching sun or heavy rains, and sometimes very badly clad, their garments tattered and torn, and they themselves debilitated and (to use a bush phrase) 'cleaned out'—that is, without a penny to call their own in this wide world.

"Almost every one who has travelled far into the interior of Australia can remember the rough-and-ready but hearty and sincere hospitality of shepherds, stockmen, bushmen, and employers ; and a note-book might be well filled with tales which they recite of their unfortunate trips to the various townships. There is not, I believe, a more generously-disposed class of men in this world (in their own way and among themselves) than Australian bushmen. I have always found them willing to help liberally a real case of distress when it has been presented to them in a proper manner. They sometimes live in the bush for years together; but when an opportunity offers, too many of them, I am sorry to say, as the fit takes them, rush off to some place—probably to Adelaide—and there squander away their hard earnings in a few weeks' or days' debauchery. Some of their greatest difficulties begin when they visit the thickly-settled districts. Very frequently, however, they are not allowed to proceed so far as the city, but get 'bailed up,' as they call it on the Sydney side, before they reach their destination; and the poor men often find, to their own and sometimes to their families' cost, that they can have the doubtful pleasure of being hocussed, drugged, and robbed without going to the city for these lamentable inflictions. Should they, however, reach it with their cheques, how often we may read in the public police reports of the way in which bushmen get rid of their money when in town! They meet with certain undesirable characters, who beguile them with drink, and lead the poor bush victim step by step into all kinds of riot and excess, until in a very short time their spoilers succeed in flattering them and cleaning them out, and then they bully them and turn them out of doors. Finally, many find themselves in the lock-up or before the magistrates, fleeced, fooled, penniless, and friendless sure enough; or, if they still retain their swag, it has to be shouldered again for a tramp through the bush, and sometimes they do not know where to go or which way to turn—poor prodigals indeed. This mode of life is not only injurious to many of our bush people and to society generally, but sets a very bad example to the rising generation, and ultimately consigns many to the Hospital, to the Destitute or the Lunatic Asylum, or to prison, while many perish in the bush. Such is the reward of sin and folly! The tendency to these evils arises in some measure from the peculiarity of bush life. Men are withdrawn from nearly every social enjoyment, and lose, from disuse, the power of measuring their wants which those who associate more with their fellow-creatures insensibly acquire. In these young colonies there is a great proportion of men destitute of friends or connections, and having literally no home, but who are yet desirous of leading sober, steady lives, and of saving their hard earnings to do good to themselves and at the same time benefit society at large. I may here observe that the proposed Home is well calculated to supply this want.

"Of late years my mind has been led to study the practicability of erecting a Bushmen's Home or Club, the establishment of which we have met here to-night to consider. I know of no better remedy for the state of things I have described than to erect such an institution, as it will (D.V.) be the means of preventing many of the evils alluded to, which all right-minded men must condemn and deplore. It will also promote the bushmen's comfort whilst residing there. It will certainly have the effect of raising them in the social scale; and I feel convinced that the Home will materially benefit the whole colony, especially the men themselves and their employers. The institution should be made a Home in the fullest sense of the word, with every requisite for innocent amusement and enjoyment as well as for business.

"I feel persuaded that the time has now come for affording bush people visiting the city and other large townships that protection and comfort which are calculated to make many of them better men, and that the good influence they will exercise directly on other bushmen will assist them to become more truly moral and independent than they now are, as their money will be better taken care of for them if they wish it, and they will not constantly have the temptations before them of indulging in the gross sensuality and drunkenness to which they are, under existing circumstances, so frequently exposed. Such an institution would not only centralize the men and cement in proper bonds the employers and employed, but would also prove highly beneficial to the settlers, stockowners, and sheepfarmers, as well as to those employed by them. What is good for the labouring men in this instance, as in all others, must be beneficial to employers also; indeed, it is to the direct pecuniary interest of all employers of labour—stockowners and sheepfarmers among the rest—that their workpeople should be sober, honest, respectable men.

"The good fruits that will (D.V.) grow out of this institution, such as making provision for the sick and unemployed, for the instruction of the young, for the preservation and comfort of the aged, &c., are more than I can possibly show in a statement of this kind, and in the short time usually allowed at public meetings for detail. Now let me ask, Why should we not establish such a Home?

"There are between 8,000 and 9,000 people at ordinary seasons employed in pastoral districts alone, and at shearing-time this number increases to between 13,000 and 14,000. There is also (at a rough calculation) between £150,000 and £200,000 paid annually in wages. Surely it is high time something should be done to improve the condition of this long-neglected large pastoral population, hundreds of whose children are now growing up in the outlying country in the grossest state of ignorance and vice, and some effort made to induce bushmen, instead of spending their cheques in spreeing when they come to town, as so many of them do, to lay their hard earnings by for seasons of distress and adversity. One very desirable object in the establishment of such a Home is, that bushmen will know, whenever they are travelling, or taking a spell, or looking for work, that they have a fixed place, which they have a right to make use of at any time as their own, at low charges, and there be far more comfortable and independent than if stopping at public-houses and such like places. In the proposed Home they will be able to keep themselves sober and respectable, meet their fellow-bushmen and friends, enjoy the intercourse natural to human beings, indulge in rational amusements and cheerful society, store any of their effects, deposit their savings, get employment probably, and feel in every sense of the word at home; being at the same time protected from those who make it their business to relieve them of their money, often leaving them to beg their way back to the bush.

"One of the fundamental principles of the institution is, that it must be made, after it is opened, self-supporting; and if properly managed and patronised by the working men, I believe it will become so. Another is, that it must be conducted on purely temperance principles. With reference to this, I can confidently affirm that the majority of the bush people are decidedly in favour of its being so; and, from my own experience of the habits of bushmen, I am equally confident that, in order to ensure its success, intoxicating drinks (in any shape or form) must not be allowed on the premises, however hard the case may be, or depend upon it drink will be the death of the Institute.

"The meeting may now desire to know with what favour this scheme has been met by the bush population generally. I beg to state that, in conjunction with my regular evangelising work, I have been collecting information and maturing a plan to remedy some of the existing evils in the bush. This plan having assumed a definite form, I have latterly been obtaining signatures and raising subscriptions towards the object. In doing all this, I have well traversed the colony of South Australia. My journeys have extended more than once as far west as the Great Australian Bight, to the north beyond Mount Margaret and Lake Hope, eastward to the Barrier Ranges, to parts of the Darling and Murray rivers, Yorke's Peninsula, Cape Jervis, and the extreme south-east, to the Gawler Ranges, and to the Western Plains—a distance of over 19,000 miles on foot. (Loud applause.) Whenever I had an opportunity, I brought the claims of such a Home as the one proposed before the people, invited discussion, and enlarged upon the contemplated rules and regulations, also the necessity of forming a Bushmen's Friendly Society, and the mode of conducting the Home, the details of which I will not now take up the valuable time of this meeting to recapitulate. I may here remark that all these matters have lately been rendered more familiar to the bush population and others by the distribution of a large number of prospectuses, addresses, advertisements, &c. In some few instances I have met with prejudice and discouragement from captious individuals, but a little explanation has generally cleared it away. The opposition to this movement has been made chiefly by self-interested parties travelling about the bush vilifying it. Letters also have been written to the press, and there is an especially bitter one in this morning's *Register*, decrying this good work, and assailing the motives of those who have so liberally given their time, talents, and exertions, in order to accomplish so desirable an object. These letters, I believe, did not emanate generally from real bushmen, but were written at the instigation of those whose sources of livelihood are not the most unexceptionable, and who began to see their questionable craft in danger. In all great changes and reforms of a social and moral nature, there are some whose interest must clash with the new order of things; and in a good work, such as this, we must expect much slander, misrepresentation, and opposition, as it is impossible that all men will see what is for their good. The result of my experience is that the men with whom I have come in contact do, as a rule, require such an institution; and those who will make use of it when built are far more numerous (since the matter has been rightly explained to them) than those who oppose the scheme.

"I must now refer to the Secretary's and Treasurer's reports for practical results and for further information. We must remember, ladies and gentlemen, that the amount subscribed has been collected within the last twelve months from amongst a hard-working class of men, many of them with numerous families and rather low wages. If we consider the large number of 1,050 who have subscribed this sum, and then add to these the names of 500 more who signed my book in favour of the movement—making altogether a total of 1,550—we shall have, I doubt not, sufficient evidence of the necessity for the Home, as well as a guarantee for its future support. There would probably have been many more names returned in favour of it, but for the pernicious effects of the prejudice alluded to, which has been excited against this movement by its secret as well as avowed enemies, who have instilled into the minds of some bushmen that the Home is being got up by the squatters to the men's disadvantage; and it is purely a question of time to disabuse their minds entirely of this idea. Let them experience the benefits to be derived from such an institution, and this notion will soon disappear, for this will be the best argument that can be used and the most successful advertisement which can be put forth, as the bushmen will listen to their own mates before they will to any one else. As a class of the community, they have so seldom had anything of a purely philanthropic nature done for them, and so little interest taken in their welfare, that many are shy, and even suspicious, about this one on their behalf. Looking at this subject in a pecuniary point of view, the Adelaide public will be particularly benefited by the first or parent Home being in the neighbourhood of Adelaide, for it will centralize here a number of bush people, and will probably bring into the city a great part of the £150,000 or £200,000 paid annually in wages to the bush people. Thus, apart from the social, moral, and other good results to the men themselves, the sum alluded to will not fall into the hands of undesirable characters, who now monopolise it for a far worse purpose than throwing it into the River Torrens, but will be conveyed into its proper and legitimate channels to benefit, and not to injure, the men who have worked so hard and so long to earn it. I have not the slightest doubt as to the success of the undertaking, if the course I have mapped out is pursued, and if the bushmen themselves are consulted and properly represented. When they have an organization of their own (which for this purpose it will be desirable to form as soon as possible), the men will become members probably by paying an annual fee as Club-money, such fee not to exceed in any case one guinea per annum. Of course this is not to apply to boarders at the Home, but to members of the Bushmen's Club. Further particulars will be given on this subject hereafter in a prospectus to be prepared for this purpose. To prove a success, I am of opinion that a small model Home should be started without delay (after a canvass of the city, suburbs, and settled districts has been made for subscriptions) with the means then at the Committee's disposal. The scale upon which the first experiment will be made must depend on the total amount of contributions towards this object. A sufficient beginning may be made with well-arranged boarding apartments and a labour office; then, as the self-supporting principle is carried out, the more applicants who present themselves the faster will be the growth of the institution.

The desire is not so much to make it a profitable undertaking as to benefit the labouring men, consequently the charges for board and lodging, &c., should be made as low as possible, compatibly with good living, comfort, &c. There is abundant proof that the institution is much required, and it will undoubtedly commend itself to the support and intellectual approval of the public generally, and to those interested in pastoral pursuits particularly, for it should be borne in mind that the colony is largely indebted to the class called bushmen for its material prosperity, pastoral pursuits having done much for opening up the country.

"The cost of such an establishment will necessarily be considerable, though, if all hands help, it can be easily raised; and it is high time that some measures should be taken to improve the condition of such a useful body of men. So deeply do I feel the importance of such a movement that, after much thought and prayer for Divine guidance, I have resolved (D.V) to comply with the wishes of personal friends, the Committee, and others (if the bushmen do not object to this arrangement) to undertake the first superintendence of the place without salary—(applause)—for a time, until it gets into good working order. I will do this to help the infant Home, and save the expense at the beginning of having to pay a large salary for this purpose, which can but be ill afforded. This will be as good a contribution as I can give. (Loud cheering.) Those only who know my habits of life, and the evangelising work to which I have devoted myself, can at all understand how the temporary abandonment of this line of Christian work will prove (not a sacrifice of principle, but) a discomfort to me. I merely mention this now to show the meeting how much faith I have in the cause. Still individual exertions can be of little avail in such a case as this; but an earnest and combined effort will in all probability result in real and permanent benefit to all who get a living, or who are connected in any way whatever with the bush people, if the proposed Home is thrown open to all who agree to conform to its rules and regulations. The Committee have not hitherto called the special attention of the Adelaide public to this undertaking, nor solicited help from station-holders, nor from residents in country towns, as they have been waiting for an expression of opinion from the bushmen through the medium of the subscription-lists, some of which have been sent in and advertised in the weekly papers; and these lists have realized the sum of £625, collected from the labouring men alone. This, I think, proves that there is an earnestness about them in the matter; and surely no settler or citizen who wishes well to the bushmen would object to contribute to the noble work we have in hand, for the evils it is intended to cure are patent to every one who has given the bushmen's case serious reflection. I would remark here that this great movement cannot be carried to a successful issue if only the bushmen take an interest in it; and as it is directly or indirectly for the good of the community at large, the public generally, and the employers of labour particularly, must please assist us, and if this combined effort is put forth, success is almost certain to be the result. I cannot conclude this statement without reference to the goodness and lovingkindness of the Lord my God, in conducting me safely through this dry and thirsty land so many thousands of miles, preserving me from dangers seen and unseen, and making me so useful to my brother-men in my day and generation. I must also refer to the valuable assistance and hospitality I have almost everywhere met with from managers, overseers, and old bush friends—high and low—throughout the pastoral districts in behalf of my work. This has made my yoke easy and my burden light. Many, many thanks to the press of South Australia for their invaluable assistance which, I trust, they will still continue towards this truly benevolent work. They will reap their fruits in due season, I doubt not. I have often had to confer with the members of the Bushmen's Home Committee, and also personal friends, and I now take the opportunity of publicly thanking them on the bushmen's behalf, as well as my own, for their very valuable assistance, counsel, and advice on all occasions, early and late, whenever it was needed. The commendation of their own consciences will be the best reward for them, I am sure. All friends of the bushmen, and all true philanthropists are earnestly appealed to, and respectfully solicited to contribute towards the funds for the erection and establishment of this noble institution when waited upon by the collector hereafter to do so. I must now leave the matter with you, feeling that I have not done the subject half the justice it deserves, and I shall be very glad to see abler persons take up the cause on the bushmen's behalf. And I pray to God, for Jesus Christ's sake, to give you all the will, and the desire, and the strength, and the power to help us build the Bushmen's Home, for 'Except the Lord build the House, they labour in vain that build it.' —1 Peter, ii. 17.—Amen. 'God save the Queen!'" (Loud applause.)

The Hon. J. H. Barrow moved—

"That, considering the success which has attended the efforts already made for establishing a Bushmen's Home, this meeting is of opinion that the time has now come when it is expedient to provide such an institution in or near Adelaide."

He said he looked upon this Home as an experiment, for he was not by any means sanguine of its entire success. There were many difficulties in its way, and many of the best causes were thwarted, and often defeated by the difficulties in their way. When the Home was first suggested he never thought it would be opposed by any persons calling themselves *bonâ fide* bushmen, although he thought it might be opposed by two or three scrub-publicans, and men of that sort. If *bonâ fide* bushmen really did oppose it, he believed that it must arise from misconception as to its object and purposes. If bushmen were to be coerced he could understand their objection; and if, when they obtained admission to the Home, they were to be debarred free egress and ingress, he could understand it; for, unless this Home was to be a sort of Club in which the bushmen could go in and out voluntarily, and be their own masters from first to last, then he would have nothing to do with it. (Cheers.) They had no right whatever to put any sort of pressure on men, even though they might say it was for their good. They must accomplish that good with their own free consent, and he supported this movement only on the clear and distinct understanding that bushmen should be as free in the Home as any gentleman who went to the York Hotel and called for what he wanted. (Applause.) They must endeavour to impress bushmen with the feeling that they were to make themselves entirely at home in their Club. They did not wish to insinuate that bushmen could not conduct themselves properly without vexatious rules and restrictions, but they desired to establish a Club, an institution where the better class of bushmen could feel themselves thoroughly at home. (Applause.) It had been stated that in the Bushmen's Home intoxicating drinks would be excluded. Of course it was not to be supposed that the bushmen who were not teatotallers were to be locked up from morning till night, so as to prevent them getting a glass of beer elsewhere; but in an institution of this kind regulations were necessary, and the Committee had determined that it was best to conduct this Home upon temperance principles, in which he thought they had done right. (Cheers.) If, however, bushmen thought they would be compelled to sign themselves teetotallers before they could enter the Home it was a great mistake, because nothing of the sort would be required of them. They would be required to conduct themselves in a decent way, and would not be at all coerced in their movements, so that he could not understand any opposition on the part of bushmen. He, like a previous speaker, had read letters in the papers, and he should like to know where those letters came from. With reference to the remarks made that this was simply a movement on the part of the squatters to oppress the bushmen and lower their rate of wages, it was his opinion that that excuse was either hypocritical or ridiculous. (Applause.) He could not see how it was to operate to reduce the rate of wages. He thought it would rather have the contrary effect. If a man, by habits of frugality had saved a little money, he was not bound to take the first job that offered itself at any price ; but it was the man who had knocked down his cheque, and had not a shilling in the world, who was obliged to take the first job that offered. (Loud cheers.) He should like those who said that the tendency of the Bushmen's Home was to knock down wages to explain how that could be. (Hear, hear.) If they were right, he was mistaken ; but he could not see how a man with £1 in his pocket was less independent than a man who had not a penny. With regard to the statement that this was simply a squatting movement, he thought that an ungracious way of putting it. A rev. gentleman had told them that the squatters should take more than an average amount of interest in the movement; and then when the squatters did take an interest in it, an objection was raised that it originated with the sheepfarmers. It was the duty of the squatters to lend this institution a helping hand, but it was absurd to call on them to do so, and then object to the movement because they helped it. (Hear.) He hoped this institution would be established, if only as an experiment. He agreed as to the analogy between bushmen and sailors, and as there were Sailors' Homes, why should there not be a Bushmen's Home? Mr. Davenport called himself a bushman, though he (Mr. Barrow) did not say that Mr. Davenport would live in the Home. (Laughter.) He dared to say that a great many bushmen like him, although they might not take up their lodgings permanently, would however identify themselves closely with the interests of the institution, and seek to carry it out successfully. The resolution stated that it was desirable to have a Home in or near Adelaide. He knew this had been a moot point, but if this Club succeeded they would soon require a similar institution in the north and in the south-east. He felt that if the movement was to become popular, a beginning must be made near the city. If they build a Home twenty or thirty miles from town, bushmen would naturally say—"You think us such children that you can't trust us in Adelaide." Bushmen, however, after spending years in the wilderness, liked to come to Adelaide, if it were only to see Burton's Circus. (Laughter.) And let them come. Then this institution, he observed, should not only be self-supporting, but self-governed. This would give the men an interest in the Home, and it was wise to do so. He hoped they would do their best to launch the Home, and he would only say that if any bushmen would give him particulars that would justify the assertions made that this scheme would lower wages and oppress bushmen, and if they would give him the names of the parties who were carrying on the plot, he would do his best to expose them to the whole colony. (Loud applause.) He believed, however, that the attempt was made by all parties in good faith, and from no sinister motives whatever. (Cheers.)

The Rev. J. L. Parsons with great pleasure seconded the resolution. The opposition to the movement, he said, was just that which might be anticipated. The class that was offering the most serious opposition was the one who would be injured by the establishment of the Home. He concurred in the remarks of the Hon. Mr. Barrow as to the institution not having the effect of reducing wages. It would enable a man to save his earnings, and the man who had money was independent—he was in a position to refuse work if the wages did not suit him. He believed, from the success that had so far attended the movement, that the time had really come when the first Bushmen's Home should be established; and before the year 1870 was far advanced he hoped the institution would be in full working order, and that it would render great benefit to the class in whose interests it was to be erected. (Applause.)

The resolution was carried.

The Rev. F. W. Cox moved—

"That this meeting, being of opinion that the establishment of a Home should not be left to the unaided efforts of the bushmen, earnestly solicits the aid of the citizens and residents of settled districts generally to assist in providing a Home in or near the city."

In an able speech the rev. gentleman commended the institution to the liberality of the public. He spoke of the bushmen's profession as being so noble and ancient that one might feel a considerable amount of pride in belonging to it; deprecated, in dealing with the men, anything approaching to patronizing, and admitted that bushmen were subject to special temptations; but hoped that those who knocked down their cheques were the exception.

Mr. J. H. Angas seconded. In consequence of ill-health he had not intended to be present at that meeting, and would not have been there had it not been for the letter signed "A Bushman of Ten Years" appearing in that morning's *Register*, to reply to which he had travelled sixty miles that day, notwithstanding the heat of the weather. He denied the allegations of "A Bushman of Ten years," affirming that the movement did not originate with the squatters, although it would have been highly to their credit had such been the case. It originated 200 miles away from Adelaide, in the bush; and before being mentioned in the city the opinion of the bushmen was taken, who, as far as his experience went, were a quiet, respectable, sober, well-conducted, and intelligent body of men—many of them men of education and genius, and competent to fill higher positions were they open to them, but in this colony genius was not always rewarded as it deserved. He was glad that merchants and others had taken the matter up warmly. It was not now in the hands of squatters solely—he did not believe it would ever be; and he trusted it would be carried to a successful issue. "A Bushman of Ten Years" showed by the statements he made that he was either very ignorant or very injudicious. He challenged him to send the name and address of that man who gave 10s. towards the Home "for fear of having to take the 'wallaby' with his wife and children." If he did so he would refund the 10s. He also challenged the writer to furnish the names of any others who had been coerced into subscribing. The Home was a free institution, and no compulsion, to his knowledge, had been used, nor would there be any used. When he noticed that the Sailors' Home was receiving liberal contributions, he thought they had no occasion to fear for the Bushmen's Home, because, whilst sailors only visited the colony now and again, the bushmen were always here, and their labours did much to enrich South Australia. (Hear, hear.) He explained that the institution would be open to all coming from the country who chose to enrol themselves as members; and stated that he had no doubt, if the thing was properly organized, it would be well supported and largely patronized. (Applause.)

The motion was carried unanimously.

Mr. N. Blyth, M.P., briefly expressed his hearty sympathy with the movement, and moved—

"That the following names be added to the existing Committee:—Hon. J. H. Barrow, M.L.C., N. Blyth, Esq., M.P., S. Davenport, Esq., T. Magarey, Esq.; and to represent bushmen—Messrs. Evan McKay, W. Coleman, Wm. Roberts, John Canham, John Quayle, Wm. Bradbury, John Gilles, Samuel Lovering, J. Lillywhite, and — Pelton."

The motion was seconded by the Rev. Mr. Lyall, who expressed his conviction that the institution was required, and stated that he had read the regulations drawn up for the management of the Home with complete approval.

The resolution was carried unanimously.

The Rev. C. Manthorpe moved a hearty vote of thanks to His Worship the Mayor for presiding, and intimated that His Worship gratuitously granted the use of the Town Hall for the purpose of that meeting, but the Committee felt disinclined to accept the offer, as they feared they could not fill it.

Mr. C. B. Young seconded the vote of thanks. He remarked that but for a misunderstanding on the part of the Committee, for which he was mainly responsible, they would have had the support and presence of His Excellency the Governor that evening. He was sure His Worship would not feel offended when he said that, pleased as they were to see the Chief Magistrate in the chair, it would have given them still greater pleasure to have seen Her Majesty's representative supported by His Worship. (Cheers.) He might say, however, that His Excellency had expressed his warmest interest in the movement, and promised to give it his support. (Applause.)

The vote was carried by acclamation, and tersely acknowledged by His Worship.

The proceedings of the public meeting then closed.

A meeting of the Committee was held next day, and

It was resolved—"That 'William' be empowered to solicit subscriptions from the residents of the city, and that he be furnished with the necessary credentials and printed statements setting forth the objects of the institution."

"William" signified his assent to the foregoing arrangements.

It was resolved—"That several members of the Committee should undertake to wait upon the leading merchants and others to solicit their subscriptions towards the Home."

It was resolved—"That the stockholders and sheepfarmers not residing in the city should be applied to by Circular to contribute to the funds of the institution, and that a statement of the amount already contributed by those employed on the stations be embodied in the Circular."

In accordance with this resolution the following Circular was distributed to friends likely to help the cause along :—

"Adelaide, December 20, 1869.

"To........................

"Sir—The scheme for establishing a Bushmen's Club in or near Adelaide having now been fairly set before the public of South Australia, and the desirableness of such an institution having been affirmed by the fact that above 1,000 men have subscribed towards it a sum of upwards of £600, the Committee have originated a systematic canvass of the city, suburbs, and country districts for the purpose of soliciting subscriptions towards the object.

"With the details of the scheme you are no doubt familiar. I have, therefore, only to intimate that I have been directed by the Committee to apply to you for a contribution.

"Should you feel disposed to assist the movement, please fill up the attached form, and forward it, with your donation, not later than 28th February, 1870.

"The Committee will furnish contributors occasionally with reports of progress, &c.

"H. HUSSEY, Hon. Sec."

[FORM ATTACHED.]

Date........................

To the Treasurer of the Bushmen's Club.

Sir—I enclose the sum of .... pounds, being my donation towards the establishment of the Bushmen's Club.

Name........................

Address........................

The services of "William" were here called upon to canvass the city from house to house at the principal places of business. When the proprietor was not in, the following note was left to be sent in or called for at a more convenient season :—

"Adelaide, December 21, 1869.

"No......

"Mr........................

"Dear Sir—I have to inform you that I have called for a contribution towards the establishment of a Bushmen's Home in or near Adelaide (see report of public meeting held 20th December, 1869), and am directed to leave this form, with a request that you will kindly state the sum you feel disposed to give towards the institution.

"Amount........................... £   s.   d.

"N.B.—Please forward this note (with the amount of your contribution) to the Treasurer, C. Sabine, Esq., Adelaide, or leave it in charge of some person (at this place) for the collector, who will call again for it as soon as possible should it not have been previously sent in.

"I am, Sir, &c.,

"WILLIAM."

A few days after the public meeting some kind but misled friend wrote the following letter to the *Register* against the temperance principles of the proposed institution :—

"TO THE EDITOR.

"Sir—As a sincere well-wisher of the success of the Bushmen's Home, and believing that its establishment would confer an enormous benefit upon the class of men for whom it is designed, permit me to offer a few observations on one point so much insisted upon by the missionary 'William.' He suggests most emphatically that no fermented liquors should be kept in the house. If this idea were carried out, it is to be feared that instead of checking intemperance it may tend, if not to encourage it, still to offer the temptation of seeking the means of gratifying a most lamentable propensity elsewhere. Of course, a bushman may be an inmate of the Home and get any amount of drink at public-houses; and to many a man the entire deprivation of fermented liquors will be a reason either for not becoming an inmate or for going out to indulge where he can.

"In moderation neither beer, wine, nor even spirit, is unwholesome ; and if the bushman could get his glass of any good liquor at the Home for a moderate price, it would be far better for him than to procure it in its generally-adulterated form. The person serving good liquors would be a domestic of the establishment, paid out of its funds, and he would have no interest in encouraging drunkenness ; on the contrary, his situation would or ought to depend upon his refusing to serve any one with an immoderate amount of drink. No 'shouting' would be permitted, and whoever asked for a glass of wine, beer, &c., would have to pay down for it.

"Instead of assisting intemperance, this plan would go far to check the vice ; and perhaps men who otherwise might continue a shocking habit would be induced to make a moderate use of that which in itself cannot injure them—which, indeed, may be almost necessary to their bodily health.

"I am, Sir, &c.,
"A Subscriber.
"December 23, 1869."

Reply to "Subscriber's" letter about the temperance principles of the place :—

"TO THE EDITOR.

"Sir—Will you kindly open your valuable columns for a few words in reply to a letter which appeared in the *Register* of 29th December, 1869, signed by "A Subscriber."

"I beg to say that there are many more subscribers and others in favour of the institution being a quiet, sober retreat than otherwise ; and surely if the men understand that it is to be conducted on temperance principles (which they do), I cannot understand why others should try to impose drink upon them, and, unasked, endeavour to throw this brand of discord into the place.

It will, I think, be quite time enough to discuss the propriety of introducing intoxicating drinks into the place when the bush people desire it themselves, without placing the very temptation it is the wish of so many of them to avoid directly in their way. It never was designed to make an hotel of it—I should think "Subscriber" must know there are plenty of them already in Adelaide—and, indeed, it never can become so, for the money has been collected from the bush people on this understanding, and if used for such a purpose as introducing intoxicating drinks in any shape or form as beverages will be misapplied.

"I am, Sir, &c.,
"WILLIAM.

"Adelaide, January 1, 1870."

The following article, in which a licensed victualler tries to persuade "William" to become "a publican himself," will, no doubt, amuse our friends. The writer expresses himself, also, that it would be beneath him to refute assertions made at the public meeting as to the hocussing, &c., attributed to part of his fraternity. He must have read deeply the hearts of wicked men to come to such conclusions as he has done in the following cynical effusion :—

[THE PUBLICAN'S ARTICLE.]

"There is a wilderness-howler who briefly designates himself 'William' who perplexes me greatly as to whether he ever had any second name, as most other people have. Was he won at a raffle, instead of being produced in the ordinary way, so that he is short of a surname ?—or, supposing 'William' to be his surname, did his godfather and godmother, in despairing to find a Christian name for such a prodigy of piety and learning, leave him without one ?—or, again, supposing 'William' ever had a second name, did he stick it up somewhere and fail to redeem it ?

"'There is a pride that apes humility.'

"'William,' I fear you have that pride in association with the intolerable cant that pervades your address read before the *amiable idiots* who proposed building a nursery for bushmen on Monday evening.

"Hear 'William :'—'So deeply do I feel the importance of this movement, that after much thought and prayer for Divine guidance I have resolved (D.V.) to comply with the wishes of personal friends, the Committee, and others (if the bushmen do not object to this arrangement), to take the first superintendence of the place without salary for a time, until it gets into good working order.'

"The inference is clear that, after the place should be got into fair working order, the superintendent should be paid; and who so fit for superintendent as he who got the place in fair working order?

"'William,' this is an old dodge. Secretaries to all kinds of schemes give their services gratuitously at first, with a prospect of a well-paid appointment after.

"Take my advice, 'William,' and a public-house, and pay down your licence-fee like a man. Then the bushmen, who love you so tenderly, on coming to town will patronize you, beyond all doubt; and, stimulated by the 'evangelizing labours' of which you boast so frequently, your brother publicans will take to psalm-singing, watering their grog, and blessing bushmen.

"The impudent assumption that there are no respectable hotels or lodging-houses in Adelaide where a bushman might reside without danger of being hocussed, robbed, and cast adrift explains itself, and is unworthy of serious refutation. It is also a gross impertinence to speak of bushmen as of so many children—helpless, without the paternal guidance of a man with a fragment of a name."

The writer of this article evidently is ignorant of the fact that "William" or any other person may assume what name he pleases for business or philanthropic purposes. Was it absolutely necessary for "William" to have two or three or even a larger number of names? He might have assumed such as Great, Bold, Magnificent, or the like, having a large number in the world to choose from. Not many persons at this our day are compelled to leave father, mother, home, and lands for Christ's sake; but even now there are some cases in families where much persecution has to be endured where a conscientious man tries to follow his Lord fully.

The following letter originated through a denial made by J. H. Angas, Esq., to a letter in the morning's paper containing an insinuation from "A Bushman of Ten Years" that the movement originated with the squatters:—

"TO THE EDITOR.

"Sir—If Mr. Angas means the idea of establishing a Home for Bushmen did not originate with the squatters, I certainly agree with him, as I have an indistinct recollection of some such scheme being set forth in your paper on the subject five years ago—the only difference, so far as I remember, being that the bushmen were recommended to form and manage their own institution without public help or squatters' help, however humble their first attempt might be; but as I never did nor can object to any movement which (whatever other faults it may have) necessarily tends to bring men into close connection with each other, and by doing so to give them a future power, it is not likely I am going to find fault.

"Were the Home to be established solely by the squatters for their own benefit—were it intended as a large boarding labour office, to regulate the price of wages, and to coerce instead of to relieve—I should still have no fault to find, simply because, instead of being isolated as they now are, bushmen would be banded together, and I believe in that case they would also act together; but it certainly surprises me that clergymen and gentlemen of very high attainments and of long and varied experience can continue to meet time after time in connection with homes and the temperance cause, and yet so lamentably neglect their duty to their fellow-men. The expression may be harsh, but it is true.

"There is a certain 57th clause in the Licensed Victuallers Act with a £10 penalty for the first breach, £20 for the second, and an extinguisher for the third. This clause is openly violated in nearly every public-house in the colony. The licensed victuallers are allowed to poison men already maddened by drink with impunity. The madman is permitted by the public and the police to reel from house to house and get fresh doses; and the end of all this is, perhaps, to lock the man up and fine him 5s.

"It is monstrous that men should be poisoned openly and publicly—that homes from this cause should be desolated—that murders should be committed and asylums filled—and yet no one interfere, much less uphold the law. This of the towns; but in the suburbs and the country there is all this, and more particularly on the Sabbath day.

"This is no case of 'informer.' Let the Temperance League appoint an agent to hunt the nuisance down; let every gentleman who witnesses the nuisance help to root it out; let every policeman be instructed to look as sharply after this as the going out of a lamp; and let every magistrate strictly enforce the penalties. The result will be, perhaps, some public-houses closed; but there will be hundreds of wretched homes made happy, and thousands of children clothed, fed, and educated, now naked, ill-fed, and ignorant.

"The man who will step forth and systematically strive to suppress this intolerable nuisance will do more general good to the community than any missionary who sought to save.

"I am, Sir, &c.,

"SPECTATOR."

—*Advertiser*, December 29, 1869.

A writer in *Licensed Victualler* of January, 1870, does not seem to agree with the foregoing letter, which he undertakes to answer in a high strain of nonsense and irony that certainly will have no effect on the class called bushmen, on whom he thinks our exertions for their happiness and welfare are thrown away. He thinks our efforts are a mere kind of philanthropic effervescence, such as he is in the habit of indulging in when he renovates and doctors up his muddled customers the morning following a night's debauch. The following are his remarks:—

"BOTHERED BUSHMEN.

"'Too many cooks spoil the soup.' The compassionate friends of bushmen are likely to commit a similar culinary misdemeanour in the endeavour to 'cook their goose.'

"One infuriated reformer—'I am, Sir, &c., Spectator'—rushes into the *Advertiser* of the 20th ultimo. A less violent philanthropist mildly invades the *Register* of the same day under the modest cognomen of 'A Subscriber.'

"'Spectator' is a man of comprehensive mind. He not only contemplates 'doing for' the bushmen, but designs to do up the publicans. He is powerful in language of the ranting kind, of which here is a specimen:—'The licensed victuallers are allowed to poison men already maddened by drink with impunity. The madman is seen by the public and the police to reel from house to house, and get fresh doses, and the end of all this is, perhaps, to lock the man up and fine him 5s.

"'It is monstrous that men should be poisoned openly and publicly; that homes from this cause should be desolated; that murders should be committed, and asylums filled; and yet no one interfere, much less uphold the law.'

"He then says—'Let the Temperance League appoint an agent to hunt the nuisance down.'

"What the nuisance is does not clearly appear in the rush of the impetuous 'Spectator's' foaming torrent of words, but it must either mean the publicans or the drunkards therein referred to. In either of which cases the 'agent' who undertook the responsibility of interfering in affairs that did not concern him might come to grief.

"That publicans are taxed, fined, and worried by oppressive laws surely should be sufficient without their having to submit to the slanderous insinuations of the canting humbugs who publish anonymously in newspapers.

"'A Subscriber' does not attack publicans in the same way as 'Spectator,' but approaches them insidiously. He does not agree with 'William' that no fermented liquor should be kept in the Bushmen's Home. This far-sighted observer thinks that bushmen possibly would not constantly remain in the Home with their feet in hot water, and their heads in a bason of gruel. He even confesses, that 'in moderation neither beer, wine, nor even spirit, is unwholesome.' He has nevertheless a great dread of publichouses, and foresees with horror that 'a bushman may be an inmate of the Home and get any amount of drink at publichouses.'

"The idea of combining the comforts of a home with the seclusion of a prison, will no doubt commend itself to the careful consideration of bushmen; in the meanwhile we find 'William,' the chief agent in the idiotic attempt to treat as children men who as a class are distinguished for their hardy enterprising roving nature, engaged in 'collecting,' which appears to be the principal aim of all missionaries."

In an article on Bushmen's Homes, the *Australasian*, after a complimentary reference to what was being done in South Australia to establish a Home for bushmen, adds the following letter commenting thereon, also upon the public meeting lately held in Adelaide :—

"Homes for Bushmen.

"Bushmen and sailors being much alike in their improvident habits, it has been often proposed to provide Homes for both when out of employment. The Sailors' Homes are succeeding admirably, and so, doubtless, would Homes for bushmen, if established on a sound principle. They would be the means of keeping many from publichouses, where the first glass of spirits often decides the question of money or no money on going away. Few are so utterly reckless as to go to such places with the intention of leaving all their money behind them, but a drinking bout once entered on, they know not when to stop. Repentance comes too late, and when his money is gone, the bushman has often no resource but to join the ranks of idle loafing swagsmen, and wander about the country for months without the chance of earning more. Many a good man is thus spoiled, for such a life must spoil all self-respect. In South Australia a movement for the formation of such Homes was commenced a year ago, and a few days since an adjourned meeting was held to receive the report of the Committee appointed at first.

"It was resolved then to canvass the country districts, and ascertain what amount of support might be calculated on from the settlers and the men chiefly interested in the subject. This part of the work was left apparently to 'William,' the Bush Missionary, who made a long speech at the meeting, explaining the steps he had taken, and the opinions prevailing amongst the men he had conferred with on the subject during his wanderings. Several had received the proposals gladly, subscribing towards the fund for the erection of a building, while many were prejudiced against it, saying that it was a squatter's project for the reduction of wages. Such ideas were as absurd as they were unfounded, for the squatters have done little to aid the movement, either with money or personal influence. Of 700 circulars asking for their aid, only 318 were returned—204 blank and 104 with subscriptions—the remainder being unanswered. Still

£644 11s. 8d. was collected principally by 'William' in small sums during his travels, and with that sum in hand from the bush and the promise with their signatures attached of 500 men to support the institution. When opened, it was deemed by the meeting time to call upon the Adelaide public for assistance. The first resolution passed recognises the important position the bushman ought to hold on account of his services to the community, and regrets that sufficient attention has not hitherto been paid to his requirements, especially when out of employment. The other resolutions affirmed the propriety of having the first Home in or near Adelaide, and that the work of raising the required funds—about £3,000—should be entered on without further delay. It is proposed to have a Savings' Bank and a labour office in connection with the institution, and if the first or central Home answers, to have branches in suitable localities. As the speakers at the Adelaide meeting were mostly clergymen, the formation of Homes was advocated for the benefit of the men themselves, but a writer in our issue of to-day recommends these as the best means of reducing the number of travelling swagsmen. His idea is that depôts or lodging-houses should be established at convenient distances apart, where men would be boarded at a moderate charge, and where they could hear of vacant situations, if in need of them. Then, no men should be hired without certificates from their last employers; in fact, that without these they should be sent to industrial establishments of some sort, where they would have to work for their keep. If these depots were established on the principal roads, and the settlers agreed to hire men only from them, of course travellers would have no excuse for calling at the stations, and might fairly be refused either food or lodging ; but unless there is absolute union amongst employers, such a system would soon become inoperative. However, the proposal is worthy of consideration, for it is only by some such means that the number of idle swagsmen can be materially reduced. On the one side Homes are recommended for the benefit of the men, and on the other for that of the masters, and doubtless there would be great gain for both, if we except those men who wish to live without work, and now very nearly succeed in doing so. One Home may do to begin with in South Australia, but in the northern parts of this colony, and the neighbouring portions of New South Wales, several would be required. However, a large fund would be forthcoming to found these if the settlers generally would only agree to devote the cost of one year's rations to travellers. Let us duly recognise the importance to the community of bushmen as a class, but not forgetting at the same time that those of them who remain idle are consumers of the wealth created by those who work, and that they ought to be cared for and rewarded according to the deserts of either section of that body."

The movement in Adelaide seems to have stirred the bushmen's case up in the sister colonies about this time, as the following correspondence extracted from the Sydney and Melbourne newspapers will show:—

"To the Editor of the *Australasian*.

"Sir—The text 'Bushmen, Swagmen' has been the heading of many letters in our journals from time to time; the theme is ventilated and discussed, and having been, so to speak, taken out to air, it is folded up and laid aside, and still the evil goes on increasing, for now we hear talk of poor laws, the increase of pauperism, and vagrancy. The evil of the present state of things is known and acknowledged on all sides, but the welfare of a large portion of the community being every one's business, ends by being no one's care.

"A short time ago I drew the attention of the readers of the *Hamilton Spectator* to a plan for forming a labour depôt and home for bushmen, and I hope there is some probability of something of the sort being tried in this neighbourhood; but as the only chance of its being productive of general good is by its being adopted over a large district at once, I would ask space in your columns in the hope that other people throughout the more settled portions of the colony may be able to judge if there would be any advantage in getting up such depôts in their vicinity. The great want in all such schemes is united action and public spirit; money is on the whole much easier to obtain, but money without the rest will do very little.

"The first step is that all employers who would join in getting up a labour depôt in their districts should give their labourers certificates upon their discharge, which might easily be rendered of no value except to the owner; and that, where it is practicable, preference be given to certificate-holders when in search of work. Then they should engage no men except from the labour depôt, and feed no travellers. This would take away all excuse for swagmen wandering through the bush on the pretence of looking for work, as it would soon be known that the only chance of getting work was by sticking to the main roads and inquiring at the different depôts; it would also considerably lessen the risk of bush fires which so often occur from the carelessness of travellers.

"Lodging-houses are to be found now in almost every township, where travellers can be boarded for sums varying from 12s. to 20s. a week; the actual cost of the provisions required by a traveller, fed as station-hands generally are, might amount to about 5s. per week. One of such lodging-houses, kept by a person in whom some confidence could be placed, might be made the labour depôt, and at this house the holder of a certificate might be boarded for 1s. a day, or about 7s. a week, if the keeper was subsidised at the rate of about 5s. a week for boarders where the average is about four, and at a proportionately less rate for a larger number. He would require to keep a register in which certificate-holders could enter the names. If any great demand for labourers arose, he could easily communicate with other depôts.

"I have given a mere outline of the plan, but I think there is enough to show the benefit of it both to employer and labourer. To the first—be they settlers, farmers, or road contractors—their servants finding the advantage to be gained by holding certificates, will have more desire to give satisfaction, and an improvement will be obtained upon the present system of picking up such men as chance sends, of whose capabilities nothing can be known. To the honest and industrious labourer it would be a bonus on his wages, for he would thus be enabled to live at a cheap rate when out of work, and, with a couple of pounds in his pocket, might travel from one end of the colony to another, knowing that if work was to be had he would be certain to hear of it.

"The cost of such a depôt would be but small—if including a fair-sized radius—to that now borne by many settlers in feeding men who neither want work nor can work, and but a trifle compared to the cost of establishing Bushmen's Homes on the Sailors' Home model.

"But some may say, this supposes all men to be honest and industrious, and that such things as knocking down cheques are quite unknown. Well, granted that all are not so, and that at the present time the loafing swagman predominates over his industrious brother, surely it is time that some means were found of curing the evil. If men will behave as children and sacrifice every consideration of the future for a few hours of drunken delirium, they ought then to be treated as children, and looked after as such, to prevent their becoming a tax on others. Could not some means be found of forming industrial establishments in different parts of the colony, having land attached to them, and different trades carried on in them, so as to be self-supporting, not managed by a staff of officials who might not have any idea of their work or interest in anything except the due return of quarter day, but by men thoroughly acquainted each with his own trade, and engaged in that alone, deriving the greater part of their income from their own exertions on something of the co-operative system? To such establishments let all men be sent for a term who are found wandering on the pretence of looking for work and cannot produce a certificate, or have no means of support, and make them work—not the 'Government stroke,' and do not feed them on the Model Prison system, but make them work for their living—and be paid and fed accordingly, or take the consequence of starvation. Pay them half the current rate of wages, more or less according to their work, and bestow the balance on the Benevolent Asylums, and thus those who are sure to inhabit such buildings will duly contribute to their support. Such an idea may be thought to savour of despotism, but better the despotism where no man is allowed to eat the bread of idleness or to starve than the freedom where he becomes a nuisance and encumbrance to others, and, for aught these others care, may be left left to die by the roadside. "Yours &c.,
"December 28." "⸺⸺⸺

[From the *Australasian* of the 15th January, 1870.]

SWAGMEN.

To the Editor of the *Australasian*.

Sir—I have always been of opinion that if in each large township some recognized home were established it would be a great benefit to the bushman; and I believe, when it came to be known that men could be hired at these depôts, the men who wanted work would stop there.

The majority of the boarding-houses in the country townships are little better than the lower class of public-house; and I firmly believe that in seven of them out of ten grog is sold, but of a rather better description than common public-house grog.

The almost daily accounts of men bereft of reason through excess of stimulants is heartrending; but here, again, it is not caused by rum, brandy, or other spirituous liquors, but by those imitations of them so commonly found in the lower class of public-house. Here, I think, our legislators and the police might help us.

If savings banks were attached to the bush homes they would be a great convenience, and lead to much real good. At present every inducement is offered to the swagman in the bush to knock down his cheque; and in some favourite localities it is a daily repetition of "Get up, Jack; let John sit down, for he is homeward bound." When John becomes Jack, he is sent off with a bottle of grog and a few shillings in his pocket, and, of course, is told that he is somewhat in debt; but still Jack declares that Old Blank is not such a bad fellow, and his next cheque shall go to him if he (Jack) can reach him.

To establish these homes there must be an entire unity amongst the employers of bush labour; even one dissentient will make it fall through. I see the swagmen are getting it hot just now because they refuse £1 per week harvesting. Of course every one knows that a man will wear out a pair of good moleskin trousers in a week, binding after a machine, and trousers are not so cheap in bush stores. Another thing, what sort of accommodation is offered? Four years ago I assisted at the potato harvest westward, and the accommodation for five men was the tilt of a light cart placed on the ground, and the open canopy of heaven.

Yours, &c.,

CARTHUSIAN.

The next meeting of the Committee was held on 2nd February, 1870, at Messrs. Goode Brothers' office.—Present Messrs. J. H. Angas (Chairman), T. Magarey, C. Sabine, H. Giles, C. B. Young, H. Hussey, and "William."

The Secretary reported proceedings since last meeting as follows :—

In compliance with the wish of the Committee, "William" has canvassed down to North Adelaide for contributions to the Home, the result of which will appear from the Treasurer's statement; the contributions received have been reported in the daily papers.

Five hundred copies of the report of the public meeting have been struck off in a separate form, and the greater part of them put into circulation.

Upwards of one hundred circulars have been sent out, soliciting contributions from stockowners, sheepfarmers, and others in various parts of the colony, and a few sent to absentees residing in England.

At the suggestion of "William," and with the approval of such of the members of the Committee as could be conferred with, the following advertisement was inserted on January 31st, 1870, for land and premises for a Home, so that in the event of any that might be suitable offering, the Committee could take the same into consideration.

"WANTED.—PREMISES FOR THE BUSHMEN'S HOME.

"Persons having Land and Buildings to sell or lease situated in Adelaide, or within about one mile of the city, which could be made available for the purposes of the above Institution, are invited to send a description of same, with terms and full particulars, without delay, addressed to Mr. H. Hussey, Hon. Sec., Bowden.

" Offers to be addressed not later than March 1st, 1870."

The offers and particulars which have been sent in will be laid before the Committee.

The Treasurer reported that up to the present time the total subscriptions amounted to £981 4s. 1d.

The principal business of the meeting was the consideration of suitable premises for the Home.

The Secretary stated that he had received some offers of premises which were quite unsuitable.

It was resolved—

"That as the offers of property sent in do not appear suitable for the purposes of the Home, the matter stand over."

"That Messrs. H. Giles, C. B. Young, C. Sabine, D. Murray, H. Hussey, and 'William' be a Sub-Committee, to be called together in the event of any suitable premises offering, 'William' to inspect and report upon same."

The Committee were not to be kept long in suspense, as the following note from Mr. James Hosking will explain :—

"Whitmore Square, February 3, 1870.

"Dear Sir—I know not what kind of premises you require for the purposes of the Bushmen's Home. Do you think those formerly occupied by Sir C. Cooper suitable? If so, I think they are attainable.

"I dare say you recollect them; they stand at the southeast of Whitmore Square. Within the last two years the large house has been made into two tenements; one contains seven rooms besides pantries and cellar (thoroughly dry); the other six rooms and an excellent cellar. There is also a detached building containing two good rooms, suitable for a kitchen and servant's bedroom. The ground in the shape of paddocks, garden, &c., measures about two acres.

"Before the subject of rental, &c., is dwelt on, perhaps you might find time to look at the premises.

"I am, dear Sir,
"Yours, &c.,
"JAMES HOSKING."

Immediately on the receipt of this note, "William" went to inspect the premises, and on the strength of his report a meeting of the Committee was called on February 5, at which Mr. Hosking attended, and stated that the premises inspected by "William" in Whitmore Square could be had in their present condition, for a term of three, five, or seven years, at a rental of £130 per annum.

Messrs. H. Giles, C. B. Young, H. Hussey, and "William" subsequently visited the premises and thought favourably of them. It was also thought desirable that the General Committee should be called together to decide upon said premises on Wednesday, 9th inst. Accordingly the General Committee met at Messrs. Goode Brothers' office, Grenfell-street. There were present Messrs. H. Giles, J. H. Angas, W. K. Thomas, C. Sabine, C. B. Young, H. Hussey, and "William." Mr. J. H. Angas (who had come to town to attend the meeting, and who had to leave in order to return by train shortly after business commenced) gave the Committee some important information relative to the leasing of Mr. Hosking's premises in Whitmore Square.

Mr. Hosking was called in and was asked if he felt disposed to part with his interest in the lease for a monetary consideration. This he declined doing, and after stating his position with reference to the lease he retired.

The Committee finding that Mr. Hosking had not the power to grant a lengthened lease of the premises, resolved that the Secretary be authorized on behalf of the Committee to offer Mr. Hosking £110 for the aforesaid premises for one year, the Committee to make the necessary alterations and repairs.

Resolved—That the name of W. K. Thomas, Esq., be added as one of the Sub-Committee for procuring premises for the Home.

Mr. Hosking having replied favourably to the Secretary's offer of £110 per annum, a meeting was held next day, 10th instant, to arrange matters; and after reading the note from Mr. Hosking, accepting the offer of the Committee, it was resolved—

"That the Secretary intimate to Mr. Hosking that the Committee agree to take the aforesaid premises, subject to the condition named in his note of February 9, viz., the Committee to make all necessary alterations and repairs, and will replace (if desired to do so) such crossfences and partitions as may be removed during the tenancy. Further, that the Committee will be prepared to take possession on March 1, proximo; that Mr. Codd (builder) inspect the premises with Mr. Giles and 'William' and report upon their present condition; also the cost of putting the place in a necessary state of repair. Mr. Hosking to prepare a draft form of agreement, and that a meeting of the Committee be called on Tuesday 22nd inst., at 2 p.m., to consider certain rules and regulations, to appoint trustees, arrange details to submit to a meeting of all the subscribers for their approval, and to appoint a Sub-Committee to carry out the details of fitting up the Club."

As it was thought necessary that the bush subscribers should be made acquainted with the movement in Adelaide, the following short local appeared in the *Observer* of February 12, 1870 :—

"We hear that the Committee of the Bushmen's Home have leased the premises in Whitmore Square, known as the original residence of Judge Cooper. The house is sufficiently commodious, and has fully an acre of ground attached to it; the situation ought also to be very suitable, and the public may hope to hear of the Home having had a very successful start."

Agreeably to a former resolution, another Committee meeting was held at Messrs. Goode Brothers' office on the 22nd February, 1870, when it was resolved that Mr. C. B. Young be chairman of the Committee *pro. tem.*, and that in this capacity he be authorized to sign the agreement for renting the premises, &c., on behalf of the Committee. It was arranged that the Committee should take the proposed rules, &c., into consideration at an adjourned meeting, held on March 1, at which meeting the constitution, rules, and regulations were also considered and several alterations made, and it was resolved that a meeting of all subscribers to the Club be held on the 17th, at White's Arbitration Rooms, at 3 p.m., notice thereof to be given by advertisement.

It will be observed that the Committee held no less than fourteen meetings up to the day of opening the Club. On March 12, 1870, a letter was received by the Acting Secretary from Mr. C. Sabine, Hon. Treasurer, tendering his resignation of that office, and stating that he would at the meeting of subscribers hand over all moneys, vouchers, &c., in his possession on the same date.

The following advertisement appeared also in the *Register*, dated from Grenfell-street, March 12, 1870 :—

"BUSHMEN'S CLUB.

"The undersigned having resigned his position both as Hon. Treasurer and member of Committee, requests that no communication on the subject of the Club, except as to past matters of finance, may be addressed to him.

"CLEMENT SABINE."

In the meantime the work was slowly but surely progressing, and on March 3 the following notice was inserted in the daily and weekly papers, viz. :—

"ADVERTISEMENT.

"A meeting of all subscribers to the Bushmen's Club will be held in White's Arbitration Rooms, King William-street, on Thursday, March 17, 1870, at 3 p.m., for the purpose of deciding upon a constitution, appointing trustees and board of management, framing rules and regulations, and taking other necessary steps for opening the Institution."

Subjoined is the *Advertiser's* report of the meeting :—

"THE BUSHMEN'S HOME.

"On Thursday, March 17, a meeting of the subscribers to the Bushmen's Home, or Club, was held in White's Arbitration Room, for the purpose of deciding upon a constitution. There were between twenty and thirty gentlemen present, and Mr. C. B. Young occupied the chair. The chairman stated that a house formerly occupied by Sir Charles Cooper, of Adelaide, had been engaged, and that it was considered most suitable for the purpose. The rules and regulations, after having been amended, were affirmed. The object of the Club is to afford a comfortable home to bushmen, with the means for social and moral improvement and healthful recreation, and to extend its benefits to other parts of the province. The Club is to be conducted on temperance principles; no intoxicating drinks are to be used or introduced on any part of the premises. The rules and regulations are to be binding on all inmates and members, with three exceptions, and cannot be altered unless by a resolution passed at an annual meeting, of which timely notice has to be given. The three clauses alluded to in the last sentence may be altered from time to time by the Board of Management, but in no case can that alteration take effect until sanctioned by the trustees. All the property belonging to the Club is to be vested in the trustees, and Messrs. J. H. Angas, D. Murray, and W. K. Thomas were appointed to act as such. In the event of a vacancy occurring in the trusteeship, it may be filled at an annual meeting by ballot. The Board of Management is to consist of three persons, who will act for a year, and another Board will be balloted for at the annual meeting. Each member of the Board is to be entitled to 10s. 6d. for each attendance, but at the annual meeting the fee may be increased or diminished. Messrs. H. Giles, N. Blyth, and C. B. Young were appointed to act as a Board of Management for the ensuing year. The annual fee of five shillings constitutes a membership, which entitles a member to various privileges. The Superintendent will be appointed or removed by the Board of Management, and it is to have the general control of the Club. An annual member of five shillings (subscription not being in arrear) is entitled to one vote for the election of trustees and members of the Board of Management. Contributors of from £1 to £5 will have one vote for three successive years; and of £5 and upwards, for five successive years. The voting at any meeting of the Club may be by proxy, and this instrument is to be lodged with the Superintendent twelve hours at least before the meeting is held. A quorum is to consist of two members at the meetings of the Board of Management, and ten at the annual meeting; and, after waiting for an hour, should no quorum be formed, the meeting may be adjourned. The Board of Management is to meet once a month to conduct the ordinary business of the institution, and the annual meeting is to take place the first week in December. The Club is to be established and maintained by annual subscriptions of members, charges for board and lodging, and contributions. Should the funds arising from the ordinary receipts be more than sufficient for the working expenses, it may be competent to set apart half the gross amount of the annual subscriptions towards the "Benefit Fund" and the other half, with profits (if any) is to be expended in enlarging the establishment. The "Benefit Fund" is for the purpose of relieving cases of real unavoidable distress among actual bushmen, in which none but members will be allowed to participate. Two auditors are to be appointed at the annual meeting. Should the receipts be insufficient to carry on the Club, an opportunity will be given for its reorganization; and, failing that, the trustees are empowered to dispose of all the property belonging to the Club, and devote the proceeds to a fund for the benefit of sick or distressed bushmen and their families. The charges for board and lodging will be fixed by the Board of Management, who will also deal with money deposits. Other rules and regulations, of a character similar to those imposed on associations of this kind, were also agreed upon. The Chairman then read a letter from Mr. C. Sabine, the late Hon. Treasurer, giving a statement of the accounts from the commencement of the Bushmen's Home up to the 12th instant, the date of his resignation, showing a balance in hand of £888 5s., and forwarding cash-book and vouchers for the amount specified. Mr. H. Hussey, the Secretary, proposed the following resolution :—" That, provided Mr. Hosking is willing, for a monetary consideration, to relieve the Committee from taking the premises in Whitmore Square, the Board of Management be not appointed, and the Club be not opened until fifty members have paid their annual subscription to the Treasurer, and that bushmen be invited to become annual subscribers. That, if fifty subscribers do not pay their subscription within six months from this date, any who may have paid by that time shall have their money returned to them, and a meeting of subscribers and contributors shall be at once called to decide upon the disposal of the remaining funds." He pointed out that it would be very unwise to start an institution of the kind, unless it was certain that there should be a guarantee for the subscriptions before the Club was opened. "William," the Bush Missionary, was very indignant that such a proposition had been proposed. He stated that five-sixths of the subscriptions had been contributed by the bushmen, who were most anxious to see the

Club started, and that as soon as possible, assuring the meeting that it would be the resort of bushmen. Mr. W. K. Thomas thought that when the bushmen saw that the Home was started, it would be an inducement to them to pay their subscriptions. After the expression of the opinion hostile to his motion, and seeing that the Committee were so far pledged in having taken the premises, Mr. Hussey asked leave to withdraw it.

A letter was read from Mr. Thomas Elder offering to give the Committee his interest in an allotment of land, situated in or near North Adelaide, for the purpose of erecting a Home there, and hoping that it would be carried out successfully, as it seemed to be regarded with so much interest by the bushmen themselves. Mr. Elder was thanked for his kind offer.

The thanks of the meeting having been accorded to the Hon. Treasurer and Secretary, Mr. Hussey (who tendered his resignation at the meeting), the Committee, and the Chairman, the proceedings closed.

The following is a copy of the Constitution, which may be interesting to the public generally, together with the rules and regulations agreed upon to be observed at the Bushmen's Club :—

CONSTITUTION OF BUSHMEN'S CLUB.

OBJECTS.

1. To rent, purchase, or erect suitable premises in Adelaide, for the purpose of affording comfortable board and lodging to bushmen, together with means for social and moral improvement and healthful recreation; also to extend the benefits of such an institution to other parts of the province.

PRINCIPLES.

2. The Club shall be conducted on Temperance principles. No intoxicating drinks shall be used or introduced into any part of the premises.

RULES AND REGULATIONS.

3. The rules and regulations annexed in Schedule A shall be binding on all inmates and members, and (except clauses 1, 3, 5) shall not be altered unless by a resolution, passed at one annual meeting of which three months' notice shall be given in two weekly newspapers.

Clauses 1, 3, 5, may be altered from time to time at any meeting of the Board of Management. But in no case shall any alteration take effect until the sanction of a majority of the Trustees shall have been obtained.

TRUSTEES.

4. All property now belonging to, or hereafter to be acquired by the Club, shall be vested in three Trustees, who shall be Messrs. J. H. Angas, D. Murray, and W. K. Thomas ; and each Trustee shall continue in office until he shall resign, become insolvent, or be absent from the colony for two years.

APPOINTMENT OF TRUSTEES.

5. In the event of any vacancy occurring in the Trusteeship, the Board of Management (to be hereafter described) shall nominate one or more persons, and it shall also be competent for any other candidate for the office to offer himself for election ; and the name of such person or persons, provided he or they shall have previously signified, in writing, willingness to act if elected, shall be submitted to the next Annual Meeting, and a ballot taken for the election of the required number.

BOARD OF MANAGEMENT.

6. The Board of Management shall consist of three persons, who shall be Messrs. N. Blyth, H. Giles, and C. B. Young, who shall remain in office until Monday in the third week of December, 1870. The members of succeeding Boards of Management shall be elected by ballot at each annual meeting ; provided, that if no quorum shall be present, then the existing Board shall continue in office if willing to act. In the event of any vacancy occurring in the Board between the annual meetings, the same shall be filled up by the Trustees. Three months before the time of election for the Board of Management it shall be publicly intimated to all members of the Club that nominations will be received by the existing Board of persons who have given their written consent to act, which will be received up to within six weeks before the annual meeting; and then the names of all such nominees shall be published, in order that the members who cannot attend the annual meeting shall have an opportunity of sending in their proxy papers. Members of the Board shall be entitled to a fee of 10s. 6d. each for each attendance, but it shall be competent for any annual meeting to increase or decrease such amount for a year prospectively.

Membership.

7. An annual fee of five shillings shall constitute membership. The person so becoming a member will be entitled to the privileges set forth in Schedule A, but will have to pay in advance for board and lodging.

Superintendent.

8. The Superintendent shall be appointed and be subject to removal by the Board of Management. He shall have the general management of the Club, and the hiring and discharging of all servants under him. The Board shall decide as to the number of servants to be engaged.

Scale of Voting.

9. The election of Trustees and of members of the Board of Management shall be conducted as follows:—Annual members of five shillings and annual subscribers of ten shillings (whose subscriptions are not in arrear) to be entitled to one vote. Contributors of from £1 to £5, one vote for three successive years; £5 and upwards, one vote for five successive years.

Proxy.

10. Voting at any meeting of the Club may be by proxy, and the instrument appointing a proxy shall be as follows:—" I, being a member (or contributor) to the Bushmen's Club, hereby appoint   of   my proxy to vote for me at any special, general, or annual meeting of the Club, until I by my presence or under my hand revoke the same.

Name—

Witness—

N.B.—This instrument to be lodged with the Superintendent twelve hours at least before the meeting is held at which it is to be used.

Quorum.

11. At meetings of Board of Management, two. At meetings for general purposes—Ten annual members or contributors entitled to vote, present personally, constitute a meeting. If there shall be no quorum within one hour, the meeting may be adjourned for any time not exceeding thirty days.

Meetings.

12. The Board of Management shall meet once a month for conducting the ordinary business of the institution, and an extraordinary meeting may be called in writing by the Superintendent, or ten members of the Club. The annual meeting of members and contributors of the Club shall be held about the third week of Decem-

ber, in each year, for the purpose aforesaid, and also for making necessary alterations in the rules and regulations, provided such alterations are not at variance with the constitution of the Club, and subject to the conditions prescribed in clause 3.

FUNDS.

13. The Club shall be established and maintained by the annual subscriptions of members, by charges for board and lodging, and by contributions. All cheques or drafts upon bankers or agents of the Club for the general expenses of the institution to be signed by two members of the Board of Management, and countersigned by the Superintendent. Amounts received as annual subscriptions, and as contributions from non-members, shall be kept distinct from other receipts. Should the funds arising from ordinary receipts suffice to defray the working expenses of the Club, without making use of amounts derived from the annual subscriptions or contributions, it shall be competent for the Board to recommend to any annual meeting that half the gross amount of such annual subscriptions shall be set apart to a fund to be called the "Bushmen's Benefit Fund," when, should the majority at such meeting support the recommendation, the amount shall be set aside for that purpose. The other half of the amount of annual subscriptions, together with any profits derived from the Club, or contributions, shall be devoted to the enlargement of premises, erection of new premises, or purchase of land for purposes of a Club, or for the establishment of branch Clubs.

BENEFIT FUND.

14. The Board of Management may establish a Benefit Society, and at their discretion relieve cases of real distress among (actual) bushmen out of this fund. Except in instances of pressing emergency, or where the regulations may otherwise prescribe, none but members will be allowed to participate. If a bushman is unavoidably in distress, such assistance may be rendered to him as the funds permit.

AUDITORS.

15. Two Auditors shall be appointed by the annual meeting.

WINDING-UP.

16. Should receipts and members' fees not suffice to carry on the Club, notice shall be given in two weekly newspapers once in each month, for six months, to afford bushmen and subscribers an opportunity to reorganize the Club; failing which the Trustees shall dispose of all property belonging to the Club, and devote the proceeds for a fund for the benefit of sick or distressed bushmen and their

Schedule A.—RULES AND REGULATIONS.
Membership.
1. The payment of five shillings annually constitutes membership. Tickets of membership will be issued, and must be produced if required. Each member will be entitled to vote at the annual meeting for the Board of Management.

Charges.
2. The charge for Board and Lodging will be—
   To members ... ... 15s. per week.   2s. 6d. per day.
   " Non-members ... 16s.   "   3s.   "
   Single meals, from 1s.

It is desirable for the interest of the Home that payments for board and lodging be made in advance. These charges to be under direction of Board, and may be altered from time to time at discretion.

Hours for Meals.
3. Breakfast at 8 a.m. ; dinner 1 p.m. ; tea 6 p.m. Meals will not be served at other hours except on arrival of persons from the Bush. A bell will be rung before each meal, and grace will be said before partaking thereof.

N.B.—Refreshments and temperance drinks can be obtained at the Club at intermediate hours.

Management, &c.
4. The authority of the Superintendent is to be recognised by all the inmates of the Club. He is to see to the carrying out of the Rules, and to the observance of order and decorum, in which the Board expect the members to support him.

5. The Club to be open daily from 6 a.m. till 11 p.m.

6. A bell will be rung at 7·30 a.m., at which time there will be morning prayer for those who like to attend.

7. Non-members requiring board and lodging, on entering the Club must furnish their names and last addresses to the Superintendent.

8. Admission may be refused to any person (whether member or non-member) who is in a state of intoxication.

9. Any inmate persistently misconducting himself will be expelled.

10. No intoxicating liquors will be allowed within the Club buildings or grounds, and any person infringing this regulation will be liable to expulsion.

11. Smoking will not be permitted within the building except in the apartments appointed for the purpose.

12. Gambling, drunkenness, cursing, swearing, and obscene language are strictly prohibited.

13. The Lord's Day is to be decorously observed.

14. No fees, perquisites, or money presents are to be given to or received by any hired servant of the Club.

15. Any person having a reasonable complaint with respect to the conduct of the Superintendent, servants, provisions, or other matters which cannot be adjusted by the Superintendent, may make known the same at any monthly or special meeting of the Board.

16. All notices, letters, &c., put into the Post Office, addressed to the party at the place of abode last notified to the Superintendent, shall be deemed duly forwarded.

APPENDIX.
THE GENERAL BENEFITS OF THE CLUB.

A vote for Board of Management.

Use of Labour Mart and Registry Office.

Savings Deposits, to deposit money for safe keeping, or in Savings Bank.

The participation, in times of distress, in the relief arising from the "Bushmen's Benefit Fund," when such fund shall be established.

A reliable business agency for correspondence and transactions of general business.

Use of Library and Branch Post-Office ; Reading-room, furnished with approved Books, Newspapers, and Periodicals.

A store for boxes, swags, &c., when away from the Club.

Recreation grounds, various amusements, the society of other bushmen, good Board, comfortable Lodgings, &c., &c., at moderate charges.

N.B.—All profits, however made, go to the benefit of the Bushmen's Club.

There are many advantages to non-members (or non-subscribers) boarding at the Club who like to make it their home, or avail themselves of its use. Bushmen are urgently requested to give it one trial. It now remains with them to say whether it shall stand or fall.

MONEY DEPOSITS.

1. All members depositing money personally must initial the entry, stating the amount paid in by them.

2. All members sending money by post must state in letter the amount of their remittances.

3. The Superintendent shall keep a depositors' book, with an opening for cash account, receipts on one side and payments on the other, with a space for initials above referred to, in which the word "letter" shall be written when remittances are received by letter.

4. All payments, of whatever amount, must be similarly initialled.

5. Repayments only to be made to the actual depositor in person, except in case of sickness or emergency, when properly certified discharges may be approved by the Board of Management.

6. All cash received shall be paid into a general account at the Savings Bank, in the name of Bushmen's Club, to be operated on by the Superintendent.

7. Depositors will be required to give a few hours' notice for all amounts required to be withdrawn exceeding £1.

8. The interest received from Savings Bank at the close of the year shall be apportioned according to rules to be then resolved on by the Board.

9. No receipts to be given by Superintendent for deposits; but depositors to be entitled at any time personally to inspect their accounts.

10. No amounts less than 5s. will be received, or repayments less than 5s. will be made.

11. A separate account will be opened at the Savings Bank for any member remitting money for that purpose, and his pass-book carefully preserved for him.

12. No person whilst in a state of intoxication to be allowed to draw any portion of his money that he may have deposited for safe keeping at the Club, and no bill or order shall be paid for him until he is perfectly sober.

How Bushmen in the Country may obtain Members' Tickets or Voting Proxy Papers.

Any Bushman sending to "William," the Honorary Secretary of the Club, Whitmore-square, Adelaide, five shillings or upwards (see scale of voting) may have sent to his address an annual member's ticket, with a voting proxy paper enclosed, if so requested. Or any subscriber of ten shillings and upwards to the Club funds (as per scale of voting) may have a proxy paper sent to any given address.

Any legacy or voluntary contribution for the purpose of relieving cases of sickness or distress among Bushmen will be thankfully received by the Superintendent of the Club.

The following is a copy of Member's Ticket :—

BUSHMEN'S CLUB.

Member's Ticket.   No..........

Date of Issue........................   Date Expires......................

This is to Certify that..
has paid his Annual Fee of..
and is hereby constituted a Member of the above-named Club for One Year, as above.

..............................Superintendent.

Adelaide....................18..............

N.B.—This Ticket is Not Transferable, and must be produced if required.

The *Advertiser's* columns contained the following letter of Mr. Hussey's, in explanation of his part in the proceedings at the meeting of subscribers, held on the 17th March, 1870:—

"THE BUSHMEN'S HOME OR CLUB.

"TO THE EDITOR.

"Sir—Excuse me for trespassing upon the little available space you have at present at your disposal, for the purpose of offering a brief explanation of one part of your report of the meeting of subscribers to the above institution.

"It appears from the report that the Board of Management were appointed prior to my proposition for postponing this part of the business. Such was not the case. At my request the appointment was deferred until the said proposition was brought forward, and then, in deference to the general opinion expressed by the meeting, I withdrew it, after which the Board of Management was appointed.

"I would also take this opportunity of stating that I consider the reduction of the members' annual fee from £1 to 5s. an impolitic one in many points of view. I think bushmen, generally speaking, have some idea of dignity and respectability, and that in order to keep up the character of their Club, they would willingly pay an annual fee of £1, if they were at all desirous of availing themselves of it. This alteration, I fear, though made, no doubt, from a desire to encourage bushmen to join the Club, will have an injurious effect upon the interests of the institution. It seems to have been overlooked that the aid to be afforded to distressed members of the Club depends mainly upon the amount of the annual fee.

"I am, Sir, &c.,

"H. Hussey.

"March 18, 1870."

In April, 1870, Mr. C. B. Young, on behalf of the Committee, signed the agreement to pay £110 for twelve months' rental of the premises in Whitmore Square, and on the 21st "William" entered into possession of the premises. On the same day the first meeting of the Board of Management took place at the office of Neville Blyth, Esq., Queen's Chambers, at 2 p.m. There were present Messrs. N. Blyth, H. Giles, and "William," Hon. Superintendent.

It was resolved to print 1,000 copies of constitution, rules, &c., for distribution and transmission to the various stations in the colony, and that 500 members' tickets, 250 voting proxy papers, and 200 cards for calling meetings, be printed also.

"That gas be laid on to the premises, and eight burners fitted in different parts of the Home.

"That the Superintendent open accounts with tradesmen in the city for the supply of necessary furniture, fittings, provisions, &c., &c., for carrying on the business of the Club."

"William's" appointment as Superintendent of the Club was signed and given to him.

"Resolved—That the fee of 10s. 6d., allowed to members of the Board of Management for attendance at meetings, be given to the Club funds.

"Resolved also—That an advertisement be issued, requesting all communications relating to the Club to be addressed to 'William,' Hon. Superintendent, after this date.

"Also that the Superintendent advertise for a good cook."

The work of fitting up the Club now began in right good earnest, and measures taken to prepare for a formal opening so soon as possible; and, in accordance with the resolutions passed at the board meeting, the following advertisements appeared in the daily and weekly papers:—

"Notice.—Bushmen's Club.—All communications relating to the above-named institution must be addressed to 'William,' Hon. Superintendent, Whitmore Square, after this date.

"By order of the Board of Management.
" April 22, 1870."

"WANTED FOR THE BUSHMEN'S CLUB. — A good plain cook (a single man), who would also be willing to make himself generally useful for a time. He must produce good testimonials as to sobriety and trustworthiness.

" N.B.—A bushman preferred.

" Apply to 'William,' Hon. Superintendent, at the Clubhouse, Whitmore Square, between 10 and 12 a.m.

" Adelaide, April 22, 1870."

The next monthly meeting of the Board of Management was held at the Club premises on May 3, at 9·45 a.m. Present—N. Blyth, Esq., and H. Giles, Esq.

The Superintendent reported that repairing, painting, glazing, papering, colouring, and white-washing were going on; also building a bath, conveying water and gas, repairing drainage, &c., had been done; that he was getting beds, pillows, sheets, and pillowcases made, and that by adopting this plan, a saving was made of about £5.

It was resolved that all accounts of the Club be paid the first week in each month, and a discount of two and a-half per cent. be received therefrom.

That a formal opening be arranged and refreshments provided, and that gentlemen and bushmen favourable to the cause be invited.

A short paragraph on this resolve appeared in the newspapers, and is here copied for perusal :—

" The Bushmen's Home or Club will probably be opened some time during next week. The quarters of the Club will be in the late residence of Sir Charles Cooper, once the Supreme Court, and a more agreeable site could hardly be chosen in Adelaide, the position being good, and the grounds spacious and well planted. At the opening as many bushmen as can attend will be invited to take part in a fitting celebration of the event, when they will have an admirable opportunity of becoming acquainted with the character of the premises, and the arrangements for the entertainment and comfort of lodgers. The Board of Management will thankfully receive books or magazines for the library of the institution."

On April 26, Mr. J. H. Angas was invited by letter to formally open the Club. The following is his reply to the Superintendent :—

"I am glad to learn that you are getting on with the preparations for opening the Bushmen's Home. I hope the cost of fitting and alterations will not be heavy. I do not know what sort of a ceremony you propose to have at the opening, but if I am able to be present, I shall willingly do what I can to assist. I purpose going to Mount Remarkable on Wednesday or Thursday week, May 11 or 12, and shall probably be away for a fortnight. In the event of my being absent from town when the Home is opened, I think Captain Bagot, as an old colonist, might be asked to preside."

It having been decided to open the Club on May 20, 1870, Mr. Angas was again apprised of this fact, but unfortunately his absence in the North covered this date.

The following is extracted from his reply to "William" on May 7, 1870 :—

"I fear, as the Home or Club will not be ready for the opening ceremony before I go to the North, it will be impossible for me to open it as you kindly suggested, and as I should have gladly done. I am pleased to hear you are going on satisfactorily, and trust the Club may prove a real success and benefit to the men we seek to aid."

On May 16, 1870, at 9·30 a.m., a special meeting of the Board was held on the premises to make preparations for formally opening the Club. Present—Messrs. C. B. Young and H. Giles. Mr. Young announced that His Excellency and Lady Edith Fergusson would pay a visit of inspection to the Club, and formally open it on the 20th instant.

It was resolved that an advertisement announcing the opening of the Club be inserted in the two daily and weekly papers. "William" undertook to call upon some gentlemen, and ask them to speak at the meeting. It was also resolved to reduce the board and lodging to fifteen shillings per week for members of the Club, and sixteen shillings for non-members.

All friends to the bushmen's cause were therefore invited by the following advertisement :—

"BUSHMEN'S CLUB.—The above institution, situated in Whitmore Square, will be opened (D.V.) on Friday, May 20, at 7 p.m.

"Bushmen and friends of the cause are especially invited. The Club will be open for inspection on the 19th and 20th instant.

"By order of the Board of Management,
"'William,' Hon. Superintendent.

"May 14, 1870."

Here follows a description of the premises and report of evening meeting, taken from the *Advertiser*, May 21, 1870 :—

THE BUSHMEN'S HOME.
THE PREMISES.

The movement originated a year or two ago to establish a Bushmen's Home has had a practical issue, Sir James Fergusson having on Friday afternoon, May 20, formally opened a Home in Adelaide. It is situated at the southeast corner of Whitmore Square, being the premises that were at one time the residence of Sir Charles Cooper. They are well adapted for the purpose, although not perhaps in every respect all that could be wished. But no doubt it is wise not to have incurred further expense, seeing that it remains yet to be ascertained whether the institution will prove a success. The Home contains in all fifteen rooms, and sleeping accommodation is afforded for about fifty persons. In connection with the building are extensive grounds, where the inmates will be able to take exercise by playing at quoits, cricket, or other games. If the undertaking succeeds, it is intended to improve these grounds, which, when done, will add considerably to the attractiveness of the place. Entering the Home from the western entrance we found ourselves in a smoking-room, in which bushmen, not members, will have the privilege of sitting.

Next to this is a labour office where the employer and the employè will meet, and further on is the waiting-room for men seeking work. Continuing our course in a direct line we passed the pantry and the servant's room on our right and left, and entered the kitchen, which is spacious, and contains a range and all other requisites. In proximity to this are the wash-house and the bathroom. Proceeding to the south side of the house where the best rooms are, we were shown into the reading-room, which is neatly furnished and has a very comfortable appearance. Various newspapers are kept, and there is the nucleus of a library, for the enlargement of which presents of books will be thankfully received. Adjoining the reading-room is the members' smoking room, which is a cosy little apartment.

The refreshment and dining rooms are capacious, and between them there are folding doors; when these are thrown back sitting accommodation is provided for fifty people. Upstairs there are two dormitories, a lavatory, and an infirmary. The dormitories are divided by curtains into a number of small compartments. The bedding and everything in these rooms were particularly clean; in fact, throughout the establishment order and cleanliness were the characteristic features, and besides there was an air of refinement which will be appreciated by the better class of bushmen. The whole of the rooms are well ventilated, and gas and water have been laid on. The Superintendent, "William," has his quarters in an outhouse, which is also used to place the stores in. The Home is managed by a Board annually appointed, which at present consists of Messrs. N. Blyth, H. Giles, and C. B. Young; and the property connected with it is vested in three trustees, Messrs. J. H. Angas, D. Murray, and W. K. Thomas. The institution is to be conducted on temperance principles, and the following notice is posted up in several rooms :—

"Swearing, drunkenness, and gambling strictly prohibited."

The means by which the Home is to be supported are the fees of the members, who have to pay five shillings annually, the charges for board and lodging, and contributions. It is to be hoped that the class for whom the Home has been established will largely avail themselves of the advantages which it offers.

Formal Opening.

Shortly after four o'clock His Excellency Sir James Fergusson, accompanied by Lady Edith and Lieutenant Fergusson, visited the Home for the purpose of formally opening it by an inspection. The vice-regal party were conducted over the premises by Messrs. H. Giles, C. B. Young, and the Hon. Superintendent. They spent about half-an-hour in the inspection, and expressed themselves pleased with the arrangements generally.

Evening Meeting.

In the evening a meeting was held in the Home, the whole of the rooms in which were lighted up and thrown open to the inspection of visitors, of whom there were a considerable number, including several bushmen. Mr. C. B. Young occupied the chair, and in commencing the proceedings said he would say a few words respecting the origin of the Home. It was not one of those things which had been got up in Adelaide to meet the wants of country people by persons who were ignorant of those wants; on the other hand, the promoters of the institution were men who were well acquainted with the requirements of bushmen. The idea of establishing the Home originated with "William" the Bush Missionary, and the Messrs. Angas; and it could not have originated in better hands, Mr. J. H. Angas having a considerable acquaintance with the people of the bush, and both gentlemen being liberal and having long purses. "William" was a bush evangelist who had travelled much and was generally esteemed. He gave a great deal of time to ascertaining the feeling of bushmen regarding the proposed Home, and the result was that he found a very large number were in favour of such an institution. They wished it to be understood that there was nothing in the shape of charity about the establishment in which they had met; it was merely bushmen raising for themselves a pleasant and comfortable Home. Now they knew that bushmen had been in the habit of coming from their stations and going to the nearest township, and there in some public-house spending their earnings. That arose from their not being able to go to a place where they would have society suited to their tastes, and amusements likely to keep them out of mischief. Considering the depressed circumstances of the colony, he thought the project to establish such an institution as the bushmen needed had met with as much success as they could reasonably expect. It was intended in the first instance to start a Home on a much larger scale. For his own part he was not sorry that they had to try the experiment in a somewhat humble way. The premises they had obtained he thought were very suitable. (Hear, hear.) He did not really think the establishing of that Home was much of an experiment, for he believed that when bushmen knew the place they would be sure to patronize it. The grand object was to give bushmen the advantages of a comfortable home at a reasonable cost. They had provided recreations of different sorts, and there was the nucleus of a library which they hoped bye-and-bye would contain many readable books. They wanted to make the institution so attractive that the inmates would not desire to seek amusement out of it. They would also have the advantage of a savings bank, which was not yet however fully established. They would likewise have the advantages of the benefit fund, and of having the officers of the institution as their agents for the transaction of business in town; and they would have a place of safety for anything they might not wish to take into the country with them. Anyone who had been over the establishment must be satisfied with the way in which "William" had fitted it up. The Committee were very greatly pleased with him, for whilst he had studied economy, he had made everything comfortable. (Hear, hear.) With regard to the funds there had been something like £1,000 collected, but only £200 or £300 had been expended, and that amount included the cost of repairing the building. He thought as soon as the place really commenced its operations and bushmen became acquainted with it, they would avail themselves of it. He hoped if that was found to be a successful experiment that similar Homes would be established in some of the northern townships. (Hear, hear.) He trusted that the movement would meet with cordial support from all who wished well to their fellow-creatures. (Applause.)

"William," having read letters of apology from Messrs. Clement Sabine and Wm. K. Thomas excusing their absence, read the following statement :—

"I respectfully beg on this, the occasion of opening the Bushmen's Club for the purposes for which it has been instituted, to present this meeting with a brief sketch of what has already been done, and what it is proposed to accomplish with the assistance of the bushmen and their friends, in connection with this institution. The original plan for a Home or Club was somewhat more pretentious than the one we are now in, and efforts were made to raise the necessary funds for its establishment. It was afterwards found requisite to depart somewhat from the original design, as there did not appear any probability of raising the required amount for a long time. The commercial depression, dry seasons, and other retarding influences prevented that amount of energy being thrown into the matter that was necessary to ensure its complete success, as designed at first by its originators. Nevertheless, a goodly sum has been raised by voluntary contributions, with part of which means this work has been carried on up to its present stage. It is intended (D.V.) at some future time, if this temporary arrangement answers, after a fair and lengthened trial, to make preparation for building a more substantial and convenient edifice. The Board of Management—Messrs. Neville Blyth, C. B. Young, and H. Giles—will, as quickly as possible, cause to be got a selection of books for the library, which is intended to be free to all inmates of the Club (under proper rules) who choose to avail themselves of it, and also a good supply of approved newspapers and periodicals. Donations of books for this purpose will be thankfully received by the Hon. Superintendent of the Club. Although the results of the general appeal to the squatters and others have not come up to the expectations of its originators, they are yet pleased and thankful to God that, through surrounding difficulties, they have succeeded in accomplishing so much as they have done with the assistance of the bushmen themselves and their friends. Further help (D.V.) at some future time will probably be required, and then all those who have been lukewarm and hardhearted will have an opportunity, if so disposed, of rendering practical sympathy with the object. We now beg to tender publicly our hearty thanks to all those true friends of the bushmen and their cause, who have by their kind sympathy and liberality assisted in accomplishing this work, and to others who have manifested much earnest and untiring zeal and self-denial, which has very materially assisted the undertaking forward. It remains with the bush people to say whether the Club this day established and opened shall take its place and rank amongst the many social institutions of our land, or fail for want of their support and patronage. It is for them (through their Board of Management) to further develop its manifold resources and advantages, in the same way as do other Clubs and friendly societies. The originators, promoters, committee, and the friends of the bushmen generally now wish the institution both 'God's speed and blessing,' and earnestly recommend that the future members of the Bushmen's Club fail not to pray Almighty God to give His blessing upon all kindred Clubs and Societies for the good of mankind, under a full conviction that without His favour resting upon any work of our hands, our labours are in vain for good. I will just add, in winding up my statement, that His Excellency the Governor and Lady Edith Fergusson have paid the Club a visit to-day, and formally opened it, expressing themselves highly pleased with the place and its arrangements. Also, that the three gentlemen constituting the present Board of Management have kindly and considerately given their fees for the year of their holding office—which amounts to the sum of eighteen guineas—to the Bushmen's Club Fund. It is to be sincerely desired that as this is the first institution of its kind established in the southern hemisphere, that so it may not be the last, and that we may have the honour (under God) of this day planting a root in South Australia that shall extend its ramifications throughout the sister colonies."

The Hon. J. H. Barrow moved—

"That this meeting views with great satisfaction the opening of the Bushmen's Club—the first of its class in the southern hemisphere—and tenders its best thanks to the Messrs. Angas and those gentlemen who formed the first or preliminary Committee, they having succeeded by considerable energy, zeal, and self-denial in bringing the matter to so successful an issue ; and expresses a hope that Almighty God will bless the undertaking, and that it may be well patronized and supported by the bushmen of South Australia." He said he did not anticipate that he should have been asked to take any part in the proceedings, till the respected Superintendent of the institution called upon him, and urged him to take the resolution he had moved. Although he would rather have seen some bushman, or some gentleman acquainted with bush life, filling his position; still, having sympathy with the movement, he had complied with "William's" request. He had listened with pleasure to the remarks of the Chairman, and to the statement of "William," which left little for him to say to recommend the Home. But he did not think it was necessary for him to say much, because those who were lukewarm and indifferent to it could only be so in consequence of their not being properly acquainted with it; for he believed, by all those acquainted with the Home, it would be appreciated. On going over the building he was gratified to see the pleasing arrangements that had been made for the comfort of the bushmen. The place was not only neat and tidy, but there was an air of refinement about it which he thought would not fail to attract the better class of bushmen—those who had refined tastes; and a great many of them had. It was a great mistake to suppose that because men lived on the outskirts of civilization, that therefore they were destitute of refined tastes. Among them there were men of education, and to many the comforts of a Home like that would be highly satisfactory. (Hear, hear.) He was of opinion that the rates of prices could not fail to commend the institution to the bushmen of South Australia. They owed a good deal to their bushmen —those pioneers who had gone out exploring the country— and they could not interest themselves too much in their comfort and welfare. (Hear, hear.) He was pleased to hear the chairman say that the bushmen, in coming to that Home, would not be accepting of charity. A charitable institution it was in one sense, so far as Christianity was charity—kindliness of heart. (Hear, hear.) It was not a refuge for the destitute; on the contrary, they hoped it would prove self-supporting, and that the bushmen would feel as much at home in it as a gentleman who went to his Club or took his ease at an inn. He trusted that it would be the successful commencement of a work that would be extended throughout the colony. It would be necessary, no doubt, to plant a Bushmen's Club in the north, and another in the south-east; but there must be a commencement made, and he did not believe they could have decided upon a better place for the first Home than Adelaide. The bushmen had contributed largely to that establishment. It had not all been done for them, but much had been done by themselves. Those who contributed were not likely to turn their backs upon the Home when they came to town. He hoped other Clubs would follow, and that bushmen would be regarded differently from what they had been—as worthy of the sympathy of their fellow-colonists. (Hear, hear.) The meeting he was sure would not refuse their thanks to those gentlemen who had manifested deep interest in the movement; and he was certain they would join in the fervent aspiration of the Superintendent, that Almighty God would bless this movement. Let them trust that the establishment of the Home would lead to a great change in the lives of many of their bush friends, seeing that there they would be perfectly free and always at home. He was satisfied that the institution would be so supported as to make it a great success. (Applause.)

Mr. David Murray, M.P., seconded the resolution. After expressing his satisfaction that a Bushmen's Club had been established in Adelaide, he observed that he thought the name Club was a very appropriate one—much better than either hotel or inn. (Hear, hear.) In such an institution bushmen could get together and talk of their common wants and work. It had been greatly needed, and he trusted, now that it had been established in the way it had been, with all the comforts of home, that it would be well supported; but he hardly entertained any doubt that it would be so supported, because the bushmen had contributed more than a half of the sum that had been subscribed, which fact proved that they would patronise the institution. The number of bushmen who contributed was over a thousand, and by doing so they showed that they desired to give the project a practical trial. The fee necessary to membership had been fixed low, and he hoped it would not prove an obstacle to any one joining the Home. It was a credit to South Australia that they were the first to establish a Bushmen's Home in the southern hemisphere. If it was successful, he had no doubt similar institutions would be established elsewhere. Thanks were certainly due to the Messrs. Angas, and so they were to "William," for his great labour in the matter, and he should be glad if his name could be included in the resolution. As nothing great or strong could be established or carried out without the blessing of God, he thought the expression of dependence in the last part of the resolution was very appropriate. He believed the institution had been established on principles which could not but be beneficial to the inmates; and he trusted it would have the effect of doing good to a class who had not, as a rule, been receiving benefit by coming to town. (Hear, hear.)

The Rev. Jas. Lyall moved—

"That this meeting views with great satisfaction, and fully approves of the establishment of a library, reading and refreshment-rooms, money depository, labour and post-offices in connection with this Club, as they will tend (D.V.) to increase the taste for mental improvement, and be the means, under God, of drawing many bushmen from social evil influences and places of amusement of a questionable character. And this meeting pledges itself to assist towards carrying out the designs of the originators of this very commendable institution."

He stated that the temptations to which their bush friends were subject on coming to town, consequent upon the privations they had to put up with, were very great. There were, it was true, men who came from the country with the deliberate intention of "spreeing," but they were not the representatives of bushmen generally, for as it had been previously said, there were amongst them many educated men, who would appreciate a Home of that kind. (Hear, hear.) In his opinion they had acted judiciously in commencing in a small way. If the institution proved successful, then something might be done on a greater scale. (Hear, hear.) The charges for board had been fixed at 18s. and 20s. per week for members and non-members respectively, which were as moderate as could be expected, and cheaper than the bushmen now paid for the accommodation they received in inns and other places. He approved of the intellectual improvement of the inmates being aimed at, and thought it would be well to have occasionally literary entertainments. He did not think too much should be expected from an institution of that kind at first, but they should be contented with small results. They should go on in faith, believing that with God's blessing the Home would be successful in the long run. (Applause.)

Mr. D. Robin seconded. It afforded him, he said, pleasure to express his sympathy with the movement. He thought it appropriate that the first resolution should be proposed by the Hon. Mr. Barrow, because, if he remembered properly, a leader which he wrote some two or three years ago had led to the formation of that Club. (Hear, hear.) He rejoiced that it had been so far successful. He was not sorry the Home had been begun on a small scale, because if it had been begun on a larger the bushmen would have thought themselves indebted to others more than they would do now. In going over the place he had been impressed with the feeling of home that was about it, and that was the feeling which should be sought to be produced—(hear, hear)—for, whilst isolated from their fellows, the bushmen had a longing for home, and till now, on coming to town, the only place to which they could go was the public house. He was glad steps had been taken to provide recreation and amusement at the Home, and he believed it would be well if they had an entertainment each week, at which recitations, readings, and a short lecture on some popular subject might be given. At such entertainments the friends of the institution would have an opportunity of rendering assistance. The utmost publicity should be given to the existence of the Home. Notices should be placed in the railway stations and in the larger country public-houses, informing the bushmen of its establishment. He hoped the newspapers would do all they could to give it publicity, and he thought there should be a standing advertisement in the weekly papers to keep it before the bushmen. He had no doubt the institution would be a success if God's blessing rested upon it. (Applause.)

The resolution was carried.

Mr. R. A. Fiveash moved a vote of thanks to the Chairman, remarking that he believed the establishment of that Home would lead to the establishment of Homes in the other colonies.

Mr. James Hosking, in seconding the motion, expressed a hope that good would proceed from an institution that had been so well begun. He believed as the comforts of the place became generally known the Home would become generally appreciated.

The motion was carried, and the proceedings terminated.

The following article, extracted from the *Evening Journal*, comments on the Bushmen's Club movement from the beginning, and gives an outline of some of the difficulties which have been surmounted in its establishment, and well describes the position of the premises and grounds:—

"THE BUSHMEN'S CLUB.

"Rather more than sixteen months have elapsed since the first steps were taken in Adelaide for the formation of a Bushmen's Club. At the meeting then held, as well as at the larger and more influential gatherings that subsequently took place, the feeling in favour of providing bushmen a place of resort on the occasion of their periodical visits to the city, was strong and unanimous. They were justly spoken of as a class peculiarly open to the worst evils connected with town life, and the great object held in view was to give them an alternative. As things are, there is practically no escape for them from those who lie in wait to pander to their lowest tastes, and ease them of their hard-earned wages. Moving about as strangers and outcasts, they naturally fall into the company of outcasts; association with them furnishes the dissipation of which they are in search.

"The movement for the establishment of the Home has had many difficulties to contend with. Among the foremost of these has been prejudice on the part of many of the bushmen. It was regarded by them as an attempt to fetter their actions during the short intervals of liberty and relaxation that they were able to steal from their monotonous work. This impression was industriously encouraged by interested persons, and it is too much to hope that it will be entirely eradicated until actual experience has shown it to be unfounded. Fixing the site of the Home has been another cause of difficulty, and to some extent of delay. It was thought by many that a place on the outskirts of the settled districts should be chosen, as offering fewer temptations to indulgence by bushmen in their besetting holiday sins; and it was seriously proposed to make the first experiment at the Burra. But the opposition by those most concerned was so keen that the plan had to be abandoned as likely to imperil the success of the undertaking. When all preliminary obstacles had been cleared off there still remained the substantial one—that funds did not flow in so freely as to warrant a large expenditure. Hard times was the fertile excuse for small contributions, and the validity of it was fully recognized by the Management. When pecuniary assistance failed they fell back upon the expressions of sympathy and goodwill which met them in all directions.

"The appeal to the liberally disposed, if it did not bring in thousands as was at first hoped, resulted in the promise of hundreds. The amount thus collected did not justify the erection of a Home, but it was a sufficient incentive to the promoters to persevere in their benevolent intentions. With the view of making a beginning they leased for a year the premises in Whitmore Square historically known as the residence of Chief Justice Cooper. These possess several of the qualifications essential to a fair trial. They are commodious, situate in a healthy part of the town pretty well isolated, and reasonably remote from the haunts which prove so fascinating and yet so mischievous to bushmen. The esplanade in front is planted with trees which, although wanting in careful tending, afford an agreeable shade and pleasing relief to the eye. On the other three sides the house is surrounded with vacant ground. Decayed or decaying fruit-trees give evidence that the greater part of this was at one time occupied as a garden. In some places shrubs and ornamental trees have triumphed over long neglect, and are still in a flourishing condition. A little care and outlay would soon impart a very different aspect to the surrounding of the place. A large plot of ground to the westward will afford facilities for the physical exercises, in which members will be encouraged to engage.

"The building itself is of irregular form. The walls are low but the roof is steep, thus enabling the formation of apartments upstairs. There are in all about fifteen rooms, some of them of considerable size, although for the most part the dimensions are limited. One of the least pretentious of all is the rough smoking-room, where callers and non-members have the privilege of sitting. Adjoining this is the labour office, where employers and employed can make their arrangements. A waiting-room alongside is available for candidates for employment. The other apartments fronting northward are the pantry, a snug servants' room, and a capacious kitchen furnished with a range and with the usual culinary utensils, and with sets of dishes. Adjacent to it is the wash-house, and beyond a tidy little bath-house numbered amongst the additions since the lease was taken. The principal rooms face the south, and are plentifully provided with light and air by large windows opening to the ground. The largest of all is the dining room, 20 x 16, which communicates by means of folding doors with a refreshment room 16 x 18. These when thrown together could on an emergency seat fifty persons, the extreme number that sleeping accommodation could be found for in the Home as it now exists. The reading-room is comfortably fitted up, and will be thoroughly stocked with newspapers, periodicals, and books likely to interest the inmates. Near to it is the members' smoking room. Upstairs there are two dormitories divided off by curtains into ten compartments. Each compartment contains a stump bedstead and the usual etceteras of a bedroom. The mattresses are stuffed with fibre; the sheets, blankets, and quilts of a coarse texture, but beautifully clean. The sleeping provision will be looked upon as positively luxurious by those accustomed to rough it in the bush. One room is set apart as an infirmary, and there is also a lavatory attached to the dormitories; throughout the entire establishment every thing is scrupulously clean and tidy. The rooms are all papered, and one or two of them carpeted. Gas and water have been laid on, but the whole of the repairs and alterations have not yet been completed.

"An outside building has been appropriated as the Superintendent's quarters and storeroom, but it will require renovation before being adapted to this new use. There is also a three-stalled stable, which, it is believed, will be found of great convenience both to visitors and to members.

"A notice prominently posted opposite the principal entrance gives a clue to the principles upon which the Club is to be conducted. It reads thus:—

"'Swearing, drunkenness, and gambling strictly prohibited.'

"No intoxicating drinks are on any pretext to be admitted, but temperance beverages are to be served out *ad libitum*. The charges made to bushmen making use of the Home appear for the most part moderate, but of course the tariff will be open to revision and modification. The formal opening takes place on Friday next, and judging from the encouraging accounts received by 'William,' the indefatigable Hon. Superintendent, the Club will be taken advantage of by the class whose interests it is intended to serve."

A friendly bushman, after paying a visit of inspection to the institution, expresses his opinion as follows:—

"TO THE EDITOR.

"Sir—Reading in the daily papers that the Bushmen's Home is about to be opened, I thought I would visit it. Yesterday I took a turn in that direction, and had an interview with the worthy Superintendent, he very kindly showing me the whole of the rooms and premises. I cannot but think, however, that the Committee might have taken the trouble to see that 'William' had some other place than a coachhouse to live in. Surely he is deserving of being cared for, though his own modesty very naturally makes him put himself in the background. Is it likely that bushmen will like to see the man who has put himself to such trouble to secure their comfort so strangely domiciled? I think not. Nor are such apartments as are set apart for him worthy the Superintendent of such an establishment as no doubt this will become.

"I venture to remark, too, that a few pounds might have been expended in putting the grounds on the south and east of the building in something like trim. Bushmen like neatness and comfort as well as other men, and having subscribed liberally towards this Home, will be disappointed at seeing the whole thing spoiled through a narrow (perhaps beggarly would be the more suitable word) parsimony. Why not put on two or three men immediately to turn up the earth, and put in a few trees, so as to make the garden grounds an attraction instead of repulsion? I hope, Sir, you will do what you can to encourage the thing being liberally dealt with, so as not to invite failure.

"I am, Sir, &c.,
"A Subscriber."

—*Express*, Adelaide, May 17, 1870.

The above correspondent was evidently not aware that "William," in arranging the apartments, was entirely unfettered in his movements by the Board of Management; and, left to choose a residence for himself, he considered the outhouse spoken of as the most suitable for his business purposes. Respecting the improvements of the garden, it was considered unwise to spend other people's money on such a short lease, and the matter was left for future consideration.

The following notice appeared in the *Chronicle* of May 14, 1870 :—

"The Bush Missionary 'William' is putting forth every effort to open the Bushmen's Home in a few days. We understand that amongst his latest sympathizers is the Right Rev. Dr. Short, who has sent a donation of £5 towards the Club Fund."

In another column of the same paper appeared the following lines, which are inserted because they are the production of a bushman :—

THE BUSHMAN'S HOME.

Come all you bushmen and listen to me,
And go look at the Club that's preparing for thee ;
It's there you'll be happy, contented and snug,
So never mind carrying your old 'possum rug.
There'll be fish for your breakfast, so nice and so sweet,
Or, if you're inclined, you can have it of meat ;

There'll be eggs and fresh butter, hot sausage and ham,
And these ought to please any common bushman.
Roast beef and plum duff on the table till two,
With kangaroos' tails made into a stew;
There'll be onions, and cabbage, and spuds in galore;
So we'll laugh and rejoice, we'll sing and encore.
There'll be games of all sorts, with swings and trapeze,
Skittles, cricket, and quoits, and whatever we please.
Then comes tea, and supper, I suppose about ten—
But the big bell will ring to tell the men when.
When our money's all done, and we feel ourselves poor,
Why, it's back to the bush we will go for some more!

SYDNEY B.

Mungibbie, S.E.

The next extract is taken from the *Register* of May 24, 1870:—

"It may seem strange to follow up a denunciation of drunkenness with a plea for the accessibility of drinks; but the following lines just received from a strange contributor, and evidently suggested by the opening of the Bushmen's Club last week, seem to me to have much strong sense, if they have little humour; and having so faithfully kept my pledge to be sedate up to this point, I gladly turn you over, my public, to another hand, lest some unseemly outbreak of jocoseness should disturb the serenity of your slumbers, and prevent the small but respectable minority of my readers who disbelieve in fun, and lament over the levity I so frequently display, from pronouncing this by far the wisest, ablest, best, and most attractive of the Crabthorn Papers:—

A PLEA FOR TOLERATION.

I like the Bushmen's Home and think that those
With whom the charitable scheme arose
Are worthy of all credit,—'tis a plan
To save from ruin many a fellow-man.
Thus when its hopeful programme met my sight
I joyfully contributed my mite;
But though I deem myself the bushman's friend
I was too far the meeting to attend,

H

And sought not on a work so broadly good
My notions from a distance to intrude,
Relying on the wisdom and good sense
Of men who merited my confidence.
I have not now the papers at my side
To give their names. Suffice it, they were tried
As men of worth ; but on a single point
I now perceive their sense is out of joint.
They give the bushman lodging and his " prog,"
But (" William" counselling) cut off his grog.
A dreary " Home !" The bushman you will find
As much for drink as eatables inclined.
He may endure the morning cup of tea,
But beer must on his dinner-table be ;
And with a glass of grog—mark what I say—
The bushman when in town must close the day.
If at his " Home" such comforts are denied,
Away he goes to seek them far and wide ;
And " Home" manipulated thus will be
A " Home" the bushmen will but seldom see.
The London Sailors' Home, with rules more wise,
Poor Jack with meat and drink at once supplies.
Twelve thousand seamen in a single year
Have used that Home, its eatables, and beer.
Till now, the question agitated there
Is this—to add some spirits to the fare.
Oh, " William," Blyth, and Young, pray make the the Club
A " Home" for drink as well as sleep and grub ;
To cheat the fell seducers of their prey,
Make it a " Home" for night as well as day.
Send not the bushman you have helped so far
Perforce to purchase liquor at the bar ;
Let him have all he wants at home, if right,
Nor drive him forth into the streets by night.
" William," your simple nature I conclude
Is somewhat innocent, however good,
Thinking to conjure into Whitmore Square
A band of shepherds, living upon air.
No, my Bush Missionary, 'twill not do,
Though C. B. Young and Murray think with you.
Better at " Home" the shepherd take his glass,
Than drink it hocussed by some painted lass.

The "Home," good "William," that has filled your brain
May do for shepherds of your earnest strain—
For pure teetotallers; but such, d'ye mind,
Without Committees can safe quarters find.
They (though their like we very seldom meet)
Are not exposed to danger in the street;
Such may the wiliest bacchanalian snub,
And rest securely though they have no Club.
But you, good brothers of the sober cup,
Must the poor shepherd as he is take up.
Give him in moderation what he chooses;
Curb him, and, mark me, he the whole refuses.

CHORUS—
(Added by a different hand.)
For he loves a drop of good beer;
He's partial to moderate beer.
And William's unwise
If ever he tries
The bushman to rob of his beer.

An old bushman, remarking on the above, speaks out as follows:—

"TO THE EDITOR.

"Sir—I was rather amused in looking over your issue of this morning's *Register* at those lines on the Bushmen's Club; but I beg to differ from our worthy friend, Mr. Crabthorn, inasmuch as he does not hold with the Club being conducted on temperance principles; but being myself an old bushman of ten years' experience, and knowing what it is to come to town with a cheque, and to 'take the wallaby' again without a copper to bless himself with, and all through the system of drinking and nobblerizing, I can speak feelingly on the subject. And I believe I speak the mind of hundreds of my fellow-bushmen—not only the constitutionally temperate ones, but also those who are most easily led to drink in town—when I say we are heartily glad that *our* Club is established on temperate principles.

"I do not think there is any analogy between the Sailors' Homes and the Bushmen's Club in respect of allowing strong drink; for the sailor, as we all know, in most ships is daily allowed his grog. Not so the bushman, who for months at a stretch drinks nothing but tea or coffee; so he will not feel the want of that to which he is but rarely accustomed; and if he wishes for a glass of beer, why he can hardly throw a stone in Adelaide without breaking a public-house window.

"But I think that every right-minded man who desires the welfare of his fellow-man will use his whole influence to stop that unmitigated evil which is filling our prisons with convicts, our asylums with luratics, our streets with prostitutes, and our homes with misery.

"So God speed the temperance cause, and down with strong drink; so says an   "OLD BUSHMAN.

"Adelaide, May 24, 1870."

About this time—it being desirable to make the institution as widely known as possible—the following advertisement was inserted in the papers:—

"BUSHMEN'S CLUB, WHITMORE SQUARE, ADELAIDE.—This establishment is now open, with room for about fifty persons. Bushmen will find many advantages at their Club, and are strongly recommended to identify themselves with it by becoming members, by payment annually of five shillings each, thus securing success to their own Society. All profits devoted to the benefit of the members. Prospectuses will be sent to all head stations for distribution, and may also be obtained from the Superintendent.

"N.B.—The charge for board has been reduced to fifteen shillings per week for members, and sixteen shillings for non-members.   "By order of the Board,
"'William,' Hon. Superintendent.

"May 23, 1870."

The *Comet* says:—

"The situation, Whitmore Square, is pleasant; the accommodation comfortable and convenient. Going down King William-street South, take the second street to the right hand, Sturt-street, follow it to the square, and there's the Club."

The Home may now be considered fairly launched for the

reception of boarders; and the first monthly meeting of the Board of Management (after the opening) was held June 2, 1870.

There were present—Messrs. C. B. Young (chairman), Neville Blyth, and H. Giles.

The Superintendent reported that the total amount received during May was £48 7s. 6d. for members' tickets and subscriptions; also that he had sent two hundred and seventeen packages of reports and subscription-lists, &c., to different stations and friends in the country. The Club had been open for seven days before the first boarder put in his appearance (Charlie, the loafer, he is well known among bushmen). A present of books from Mr. H. Giles to the library had been received, also a number of magazines and other suitable books from Mr. J. Chapman. Letters had been received from bushmen and others respecting the Club, some of them speaking in very encouraging terms. During the past month one man had made an opening in the Savings-department, by sending his money to be taken care of for him. There had been a large number of visitors to the Club. The premises were generally approved of by bushmen, who had favoured the institution with a call, and by the end of May there were thirteen members belonging to the Club. A few tickets had been sent to Mr. Samuel Lovering, of Willowie Station, at his request, for sale amongst his mates. (Since that time this zealous young man has sold about seventy members' tickets.)

On June 18 the following short paragraph appeared in the papers:—

"THE BUSHMEN'S CLUB.

"We are informed that 'William' the Hon. Superintendent has been kindly presented by Mr. Howell, bookseller, Rundle-street, with seven or eight pounds' worth of illustrated London newspapers (in monthly parts) for the instruction and amusement of the bushmen at the Club. The men are, we hear, beginning to patronize their own institution, and this timely donation will no doubt be appreciated by them as it deserves."

It is pleasing to read the following letter from a bushman after the dissemination of so much prejudice against the institution. It gives his first impression of the Club after becoming a member and an inmate :—

"TO THE EDITOR.

"Sir—May I through the medium of your paper try to convey to my fellow-bushmen the great advantage they would derive by supporting their own Club?

"I came to the Club on my arrival in town to give it a trial, with the impression on my mind that the rules and regulations would make it too much of a barrack sort of life for a bushman to be comfortable in it. But I have had good reason to change my mind since I have been residing here. Every comfort and amusement is provided which bushmen could desire, and every facility is held out which could induce them to make themselves feel at home.

"I heartily wish all my fellow-countrymen coming to town may give it only one trial.

"A desire to serve my class prompts me to write this letter, and on my next visit to Adelaide I hope to enjoy the further recreations and amusements the Hon. Superintendent will provide for the entertainment of the inmates.

"In conclusion, I beg to thank the Hon. Superintendent and the many kind friends of the institution who have helped and are still helping it forward ; for I think it no small boon to be enabled to spend my time in such rational amusements as our own Club is now calculated to promote.

"I am, Sir, &c.,

"DANIEL E. CLUCO.

"June 27, 1870."

On July 2, 1870, the Board held their usual monthly meeting. The following is extracted from the minutes :—

There were present Messrs. C. B. Young (chairman), and H. Giles.

"The Hon. Superintendent reported that J. H. Angas, Esq., had paid a visit to the Club, and had taken supper there ; that he had warmly expressed his approbation and gratification, and bade the Superintendent to tell the Board of Management that he felt very highly pleased with the place and its arrangements, and he hoped that God would make it a great blessing to the bushmen of Australia; that he would help it in every way he could by recommending his men to stay at the Club whilst in town. He wished him also to say that he thought it desirable to post placards up at all the railway stations, and every means taken to make the institution known and popular; that Alexander McCulloch, Esq., of Gottlieb Wells, had presented to the Club a subscription of £7, and N. Blyth, Esq., £5; that donations of books, papers, and periodicals had been received from Messrs. Howell, Capt. Bagot, and T. Magarey, and a basket of good books from an anonymous lady. The Superintendent suggested to the Board the necessity of preparing circulars expressly for the shearing season, copies to be sent to all the known sheds in the colony, and that placards, according to Mr. Angas's suggestion, should be placed at the different railway stations. The labour-office should be opened as soon as possible, and advertised when it was so,—and he asked permission from the Board to open it. He also reported that more bedding was needed, and that it would be necessary to engage another servant for the Club, as the work was increasing.

"Number of members' tickets issued to date, forty-two. Number of weekly boarders at Club, five. Total amount of receipts from all sources, £30.

"It was resolved—That a suitable placard be prepared, and that a copy be posted at the following railway stations:— Kooringa, Saddleworth, Gawler, Kapunda, and Adelaide. That the Superintendent open the labour-office as soon as convenient. That more bedding be procured. That the thanks of the Board of Management be tendered to the abovementioned gentlemen for their kind donations of books, &c., &c."

The following is a report of the first cricket match played by the bushmen of South Australia. The *Register* says :—

"BUSHMEN'S CLUB.—A rather novel sight was witnessed on the South Park Lands on Saturday afternoon, July 2, a cricket match being played by a number of inmates of the Bushmen's Club. The game was carried on in a spirited manner, and, considering that the men were mostly novices in the art, they handled the willow creditably. One worthy bush veteran of between sixty and seventy years surpassed the younger members in feats of speed and agility, and all evidently enjoyed the sport. We hope to see more of such recreation among that long neglected class—the bushmen. It cannot but be gratifying to the friends of the institution to know that it has already become of great service to those for whom it is intended."

Extract from the *Advertiser* :—

"On Saturday, July 2, a cricket match was played on the South Park Lands by the inmates of the Bushmen's Club. The wickets were pitched early in the afternoon, and the game was kept up with great spirit and fair skill for some hours. The mirth was genuine and boisterous, and one pleasing feature in the scene was the open friendship displayed towards each other by all the players—men who perhaps had never seen one another before—showing the spirit of fraternity existing among South Australian bushmen."

From *Advertiser*, July 20, 1870 :—

"We are informed that a draft of a circular and subscription-list has been approved by a meeting of bushmen at their Club, held on Saturday last, urging on their mates not to stand aloof, but to come forward and patronise their own Society. After a debate on the subject it was resolved that the circular, &c., be further submitted for the approval of the gentlemen composing the Board of Management at their next meeting, and for permission to send copies to the different stations in the country so soon as shearing commences. The expediency of opening the proposed labour-office in connection with this Club was also strongly urged by all present. We are assured that the Club is growing in favour, and getting better understood by the bushmen, and that it really bids fair to become one of the permanent social institutions of the land."

The two following paragraphs in praise of the Home have also been taken from the *Advertiser* :—

"BUSHMEN'S HOME.

"Jas. Allen states that with his son he has visited the Home, and writes, as a friend of bushmen, that its comforts and conveniences far exceeded his expectations. Among the advantages enumerated by him are, that the living is good, accommodation cleanly and excellent, shepherds' dogs are well cared for and fed, and there is an air of comfort. He then highly eulogizes the Hon. Superintendent, 'William,' and strongly advises bushmen to use the Club.

"July 29, 1870."

"Bush" corroborates the congratulatory statements of a previous writer on the comforts of the Club, and then continues :—

"If its members, however, really intend it to become a place of accommodation for all who come, provision must speedily be made for the influx that may be expected after shearing. That will be the season for testing its value— when bushmen come to town with their cheques. I desire from my heart that no more such cases as that of 'O'Dea v. Boddington' may again disgrace our social circle, and that this institution may prove a permanent blessing to very many.

"July 30, 1870."

The meeting of the Board of Management was held on August 2. There were present—Messrs. H. Giles (chairman) and Neville Blyth.

The Superintendent reported that agreeably to resolution passed at last Board meeting he had made applications to the proper authorities for permission to exhibit placards at the six principal railway stations gratuitously, which was kindly granted by the Commissioner through Mr. Bonney ; likewise the receipt of some valuable books and six mounted maps from Dr. Mayo, and a further supply of papers and periodicals from Mr. Howell of Rundle-street. That he had prepared a circular, &c, for the coming shearing season, which was laid on the table for approval and authority to publish and post when necessary, also two forms of Books for the labour department, requesting suggestions as to the amount of fees to be charged for registry, &c. That several sheepfarmers had visited the Club during the month and all expressed themselves highly pleased (except as to size) with the institution and promised their support. That several letters from Bushmen had been received speaking in glowing terms of the Club. He had also been compelled to add six more beds, &c., the arrangements having been made for only twelve men, and this was not found sufficient as fifteen men had been stopping at the Club at one time. That copies of rules of the Club were forwarded to Mr. Inspector Bee (per request of Commissioner Hamilton), to be posted up in the cells, &c., of the different Police-stations. That, as the shearing time was drawing near and slack times anticipated, it would be advisable on such an opportunity to prepare for a large influx of inmates after shearing.

Total number of tickets issued, sixty. Total amount of receipts for the past month, £28 5s. 1d.

Resolved that the Superintendent acknowledge the receipt of books, maps, &c. That the circular for the shearing sheds be printed and circulated, and that the Labor-office forms be agreed to.

The *Advertiser* gives the following:—

" It is pleasing to learn that the Bushmen's Club has met with very gratifying success since its establishment. Several letters have been received by the Superintendent from bushmen, expressing their interest in the institution, and their intention to patronise it. Gentlemen also engaged in pastoral pursuits have visited the Club, and expressed their entire satisfaction with the arrangements. They have also promised what support they can give by means of recommending the Club to the men whom they may employ at shearing time. We hear that sixty members' tickets have been issued; that there are now seven men in the Club; and that the largest number boarding there at one time has been fifteen. We learn that the premises are found to be rather small; and, as a great influx of boarders may be expected after shearing, the present is urged as a desirable time in which to improve and enlarge the building. Placards have recently been placed, by kind permission of the Commissioner of Public Works, at the several railway stations, by which the advantages of the Home are set forth for the information of bushmen travelling townwards. Very great praise is due to the Board for their untiring exertions in promoting the comfort of the boarders, and in holding out the benefits of the Club to bushmen generally. The inmates also experience much kindness and consideration from the Superintendent, 'William.'

"Before closing this notice we may mention that the Board are desirous of expressing their acknowledgments to Captain Bagot, Dr. Mayo, and Mr. J. Howell, for the contributions of maps, books, &c, which they have made to the institution."

August 3, 1870.

The following is a copy of the placard alluded to. It was printed in large letters on a sheet two feet by eighteen inches in blue and red colours:—

"BUSHMEN'S CLUB, WHITMORE SQUARE, ADELAIDE.

"*Notice to Bushmen.*

"The Board of Management of the Bushmen's Club are desirous of making that institution as extensively known as possible. They therefore invite bushmen visiting Adelaide, and desiring peace and comfort during their stay, to make it their Home, and test its advantages for themselves, feeling satisfied that they will then report favourably to others on their return to the bush.

"That visitors to town may the better understand the locality of their Club on their arrival, they are hereby informed, that on reaching the Morphett-street platform at the Adelaide station, they might proceed through Morphett and Brown-streets till they get to Whitmore Square, at the south-east corner of which the Club stands; or they can procure a cab at the station and ride to it, taking their luggage with them.

"The Superintendent will be glad to welcome the new comers, and will not be slow in offering them the many advantages of the institution."

Then follows the terms of membership, charges, &c. The placard is signed—

"For Board of Management,
"WILLIAM,
"Hon. Superintendent Bushmen's Club.

"Adelaide, 1870."

The *Register* comments on the Board meeting held August 2, as follows:—

The present number of members is sixty, and there have

been in the Home already at one time as many as fifteen inmates, but a larger influx is expected after shearing, and further accommodation is acccordingly to be provided. Circulars are about to be distributed throughout the shearing sheds, directing attention to the advantages and comforts provided by the institution, and several squatters and bushmen who have visited the Club during the past month have expressed great satisfaction with the design and arrangements, as well as a determination to aid in every way the furtherance of the objects aimed at. A number of additional books and periodicals have been presented to the library, and more room is to be afforded for those who are fond of reading. Among the intended auxiliaries to the Club is the early opening of the contemplated labour office.

August, 1870.

In accordance with a resolution of the Board, circulars and subscription-lists were printed and circulated, of which the following are copies :—

"BUSHMEN'S CLUB, WHITMORE SQUARE, ADELAIDE.

"*To the Shearers, Bushmen, &c., of South Australia.*

"Dear Friends—Being unable from press of business at the above-named institution to visit the different stations and sheds this season, and it being the only time of the year when large numbers of bushmen are drawn together, I have taken advantage of this opportunity to suggest to the members of the Club and the friends of the institution the desirability of the bushmen and shearers holding a special meeting at each shed or station in the country, for the purpose of forming a Committee of their own for furthering the interests of their own Society. This can be done by obtaining the names of bushmen, &c., who are desirous of becoming members on payment of five shillings annually, and sending the money for the tickets and voting proxies to the Superintendent, who will forward them to any given address by mail ; by opening a subscription-list (as per form enclosed) at each station or shed yourselves ; by extending a knowledge of the Club among your mates ; and by patronising it when they come to town. Bushmen, hearty co-operation and union are now needed to follow up the work begun, and pecuniary assistance is solicited from all who desire the real prosperity of the Bushmen's Club.

"Those persons who have been already benefited by the institution, and others who have enjoyed its comforts and advantages, will be better able to explain to their mates further particulars about the place, &c., than can possibly be done on paper.

"It is intended (D.V.) for the first time in the history of the colonies, to hold a Bushmen's Annual Festival or Reunion some time in December next (if funds are forthcoming) in connection with the Club, to which all bushmen and friends who can make it convenient to attend, will be publicly and respectfully invited.

"Any of the gentlemen managing the stations, &c., will, without doubt, feel a pleasure in co-operating with you in this movement, by transmitting for you any amount you may be desirous to send for the good of your Club.

"Wishing you all a good season and a good clip, and that the blessing of Almighty God may rest on the work of our hands, for Jesus Christ's sake,

"I have the honour to be
"Yours very faithfully,
"'WILLIAM,'
"Hon. Superintendent Bushmen's Club.

"P.S.—Care must be taken to spell the five-shillings members' names correctly, also to state whether their tickets are to be sent to them, and where, or whether they are to be kept at the Club for them.

"FORM OF SUBSCRIPTION-LIST.

"BUSHMEN'S CLUB, WHITMORE SQUARE, ADELAIDE.

"*Collecting List for Shearing Season*, 1870.

No.———

Address (or name of station)..........................
Name of manager or collector..........................
Date of collection..........................

"N.B.—The names of all subscribers will be published in the *Observer* and *Chronicle* weekly during the shearing season, as a receipt for the money.

Names of Subscribers, &c.	Amounts.			For Members' Tickets or Subscription.	State here the Address where the Member's Ticket and Voting Proxy are to be sent, or if they are to be left at the Club.
	£	s.	d.		

To interest the managers and overseers of the stations, and induce them to assist in the movement, a copy of the following circular, accompanied with aforementioned letter and subscription-list, was sent to each :—

"BUSHMEN'S CLUB.
"*To the Manager or person in charge of the Station.*
"The Board of Management of the above-named institution—Messrs. N. Blyth, C. B. Young, and H. Giles—respectfully request that you will please co-operate to carry out the design of the enclosed circular and subscription-list; or failing yourself, will you kindly appoint a responsible or trustworthy bushman to do it.

"Believing the goodness and importance of this movement on the bushmen's behalf needs no apology to you, and will be a sufficient excuse for trespass on your valuable time and kindness,
"I am, Sir,
"Your obedient servant
"*Pro* Board of Management,
"'WILLIAM,'
"Hon. Superintendent Bushmen's Club.
"Adelaide, August, 1870."
"N.B.—The labour-office in connection with this Club will be opened so soon as arrangements are completed."

After much agitation on the subject, the Club labour-office was finally opened. See following advertisement :—

"BUSHMEN'S CLUB.
"TO EMPLOYERS OF BUSH LABOUR.
"The managing Committee have completed arrangements for opening the labour-department connected with this institution.

"Bush labour only can be obtained at this office. All orders for men, &c., by post, telegraph, or otherwise, carefully and punctually attended to, and executed if practicable.

"Employers in want of hands are respectfully informed that men, &c., can be hired under any private form of agreement sent in, that a good class of labour may be obtained at this office, and they are requested to give it a trial. Fees low. Office hours (working days) from 10 to 12 a.m., and from 2 to 4 p.m.

"By order of Board of Management,
"'William,'
"Hon. Superintendent of Bushmen's Club.
"Whitmore Square, Adelaide, August, 1870."

To show that the bushmen were beginning to spend their spare time in a rational and sensible manner, the following short notice clipped from the *Register*, August 25, 1870, is here inserted for perusal :—

"Bushmen's Club.—On Saturday, August 20, the inmates of the Home numbering sixteen or eighteen bronzed, able, hearty fellows turned out on their usual recreation grounds, the South Park Lands, for a game of football. They were matched North v. South-east. It would have delighted many friends of bushmen to witness the scrambling, tumbling, busters, and boisterous mirth of these hardy colonists who by mutual consent seem to lay aside for a time their manhood to become boys again; it was a time of real hearty enjoyment, some of them exclaiming that they never had such jolly fun in their lives before. The game would have been continued much longer than it was but for the slippery state of the ground, and the wind rising rather high for the ball to spin well. As several leave in a day or two for the shearing, the result of the game cannot be decided until after their return.

"Great commendation has been bestowed by the men on the Board of Management, as they have left nothing undone that would add to the comfort, instruction, or amusement of the inmates. We learn that arrangements have been completed for the opening of the bush labour-office in connection with the institution, and doubtless this will be an auxiliary, the value of which will be appreciated by employers and employed."

The following are extracts from the proceedings at the monthly meeting held on September 1st, 1870 :—

There were present Messrs. N. Blyth (chair), C. B. Young, and H. Giles.

The Hon. Superintendent reported that though the Club was passing through the dullest part of the year (for the work in hand), that there had been no diminution in the amount of receipts for the month as was anticipated, but rather an increase. That more furniture, bedding, and other necessaries had been obtained to keep pace with the growing requirements of the institution; that the partition in the reading room had been taken down with the assistance of some of the inmates; and two rooms thrown into one, thus giving the place a cheering, light, airy and comfortable appearance, and making it capable of accommodating about forty readers. That, according to a resolution of last meeting, there were forwarded to the various sheds, stations, and friends of the Bushmen's cause over 200 circulars, subscription-lists, and a few remaining placards. That the labour-office had been publicly opened by advertisement. The Hon. Superintendent also respectfully suggested to the Board the desirability of enlarging in some way the sleeping, dining, and smoking accommodation, and that it was necessary to take this matter speedily in hand, as it was incumbent to make more provision for the large influx of boarders expected after the shearing was over, and that some kind of gymnasium should be fitted up in the paddock. The Hon. Superintendent also mentioned that he had received a large number of letters from men in the bush, promising to stay at the Club when they came to town, but the best evidence of its growing popularity would be found in the steady increase of members. That N. Blyth, Esq., had presented some very valuable books to the Club, but as bushmen are such great readers, that a larger stock of books, newspapers, English and Colonial, &c., would soon be required. That the Mayor of Gawler, E. Clement, Esq., the Chairman of the District Council, and other gentlemen had visited the Club during the month, and without exception expressed themselves pleased and gratified with the place, some of them suggesting that it was too small for the object aimed at.

"Number of members' tickets issued to date, 116. The highest number at one time in the Club during the month, 20. Receipts from all sources, £51 12s. 11d.

Resolved—That with a view to increase the accommodation of the Club, Mr. J. Hosking, the lessee, be communicated with to ascertain upon what terms the property now held may be purchased, or leased for a term of years. Answer to be considered at a meeting in a fortnight's time, to which the trustees, Messrs. Angas, Murray, and W. K. Thomas should be invited. Also resolved that some gymnastic and athletic appurtenances be produced. Resolved that a late English paper be obtained upon the arrival of English mail."

A bushman in the Far North writing to the *Advertiser*, says as follows :—

"Sir—I rejoice to find that the Bushmen's Club is gradually being freely patronised by and becoming popular amongst bushmen—the class for whose special benefit it was (by dint of much energy and perseverance evinced by 'William,' the Hon. Superintendent, and others) established.

"There can be no doubt whatever that such an institution is much wanted. It will be the fault of the bushmen themselves if they allow it to fall to the ground, as it were, for want of support.

"This being shearing season, and consequently the bushmen's pecuniary harvest time, I would strongly recommend them, one and all, to become members. Five shillings annually is a very trifling fee for constituting membership. A few extra shillings, or even a one-pound note, as a present to the funds from every member are greatly needed, and would scarcely be missed during or after shearing time.

"I don't preach what I don't practice. I am a member, and intend to give whatever subscription I can afford during the season when the lists are sent round.

"I heartily approve of the Bushmen's Club. I believe that it will tend to bring employers and bushmen together on better terms. It will not lower wages as supposed. Comfort and economy will be the order of the day; and all will go, I hope, merrily as a 'marriage bell.'

"I conclude with best wishes for the prosperity of the Club, and hoping that all bushmen will join and support such a praiseworthy and deserving institution.

"I am, Sir, &c.,

"AN EDUCATED AND BONA FIDE BUSHMAN.

"Far North, September 3, 1870."

A special meeting of Trustees and Board of Management (as resolved at last meeting) was held on September 15, to consider the propriety of enlarging the accommodation of the premises. Present—Messrs. H. Giles (chairman), N. Blyth, and W. K. Thomas.

Extracts from the minutes were read, also Hon. Superintendent's report to the last meeting of the Board of Management.

The Hon. Superintendent, "William," reported that he had seen Mr. Jas. Hosking, and his letter was read, offering the property required for the use of the Club at £1,300. After reading extracts from a letter received from Mr. Angas and examining the property, the subject of the purchase was considered, and it was agreed to hold an adjourned meeting, the day to be fixed by "William." It was resolved that bedding and furniture should be provided by the Superintendent for the accommodation of forty men in all.

The proposed adjourned meeting was held on September 28, 1870. There were present — Messrs. C. B. Young (chairman), J. H. Angas, N. Blyth, and H. Giles.

The letter from Mr. J. Hosking was again read, offering the house and grounds for £1,300.

Resolved—That a deputation consisting of Messrs. J. H. Angas and N. Blyth call on Messrs. Hart and R. B. Smith on the subject of the two acres at North Adelaide, offered by T. Elder, Esq., as a site for the Home. Committee to meet at Mr. Giles's office on the 30th instant, at 2 p.m., and report progress.

Resolved also—That an advertisement be inserted four times each in the *Observer* and *Chronicle*, and four times each in the *Register* and *Advertiser*, appointing the time of annual meeting, and calling for nominations, &c., as per clauses 6 and 12 of the Constitution of the Club.

Total number of members' tickets issued to date, 137. Total receipts for past month, £22 6s. 11d.

The Constitution of the Club requiring that three months' notice of the general annual meeting should be given in the newspapers, the following advertisement to that effect was issued :—

"IMPORTANT NOTICE TO BUSHMEN, &c. — The annual general meeting of the members of the Bushmen's Club will be held (D.V.) at their Club-house on Wednesday, the 21st day of December next, at 7 p.m., for general business, and to elect a Board of Management in the place of Messrs. N. Blyth, C. B. Young, and H. Giles, who retire, but are eligible for re-election."

"FURTHER NOTICE. — Members of the Club, and other qualified persons, proposing to offer themselves as candidates, must signify their willingness to act if elected (in writing) to me on or before Thursday, the 10th of November next. (See Constitution, clauses 6 and 12.)
"By order of the Board of Management,
" 'WILLIAM,'
" Hon. Superintendent Bushmen's Club.
" Bushmen's Club, Whitmore Square, Sept. 29, 1870."

Extracts from minutes of meeting held November 7, 1870. Present—Messrs. H. Giles (chairman) and N. Blyth.

The Hon. Superintendent, "William," reported that one ton of hay had been saved from off the premises; that on October 22, G. F. Angas, Esq., J.P., in company with other gentlemen, called at the Club and desired "William" to mention to the Board of Management that he would give another £100 to help the institution forward when needed, also some good books, and to say that he was very much pleased with the establishment and its arrangements. He reported also that an old man named Thomas Johnston (friends unknown) became insane and was removed to the Hospital and thence to the Lunatic Asylum, and that his Bank pass-book for a considerable sum (about £109) was sent to him to the Hospital and his receipt obtained for it. On the suggestion of Mr. Giles, he (the Superintendent) had applied to Mr. D. Robin, who had kindly consented to get another gentleman to audit the accounts; also that he had spoken to Mr. J. H. Angas about presiding at the annual meeting. Mr. Angas suggested that Mr. Maughan should be asked to give a lecture, &c. N. Blyth, Esq., reported that after conferring with Mr. J. H. Angas, he thought it desirable to await Mr. T. Elder's return before taking further action with regard to the site.

Total number of tickets issued to date, 248. Total amount of receipts from all sources, £72 8s. 11d.

Respecting Mr. Angas's promise the press made the following remarks :—

"'William,' the Hon. Superintendent of the Bushmen's Home, informs us that Mr. G. F. Angas paid a visit to the Home on Saturday, and expressed himself highly pleased with all the arrangements. With his usual liberality, Mr. Angas promised a donation of £100, and a present of books. This is a good example that might be followed by gentlemen interested in pastoral pursuits."—*Express*, October 25, 1870.

The *Evening Journal* of November 9, 1870, has the following regarding the above monthly meeting :—

"BUSHMEN'S CLUB.—We are informed that at the meeting of the Board of Management on Monday, November 7, there was reported an increase of 111 annual subscribers, making a total number of 248 on the Club-roll. A strong muster of bushmen is expected at the annual meeting and festival to take place in December. The institution has already met with a fair measure of support, and much good has been accomplished by it during the present shearing-season—the men who have taken up their abode in the Club having enjoyed the advantages of a comfortable home, and availed themselves of the arrangements for taking charge of their money until required for them; this has saved many from those who have hitherto being accustomed to prey upon them. We understand that Messrs. C. B. Young, N. Blyth, and H. Giles will be nominated again as a Board of Management, these gentlemen having consented to act in that capacity. The interests of the Club could not be placed in better hands. Bushmen, who have qualified themselves as members, are expected to send in their voting proxies if they cannot attend personally at the annual meeting."

It was considered necessary to change the day of annual meeting. See the following notice :—

"Bushmen's Club.
"important notice to bushmen.

"The annual general meeting will be held at the Clubhouse on Friday, 16th December next, at 7 p.m., instead of the 21st, as previously advertised. Persons holding proxies intended to have effect are requested to send them to 'William,' Hon. Superintendent, by that date. (See Constitution of Club, clauses 6 and 12.)

"By order of the Board of Management,
"'William,'
"Hon. Superintendent Bushmen's Club.
"November 21, 1870."

The following will explain itself :—

[ADVERTISEMENT.]

"Bushmen's Club.—At the request of a number of bushmen, the Board of Management have decided to give them a trip to the Bay on the day of their annual general meeting, 16th December, inst.

"Provisions, music, and amusements will be provided.

"Bushmen in town, who are not inmates of the Club, wishing to participate in the day's recreation, are invited, and will please send their names, or apply personally to the Hon. Superintendent on or before the 14th inst.

"No charge.

"The annual general meeting will be held (D.V.) in the evening, at 7 p.m. J. H. Angas, Esq., J.P., has kindly consented to preside.

"N.B.—Arrangements will be made for the return of the excursionists in time for the meeting.

"Further notice on 15th instant.
"'William,'
"Hon. Superintendent Bushmen's Club.
"December 10, 1870."

The usual monthly Board meeting was held December 2nd, 1870. There were present Messrs. H. Giles (chairman), N. Blyth, and C. B. Young. "William" reported that G. F. Angas, Esq., J.P., had (according to promise) sent a collection of about thirty books as a present to the Club, and that J. H. Angas, Esq., had kindly consented to preside at the annual general meeting; that, as the annual meeting was drawing nigh, he had been drafting the report, preparing resolutions, &c., and now asked the Board's permission to hold an annual festival or picnic on the day of the evening meeting and invite absent bushmen and friends. It was resolved, during the meeting, that an iron safe be purchased for the security of the funds placed in the Superintendent's hands. Also, it was agreed to meet on the 13th inst. at 9.30 a.m., to consider the annual report, &c.; this was done, and the report of Board of Management, balance-sheet, and resolutions for the annual meeting were read, considered, and adopted.

Total number of tickets issued to date, 263. Total amount of receipts from all sources for the month, £54 13s. 9d.

The following extract from the press says :—

"BUSHMEN's CLUB.—A meeting of bushmen was held at the Club-house, Whitmore-square, on Friday evening, to consider the best means of providing amusement and recreation on the day of the annual general meeting, December 16; Mr. W. Colman was in the chair. Mr. Allan Cameron suggested that a ride to the Bay and a picnic, with amusements, such as cricket, quoits, and football, or a sail, would be the most suitable, the party returning in time for the meeting at 7 p.m. Mr. John Edkins seconded the proposal, which was carried unanimously. It was proposed by Mr. William Walters that bushmen in town, not inmates, desirous of participating in the festivities, be invited to communicate with 'William', the Hon. Superintendent, on or before the 14th inst. Seconded by Mr. Thomas Marshall and carried unanimously. Mr. John Nolan moved that the Hon. Superintendent be requested to confer with the Board of Management, for the purpose of carrying out these resolutions if practicable. Seconded by Mr. F. Miller, and also carried. Thanks to the Chairman, proposed by Mr. James Wheeler, seconded by Mr John Bramley, closed a lively but orderly meeting. Since the meeting arrangements have been made, and these are announced in our business columns."

December 15, 1870.

ADVERTISEMENT.

BUSHMEN'S PICNIC.—The picnic party will leave the Club House, Whitmore-square, at 8.45 a.m. punctually, on 16th inst., for the grounds of Sir George S. Kingston, Marino, leaving that place for home about 4 p.m. A band has been engaged.

"WILLIAM," Hon. Superintendent.

Another advertisement on December 16th, 1870, gives the following notice :—

"BUSHMEN'S CLUB.

"The following gentlemen—C. B. Young, Esq ; N. Blyth, Esq ; H. Giles, Esq.—will be nominated for the Board of Management, at the Annual Meeting this evening.

"WILLIAM," Hon. Superintendent.

Whitmore-square, December 16, 1870.

In the *Evening Journal* for that day appeared the following paragraph, speaking of the arrangements of the picnic party :—

"This morning at 9.30, the inmates of this institution proceeded from the Club-house to Glenelg, in one of Cobb & Co.'s large omnibuses for their first picnic. In addition to Schrader's Band, there were 37 passengers on the coach, amongst whom were 16 Club boarders, the others being outside members and friends. As 'William,' the Hon. Superintendent, was not able to accompany them, two of the men were appointed field marshals. On arriving at Glenelg, sports such as quoits, cricket, football, and other games, were indulged in. Arrangements have also been made for refreshments, and the party is expected to return to town by 5 o'clock."

Here follows an account of the proceedings at the Annual General Meeting as taken from the *South Australian Advertiser*, Saturday, December 17, 1870 :—

Bushmen's Club.
THE PICNIC.

For some days past an advertisement might have been seen in our paper announcing the annual meeting of the Bushmen's Club. In a community such as this the existence of such an institution stands out like a cheering omen—we have so long looked at bushmen when in town somewhat after the fashion in which we were accustomed to regard paid-off sailors in the old country after their long voyage over the briny deep. Drunken rollickery and obscenity, while cash remained "in the locker," was the rule; the votaries of Bacchus being insensible alike to precept and example of temperance or virtue. Under the fostering and general influence of this institution a different state of things is being inaugurated. Hundreds of men have given in their names as members, have paid their subscriptions, and are deriving, under its regulations, advantages that no institution before brought within their reach. On Friday morning, at an early hour, passers by the Club-house might have seen that a red-letter day had arrived—that something more than ordinary was about to take place. From a pole, fixed at the north-western boundary and stretched across the ground, a long line of flags and streamers floated in the breeze, while near a number of bushmen were seen talking earnestly together, not looking as if just recovering from some debauch, but as sober and thoughtful men—contrasting favourably with those scenes that we have witnessed on more than one occasion in the past. About half-past 8 o'clock one of Cobb & Co.'s large omnibuses drew up at the entrance to the Club-house, and shortly after the bushmen and their mates, in number about forty—accompanied by a band of music and banners—started off right joyously for the Bay. Here some of them enjoyed themselves at cricket, football, quoits, and similar amusements, whilst others made one or two excursions on the "briny." All seemed to thoroughly enjoy themselves, and refreshments of all descriptions were plentifully supplied. The party returned to town about 5 o'clock.

THE EVENING MEETING.

The annual general meeting of the members of the Club was held at the Club-house, Whitmore-square, on Friday evening, December 16. There were about twenty bushmen present, and there were also several visitors, including the Private Secretary. Mr. J. H. Angas, President of the Club, occupied the chair, and in opening the meeting expressed the pleasure he felt at being President. It was now about twelve months ago that several persons interested themselves in the welfare of the bushmen, and were requested to form this institution. The result as far as they could judge had been most satisfactory—more satisfactory than perhaps even the most sanguine had anticipated. When they took into consideration that the past had been one of the worst years in South Australia, it would be seen that the report was favourable, not only to the bushmen, but to the gentlemen who had exerted themselves on behalf of the Club. He was glad so much interest had been taken in the Club; and he acknowledged with gratitude the services of their Hon. Superintendent "William," without whom they could not have got on. (Applause.)

Mr. H. Giles then read the report, as follows:—

"Your Board of Management, in presenting their first report, are happy to state that a fair amount of progress has been made in the establishment of the Club since its formal opening in May last by His Excellency and Lady Edith Fergusson.

"There is every reason to believe that there is cause to congratulate the members and friends of the Club upon the success of its proceedings. So far a good work is being carried on, and that hereafter it will be (D.V.) amply proved that the labor and expenditure have been well bestowed.

"To enable the Committee to give the matter a fair trial, the present premises were engaged by the year at a rental of £110, which has been a serious drain upon the resources of the Club, but as it was absolutely required, the expense cannot now be regretted.

"The Board strongly recommend cordial co-operation among the bushmen and their friends to secure a freehold property for the Club premises, and trust that another year will not be allowed to pass without providing a building more

I

suitable to the requirements of the large number of members that may be reasonably expected will in future compose the South Australian Bushmen's Club.

"Making every allowance for the time naturally absorbed in the formation of such a Club, and considering the peculiarly depressed state of every branch of industry which characterised the past year and those which immediately preceded it, we may derive encouragement from the fact that we have, as a Club, a comparative large list of members, namely 285.

"The Club was started in May last with complete accommodation for 12 persons; this has been gradually increased up to 24, and further additions will be made as applicants present themselves.

"The labor-office in connection with this Club has been opened; but owing to its having been started late in the season, very little business has yet been done in this department. Advertisements have been inserted in the papers calling attention to this fact, and circulars have been sent to the different stations, soliciting employers to give the Club Labor Office a trial. There is very little bush labor engaged at this time of the year in the city. We have no doubt that as lambing and shearing again approach, the Club will be favoured by the squatters, &c., with a fair share of their patronage, and orders for hands may then be expected. And here we would respectfully appeal to the sheepfarmers, &c., to let us have their hearty co-operation in this movement, as with such a united effort the Club, we feel confident, in a little while can be made entirely self-supporting.

"Circulars and subscription-lists were sent round to the men during the shearing season. Only a very few have been yet returned, with small results.

"In the Postal department a very large number of letters, &c., have been received and forwarded to their destination or retained at the Club, as desired, without extra charge. This is a great boon to many bushmen travelling about who have no friends or fixed place of residence in the colony.

"In the Savings department there has been great good done in preserving the bushmen's money, as the following account will show :—The total amount of property, deposited for safe keeping in cheques, pass-books, cash, &c., £1,372 16s.

2½d. ; drawn out by instalments £1,213 17s. 8½d. ; leaving still in custody £159 4s. 6d. There have been 151 weekly boarders accommodated ; there have been 35 travelling bushmen relieved with board and lodging, and the greatest number at one time in the Club has been 21. Experience proves that it would have been better for the Club had it been more central or nearer the North Terrace; it should not be on any consideration further away than it now is from the centre of the city and should be nearer if possible.

"The Library has steadily increased to about 100 readable books, besides periodicals, magazines, files of papers, &c.

"Reverting to the preliminary and painstaking exertions of the gentlemen with whom the desire to form such a Club for the bushmen of South Australia originated, the least we can do is to remember them on this fitting occasion, and publicly acknowledge our thanks to them, and all those who became associated with them in founding this institution, which has not its counterpart in any other colony, and trust that their object being thus far accomplished, and the early impediments to its usefulness greatly overcome, the Bushmen's Club may continue to exert a beneficial influence in a more extended sphere for the future.

"It would not be advisable, did time permit, here to recapitulate all the various incidents attending the formation of the Club before it could be said to be fairly established.

"We trust also that the proceedings of the past year will have clearly demonstrated to the minds of bushmen that the interests of the employer and employed are identical. A unanimous assent to this opinion will, no doubt, facilitate the usefulness of the institution for the future.

"In conclusion, we would again repeat with firm assurance that the members and friends of this Club have every reason to congratulate themselves upon the result of its transactions so far."

Mr. Giles then read the financial statement, showing the receipts to have been £1,254 19s. 3d. ; and the expenditure £690 0s. 6d. ; thus leaving a balance in the Bank of £564 18s. 9d. He remarked that they had great cause to be thankful for the care and attention to the interests of the

Club shown by their friend "William," and drew the attention to the lowness of wages account, stating that "William" had given his time and services gratuitously.

The Chairman advised the bushmen to support their own institution, and pointed out that the investment of their money through the medium of the Club secured many advantages.

Mr. D. Murray moved—"That the report and financial statement now read be adopted, and published for the information of absent members, under the direction of the Board of Management." He attended the first meeting held to get up this Club, and also the last meeting, and he confessed that he had been rather doubtful as to the success which would follow the establishment of the institution—the response generally being so meagre—but he was glad the bushmen themselves had responded, and had shown that they had confidence in it before they had but barely heard of it. The response of the general public was not encouraging, and it was with fear and trembling, so to speak, that he saw the institution opened. He felt now, however, that it was a success, independent of any of the rich people of Adelaide, and that its success was likely to be permanent, inasmuch as the bushmen themselves had taken an interest in it. He was glad that during the six or nine months the Club had been carried on, although under such bad circumstances, it showed such a small loss. He felt that that small sum could not be called a loss, but he hoped that at a future meeting they would be able to show a large profit. Of course this was dependent on the economical way in which it was carried out. If they had carried it on as a large hotel or something of that sort, it would have had to be given up, but through their friend "William," and his excellent management, they had the satisfactory and good result shown that night. There was a great thing in having minor institutions connected with the Club, such as a labor-office, savings-bank, &c. He did not wonder that so much money had been taken out, because of the prevailing dulness of the past year, but he thought next year they would have more depositors. He trusted that the labor office would be of service to the sheepfarmers and also to the bushmen. The employers would be able to get the best of servants, and good servants would get good masters. (Applause.)

Mr. H. Hussey, in seconding, remarked that when the Club was started he was not so sanguine about it as some were. He did not think that they had a sufficient guarantee, and perhaps he ought to feel a little embarrassment in rising. However, he had much pleasure in acknowledging his fault, and he could now say that it was sometimes better by far to do a thing than to have so much talk about it. (Hear, hear.) He thought they had a little too much cutting and carving about the thing; but now, having taken in sail, he believed they had reduced it to workable order, and that had caused its success. He was down at the Port the other day, and saw the Sailors' Home, which was started before that Club, and saw a great deal of bricks and mortar, and he thought of that Club, which though started since, had taken the lead of the Home. He hardly wondered as to there being a little backwardness in putting money in their Savings Bank, but there was no doubt that it was quite right they should have such a thing; it was quite right that the bushmen should have a safe investment, and he thought it would be a good plan if land could be procured and a building erected. He thought bushmen might deposit money, and receive bonds till the building could be erected. Money, however, could be given out as required, as at present.

The resolution was put and carried unaminously.

Mr. James Smith moved the next resolution as follows:—
"That this meeting renders thanks to Almighty God for the measure of success which has attended this experiment on the bushmen's behalf, and expresses an earnest hope that renewed efforts may be made for the social and moral welfare of the bushmen of Australia." He was thankful to speak on the resolution, and first he noticed that it placed the acknowledgment of success where it should be. They all knew that no undertaking could be initiated and carried on successfully unless God was recognised in it. If they commenced it, trusting in their own efforts, they would find that they would come to naught. He was sure that the meeting would join heartily in this resolution. The second part re-

minded them that the moral as well as the temporal welfare of their fellow-colonists needed attending to. He pointed out the temporal advantages resulting from a Club of that sort, and the other blessings accruing, and concluded by saying that perhaps bushmen would go from this institution to the other colonies, and the relation of their experiences in it might tend towards the making of provision for the welfare of bushmen in those colonies also. (Applause.)

Mr. W. K. Thomas seconded, saying he felt great interest in this institution, and was one amongst those who took an interest in its establishment, and more or less was sure of its success. He need not say how pleased he was to see that it had met with such success. He thought that report was the best speech of the evening, it contained so much encouragement—so much that would doubtless induce bushmen when they read it to take greater interest in the institution, and he was sure that all he or the other speakers might say would not have so much weight as that report. He thought they should render thanks to God for the success which had been met with. Now was the day of small things, and the success they had met with was, he was sure, largely due to the persistent energy of "William," and to the prudence and energy of the Board of Management. (Hear, hear.) Going on so well, he had no doubt in the future it would be a greater success. Bushmen who had been there would go back and communicate their experience to others, and so induce them to try it. He hoped the Board of Management would be soon able to build, especially considering Mr. Hussey's suggestion.

The resolution was unanimously carried.

Mr. W. Colman (a member) moved the next resolution, as under :—" That the thanks of this meeting are due, and are hereby tendered, to the Board of Management (Messrs. C. B. Young, N. Blyth, and H. Giles); also to the Auditors (Messrs. Steele and Robin), and that the same gentlemen now nominated be again appointed for the ensuing year." In doing so he said—With respect to the gentlemen named in the resolution which I have the honour to bring forward, namely, C. B. Young, N. Blyth, and H. Giles, I believe I only speak the minds of the majority of the bush people when I say that they have laid the bush people of this colony under lasting obligation, and a debt of sincere gratitude is due to them for their disinterested and unselfish kindness. It is very certain that if they had not the bushmen's welfare and greatest good at heart, they would not have given (gratuitously, as they have done) so much valuable time and labor on their behalf. It is to be hoped that the bush people will appreciate this as it deserves, and I think they will. Respecting the resolution itself; I am heartily glad that they have consented to act as a Board of Management for the Club another year, and I have very great pleasure in again repeating the resolution entrusted to my charge. (Applause.)

Mr. T. O'Connell seconded, and the motion was carried with acclamation.

The Chairman said he was glad they could speak so well on on behalf of the others; and if they had anything to suggest to the Committee they would be glad to give it every attention. The work the gentlemen of the Board had performed had resulted satisfactorily, and he rejoiced that they would be reappointed, for he knew they had the interests of the bushmen at heart. There were about 7,000 bushmen in the colony, most of whom were single men, and if every one of them were to give £1, they would be able to erect a handsome building, and it would be their own, for there was no vested interest in the institution; if any land was bought, if any institution was built, it belonged to the bushmen, having been bought with their own money.

The resolution was carried.

Mr. Giles apologized for the absence of Messrs. Blyth and Young, and returned thanks for the feelings the resolution expressed. He mentioned circumstances which led him to be interested in the formation of this Club, and stated that Mr. Angas had behaved nobly towards them. He had given £100, and had promised £100 more. Mr. Elder, also, had not forgotten them, for he had been endeavouring to negotiate for a piece of land on which to erect Club premises; and when he came out no doubt there would be a final settlement.

Mr. Gore moved—"That the thanks of this meeting are due to J. H. Angas, Esq., J. P., for presiding; and it is gratifying that the bushmen themselves continue to take so much interest in this movement, as their example is calculated to further the best interests of the institution." He spoke in high terms of Mr. Angas, and also of "William." In commenting on what the latter had done, he said whatever satisfaction there might be in a man's own mind in knowing the good he was doing, that no less exonerated them from acknowledging what their friend "William" had done. He first walked through the length and breadth of the colonies, and felt and suffered with bushmen. He (Mr. Gore) felt, looking at this, that there was a nobleness in man. He then came down to the city, and having obtained the assistance of a few gentlemen, his work assumed a practical form. He was glad to see that "William" had used the public press, which was the best way of bringing the Club into notice. He thought it would be very desirable to have a building like the Sailors' Home, and he did not see why they should not have a building equally as good. (Applause.)

The Hon. T. Reynolds seconded, remarking that he noticed thanks were not rendered to other pastoral lessees of the Crown who had done a good deal in support of the institution. Referring to "William," he termed him the life and soul of this institution; and concluded by saying that if a building was to be erected the bushmen alone would not be called on to contribute, but would receive support from others. The motion was carried; "William's" name, which was added, being received with loud and prolonged applause.

Both the Chairman and "William" acknowledged the vote, the latter reading his reply as follows:—

"I desire now with your kind permission, Mr. Chairman and gentlemen, to make a few remarks respecting the organization of this Club, and the wants it is designed to meet. All who know anything of the social and moral condition and habits of the bushmen know that they suffer incalculable disadvantage for easy recreative intercourse with their fellows, which can only be indulged in under circumstances which expose them to baneful temptations. When on the stations, their huts for the most part cannot supply this great want: crammed for room as some of them are, deficient in most of the accommodations necessary to comfort; ill-ventilated, ill-lighted, intolerably close in summer, inadequately warm in winter, fit neither for solitary reading, nor for cheerful converse with friends. There are needed for this class of men such clubs as this in which they may obtain—away from the demoralizing influences of the public house—precisely the same kind of advantages as gentlemen usually find in their clubs. Bushmen, not less than others, require to meet each other; sometimes for business, sometimes for conversation, sometimes for refreshment, or amusement, or mental improvement; and until quite recently such meetings could nowhere be arranged but in connection with a certain amount of expenditure in intoxicating beverages. This Club has been organized for the purpose of rescuing bushmen from these special disadvantages of their position—an object which few will deny to be both pressing and praiseworthy. The Club undertakes to do nothing for the class whose benefit it seeks which they can more properly do for themselves. Its business is to put bushmen themselves in the way of securing to their use all the social appliances required by their position; it leaves it to them to find the necessary means, to subscribe to the rules and conditions, and to govern the interests of the institution through their Board of Management. It acts chiefly with a view of awakening attention to the desirableness of establishing such clubs, of assisting them when formed by personal visits, correspondence, and the counsels of experience, and of developing its capacities for usefulness by co-operating one with another, and with a common central establishment. This is just the kind of aid which bushmen will most readily recognize and appreciate —aid which is stimulative and regulative of their own self-reliant exertions. They do not like to be treated as mere children in leading strings. They are thankful for such guidance as may be vouchsafed to them. Show them how they can help themselves, and you confer upon them a boon far more valuable than any amount of assistance which entirely supersedes their own efforts. The mode in which the promoters have planned and hitherto conducted their enterprise presents a favourable example of the modest reticence which men who aim at the welfare of their fellow-men by means of a scheme of benevolence are, I am sorry to say, too apt to forget. It must be remembered that wisdom and philanthropy do not always go hand in hand. The best impulses of the heart are too frequently frustrated by the mistakes of the head. Many a social and moral reform, the object of which commands general approbation, has utterly failed. Some have even done more harm than good, owing to a singular want of adaptation of the means to the end. This Club under the blessing of God has met with a fair measure of success, all things considered. It has been comparatively but a very short time in existence, and only a little over six months in working order; but it has already accomplished quite enough to prove its qualifications for doing much more good. In conclusion, I beg from my heart to thank publicly the Messrs. Angas, Young, Blyth, and Giles; also the numerous gentlemen and friends who have so nobly and cordially promoted the objects of the Club by presiding over our meetings, by initiating or taking part in the various subjects of discussion, and by furnishing much valuable information, or in other ways assisting our efforts. And I do trust that a like unanimity may ever exist among those who enjoy a position which thus enables them to assist those who are toiling on in an honourable endeavour to increase the morality, and consequently the happiness of their adopted country, for the establishment of themselves and those dependent upon them. For myself, I feel I am in honour bound not to leave the Club in this present and critical stage of its existence; and on the requisition of many friends and members of the Club, I will (D.V.) give it for the Lord's sake a free helping hand for a while longer. I cannot at present promise any given time; I can only say that if it flourishes I shall withdraw, and leave to others the honour of working it out, but if it is likely to fail, I shall stand by the wreck to the last."

Mr. T. O'Connell, one of the members, suggested that a building more centrally situated should be provided for the Club.

The Chairman, in replying, pointed out that the way to make the Club progress was to double the number of subscribers. With regard to the building, he intimated that they had been trying to get a suitable site; and he also thought it would be better to have it more in the centre of the city, or near the Railway station. In conclusion, he trusted that that day would be only the beginning of many happy and pleasant days which they would be able to spend in such enjoyment and desirable recreation as they had on that occasion experienced.

The proceedings then terminated.

The next thing we hear of the Club is through the following short newspaper extract speaking of its continued success, and a letter signed "Bushman," bewailing the folly of many men coming from the country seeking to make the acquaintance of their enemies in town in preference to their friends at the Home, as also their treatment by the Adelaide cabmen:—

"THE BUSHMEN'S CLUB.—For several days lately there have been about twenty-six inmates at this institution, and there has been a difficulty in providing accommodation for the increasing members who are desirous of sharing the comforts of the Home."—*Evening Journal*, January 14, 1871.

The "Bushman's" letter referred to above:—

"TO THE EDITOR.

"Sir—Hearing of your goodwill towards the working classes of this colony, I respectfully ask you to open your valuable columns for a few words respecting the Bushmen's Club. Coming from a bushman, it may be all the more acceptable to some of your readers. You no doubt are aware that the Bushmen's Club has been opened about eight months; and I am sure you will be glad to learn that it is still progressing, with a fair share of success, to benefit the class whose name it bears; and not only bushmen, but working men of any class. There has been some opposition to this movement, some of the men for whose greatest good this Club has been instituted blindly refusing to participate in its many advantages, and sooner than accept of its invaluable privileges and benefits rush off into some of the undesirable places which abound in Adelaide, and following the old custom of shouting for all loafers, &c., are soon compelled to take the wallaby-track instead of the railway track to search for employment, with the bitter consciousness of having again acted the fool.

"How is it that working men persist in refusing that which is for their benefit, and so greedily take hold of that which they know in their hearts cannot be for their good? I have noticed the backwardness of some of them to take advantage of this useful institution. Bushmen on their arrival in Adelaide are in most cases met either at the trains or busses by a warm friend from the Club who is willing to direct him to it. But I know by experience they too often turn away from their best friends to those questionable characters, who think that every penny the bushman is possessed of by right belongs to them, and therefore leave no means untried to possess themselves of their hard earnings. Then, and not till then, does the unfortunate man deplore his lamentable condition. Then, and not till then, does he know that if he had stopped at the Bushmen's Club he would have escaped all that. If any man thinks there is ought wrong at the Bushmen's Club let him ask any respectable man, and in nine cases out of ten he will get for answer—'The Bushmen's Club? Why, my good fellow, there never was in Adelaide a better place for you to stop at. Go there, by all means, go there, and you will never regret your choice. Your bush friends are there to receive you; men of your own class are there, with whom you can associate without fear of being fleeced. You will find much there for your good. I advise you to go there, and try whether it is so or not.' In conclusion, I would caution all persons coming from the country not to be decoyed by false representations, but go and see for themselves. Another thing I am credibly informed is, that men have entered cabs with the intention of going to the Bushmen's Club, Whitmore-square, who have been put down at other places. Asking pardon for trespassing so much on your time and space,

"I am, Sir, &c.,
"BUSHMAN.

"Adelaide, January 27, 1871."

A clipping from the *Northern Argus* also speaks of the ill-practice of "cheque melting" as follows:—

"This ceremony has been rather frequent of late in Clare, and those engaged in it—principally shearers from northern runs—have, instead of visiting the Bushmen's Club, or conducting themselves like rational beings, been conspicuous in free fights and unlimited brawls."

The following is a letter from a bushman living in New South Wales, as taken from the *Evening Journal*, February 2, 1871:—

"BUSHMEN'S CLUB.—This institution is fast acquiring celebrity and popularity. The following letter, just received by one of the first Committee, will show how the action taken in South Australia to found the Bushmen's Club has met with approval in the neighbouring colony:—

"'Momba, New South Wales, January 6, 1871.

"'Honoured Sir—Having accidentally seen a printed copy of the address to bushmen by "William," I cannot keep back —being a bushman myself—my admiration and humble thanks for the gracious interest taken in trying to provide a home for the lonely ones of the bush by a few of the good men of South Australia. Dare I hope that the rules and regulations of your establishment permit a stranger (who feels a lively interest in the welfare of all bushmen) who lives at present in this colony—New South Wales—to be an annual subscriber to your home? I may not have an opportunity of visiting your establishment perhaps for a long time; but let that be as it is, I may, in the meanwhile perhaps have the opportunity of engaging the interest of my fellow-bushmen in behalf of their own benefit in your established home. I do not know if enclosed cheque for £5 is sufficient for an annual subscription; if not, will you oblige me by letting me know? and if it should be more money than required, please will you oblige me, Honoured Sir, to let it go to the benefit of the Home. May I humbly ask if you in your kindness will send me a copy of the regulations of your place, which by showing to my fellow-men hereabout may lead through it, I humbly hope, to some benefit to themselves; for, alas, it is sorely needed to take them by the hand and show that there is yet something better on this earth than only harshness, coldness, mistrust, &c., &c. May Almighty God in all his goodness be with this beautiful undertaking of yours!

"'I remain in all sincerity, a humble bushman,
"'JOSEPH SELIGMANN.
"'To the Treasurer and Secretary of the
Bushmen's Home, Adelaide.'"

At the first meeting of the Board of Management for the year 1871, which was held on the 3rd of February, there were present Messrs. C. B. Young (chairman), H. Giles. The Hon. Superintendent reported that in December, 1870, 1,000 reports of annual meeting had been printed, and many sent to members and friends of the institution; that an act of theft had been committed by one of the boarders (not a bushman he was happy to say) of three books from the Club library, which had been presented by G. F. Angas, Esq., named respectively "Faith and Victory," "Memoirs of Eminent Christians," and "The End of all Things"—the thief was arrested, pleaded guilty, and was sent to gaol for four months; that a "runner" had been attached to the staff to meet the trains, steamers, busses, &c.; that he had been compelled to again increase the quantity of bedding, &c., as twenty-four boarders had arrived, and there was a probability of more coming, and he pointed out that more sleeping accommodation was absolutely necessary; that he respectfully asked for another servant to keep the establishment up to the mark, as the work was increasing; that the drainage was bad, and had been imperfectly remedied; that sand and gravel was necessary to harden the ground around the house before the rains set in; and that it would be necessary to obtain a larger range for cooking, as the old one was too small and fit only for an ordinary private family, and not for a large number of men. Receipts from all sources, £81 16s. 4d. Total number of tickets issued to end of December, 292. He further reported that in the month of January, 1871, the disposable number of beds had increased to 30; that Mr. S. Tomkinson had sent a few books and periodicals to the Club; that the Club property, estimated at £300, had been insured; that he had called on

Mr. Hosking (as desired by the Board) and that gentleman had agreed that the tenancy should be continued at the former rate, viz., £110, for the remainder of his lease; and that some arrangement should be made respecting parents in the bush sending their boys to school in the city. Receipts from all sources for January, £70 8s. 4d.; tickets issued to date, 303.

The sum of five guineas having been subscribed for a flag among the inmates of the Club, it was resolved by them, with the consent of the Management, to make the hoisting of it a public and formal matter, to which their mates in town were to be invited. See the following advertisement:—

"NOTICE TO BUSHMEN.—Bushmen and their friends are informed that the United Bushmen's Club Flag will (D.V.) be formally hoisted on Friday, 17th instant, at 2 p.m. There will afterwards be games, &c., on the South Park Lands, and in the evening an amateur entertainment at the Club. Several gentlemen have consented to give their services gratuitously. All bushmen and their friends in town, whether members or not, are respectfully invited. Further particulars this evening.

"'WILLIAM,' Hon. Superintendent."

The evening papers, to draw attention to the entertainment, had in their columns the following announcements:—

From the *Evening Journal:*—"Bushmen's Home.—All bushmen now in Adelaide are invited to an entertainment to be given this evening at the Club-house, Whitmore-square. In the afternoon the United Bushmen's Club flag is to 'unfurl its blasonry,' and a number of games are to be played upon the South Park Lands."

From the *Express*—"This afternoon the United Bushmen's Club flag will be formally hoisted. Games, &c., will follow on the Park Lands, and there will be an amateur entertainment in the evening at the Club-house."

Here follows the description of the proceedings at the hoisting of the flag, as taken from the next day's *Express:*—

"THE BUSHMEN'S CLUB.—This institution, which has been established about fourteen months, has been attended with very considerable success, and is, no doubt, exercising a beneficial influence. The number of inmates at the present time is twenty-six. On Friday afternoon the ceremony of formally hoisting the Club's flag took place at the Home, Whitmore-square, in the presence of between thirty and forty bushmen. The ceremony was performed by Mr. D. Murray, M.P., and on the flag reaching the top of the pole the bushmen gave three hearty cheers, and the Concordia Band struck up 'Home, Sweet Home.' The flag, which has been purchased by the inmates, is a very pretty one. The colours are red, white, and blue, and on it are the words 'United Bushmen's Club.' Amongst the visitors were the Rev. Jas. Lyall, and Messrs. W. H. Charnock and Jas. Smith. After the hoisting of the flag,

Mr. Murray said he was pleased that they had succeeded in inaugurating such a Club, but his pleasure was still greater in knowing that the hoisting of the flag was a signal that the institution was to be a permanent one. During the past year it had been an experiment. Now, however, the case was different, for the institution had reached a stage when it might be considered to be self-supporting, which could not be said of clubs of a higher standing than the Bushmen's Club, for appeals had often to be made to the members for contributions to defray the expenses. He congratulated them on the fact, and also that it was likely to be a permanent institution, and one likely to be of benefit to South Australia. It was likewise probable that it would have an influence for good beyond the limits of the colony. He would mention that "William," the Hon. Superintendent, had received a letter from a gentleman in Western Australia (Mr. E. H. Lawrence) asking to be furnished with particulars of the Home, with a view to the establishment of a similar institution in that province. It was gratifying that their example should be followed; and he trusted that they were commencing a movement which would be taken up in all the colonies, and be productive of immense advantage. It was necessary that bushmen, as well as sailors, should have their Home or Club to which they could go; and he believed that the former were in a better position than seamen to maintain and derive benefit from such an institution. He visited the institution on the previous evening, and was pleased with the appearance of comfort he found. He was confident that the accommodation was superior to that of very many hotels, and he believed the inmates agreed with him, for those he saw seemed to be enjoying themselves. The words on the flag "United Bushmen's Club" met with his approbation. He believed that it was a united club, and that it would occasion a feeling of unity among the bushmen that had not previously existed —a feeling that would lead to beneficial results. The aim of the Superintendent now was to provide increased accommodation, especially better sleeping accommodation. He trusted that this year, which was more favourable than its predecessor, the Committee would be able to provide more accommodation, so as to be able to accommodate from fifty to sixty men. He congratulated the bushmen upon the success of the institution because it was their own movement; what had been attained was not the result of the efforts of employers, but of the efforts of the bushmen themselves; consequently they had a right to call the Club their own. They raised the money for commencing the institution, and they had contributed the necessary funds for carrying it out; and with them rested all the merit. He would conclude by asking them to give three cheers for the Bushmen's Club.

Cheers were then heartily given for the Club, for "William," and for Mr. Murray.

The Rev. James Lyall did not know that he could add anything, but he would say that he heartily rejoiced in the success of the movement. The institution might now be regarded as having been established on a sure foundation, and it was a source of great pleasure to him that the movement had been so cordially entered into by the bushmen. The Club was in no way a charitable institution: the bushmen could go there just the same as other men went to their clubs. He wished the institution success, and prayed that God would bless it, and that it might lead to much good in this colony, and as an example be a means of benefit in the other colonies. Great credit was due to "William;" his perseverance was deserving of all praise, and the success of the institution must be very gratifying to him.

Mr. Murray explained that Mr. J. H. Angas, who was to have hoisted the flag, had been prevented from doing so by indisposition.

The proceedings then terminated.

Later in the afternoon an adjournment was made to the South Park Lands, where games of cricket, quoits, and football were engaged in; and, judging from the zest with which the bushmen entered into the sports in spite of the hot weather, they seemed thoroughly to enjoy themselves. There were among the visitors a number of city Arabs, who were enticed to engage in three-legged races and other sports, much to the amusement of the bystanders, and apparently reaped a rich harvest. In the evening a supper was given at the Club-house, at which a large number, including many visitors, sat down. An amateur entertainment followed, and Mr. C. B. Young, J.P., presided. In opening the proceedings, the Chairman remarked that it was with very much regret he had to announce that the President (Mr. Angas) had, in consequence of indisposition, been prevented from taking part in that evening's proceedings. A substitute had been found to hoist the flag in Mr. David Murray, M.P.; and now they had his unworthy self in the chair. The flag hoisted that afternoon—on which were the words " United Bushmen's Club"—was intended as an emblem of the union that it implied. He hoped the sentiment would be thoroughly endorsed by all the members, and that all would see the unanimity that existed. It was an advantage to men to be able to meet—not as they used to do formerly in public-houses to knock down their heavy cheques in drink, but in a place where social intercourse and healthful recreation could be obtained. He might say that the Club had been as successful as the most sanguine could have anticipated. They did not expect to see a large number of people in the Home, for that would show that the state of the colony was not very prosperous, but it was intended that men coming down to Adelaide for a little spell should have some place to come to, where they would be properly looked after and comfortably provided for. It was the endeavour of the Superintendent to promote the happiness of the inmates, and in that he had certainly succeeded. There were now three hundred and sixteen subscribers to the Club, which looked as if the advantages offered were thoroughly appreciated. They must see that the institution had outgrown itself, and that the Board of Management had long considered the present premises too small; and had there not been obstacles, a larger place would have been obtained, or the present premises extended; but they hoped, however, that in time something would be done in that way. He was not aware of the Superintendent being obliged to close the doors to any applicants on account of this: and what they required was a large and airy place, with dormitories capable of accommodating fifty persons at least. The pecuniary matters had also been satisfactory, for the Club was self-supporting. The promoters intended to build a "Bushmen's Home," but they wished to see how things would be managed on a rather small scale before undertaking so great a responsibility. Now, seeing how bright were the prospects, he hoped considerable extensions would be made, and that the Club would not only continue to be self-supporting, but that a sufficient sum would be left to become the nucleus of the building fund. He had paid the Club several visits, and the management under the Superintendent "William" appeared to be a credit to him, and he was sure "William" was gratified with the present position of affairs. He was sorry to say that their labour-office was not valued, nor did persons avail themselves of its advantages as could have been desired. It did not seem to be remembered that in such a place there always was an opportunity of engaging good men. The Committee had hoped that the business of a labour-office would have been carried on, and that persons requiring bushmen would come and suit themselves. No heavy charge was made to those seeking employment. He hoped they had spent an enjoyable day. Several recitations were then given by amateurs—one especially, entitled "Tarnation Strange" evoked much merriment, and all seemed to be appreciated. The entertainment concluded with a temperance ditty, the company joining in the chorus. The Chairman remarked that two or three pieces having reference to temperance, which had been given that evening, reminded him that he had omitted to state that the Club had been established on temperance principles. Many persons favourable to the movement considered that this would have a prejudicial effect, but it would be seen that "William" was quite right in making such a provision. Refreshments, provided in an adjoining room, having been partaken of, the proceedings terminated.

The Club was rapidly progressing at this time. On the night of February 26, 1871, two men applied for admission. The beds were all engaged, and as they did not feel disposed to rough it for the night they refused to accept the accommodation proffered, and took upon themselves to make their grievance known by a letter to the papers. It will be seen by this that it was really necessary more room should speedily be provided.

"TO THE EDITOR.

"Sir—I have read a great deal in your papers about the Bushmen's Club, but, generally speaking, it has been all in praise. Though agreeing with much that has been said, I cannot but think the time has come for making increased accomodation for the members. Last week the Club House was so full that beds had to be made on the floor. If the institution is to maintain its hold on the men who have enrolled their names, additional sleeping-rooms must be provided, and that without delay. I hope a hint will be deemed sufficient.

"I am, Sir, &c.,

"BUSHMAN.

—*Express*, February 27, 1871."

The following on the above is taken from the Notice to Correspondents in the *Advertiser*:—

"The Bushmen's Club.—We have made enquiry respecting the letter from two bushmen, and are informed that they applied at the Club late in the evening, when there was no room to spare. If, however, they will try again at a more reasonable hour they will find good accommodation and a hearty welcome."

A few days later the same paper had the following notice:—

"Bushman.—We cannot open our columns day after day to explain why two bushmen, who arrived late at the Club, and when it was full, failed to secure accommodation. The same thing might happen at the best-regulated hotel."

The next monthly meeting was held on March 2, 1871. Present—Messrs. H. Giles (chair), C. B. Young. The usual monthly accounts were passed for payment, &c.

"William," the Hon. Superintendent's report showed that the highest number yet reached (33) was attained during the past month. On February 6 he had received from Mr. J. Hosking a letter, contents as follows:—

"February 6, 1871.

"Dear Sir—Sir Charles Cooper's trustees have this day informed me (through their agent Mr. Spence) that no extension of time will be given as regards the Whitmore-square property—in other words, that Sir Charles Cooper wishes the property sold; and that unless 'the right of purchase' under which it is now held is exercised within the term named in the lease, the Trustees must have possession, that they may sell it themselves. You will see, therefore, that I cannot offer to extend the present tenancy beyond the 1st of July next—that will be just four months over the twelve months—the terms to be similar in every respect to those in the agreement now in force. If this meet your approbation a fresh agreement can be made out for the said term.

"I am, Sir, &c.,

"JAMES HOSKING.

"To 'William,' Hon. Superintendent of Club."

The Superintendent's report goes on to say that a note was received on the 20th February, from the same gentleman to the Board of Management.

"William" suggested that the trustees of Sir Charles Cooper be waited upon, and enquiry made as to whether they positively refuse to let or lease the premises for the use of the Bushmen's Club, it having been rumoured that the property was to be cut up and sold in building allotments at the expiration of Mr. Hosking's lease, if he (Mr. Hosking) did not exercise his right of purchase, that steps might be taken to procure (in good season) some other suitable place; he suggested that a building fund would probably be the best way out of the present difficulty, a kind of Joint-Stock Company, formed among the bush people and their friends—scrip or shares might be sold to the amount of say £2,000. He did not think it would be a difficult matter to sell this amount among 7,000 bushmen, if the shares were placed at about £1 each. He was afraid that if the arrival of T. Elder, Esq., was awaited from England, it would perhaps place the Club in jeopardy, as the term of the lease and tenancy was growing so short. The bushmen were agitating to hold a meeting among themselves at the Club, to devise some scheme for raising money to secure the present premises and extend operations, and seemed anxious to do all they could to strengthen the hands of their friends, and they were only awaiting the result of the present Board meeting, so as not to compromise the Board in any way. "William" stated that the Club at its present size could not make much profit supposing it to be always full, and that a large dormitory was particularly needed to accommodate about 50 persons; also that there was now no indoor smoking-room, there having been two at the beginning, but they had become of necessity merged—one of them into the dining apartment, and the other for sleeping accommodation—and that the year's tenancy would expire on the 14th April, and a new arrangement would then have to be made as regarded the premises. Total receipts for the past month, £86 4s. 3d.; number of tickets issued, 324.

Resolved by the Board of Management—

"That, as the Superintendent had been applied to by bushmen who were willing to contribute to raise a fund for the purchase or erection of a suitable building, he is hereby authorized to raise funds in the way he considers best, and thus provide for the fuller prosperity of the Club."

Mr. Hosking replied to the Board's enquiry about the premises, that the tenancy can be retained until February 1, on the terms at present in force. The Board of Management stated that they were not in a position to offer to purchase the property at that time, but would be glad to continue the tenancy as proposed by Mr. Hosking.

On the evening of the day after the usual monthly meeting the bushmen assembled on the premises to consider the best means of raising funds for the purpose spoken of in the above report. The result will be seen from the following day's paper, as under:—

"A meeting of the members of the Bushmen's Club was held at the Home, Whitmore-square, on Friday evening, March 3, to take into consideration the necessity of raising a Building or Extension Fund; also, the best means to adopt for the attainment of the object. There were twenty-five bushmen present, and Mr. Edward Clifton, one of the members, presided. He said he thought they as well as himself understood the object of the meeting, which was to raise a sufficient sum for the purchase of the property for a Bushmen's Home. Every true-hearted bushman, he was sure, would desire to see this object attained, but it was for the meeting to say whether the funds should be raised by the issue of shares confined to the members of the Club, or whether they should be raised by general subscription. The Home wanted extension, but he did not know how that desired object was to be attained if more bushmen did not come forward and join the Club, which was a most deserving institution, and worthy of all support. They had received a good deal of assistance from outside, but he would appeal to the bushmen for their co-operation. The Honorary Superintendent, "William," read the minute of the Managing Committee as follows:— 'The Honorary Superintendent has been applied to by bushmen who are willing to contribute to or raise a fund for the purchase or erection of a suitable building. He is hereby authorized to raise funds in the way he considers best, and thus provide for the further prosperity of the Club.' Mr. James Campbell moved—'That steps be taken to secure this property, or a portion of it, for the purposes of the Club.' Mr. John Campbell seconded. Carried. 'William' then read a letter from Mr. James Hosking, who held the lease of the property, stating that the trustees of Sir Charles Cooper had that day informed him that no extension of time would be given as regarded the Whitmore-square property. He wished the property sold, and unless the right of purchase under which it was held be exercised within the term named in the lease (1st July), the trustees must have possession, that they might sell it themselves. Mr. T. O'Connell moved —'That a regular canvass for subscriptions be made throughout the bush, and that if sufficient money be not raised in this way, the subscriptions be returned if desired, and funds raised in another way.' Mr. R. East seconded the motion, which was carried after a little discussion. Mr. Potter moved, and Mr. Burton seconded—'That a Sub-Committee of three, including the Hon. Superintendent, be appointed to draw up a circular to the bushmen of Australia, appealing to them all on behalf of this institution, and to take such other steps as may be needed for the furtherance of the work; also that this meeting respectfully suggest to the Board of Management that a circular emanating from them might be advantageously sent to the sheepfarmers, stockowners, managers and overseers of runs, soliciting their co-operation, and asking them to use their influence, and kindly undertake the transmission of any sums of money that might be collected among the men to the Superintendent in Adelaide.' A Sub-Committee, consisting of the Hon. Superintendent and Messrs. Stewart and Watson, was appointed. Mr. A. R. Stewart proposed and Mr. Clark seconded—'That "William" be respectfully requested to undertake the management of this matter on the bushmen's behalf, and see to the carrying out of the wishes of this meeting in detail.' Carried. Mr. James Campbell moved—'That all amounts of £1 and upwards be advertised in the *Observer* and *Chronicle* as a receipt for the money.' Mr. John Campbell seconded, and the motion was carried. Mr. East moved a vote of thanks to the Press, and in doing so said bushmen owed a great debt of gratitude to the Press of the colony for its influence. Mr. Peter Campbell, shearer's cook, seconded the motion in laudatory terms, and it was carried. A vote of thanks, on the motion of Mr. A. R. Stewart seconded by Mr. T. O'Connell, passed to the Chairman closed the proceedings. A subscription-list was at once opened for the attainment of the desired object, and several names attached."

The following is a copy of the address prepared by the Sub-Committee for distribution among the bushmen of the colony, as resolved at the meeting held March 3, 1871:—

"Bushmen's Club, Adelaide.

"Brother Bushmen and Friends—We, a Sub-Committee appointed at a meeting of bushmen, held at the Club on March 3, 1871 (see enclosed report), appeal to you all on behalf of your own best interest, to come forward and support and patronize your own Society, and thus at once and for ever put a stop to the false arguments of those who say that the bushmen of South Australia never will support a Club of their own, nor any other good thing. A trial of about ten months has proved what the Club is capable of doing for all those who make it their home. We would not at this time ask your support, but we are satisfied that the time has really come for us one and all, married and single, as bushmen, to come forward and support our own Society.

"We speak to you as brother bushmen. We are bushmen, and we appeal to you all as such, and we also appeal in a good cause. We have fully identified ourselves with the Club as members; we have seen how it is managed, and we are perfectly satisfied with it; we have partaken of its advantages, and we know with your kind help what it is still capable of doing for the best interests of bushmen generally.

"That our Club has not got enemies, secret and avowed, we dare not say; for what movement for good was ever without enemies? But we may safely say that while its enemies are few, its friends are many. Come forward then, all you who are lukewarm and half-hearted, and fully identify yourselves with us to further this movement. This is to be done by helping us with your hearty co-operation—not only in the matter of money, but in making the Club your home on your visits to town, and making it known among others. We are sure that if you were fully aware of the comforts to be obtained, and the benefits to be derived by so doing, there would be no necessity for this appeal. Ask any men you know, who have been stopping at the Club, and they will be far better able to tell you of its many advantages than we can possibly do; but as space is rather limited, 'the least said the soonest mended,' we would rather let the institution prove itself.

"No man who is a thorough true-hearted bushman will or can withhold a helping hand from this most worthy undertaking on the present occasion, for there is a rather high rental, which hangs like a millstone around our necks, and if with this drag we can hold our ground, what may we not expect when this obstacle is removed? Cramped as we now are for room we shall never be able to carry out the original intention of establishing a fund for the relief of aged, sick, or distressed bushmen. Recollect, the rent and rates amount to about £120 per annum. If we were in a position (instead of paying this amount away) to bank it, we should soon be able to help the aged and worthy members of our own class.

"We wish now to say a few words to the married people in the bush. A man may be married, but that does not prevent his being a bushman. We hope to see a larger number of our married friends assist in supporting this Club, and helping us with their mites, and by doing so show that their interests are identical with their single mates, and that in helping us they are indirectly helping themselves.

"There are thousands of bushmen in this colony, and if each man would come forward and subscribe what he could afford, an institution could be provided second to none in the country. Bushmen! stand by and help us with your willing hearts and hands to build or extend our Club, which shall take its place in the history of the colonies, and you will have the honour of helping to establish upon a firm basis a noble institution, which has not its counter part in the southern hemisphere.

"Let no bushman who reads this appeal say that he is ignorant of the design of this collection, but put his shoulder to the wheel. There will be subscription-lists sent with these circulars to each known head-station in the colony, and we would respectfully ask you all to place your names upon them without delay.

"Many and great difficulties connected with the Club have by God's help been overcome, and with His further blessing upon our labours we hope for a speedy solution of the present question.

"Bushmen, your Club is not in danger, but we want more room; we want to enlarge the present accommodation; we want to be free, to be enabled to do more good than it is possible for us to do in our present confined condition. The house is not sufficiently large to accommodate more boarders than sufficient to pay its way, which it will do if always filled. We therefore ask you to help us with liberal subscriptions and willing hearts, to extend in some way our present boundaries, to help us to buy or build a more suitable Club-House, and extend our operations, so that we may be able to heartily welcome as many of you as may come to stop at the Bushmen's Home.

"WILLIAM WATSON,   } Members
"ALEXANDER R. STEWART, } of Sub-
"'WILLIAM,' Superintendent of Club, } Committee.
"March, 1871."

The foregoing address was sent to the sheepfarmers, managers, &c., accompanied with a report of the meeting and the following circular:—

"Committee-Room, Bushmen's Club, Adelaide.

"Respected Sir—A scheme for raising subscriptions in aid of a Building or Extension Fund for the above-named Club having now been fairly set before the public, and the desirableness of the movement affirmed by the bushmen themselves, with the details of which you are no doubt familiar, I have, therefore, only to intimate that I am directed by the Board of Management—Messrs. C. B. Young, N. Blyth, and H. Giles—to forward to you a subscription-list (see report of meeting enclosed), and respectfully ask you to co-operate with them in making a systematic canvass among the people in your employ, and to use your best endeavours to induce them to contribute to this desirable object.

"The cheque for the amount contributed by the men should be sent in with each list to 'William,' Hon. Superintendent of the Club, Adelaide, to prevent unnecessary expense and anxiety, and to enable the Board to make the necessary arrangements for effecting the object contemplated.

"As each list sent out is numbered and registered, it is requested that great care be taken that they be returned by the 31st day of May, 1871 (blank or otherwise), that they may be accounted for, and scratched off the register; or if mislaid or lost, a few words written to that effect will be very thankfully received. The Board will furnish contributors occasionally with reports of progress, &c.

"N.B.—Will you please either to distribute or nail up in some conspicuous place the papers enclosed with the list for the information of the men, and in this way further the movement. Managers and overseers are not asked to be continually putting their hands in their pockets; what is wanted is their hearty co-operation in this matter, as it is felt sure that with this combined effort, if a thorough canvass is made among the bushmen, means will be forthcoming to make the Club entirely self-supporting in the future.

"Believing an apology needless for trespassing on your valuable time in so good a cause,

"I am, respected Sir,

"On behalf of the Board of Management,

"'WILLIAM,' Hon. Superintendent B. Club.

"March, 1871."

The printed reports of the meeting held on 3rd March had appended to them for the general information of the bush people the following:—

"LABOUR DEPARTMENT.

"All kinds of Bush Labour can be obtained at this Club. All orders for men—by post, telegraph, or otherwise—carefully and punctually attended to, and executed if practicable.

"Employers in want of hands are respectfully informed that a good class of men may be obtained at this Labour Office, and they are requested to give it a trial and patronize it.

"FEES.

Members on registry	1s.
Do. on engagement	1s. extra.
Non-Members on registry	1s.
Do. on engagement	2s. 6d. extra.

"Employers sending for men should give all possible time to select them, and the maximum rate of wages to be given.

"N.B.—You will observe there is no fee charged to the employers for hiring labour, their custom being desired.

"Bushmen's Club, Whitmore-square, Adelaide."

Respecting the circular drawn up by the Sub-Committee appointed for that purpose, the *Register* had the following kind remarks:—

"THE BUSHMEN'S CLUB.—We learn that the Sub-Committee appointed at a meeting of bushmen, held at the Club on March 3, are distributing throughout the stations copies of the proceedings, accompanied by a circular appealing for increased help and sympathy. As the movement to which we now refer has been initiated, and is being carried out by bushmen themselves, apart from the other supporters of the institution, the representations made and arguments adduced are likely to have weight with such as have not hitherto identified themselves with the Home. The present appeal is a hearty and stirring one, grounded upon the benefits already conferred by the Club, its proved usefulness, and the advantages which a more general support would enable the conductors to offer. The Committee speak feelingly of the need for increased room. What is needed is a wider field and the power to do more good. The Home is an established fact, and there is little fear that those who once visited it will afterwards place themselves in the hands of crimps and spungers, but accommodation is needed for larger numbers, and the benefits procurable, apart from residence, required to be made more widely known. The Sub-Committee of bushmen, to secure the objects they seek, have done wisely in sending out these documents, and we wish them every success in their laudable endeavour."—March 9, 1871.

The following are the *Advertiser's* remarks on the same subject:—

"A Sub-Committee, recently appointed by the members of the Bushmen's Club, has drawn up a circular for distribution amongst bushmen throughout the colony. The circular is signed by Messrs. Wm. Watson, Alexander M. Stewart, and 'William,' the Hon. Superintendent of the Home, and urgently appeals to all bushmen for their earnest and practical co-operation on behalf of an institution which is calculated to benefit them so largely, and afford comfort to them on their visits to Adelaide. It is pointed out that the Club has already proved a success; but the Committee are desirous of extending the influence of the Home by securing a more suitable Club-House, where a larger number of lodgers may be accommodated. This, however, cannot be accomplished without money, and bushmen—both married and single—are therefore appealed to to subscribe to the Home, so that the Committee may be in a position to enlarge the present premises, or purchase another place. Circulars, accompanied by a report of the last meeting of the Club, are to be forwarded to every known head-station in the colony, respectfully soliciting the subscriptions of bushmen in behalf of the Home."—March 9, 1871.

A few days after the meeting held by the bushmen on March 3, a temperance lecturer, late a shearer's cook, who was present at that meeting, commenced an agitation among the inmates to subvert and overthrow the existing order of things at the Club, and introduce a new system more agreeable to his own way of thinking. The Hon. Superintendent considered it his duty to report all the circumstances of this case to the Board of Management. The whole affair proved such a failure, and the absurdities of the movement were afterwards so thoroughly transparent and exposed, that the particulars of what might have turned out a serious matter to the bushmen if the instigator had had the power to make it so, will no doubt be acceptable to the reader.

First, attention was called by the Superintendent to the fact that the whole transaction was contrary to the existing Rules of the institution under which Campbell, as well as all other members, were admitted to partake of the benefits of the Club. It is distinctly stated in those Rules "That if there are any reasonable complaints that cannot be adjusted by the Superintendent, it should be reported to any monthly or special meeting of the Board." The agitator, who persuaded a couple of inmates to act with him, went round to each individual boarder in the Club with an advertisement of his own framing, designed to call a general meeting to carry out his own views, at the same time collecting money-subscriptions from the inmates, to enable him to give this advertisement publicity; when this was done, the said advertisement was brought to the Superintendent, and he was told that it was to be inserted in the newspapers; that it was only as a matter of form and compliment that it was shown to him, and that whether he signed or approved of it or not, the meeting would be called, anyhow, on their own account, to alter the present arrangement. The idea was to form a Board of Management of their own choosing—no doubt with a view to get the control of the funds into their own hands if possible, to oust all the present officers and servants, and choose their own. Unfortunately for the success of their movement, the advertisement bore the signature of only two members of the Club according to the constitution, who seem to have been cajoled into the plot by over-persuasion, and induced to believe that this revolutionary movement was for their good. The Superintendent called attention to the fact that it would be an illegal and improper meeting, and that any resolution passed could have no effect without the sanction of a majority of the trustees; and pointed out that the advertisement produced had only the signature of two members, the other eight who had signed being non-members of the Club. He also stated that if any such advertisement should appear publicly, he, as Manager of the institution, and on behalf of the absent members, would put in a counteracting advertisement; and even if there should be such an illegal meeting got together, it should not be held on the Club premises. He further told them that if they should succeed in holding a meeting anywhere else, their resolutions would be valueless; while, if they carried out the idea of having a paid Superintendent—which was one of the points they insisted upon—that he would certainly not accept it, but would give up his connection with the institution altogether.

It would not be just to absent members of the institution for any person to alter the constitution, rules, or management, or right to leave it in the power of any ambitious or unprincipled man or clique to raise a disturbance, and make others dissatisfied with the institution.

The Hon. Superintendent ought to have been consulted in such a matter as a reorganization of the Club or rules, since he held the proxies on behalf of more than fifty members of the Club. Of course, a movement such as this once fairly set on foot, with some little organization, might give considerable trouble, though the promoters could not by any means possibly establish themselves in control of the Club, and eventually remain its masters. But a guard was set against this at the Annual Meeting in December, 1871.

Enough has now been stated for the reader to see through this manœuvre, and it is unhesitatingly affirmed that never was there such a shipwreck of a movement as this proved to all concerned in it. When the matter was officially dealt with, the number of adherents dwindled down to the agitator alone; he had to return the subscriptions gathered for the advertisement, and those who were carried away by him were thoroughly ashamed of themselves for the part they had taken. Most of them apologized to the Superintendent, and afterwards, when becoming members of the Club, to prove their sincerity entrusted him with their proxy papers, to use as he deemed best for the interests of the Club.

It may be added here that the simple firm front shown by one energetic friend of order in the Club caused the whole movement to collapse, and it turned out one of the veriest shams ever exposed. The ring-leader left the Club without making one real friend, despised by the men he had deluded; and it is a scandal even now to think of such an outrageous pretension to disorganize the Bushmen's Club. Still this undertaking has produced one good effect, for since then no movement of this kind could find acceptance among the bushmen anywhere, for any suggestion of interference with the management of the institution is scouted in the bush, in the Club itself, and in the city or wherever made.

Immediately after the foregoing attempt the following public notice appeared in the *Evening Journal* of March 8, 1871 :—

"Mr. Peter Campbell, temperance lecturer, &c., announces that he is a member (No. 35) of Bushmen's Club, but not connected in any other way either with that club or 'William.'"

As a set-off to the above, the following will no doubt be read with interest :—

"The Bushmen's Club.—Some friends, evidently bushmen, have anonymously sent to 'William,' the Hon. Superintendent of the Bushmen's Club, a watch and chain, and a purse with money. The recipient intends to sell the watch and appendage, the proceeds of which, with the cash received, will be devoted to the relief of sick or distressed bushmen. The new diggings have made havoc among the ranks at the Home, three different parties of experienced diggers having left for Ulooloo Creek. The last batch of five sober, steady, and well equipped workers, with tents, &c., started on Monday. They are not the sort who waste their substance in riotous living and then go penniless, homeless, and friendless wherever an empty pocket and a confused brain drive them; but men who shepherd their money as well as their sheep. The result is that this class are able to move off in any direction from their Club when what appears to offer advantages comes before them. The Club has benefited many, and it is sincerely hoped that bush people will continually patronise their own institution, not forgetting that subscription-lists for extending its work are lying open at every known head station in the colony."—March 28, 1872.

The following letter on this subject signed "Hope," appeared the next day :—

"TO THE EDITOR.

"Sir—The paragraph in your issue of yesterday, referring to a watch, &c., having been forwarded by unknown friends to the Hon. Superintendent of the Bushmen's Club, gives me a pleasure greater than I can describe. Soon after the Club was started I visited it, and saw enough to convince me that the undertaking would prove successful. The result proves that I was not too sanguine. Abundant evidence is given that the men for whose benefit and comfort it was set on foot hold it in high appreciation. I believe, Sir, that from this Club a great institution will spring. The Hon. Superintendent, at the time I visited the Club, spoke of making provision for worn-out or afflicted bushmen, of providing a home for orphan children, and of properly educating such as had not the means. Of course, such an institution cannot be expected to reach maturity in a few months; but if past successes may be taken as an augury of the future, there is no reason why it shall not embody within itself a vitality that shall cause it to shed its blessings over the whole of our Australian Colonies. When Müller, of Bristol, commenced his first 'Orphanage,' he little dreamt of the gigantic proportions that his philanthropic plans were to assume; nor can 'William' now tell what under God's blessing will open up from this Bushmen's Club.

"Sir, I rejoice in the success of this institution. I have seen a great deal of bushmen, and confess that at one time I thought it just as likely that a leopard could change its spots as that a cheque could be held by one of them for any length of time, without undergoing the 'melting-down' process. No sooner did the bushman receive it than a thirsting for drink sprang up in his soul. As soon as possible the fatal glass found its way to his lips, and as long as cash remained his companions were the scum of our towns and villages. How frequently the poor wretch has fallen a victim to the delirium that attaches to alcoholic excess multitudes of sorrowing relatives will ever remember. Such deaths are lamented with a bitterness even greater than if, having 'been lost in the bush,' the bushmen's bones 'lay bleached on some dreary wild.'

"The fact that there are now hundreds of subscribers to the Bushmen's Club plainly indicates that a better day has dawned. These men are really bushmen, desirous of husbanding their means, and many of them of living reformed lives. Their respect for the Manager is often spoken of; and no doubt the small present anonymously forwarded by some one must be taken as an individual proof. I hope, Sir, that this watch will not be sold, though the object named to which the money would be devoted was in every way praiseworthy; I would say, let it be kept as a memento of the unknown donor's good will. Success, then, to the Club, and may its friends work on.

"I am, Sir, &c.,

"HOPE."

At the monthly meeting held on the 1st April, 1871, there were present Messrs. N. Blyth (chair) and H. Giles.

"William," the Hon. Superintendent, reported that he had been placed in a position to make an offer of £1,700 and a bonus of £20 for Mr. Hosking's right of purchase;—this he was sorry to say was declined, on the ground that the present lessee did not intend selling the entire property but would entertain offers for a short lease.

"That agreeable to resolution of former meeting, to make a thorough canvass of the Bush for subscriptions for a building or extension fund, he had sent out a number of circulars and subscription-lists to the stations, &c., returnable 31st May next, that he had heard the lists were doing pretty well, but he did not think so much money would be raised by subscription as by issuing shares; that the bushmen, as a rule, desired to try what they could do among themselves in their own way, and wishing, if possible, to keep the Club in their own hands for their own particular class, instead of by a system of shares sinking the institution among outside shareholders; that Mr. Angas kindly offered to lead off the lists with £100, but it was thought advisable to await the result of the present appeal to the bush, and see what the bushmen intended doing before further steps were taken in town in the matter; that Mr. Alexander MacCulloch, sen., of Gottlieb's Well, had paid the Club a visit, and expressed himself pleased with the arrangements; that there was at present a small number of inmates at the Club, this being accounted for by the fact that lambing season had begun, and the Ulooloo diggings had just broken out, and it was likely under those circumstances that business at the Club would be dull for a time; and also that more bedding would be required, as the winter was approaching. Total receipts for the past month, £73 3s. 3d.; total number of tickets issued to date, 334."

The monthly accounts were examined and passed, and ordered to be paid as usual.

It was resolved by the Board that the address to bushmen signed by the members of the Sub-Committee appointed at a meeting held at the Club, and a circular from the Board of Management addressed to the managers of stations, &c., should be circulated.

To call the bush people's attention to the circulars and subscription-lists for the purpose of raising funds, &c., the following notice was inserted in the newspapers:—

"Bushmen's Club.

"Important Notice to Bushmen.

"Bushmen are informed that circulars and subscription-lists have been sent to all known head-stations in the colony for the purpose of raising a Building or Extension Fund, and they are hereby urgently requested to add their names to them without delay, as the lists are returnable on the 31st May instant; or the Honorary Superintendent, 'William,' will thankfully receive any sums direct from persons wishing to contribute towards this very desirable object.

"'William,'
"Hon. Superintendent Bushmen's Club.
"Whitmore-square, April 7, 1871."

The following extracts are taken from the *Express*, April 26, 1871:—

"The Bushmen's Club.
"[Communicated.]

"There are many things which go to prove at this stage of our existence as a Bushmen's Club—and it may not be amiss to further enlighten our friends on the subject—that a little energy well and judiciously directed may suffice to originate and establish one of those important and useful institutions. The history of the Bushmen's Club established in Adelaide shows marked progress since its inauguration, and only let the need of some such place of resort in the sister colonies be once felt, and the advantages afforded by such institutions to working men be known, and become apparent, and there will probably be no lack of patronage. Although a large amount of publicity has been given to this Club, there are yet hundreds of bushmen who know more about their old haunts than their own Club. It is for the benefit of those that this is written.

"Of the vast sums which are spent every year in drink it

is estimated that nearly one-half comes out of the pockets of the working classes; and if all the glittering sovereigns spent by bushmen alone in drink were laid side by side, how many such Clubs might be literally paved with gold? How much could be done towards improving the social condition of the people if those sums could be collected, and devoted to some such worthy object as this?

"This Bushmen's Club is supported by the fees of members—5s. annually—the charges for board and lodging, and by contributions. The establishment is managed by a Board of three, annually appointed by the members of the Club, and the property connected with it is vested in three trustees—Messrs. J. H. Angas, W. K. Thomas, and D. Murray—appointed by a public meeting of all the original subscribers. Many bushmen are attracted to the Club as well by its popular form of government as by the advantages it offers, and the low rate of the annual subscription, viz., 5s., and board and lodging, which is fixed for members of the Club at 15s., and non-members 16s. per week.

"In such Clubs it is always desirable that those whose interests are most concerned should have the largest share of control. It is intended as the winter advances that there shall be, if possible, opportunities given for instruction and amusement. Arrangements will be probably made for courses of lectures on interesting and scientific subjects, somewhat after the following plan:—

"On Monday evening—A Singing Class;
"Tuesday—A Temperance Meeting;
"Wednesday—A Debate;
"Thursday—Lectures;
"Friday—Readings or Recitations.

"Many who have visited the Club have been struck with the appearance of a number of bronzed able hearty weather-beaten men—some growing grey, and others in the prime of life—respectably clad, and comfortably seated in a clean and airy, but plainly furnished room, many talking together, some playing at chess or draughts—which seem to be their favourite games—and the younger ones exercising themselves at athletic sports, quoits, &c., out of doors. On Sundays a simple unsectarian religious service is held by the

Superintendent for the benefit of those who cannot or do not attend church or chapel, in the Reading-room mornings and evenings; the newspapers are removed, and religious publications placed upon the table. The rules positively forbid the use of any intoxicating drinks on the premises; also all gambling or profane language; and although only a minority of the men are total abstainers, experience has proved very forcibly to the minds of most bushmen and their friends that the Club works better without those drinks, that though some of them at first wished for their introduction they are now to a man against them. Such influences must do good. Bushmen have been heard to say that it is a blessed place— not only good food for the body, but also good food for the mind—that they have no anxiety now about their money, for if they had a hundred notes in their pockets when they enter the Club it would be taken care of for them; others have said that if anything were to happen to shut up the Club now it has once been started it would be one of the greatest calamities that could happen to the bush people; others have spoken of the debt of gratitude specially due to the promoters and friends of the movement, who came forward so nobly to help the institution forward.

"There can be no question about the management of the Club being thoroughly appreciated by thoughtful men, as is proved by its progress, and the harmony, decorum, and good feeling which have with but few exceptions constantly prevailed among its inmates, as also their again returning to partake of its advantages. In all movements of this kind there are certain to be a few captious individuals, and the purest management will not prevent this. Later experience of the Club has shown that, as with all good and benevolent enterprises, there is need of much patience and wisdom to surmount all the difficulties which arise when the novelty of the undertaking wears away. Numerous illustrations might be given of the real good that is being done by the establishment of this Bushmen's Club, and the grand question after all is how to make it self-supporting. If what has now been said on this subject will cause bushmen to stop and consider what is for the greatest good, and be the means of stirring them up to action, and induce those that are lukewarm and half-hearted to go forward and place their names on the subscription-lists which are now lying at the stations in the country, for raising a Building or Extension Fund, it will be furthering a good work in hand, which will eventually redound to their benefit in saving the present large rental, and thus make the institution entirely self-supporting in the future, as well as form a Benefit Fund, which is very much needed for the relief of sick and distressed bushmen."

The following is extracted from an article in the *Register*, dated April 28, 1871:—

"We have on previous occasions alluded to the usefulness of the Bushmen's Club, but a few further remarks respecting an institution which has achieved so much good, and which needs to be known far and wide, will not be deemed out of place. An endeavour is now being made to make the establishment self-supporting, and for this purpose subscription-lists have been forwarded to all the head squatting stations in the colony. Should bushmen and squatters regard the benefits of the Club in a right light, there is very little doubt but that a handsome nucleus to a fund for erecting a suitable building would be speedily raised. This, with contributions from friends in Adelaide, might be sufficient to enable the promoters to undertake the purchase of premises, or the erection of a home suitable for the objects of the Club. If this desirable result could be secured the large expenditure now incurred for rent would be saved, and the institution would doubtless be able to support itself entirely.

"We are glad to hear from 'William,' the untiring friend of the bushman, that arrangements are in progress for providing the inmates with instruction and amusement, during the long evenings of winter.

"It is to be hoped that care will be taken to prevent the meetings becoming wearisome, and that the lectures will be such as shall prove interesting as well as informing. The success of these week-night gatherings will greatly depend upon the wisdom which is displayed in their management, and in the character and mode of the teaching adopted. Amusement and instruction must not be divorced, and as far as we can gather, there is no intention to do so. The promoters so far have done all they can to meet the rational needs of human nature. The rooms are clean and airy; chess and draughts, periodicals and books are provided inside, while outside all sorts of athletic sports are available. On Sundays, 'William' informs us, a simple unsectarian religious service' is conducted by himself, and religious publications are substituted for secular. Intoxicating liquors are not sold or admitted into the institution, and although at first some of the bushmen demurred to this, yet now they are quite reconciled to the decision of the promoters, and think they have acted very wisely in the matter. To have introduced strong drink into the Club, and to have dispensed it to some of the inmates and not to others, which must have been done, would have operated very injuriously to the interests of the establishment, and therefore the best plan was to exclude it altogether. Gambling is also prohibited; but because these two evils are excised bushmen must not be led away with the notion that the institution is a dull uninteresting place, where little freedom is allowed, and the play of the spirits kept in continual check. This is a mistake, for the greatest liberty is permitted consistent with moral and rational good. There is scarcely a bushman that has entered the Club who has not acknowledged its benefits, and, conducted as it is—offering a good home and good food for the body, with ample recreation for the mind—it cannot fail to exercise a beneficial influence upon a class of persons most of whom have hitherto had no abiding place when they came into the city, and who have consequently too often wandered away into haunts of vice where they have lost both health and money. We rejoice at having another opportunity of wishing the establishment God speed, and trust that the effort now being made to raise a fund for building purposes will receive an ample measure of support from those who are more particularly concerned in its welfare."

At the usual monthly meeting held on the 2nd May, 1871, there were present Messrs. N. Blyth (chair), H. Giles, C. B. Young.

The Hon. Superintendent reported that there had been a falling off in the receipts, it being lambing season, so that the bushmen were generally employed, and the slack business time afforded an excellent opportunity to prepare for a large influx of men when the reaction takes place, to have everything in readiness; that it would be advisable to call a meeting, after the return of the subscription-lists, to take into consideration the best means to adopt respecting the property, whether further efforts should be made to purchase it altogether or only a part of it, or whether a lease should be obtained, and a temporary dormitory added to the present premises; that Messrs. Charnock and Turnbull, and two Quaker gentlemen had kindly presented some books and English newspapers; that a letter had been received from E H. Laurance, Esq., Resident Magistrate, Greenough, Western Australia, returning thanks for a supply of reports, addresses, &c., &c., forwarded to him by last March mail; that the Club was growing in favour with bushmen, and the duty of all interested evidently was to prepare ample accommodation to make the undertaking pay; and that in consequence of the anticipated increase more bedding would be required. Total receipts for past month, £49 10s.; total number of tickets issued, 341. The usual accounts were examined and passed for payment.

Resolved by the Board—That a meeting of Trustees and Board of Management be convened some time in the month of June, to take into consideration the question of the future position of the Club in respect to the present building, and the desirability of either attemping to purchase the freehold or taking a lease, and building a dormitory, or procuring premises in some other situation; that Mr. T. Elder be invited to attend the meeting, as that gentleman had formerly made a liberal offer of assistance.

The following advertisement was inserted to stir up the holders of subscription-lists to be punctual in returning them :—

"IMPORTANT NOTICE TO HOLDERS OF THE BUSHMEN'S CLUB SUBSCRIPTION-LISTS.

"It is respectfully requested that holders of subscription lists will be very punctual in returning them, filled up or otherwise, by 31st day of May next, as it is a matter of great importance to the Board of Management and the bushmen that the result of the canvass should then be known, prior to to a meeting of trustees, &c., to be held in the beginning of June, to take into consideration the future position of the Club.

"WILLIAM,'
"Hon. Superintendent Bushmen's Club.
"Adelaide, May 2, 1871."

"THE BUSHMEN'S CLUB.
[From the *Evening Journal*, May 4, 1871.]

"A meeting of the Board of Management of this institution was held at the Club-house on Tuesday, May 2. The Board acknowledged with thanks the receipt of a number of newspapers and periodicals from Messrs. Charnock, Turnbull, and Barrett, and a valuable box of books from Messrs. Platts & Co. It was stated that there had been a decrease lately in the number of inmates, there being now twenty, which was to be accounted for by this being the lambing time. A large influx might be expected when the season was over. A letter was produced by 'William' from Mr. E. H. Laurance, Resident Magistrate in Western Australia, which after thanking him for documents in connecting with the Club forwarded in March, said 'They convey ample information to guide the formation of a similar Club here, should such a scheme be deemed feasible. I will not fail to send you local notices that may appear in regard to your institution, and to acquaint you with any practical action that may result here. With our small, scattered, and rather poor population I see many difficulties, but the desirability of such a Club to divert some of the money earned in the bush from being spent in drink is daily present to me and others.' Captain Scott, Police Magistrate of Sydney, also wrote to 'William,' promising to distribute the documents sent to him among the squatters, and stating—'I feel a deep interest in the establishment of a similar institution in Sydney, as from my position as Police Magistrate I see the enormous amount of misery which homeless shepherds and stockmen are subject to by being dragged and robbed by fiends in the shape of women, who allure them to destroy. Nearly two years ago

I attempted to form such a Home in Sydney, got the subject well ventilated through the public Press, and wrote about 150 letters to squatters, police magistrates, and merchants, and the result was a miserable failure, £4 10s. being the whole amount subscribed, which I returned to the different donors, paying all the expenses of advertisements, stamps, &c., out of my own pocket. I am so occupied all day I have no leisure to canvass the city. Perhaps this fact may account for a portion of the failure. No doubt with your energy and perseverance you might succeed in forming such an institution in Sydney. It will be a step involving a considerable amount of risk and expense. I shall at all times gladly receive any account of your continued success." These extracts are sufficient to show that a lively interest is felt outside of South Australia, and that the idea of Homes in the different colonies for wandering bushmen may eventually be realized. The Club in Adelaide is growing daily in favour with the bushmen, and with a view to making a strong effort to increase the accommodation and cause the undertaking to pay, it was resolved by the Board of Management to call a meeting of trustees and others at the beginning of June. As the subscription-lists are returnable on May 31 the result of the present canvass will probably be then known, and the meeting will be to consider the future action of the Club in respect to the present building, the desirability of either attempting to purchase the freehold, or take a lease and build a dormitory, or else procure premises in another situation. It may be mentioned that Mr. Joseph Seligman, of Momba, near Wilcannia, New South Wales, who a short time back sent a contribution of £5, has lately forwarded a cheque for £7 15s., being the subscriptions of several bushmen, and £5 of his own."

The *Northern Argus*, May 19, 1871, says :—

"The Bushmen's Club, in Adelaide, is to be congratulated on its success in establishing itself as it has done, for this is the only colony where an attempt of this sort has succeeded. The Police Magistrate of Sydney tried the experiment about two years ago. He says that he wrote about 150 letters to squatters, police magistrates, and merchants, and the result was a miserable failure, £4 10s. being the whole amount subscribed, which he returned to the different donors, paying all the expenses of advertisements, stamps, &c., out of his own pocket. It is therefore something for bushmen to be proud of that they have a Club of their own in South Australia, where they can enjoy in the same way, according to their station, the same conveniences that gentlemen do in their clubs. Subscription and members' lists are now circulating throughout the colony, with the object of raising funds to build a new club-house or to enlarge the old one. Particulars, as to the advantages, &c., of membership, may be obtained of 'William,' Hon. Superintendent, Bushmen's Club, Whitmore-square, Adelaide."

It being deemed advisable to furnish absent members of the Club and friends of the institution with a short account of progress, the following is a copy of the report taken from the *Advertiser* :—

"The following information has been handed to us by the Hon. Superintendent, 'William,' and will without doubt be acceptable to the up-country population and true friends of bushmen generally, while it will probably surprise many that such a work is going on in our midst so quietly :

"Readers will remember that the Bushmen's Club was formally opened by His Excellency, and since that day its promoters and untiring friends have not been idle, as is abundantly proved from the subjoined synopsis of transactions up to 20th May :—

"The number of members on the roll has gradually increased to 355 ; total of weekly boarders entertained, 346 ; casual boarders, say 200 ; and about 60 travelling bushmen have been temporarily relieved. The greatest number of inmates at one time has reached 33.

"The expenditure has been on an average about £100 per month—this including the cost of furnishing the institution. The property belonging to the Club is insured for £300.

"The total value handed to the Superintendent for safe keeping during the period, of cash, funds as per Bank pass-books, cheques, &c., amounted to £3,458 18s. 3¼d. ; and the deposits of this kind in charge on 20th May were worth

£770 3s. 11½d. The entire sum drawn out by instalments was £2,688 4s. 4d., and number of depositors 174; thus giving an average of nearly £20 each. An immense host of letters, book parcels, and newspapers (English and colonial), have passed through the Club Post-Office to their destination or been retained as requested until sent for, and all unclaimed letters were advertised at the end of the year.

"The business in the labour department has been trifling compared with what may yet be expected. At the present, settlers prefer hiring men at their doors rather than send to Adelaide, and having to pay their expenses to the stations. There are very few inmates at the Club just now, most of the hands being under engagements during lambing. But this dulness will end in a month or two, when a large influx may reasonably be expected.

"It is very necessary that ample accommodation should be speedily provided by the Trustees and Board of Management to meet the anticipated demand for room.

"The subscription-lists for either building a new Clubhouse, or extending the present one, are returnable on May 31, and it is sincerely desired that the bushmen of South Australia will not hang back from assisting to promote such a really good work. This is a matter of much importance to them all as a class, and the Committee hope that they will with willing hearts substantially help on this noble institution, for it has proved itself to be such to all minds not blinded by prejudice, and capable of doing great good to the future.

"As a general rule the members and inmates have conducted themselves in a sober, quiet, orderly, and fraternal manner, and many new and lasting friendships have been formed at the Bushmen's Club among the men.

"It appears but a simple question of time for this institution to become the centre of attraction to bush people. The Superintendent has been enabled to send a few cases of sickness to the Hospital, and some for private treatment, through the consideration and kindness of Messrs. Angas and other friends. When the Club becomes stronger it would be well to pay a yearly sum for a stipulated number of beds in the Hospital. But this and many other improvements, such as a Benefit Fund, &c., are matters for consideration when the property is secured and the Club firmly established."—May 27, 1871.

The next Board meeting was held on June 2, 1871. Present—Messrs. N. Blyth (chair), C. B. Young, and H. Giles.

The Hon. Superintendent reported that business was very slack on account of lambing, and that it probably would be for a month or two longer; that he had advertised for the subscription-lists which were sent out in March last, and all unclaimed letters lying at the Club, as also to warn the members whose tickets had fallen due for renewal; that there had been twenty-three subscription-lists for Building and Extension Fund returned with money to the amount of £111 14s. from 172 subscribers; that Messrs. Grant & Stokes had kindly put themselves down as annual subscribers of £10 10s.

It was resolved by the Board that the £111 14s. received for the building and extension, and all subsequent subscriptions for this purpose, at present be paid into the Savings Bank in the names of "William" and Mr. H. Giles. Messrs. D. Murray and W. K. Thomas, trustees, having joined the meeting, it was resolved, after full consideration of the question of premises, that "William" should see Mr. J. Hosking, and enquire the terms on which he would sell his right of purchase, or in the event of his exercising that right himself, the terms on which he would lease the premises as at present occupied for a term of five years. The usual monthly bills were examined and passed. Receipts from all sources for May, £66 18s. 1d.; number of tickets issued to date, 365.

The reader will see by the following that there are some friends who take an interest in the intellectual welfare of the men:—

"'William,' Hon. Superintendent, desires to return thanks to the kind friends at Lower North Adelaide, who have presented through Mr. Alfred Gore a lot of very valuable books for the Bushmen's Club library, including 'Goldsmith's Animated Nature,' illustrated, and complete, in eight volumes; also Robertson's Historical Works, in eleven volumes, &c. This is a very acceptable gift, and will no doubt be highly appreciated."

Extracts from minutes of special meeting held at Mr. C. B. Young's office, June 21, 1871:—Present—Messrs. D. Murray (chair), C. B. Young, and H. Giles.

A letter was read from Thomas Elder, Esq., regretting his absence, also a letter from W. K. Thomas, Esq., expressing his agreement with proposition to buy the property. A letter from Mr. James Hosking was read, offering the property at present occupied without the stable at a rental of £100 per annum, or to purchase it for £1,000. After taking into consideration ways and means it was moved by C. B. Young, Esq., and seconded by H. Giles, Esq., that the property be purchased, which was agreed to. "William" was deputed to inform Mr. Hosking that his terms were agreed to, and that Messrs. Scott & Bakewell, solicitors, were appointed to prepare the conveyance.

On 5th July the usual monthly Board meeting was held. There were present Messrs. N. Blyth (chair), C. B. Young, and H. Giles. The minutes of the special joint meeting of Trustees and Board, held on June 21, were confirmed.

"William," Hon. Superintendent, reported that it was now the dullest time of the year for the institution, as the amount of receipts would show, but that in a month or two the bushmen would begin to come to town, and he believed that as there would be now no rent to pay after a little while the Club he hoped would work on its own merits and profits; that he had advertised the subscriptions, £133 18s. 6d., received from the bush for the Building and Extension Fund, and that he had paid it into the Savings Bank, and also had advertised for all straggling lists; that according to arrangements come to at the special meeting he had informed Mr. Hosking that his offer was accepted, &c., in writing; that he had written a long explanatory letter to G. F. Angas, Esq., and that in reply he believed that gentleman had kindly agreed to a lend on a promissory note of the Trustees £500 for twelve months without interest; that he had also written to J. H. Angas, Esq., reporting progress, that in reply he (Mr. J. H. Angas) had sent a very kind and sympathising letter with cheque enclosed for £100; that Mr. Hosking had informed him ("William") that the property was insured in the Imperial Office for £800, at the rate of 6 per cent. per annum, and that the policy should be renewed on the 1st July, 1871; that special permission had been obtained from the Company to use the building for the Bushmen's Club; that a first-class cooking-stove was needed, also a good fence around the property (iron, if possible); that it would be advisable to prepare a plan of dormitory and decide on a spot to build it upon; that the drains required attending to, and the garden walks and other odd jobs done to improve the place. Total receipts for past month, £45 5s.; total number of tickets issued, 386.

A communication was read from Mr. J. Hosking, asking if the purchase-money, £1,000, would be ready on the 10th instant, also a notice that the land was being brought under the Real Property Act by Sir Charles Cooper.

It was resolved by the Board that Mr. Hosking be informed that the money would be ready immediately the conveyance was ready for completion by the Trustees; Mr. H. Giles undertook to pay the insurance premium on the premises; builders to be applied to to give an approximate estimate of the cost of a dormitory something like the plan "William," Hon. Superintendent, submitted for the approval of the Board.

The following is taken from *Advertiser*, July 13, 1871:—

"THE BUSHMEN'S CLUB.

"The following communication respecting this useful institution has been supplied to us:—

"Many persons in the other colonies, as well as in South Australia, will be glad to learn that by the favor of God, and the indefatigable exertions of the promoters and friends of the Bushmen's Club, a sufficient portion of the late property of Sir C. Cooper has been secured for the Club, that is to say a piece of land having 246 feet frontage to Whitmore-square, with an average depth of about 120 feet, including the large dwelling-house, the cottage at present occupied as an office, store, &c., by the Superintendent, outhouses, &c., for the sum of £1,000 cash. When all the funds were drawn together the Board of Management found that the amount available was between £500 and £600. This was not enough, as the £1,000 had to be paid, and on a certain day. In the dilemma applications were made to the aged Christian philanthropist, G. F. Angas, Esq., and his son Mr. J. H. Angas, which was not in vain. Their truly benevolent bands were ready to assist in this good undertaking, and Mr. G. F. Angas at once sent a donation of £100, and a promise to lend on a promissory note of the Trustees, £500 without interest, for twelve months. This generous offer, with the addition of another donation of £100, from Mr. J. H. Angas, places the Club in a very favorable position. This purchase will release the Board of Management from the late heavy rental of £110 per annum, and enable them to put up a good dormitory, and make sundry alterations and improvements which are much needed to add to the comfort of the inmates and improve the house and grounds. The building is insured in the Imperial Office for £800, and the property of the Club in the Marine Office for £300. Much credit is due to the Trustees—Messrs. J. H. Angas, D. Murray, and W. K. Thomas, and to the present Board of Management—Messrs. N. Blyth, H. Giles, and C. B. Young, for their unremitting gratuitous exertions, not only to make the institution an established fact, but to make it if possible self-supporting. The bush people and all interested in the institution will be very pleased to hear that to complete the work, their old and tried friend 'William' has guaranteed to the Trustees and Board to superintend the progress of the Club gratiutously for two years certain (D. V.). This is indeed a noble gift at this stage of the Club's existence. The institution is rapidly growing in favour, and now numbers 390 members on the roll, and is becoming more and more useful to the bush people. It is sincerely to be desired that the many flockmasters and gentlemen in this colony interested in pastoral pursuits, and having at heart the welfare of their employès, will on this occasion come nobly forward and assist. It is also to be hoped that the bushmen, and the friends of the bushmen generally, will make a strong effort during the next twelve months to clear off the £500 mortgage so kindly lent by Mr. Angas, and thus set the Bushmen's Club entirely free. The Hon. Superintendent 'William' will be glad to receive donations or subscriptions from all friends to this cause, as well as from those who have hitherto entertained doubts as to the success of the institution."

The *Register* of July 13, 1871, in an article on the affairs of the Bushmen and their Club, says :—

"Slowly but surely the Bushmen's Club is being established on a permanent basis. It is but two or three years since the question of providing in Adelaide a comfortable home for a large and ill-cared for class of the community was mooted, and the object sought has become an accomplished fact. Bushmen have now in the city a place that they can call their own. Whenever they are required by business, or by the exigencies of a somewhat precarious occupation, to visit the metropolis, there is an asylum where they can not merely rely upon a friendly welcome, but where they have a right to enter. The only formula through which they have to pass are to enrol their names and pay a trifling sum by way of entrance fee. This done, they are entitled to the freedom of the Home, and may take up their residence in it. Care was taken whilst the rules of the institution were being framed to make them as little irksome as possible, and experience has proved their suitability to the requirements of the case. The rate charged for board and lodging is exceedingly reasonable, the food supplied and the accommodation provided are unexceptionable, and the restrictions imposed do not interfere with the proper personal liberty of the inmates. As in all well-regulated families, certain rules have to be conformed to, but they sit lightly upon those who are disposed to regard the retreat as a Home. Very prudently the management interfere as little as possible with the internal affairs of the establishment, leaving it to the Superintendent and the bushmen themselves to carry into effect the idea with which the Club was started. How successful this policy has been events have shown.

" It will be remembered that when the Board took a lease of the building in Whitmore-square, once occupied by Sir

Charles Cooper, their avowed intention was to give the Home a trial. The pecuniary support they had received, although liberal, did not warrant them in going to great expense, and they wisely thought that a year or two would prove whether their philanthrophic efforts would be rightly appreciated. A few months ago the friends of the institution were made aware that the experiment had been so far satisfactory, and that the Board had resolved upon purchasing the fee-simple of the property. The balance of funds in hand, supplemented during the last few months by special contributions from bushmen, amounted to between £500 and £600 towards the £1,000 required. An application was then made to Mr. G. F. Angas, who, with his accustomed liberality, not only forwarded a donation of £100, but agreed to lend upon a promissory note £500 for twelve months without interest. At the same time Mr. J. H. Angas presented a cheque for £100, so that the Trustees —Messrs. J. H. Angas, D. Murray, and W. K. Thomas—not only found themselves in funds to pay down £1,000 cash, but also in possession of a credit balance of about £250.

"The purchase has been effected, and the Club is now seised of a piece of land with a frontage of 246 feet to Whitmore-square, and an average depth of 120 feet, together with the large dwelling-house, cottage (now used as offices and store by Superintendent), outhouses, and other appurtenances.

"The immediate effect of this transaction will be to relieve the Board, which now consists of Messrs. N. Blyth, H. Giles, and C. B. Young, from the heavy annual rent charge of £110, and enable them to carry out in their own way many alterations which have been required from the first, but which they felt indisposed to make upon leasehold property. It is intended, without loss of time, to put up a convenient dormitory, and make other improvements about the house and grounds, with a view to promoting the comfort of the inmates. The premises are already insured for £800, and the property of the Club for £300.

"The Board of Management and the Trustees have, without the incentive of fee or reward, given unremitting attention to the duties of their position, their aim being first to make the Home attractive, and secondly to make it, if possible, self-supporting. In all these efforts they have had the cordial co-operation of the Hon. Superintendent, whose unwearied and self-denying labors have contributed much to the success of the institution. Had the superintendence fallen into the hands of a man less esteemed by the bushmen, less able to understand their difficulties and assist them with his advice and sympathy, it is more than doubtful whether the Club would have attained its present popularity. This being the case, it is gratifying to know that 'William' has agreed to remain at his present post without salary for two years more, in order to complete the work which he has undertaken, and see the Home established as one of the institutions of the land. The intrinsic merit of his offer is not at all lessened by the fact that he takes a strong personal interest in the class benefited by the Home. Whilst he has had charge the number of members has advanced to 390, and the advantages of the Club have become more and more extended. There are still many flockowners and persons interested in pastoral pursuits who have done little to aid the good work, and it would be a gracious act on their part to give something to the institution, if only by way of thank-offering for returning prosperity. It must be of service to them, if for no other reason because it affords them a ready means of coming into contact with the men they require for station hands. There is no cause for fear that their donations will be either misapplied or unnecessary. The £500 so freely lent by Mr. Angas ought to be returned by the end of the twelvemonth, and there are many expenses connected with improvements to the buildings and so forth which will have to be met. The Honorary Superintendent intimates that he will be happy to receive contributions from those who formerly stood aloof from the institution as well as from its staunch friends;

"The Board have at length seen their way clear to the initiation of a Benefit Fund for the use of members who have become incapacitated for work either by old age or illness. This was one of the objects prominently placed before the public in the prospectus of the Club, and if carried out will be of immense advantage. Improvidence is one of the most conspicuous weakness of bushmen, and does much to aggravate the ills to which as a class they are peculiarly subject. It will therefore be a real charity to give them facilities for making provision against infirmity and bad times. As the Club becomes older and more consolidated the sphere of its usefulness becomes more extended, and we heartily recommend it as an institution worthy of the support of the benevolent.

The following letter, which appeared two days after the former article, will no doubt be acceptable to the general reader :—

"THE BUSHMEN OF SOUTH AUSTRALIA.

"TO THE EDITOR.

"Sir—As bushmen have been more or less before the public for the last twelve months, perhaps it is only reasonable that the majority of the good people of Adelaide should hear something about them as they are and ought to be. Most people think that those reckless-looking drunken men they see occasionally rolling in the gutters are a fair type of the bushmen; and though I must confess this is true in a measure, still I would raise my voice against this libel on a great many of those who are in a true sense 'nature's noblemen,' ready with heart and hand to help everything which bears the impress of philanthropy. Those are the men who in their own sphere are earnest workers for the cause of reform among their own class, and those are they who I hope may live to see the day when bushmen will be respected throughout the length and breadth of Australia. A few words about the first-mentioned class of bushmen—I mean those who of their own free will become the prey of the many 'sharks' who, in spite of all laws, consider the improvident bushmen their pray. How well they manage, the records of our Police Courts best testify. It seems almost impossible to do those men any good; yet time and patience work wonders. Perhaps men may not always be led by those whose only desire is to transfer the hard earnings of the bushmen from his pocket to theirs. Ask Mr. Beddome what is a bushman. He will tell you, "Oh! they are the biggest set of fools I ever came in contact with. They are men who will turn from their best friends to the denizens of Light-square, as I know to my sorrow and their loss." Whilst admitting this to be true, still we must not condemn the innocent with the guilty. Whilst there is much that is foolish and improvident about bushmen, they are as a class a noble, generous lot of fellows, with a heart ever ready to feel for those who may need their sympathy, and if there is one thing more prominent than another in them it is gratitude, and I am sure there is many a heart amongst them at this moment throbbing gratefully to those noble disinterested gentlemen who by their acts prove that the bushman is a man and a brother, and that they are ready to help him if he will only help himself. Let us then do as those gentlemen would have us do—steer clear of the vile crew who too long have robbed us, and become a living proof that we never forget our friends. The disinterested interest taken in us ought to be an incentive, and noble incentive, for us one and all to work earnestly for the object in view— that is to help to amalgamate into one all classes of bushmen, and thus make ourselves a Home, independent alike of the many sharpers, *alias* friends, *alias* publicans, who for upwards of thirty years have fattened on us. A few words more, and I have done. Bushmen are not wanting in gratitude, as future experience will prove. With 'William' at the helm we will yet, with God's help, prove that the United Bushmen of South Australia are a class who are able and willing to discern friends from foes, and thus we will prove that we are able to respect ourselves, and make others do so likewise.

"I am, Sir, &c.,
"BUSHMAN."
—*Register*, July 15, 1871.

It having been mooted occasionally from the beginning of this movement that there should be a benefit fund in connection with the institution, it was now considered desirable, at the request of a number of bushmen, that some steps should be taken to initiate the affair; in consequence of which the following advertisement was inserted in the newspapers, as a preliminary step:—

"To the Bushmen of South Australia.

"The property of the Club being now secured, the next step is, if possible, to establish a Benefit Fund.

"Members of the Club, or any bushmen, are respectfully requested to communicate with me on this subject before the end of August next, and express their views, also state the amount they are willing to subscribe for this purpose either weekly, monthly, or yearly to secure help in old age, or times of sickness or distress.

"'William,' Hon. Superintendent.
"Bushmen's Club, July 11, 1871."

On the 2nd of August, 1871, the next annual Board meeting was held. There were present Messrs. C. B. Young (chair) and H. Giles.

The Hon. Superintendent reported that he had obtained a Flavel's kitchener, for the kitchen, at a cost of about £22; that a man had been engaged to put the drains in better order; that he had engaged a man to go round the sheds during the shearing season to take the names of persons desirous of giving money to assist in paying off the debt on the property; that he had had an interview with J. H. Angas, Esq., and it was considered that the best plan was to send the acting agent to Mount Remarkable by mail—Mr. Angas promised that his Manager at Willowie, Mr. F. J. Whitby, should be communicated with to provide a good horse for the journey; an address had been prepared for the Collector by "William," to read to the men, and other things needful for his work had been supplied, and an advertisement to the bush people, calling attention to his work, inserted in the newspapers; that preliminary steps had been taken during the past month to initiate a benefit fund for aged, sick, and distressed bushmen, independent of the regular Club funds. Total receipts for July, including subscriptions and loan from Mr. Angas, £1,161; total number of tickets issued, 397.

Resolved by the Board—That a cheque be signed for £1,000 to pay for property, as a letter had been received from Messrs. Scott & Bakewell, solicitors, stating that the conveyance would be ready in a few days.

Copy of the advertisement calling the attention of the bush people that subscriptions would be collected during the shearing season of 1871:—

"BUSHMEN'S CLUB.

"The members of the Club, and bush people generally, are hereby informed that John O'Connell (member of Bushmen's Club) is authorised to obtain the names of persons, with the amounts they are willing to subscribe toward the above-named institution, and hand them over to the Managers, &c., of the different stations or sheds during the shearing season, 1871.

"He will at once commence in the North.

"*Pro* Board of Management,

"'WILLIAM,'

"Hon. Superintendent Bushmen's Club.

"Adelaide, July 29, 1871."

The following appeared in the *Advertiser* of August 9, 1871:—

"The Bushmen's Home is making substantial progress, and bids fair to be one of our most useful public institutions. There are now between three and four hundred members, and 'William,' the Hon. Superintendent, continues to receive fresh promises of adhesion and support. The Club has attracted attention even in New South Wales, and among his recent correspondence 'William' has received an earnest and sympathetic letter from a shepherd in that colony, who expresses the warmest interest in the Club, and has already remitted about £10, which he has collected towards its support.

"The Club has already done much good, and will doubtless be the means of preserving many bushmen from those degrading excesses by which so many worthy men have wasted their hard-earned savings, ruined their health, and prepared for themselves a future of remorse and wretchedness. God help them."

A special meeting of the Trustees and Board of Management was held at Mr. D. Murray's office on the 9th August. There were present Messrs. D. Murray (chair), J. H. Angas, and W. K. Thomas (Trustees), and Mr. H. Giles representing the Board of Management.

It was agreed to request Mr. Scott, solicitor, to tender the purchase-money for the Whitmore-square property, and to decline further payment of interest. Plans of dormitory were examined, and that of Mr. Peter Cumming, architect, approved. It was agreed to ask tenders when the means were forthcoming, as only £125 was at credit of current account, it being considered necessary to raise at least £400 before commencing work. "William," Hon. Superintendent, was instructed to get an estimate of the fence around the property, iron and paling. The monthly accounts were examined, found correct, and passed for payment.

The next meeting of the Board was held at the Club on September 2. Present—Messrs. N. Blyth (chair), C. B. Young, and H. Giles.

Minutes of meeting of Trustees and Board held on 9th August were confirmed.

The Hon. Superintendent reported that there had been 444 tickets of membership issued since the opening of the Club, and that as there was not sleeping accommodation for a fair proportion of that number it was absolutely necessary that more room should be obtained, and that the capabilities of the institution were cramped for want of sleeping accommodation; that he had made enquiries and calculations about the fencing, &c., as requested—the charge for iron of 130 sheets to the ton was £25, and that sufficient to go all round the property would cost about £58, also that there was another kind (black iron) which would cost about £42; that Mr. Whitby, of Willowie, had provided a horse for the acting agent, that it was too early yet to give opinion as to result of the canvass for subscriptions; that it had been found necessary to frame a few new rules, and a new clause for the constitution of the Club, and with the sanction of the Board they would be hung up in the Reading-room for three months, and if passed at the meeting in December be incorporated with the regular constitution and rules; that Mr. Hosking had informed "William" that the money—£1,000 cash—had been received for the property; that two men sent from the Club to the Hospital had died during the past month, both of them had a little money—one named Anderson left a wife and family, his effects were sent to them; the other, named T. Kelley, left in custody of Hon. Superintendent £14 16s., and having no friends in this country, and no clue being found to his relations, the Superintendent requested to know what to do with it. Total amount of receipts for past month, £80; number of tickets issued, 444.

It was resolved by the Board that the money deposited in the hands of " William " by an inmate, who had died in the Hospital, and as far as known has no relations or friends, be handed to the Curator of Intestate Estates; that the rules and new articles for the constitution be approved.

Mr. H. Giles reported that the purchase of the property had been completed, the money paid, but the deeds not yet ready; that temporary repairs had been done to the fences, and new posts and palings put where required.

On the 5th September a joint meeting of Trustees and Board of Management was held, to take into consideration the propriety of erecting a dormitory. Present—Messrs. D. Murray (chair), J. H. Angas, W. K. Thomas (Trustees); H. Giles, Esq., representing the Board of Management; Mr. P. Cumming, architect; and " William," Hon. Superintendent.

It was agreed to invite tenders for the erection of a dormitory according to Mr. Cumming's plan, and afterwards to decide upon the erection of the whole or half according to the prospect of funds coming in. It was agreed also to make an effort to raise by voluntary subscriptions the sum of £500, and to petition Parliament to supplement to a similar extent the sum thus raised. It was agreed to modify the architect's plan by reducing the width of the building to twenty-five feet, thus reducing the number of bedrooms to twenty in place of twenty-four, and that the Board of Management act as a Building Committee.

The following is a brief newspaper report of the late important transactions of the Club :—

" For some time past the want of more sleeping accommodation has been severely felt at the Bushmen's Club, but hitherto the uncertain state of the property has prevented any action being taken in this matter by the Board of Management. We are informed now, however, that steps have been taken, and that on the 9th August last, at a joint meeting of the Trustees and Board, plans of a dormitory were examined, and that of Mr. Cumming, architect, approved. As only a small sum of money was at the credit current account in consequence of the late draft of £1,000 cash, which was recently paid to secure the property, it was considered necessary to postpone the matter for a short time, and endeavour to raise £400 before commencing building. Subsequent events have proved, however, that a large number of bushmen may be reasonably expected after shearing, &c., and there being 444 tickets issued from the Club it has called forth the undaunted energy and perseverance of the bushmen and their friends, who determined to make another effort to overcome the difficulty, for which purpose a meeting was held on September 5. Present—Messrs. D. Murray (in chair), J. H. Angas, and W. K. Thomas, Trustees; Mr. H. Giles representing the Board of Management; 'William,' Hon. Superintendent of Club; and Mr. Cumming, architect. After a short debate on the subject, it was agreed to erect a dormitory according to Mr. Cumming's plan, and afterwards to decide upon the erection of the whole or half, according to the prospect of funds coming in. It was agreed also to modify the plan under the circumstances by reducing the width of the building, thus reducing the number of small bedrooms to twenty—the Board of Management to act as a Building Committee. 'William' reported to the meeting that Mr. Thomas Elder had that day paid the Bushmen's Club a visit for the first time, having been absent in England, and expressed himself highly pleased with the place and its arrangements. We trust that the bushmen themselves will not be backward in supporting with their subscriptions and patronage their kind friends in Adelaide, who have taken such a deep interest in their welfare as a class. The Hon. Superintendent will be glad to receive subscriptions from any friends desiring to aid the good work. We hear that a large muster of bushmen may be expected at the annual picnic this year, of which due notice will be given. The matter of the Benefit Fund is still under consideration. 'William' reports that a few subscriptions are beginning to come in from the bush; he has also received a letter from the acting agent speaking in encouraging terms of the prospects of the Club this season, but as shearing has not yet begun on some stations it would be premature to speak positively as to results. Another month or two will probably show what the bushmen will do."—*Express*, September 7, 1871.

J. H. Angas, Esq., having called "William's" attention to an application addressed to the Municipal Corporation on the 5th September, 1871, as follows:—

"James Hosking requested that the plantation at the south-east corner of Whitmore-square might be removed. Referred to the Public Works Committee, with power to act;"

The following correspondence took place upon the subject:—

"Bushmen's Club, September 11, 1871.

"To His Worship the Mayor and Corporation
of the City of Adelaide.

"Your Worship and Gentlemen—The Trustees and Board of Management of the above-named institution regret to see an intention on the part of the Corporation to clear away the plantation at the south-east corner of Whitmore-square, and beg to request that the portion in front of the Club premises may not be removed.

"Names of Trustees, { J. H. Angas.
W. K. Thomas.
D. Murray.

"Names of Board of { H. Giles.
Management, N. Blyth.
C. B. Young.

"I have the honour to be, Gentlemen,
"Your obedient servant,
"'WILLIAM,'
Hon. Superintendent Bushmen's Club."

"Town Clerk's Office, Town Hall,
Adelaide, Sept. 14, 1871.

"Sir—I have the honour, by direction of the City Council,

to acknowledge the receipt of your letter of the 11th instant, having reference to the preservation of that portion of the planted enclosure immediately in front of the Bushmen's Club, Whitmore-square, and in reply am instructed to say the Council has decided to remove only about 50 (fifty) feet at the northern end, and the same space at the southern end, leaving that portion you refer to intact.

"I have the honour to be, Sir,
"Your obedient servant,
"THOMAS WORSNOP, Town Clerk.
"To 'William,' Hon. Superintendent
Bushmen's Club."

Again, on the 13th September (the same month), a special meeting was held at Mr. Cumming's (the architect's) office, to decide upon a tender for building the said dormitory. Present—Messrs. D. Murray and W. K. Thomas, Trustees; N. Blyth and C. B. Young, Board of Management.

It was agreed, after considering ways and means, that Mr. D. Murray should call on T. Elder, Esq., and other gentlemen, and endeavour to raise £200—if successful, the entire plan of the dormitory to be carried out; failing this, one-half to be proceeded with.

At the suggestion of Mr. Angas, it was agreed that C. B. Young, Esq., draw up a petition to be presented to Parliament; "William," Hon. Superintendent, to furnish such information as required.

In the *Register's* Parliamentary report of 20th September appeared the following paragraphs:—

"Mr. Glyde, in the absence of Mr. Murray, presented a petition from the Trustees and officers of the Bushmen's Club, praying that £500 be voted to subsidize the funds of the Club.

"Received and read."

"Mr. Glyde to move—'That Petition No. 46, presented on 19th September, from the Trustees of the Bushmen's Club, be printed.'"

Touching upon this matter the *Express* of September 22 adds:—

"The Trustees and Board of Management of the Bushmen's Club have felt themselves bound to make arrangements to increase the accommodation, in consequence of the continual growth of the institution. Nearly all the bushmen being out of town at the shearing, &c., and the need being specially urgent for more sleeping accommodation against their return, the present opportunity is considered a very favourable one for building a new dormitory, the foundation stone of which will be laid on Saturday. The new building and its arrangements will add much to the comfort of the inmates, giving more space, and enabling each man to have his own sleeping apartment. There are many improvements contemplated; some of them are partly carried out, and when completed former inmates will scarcely recognise the old place. We see by the Parliamentary Notice-paper that Mr. Glyde, M.P., has given notice of motion for a supplementary grant of £500 towards the institution. This is as it should be, for it is an institution that deserves the countenance and support of the colonists generally."

The *Evening Journal* of same date also furnishes the following:—

"As we lately stated, the Board of Management of this Club have, owing to the increased interest taken in, and the healthy growth of the institution, been induced to make arrangements for providing more accommodation at the Home in Whitmore-square. As nearly all the Bushmen are at present busily engaged at the stations in clipping the sheep, and a large influx is expected so soon as the wool season has closed, the present seemed a suitable time for supplying the additional sleeping room that is urgently needed, and the dormitories, the number and size of which have been previously noted, are on the eve of being erected. Masons and other workmen are now engaged in clearing the space, and preparing for the laying of the foundation-stone of the new wing. Many improvements are also going on, and when former inmates return it is believed that the old place, comfortable as it was, will have been so thoroughly renovated and brightened up as to be scarcely recognisable. Under the altered system, and the increased space, each lodger will be able to get a separate room, and keep the key while he remains in town, so that it may be for the time his own castle. The friends of this useful and now thoroughly established affair are glad that Mr. L. Glyde, M.P., has taken action to endeavour to secure a grant of £500 to aid the promoters. The institution deserves to be well treated, for those who have to do with its establishment have certainly worked with spirit, and given with liberality. Prejudices had to be met, fought, and defeated, and objections to the Club or its operations are seldom if ever heard. The bushmen have themselves contributed generously, and are identifying themselves with the Home in greater numbers than ever; they, however, still claim the countenance, and to some extent the help of others."

All things being now ready to commence the new building, it was thought advantageous to the success of the undertaking that the foundation-stone should be formally laid, and the following invitation was inserted in the public papers:—

"BUSHMEN'S CLUB.

"*General notice to bushmen and their friends.*

"The foundation-stone of the new dormitory will be laid (D.V.) on Saturday next, 23rd instant, at 2 p.m. All friends respectfully invited. No collection.

"'William,' Hon. Superintendent, &c."

The following is the *Advertiser's* report of the ceremony:—
"Since its commencement the Bushmen's Club has been a continued success; and the Board of Management, finding the urgent necessity of providing increased accommodation, determined to add a wing to the western portion of the premises. Mr. Cumming, the architect, was deputed to draw up plans for the addition, and tenders were called— that of Mr. Farr, for £440, being accepted. The building is intended to be used as a dormitory. It will be fifty-six feet long, twenty-five broad, and thirteen feet to the tiling. The average height of the roof will be seventeen and a-half feet, and there will be no ceiling. This will allow ample space for ventilation, so as to give bushmen an equivalent for the open

huts to which they have been accustomed while living in the country. It will contain twenty separate sleeping rooms, with the necessary fittings. The walls will be of Glen Osmond stone, with cement dressings, and the roof of galvanized iron. It is intended, we believe, as the Club increases, to add another wing on the opposite side of the main building. On Saturday afternoon, September 23, the ceremony of laying the foundation-stone of the new dormitory was performed by Mr. D. Murray, M.P.; Mr. C. B. Young and other gentlemen being also present. The grounds were very tastefully decorated with flags and banners, which gave them quite a holiday appearance. Schrader's Band was also present, and enlivened the proceedings. Shortly after 2 o'clock—a number of persons having assembled, and Mr. Murray having taken his position—the Hon. Superintendent, 'William,' said he had a short address to present to Mr. Murray. He then read the following:—

"'To David Murray, Esq., M.P.—We, the members of the Bushmen's Club of South Australia, request that you will on this special occasion accept of the accompanying trowel, not for its intrinsic value, but as a slight manifesto of our esteem and regard; also as a remembrance in time to come of this happy event, namely, of laying the foundation-stone of the new dormitory. May Almighty God bless you with peace, prosperity, and happiness; and the institution itself with His favour.

"Signed on behalf of the members,
"THOS. WARD,
"JOHN STEWART,
"TREELOVE HAMMOND.'"

"Mr. Murray thanked 'William' on behalf of the members of the Club for their address. He certainly felt he was greatly honoured in being asked to lay the foundation-stone of the new building. Such an event as that augured well for the future of the Bushmen's Home, and was he thought the precursor of better things to come. He hoped the comforts and accommodation of the Home would recommend it to bushmen. He quite expected that there would be a large increase in the attendance of members, who already were numerous, and that some who came from curiosity would be induced to stay. He trusted that the Home would be a permanent Home and increasingly useful, and that the building would increase the comforts of the bushmen. He again thanked the members of the Club.

"Mr. Archibald Duncan here presented a silver trowel to Mr. Murray on behalf of the bushmen. It was manufactured by Mr. Steiner, Rundle-street, and on it were engraved the words, 'Presented to David Murray, Esq., M.P., by the bushmen of South Australia. September 23, 1871. 1 Peter, ii. 17.

"Mr. Murray expressed his thanks for this token of esteem from the bushmen of the colony, and Mr. T. Hammond again thanked Mr. Murray, on behalf of the members, for the interest he had taken in the Club.

"Mr. Murray briefly acknowled the compliment, stating that the Club was greatly indebted to 'William' for its success.

"A bottle containing copies of that day's *Register* and *Advertiser*, a portrait of Mr. J. H. Angas, a promoter of the work, on the back of which the words 'Promoter of good' had been written, and the following document:—'This stone was laid by David Murray, Esq., M.P., on the 23rd day of September, 1871, in the thirty-fifth year of the reign of Her Majesty Queen Victoria, and the third year of the Governorship of Sir James Fergusson,' having been deposited in a space under the stone, it was lowered into its place. Mr. Murray declared the stone well and truly laid, and then proposed cheers for the Bushmen's Club, which was heartily responded to—the Band playing the National Anthem. Cheers were also given for the absent members; Mr. J. H. Angas, the President; the Hon. Superintendent, 'William;' and Mr. Murray. The company then adjourned to the main building, where refreshments had been laid out, and after partaking thereof the proceedings terminated."

The next meeting of the Board of Management was held on the 3rd October, 1871. Present—Messrs. C. B. Young (chair), and H. Giles.

Minutes of preceding meeting were read and confirmed; vouchers called over, and found correct.

The Hon. Superintendent reported that he had paid over to the Curator of Intestate Estates, as per order of Board, on account of James Kelley, deceased, £14 16s., for which amount he held the receipt; that the fences were partially repaired; that he had called on T. Elder, Esq., who promised to visit the Club, and also to see Mr. N. Blyth about his vote; that Mr. Angas had sent " William" a letter, directing him to bring before the notice of the Board the fact that the Corporation were disposed to remove the shrubbery in front of the premises, and to take the necessary steps to prevent it—this had been done; that the labourers and masons had been employed during the past week about the dormitory, the foundation-stone of which was laid by D. Murray, Esq., on the 23rd September, 1871; that a movement had been made to get a supplementary grant of £500 for the Club from the Government placed on the Estimates; that he was now of opinion that the subscriptions from the bush after all expenses were paid for collecting, would be very small; that on the 29th September a young man named William Costello, without any known friends, was sent to the Hospital, and died the same evening; that according to clauses 6 and 12 of the constitution it was time to give notice of the approach of the annual general meeting, and the nomination of candidates for Board of Management. Receipts from all sources, £87; total number of tickets issued, 506.

Resolved by the Board that the annual general meeting be held on Friday, 22nd December, 1871.

The following advertisement was inserted:—

"Notice to Bushmen.

"The annual general meeting of the Club will be held (D.V.) at the Club-house on Friday, December 22, 1871, for general business, and to elect a Board of Management in the place of Messrs. N. Blyth, C. B. Young, and H. Giles, who retire, but are eligible for re-election.

"Further Notice.—Qualified persons proposing to offer themselves as candidates must signify their willingness to act if elected in writing to me on or before 10th November next. (See constitution, clauses 6 and 12.)

"By order of the Board of Management,

"'WILLIAM,' Hon. Superintendent.

"Bushmen's Club, Whitmore-square,
October 3, 1871."

Respecting the Government grant to the Bushmen's Club, the *Register* of 29th September had the following remarks:—

"THE BUSHMEN'S CLUB.—The Trustees and Board of Management of the Bushmen's Club have presented a petition to the House of Assembly, which has been printed on the motion of Mr. Glyde. It represents that upwards of £1,500 has been subscribed for the purchase of premises for the purposes of the Bushmen's Club, and that a further sum of £1,000 is required to extend the building in order to meet the increasing demands for accommodation. It therefore prays that a sum of £500 may be placed on the Estimates for 1872, in order to supplement the amount raised by private subscriptions. Considering the great benefits to the moral and social welfare of the bushmen which the Club offers, and considering also the energetic spirit of self-help which the bushmen themselves have displayed in their contributions to the funds, we do not think a more deserving case could be submitted to the Assembly, and we trust it will receive favourable consideration when it is brought forward."

The following is a copy of the debates as reported by the *Advertiser*, October 7, 1871:—

"THE BUSHMEN'S CLUB.

"In Committee.

"Mr. Murray moved—'That an address be presented to His Excellency the Governor, praying His Excellency to cause a sum not exceeding £500 to be placed on the Estimates for the year 1872, for the purpose of supplementing contributions in behalf of the Bushmen's Home.' (See Petition, House No. 88.)

"He anticipated very little opposition to this motion, as he advocated not any local interest, but the claims of a class.

who he thought every class of the community must feel they had an interest in. It was needless for him to point out that to a large extent the bushmen were destitute of many blessings which persons possessed in the settled parts of the colony, and were therefore entitled to their consideration; but he might mention that the assistance of Parliament had been granted for a Home of another class of persons in the colony—the Sailors' Home. Those who would be benefited thereby, however, had not the same claims upon the colony as the bushmen had, inasmuch as the sailors only came to the colony now and then, whilst the bushmen were continually with them; and being absent from the settled districts, especially town, and visiting it only once a year, he thought it the duty of the Government to assist the colonists and the bushmen themselves by providing some kind of a Home for them. The bushmen had done all in their power to provide themselves with such a Home, having collected £600 in small sums from over 2,000 of their number, and the public had already supplemented that amount so as to make a total of about £2,000, which had been expended on the Home and providing the necessaries for establishing it. Its success had been proved during the eighteen months in which it had been established by there having been from a dozen to thirty inmates constantly inhabiting it, and the bushmen had shown their appreciation of it by returning to it again and again. The Committee of the Home had already taken steps to increase its accommodation by building a new dormitory, which would cost something like £500, and they were endeavouring to complete the purchase of the property comprised by the Home, which would take another considerable sum, and they only asked the House to grant them a sum not exceeding £500, which they would supplement by contributions from the public to a similar extent. He felt that the bushmen had a stong claim upon the Government, inasmuch as they were a large portion of the community, connected with one of the largest industries in the colony, who had received no sort of assistance from them yet. He thought it was a very creditable thing that a Home of this sort should be established first in South Australia, and the other colonies were making enquiries with a view of establishing similar Homes there. Already the sum of £5,000 had been lodged in the Home by the bushmen themselves, which might have been spent in a way not at all conducive to their interests had they not had the Home to go to, which also enabled them to receive letters, to have communication with others, to use it as a place where they could obtain employment, and for many other purposes. He felt that every member of the House as well as himself should have the interests of the bushmen at heart, and that they should consider it only a privilege to lend a helping hand to those who were willing to help themselves.

"Mr. Coglin had much pleasure in supporting the motion. If there was one body of men more deserving of the consideration of the public than another it was the bushmen, and he thought the establishment of a Home for them was a step in the right direction. It would keep them from going to hotels, and other places where they would spend their money foolishly, and regret it in their more sober moments. He was very glad it was an abstemious institution, and he thought they could not do better than assist those gentlemen who had so kindly formed themselves into a Committee to establish it.

"Mr. Boucaut, before he said he would vote for the motion, asked the hon. member in whom the Bushmen's Club was vested, and, supposing the Club was broken up tomorrow, to whom the benefit of the £500 would go?

"The Treasurer (Hon. J. Hart) said there appeared neither in the petition nor in the motion any guarantee that the sum asked for was absolutely for a building which would be like the Sailors' Home at Port Adelaide, which was in trust for all time, and therefore could not by any possibility be sold or made away with. The Sailors' Home also provided accommodation for the Shipping Master and his clerk, so that it was a Government establishment so far as that was concerned; and although something like £4,000 had been contributed by private subscription and laid out upon it, the whole amount subscribed by the Government was only £1,000, so that the circumstances of the cases were not similar to those represented by the hon. member for the city. He thought it would be a good thing to have in connection with the Bushmen's Club some similar arrangement to the Shipping Master's establishment at Port Adelaide. During his visit to Melbourne he had gleaned some information with regard to the system lately establised in California—that of the Government finding a Registry Office without fee for people out of employment. It had proved very successful, and there was some talk of adopting something of the kind in Melbourne, and if such an office could be arranged for in the Bushmen's Club building, the Government would see their way more clearly to vote for the sum now asked for. They, however, would not be able to do so unless they were informed that the building was vested in the hands of trustees, so that it could not be sold, and that the whole of the Government expenditure would be on the additions to be made to the building, otherwise it might be devoted towards the support of the institution, which of course the Government could not admit.

"Mr. N. Blyth could inform the Government that the whole of the money was to be applied to enlarging the building, that the building was vested in trustees for all time, was freehold property, and was tied down against any malappropriation the same as similar institutions. As for the institution asking for any sum to carry on operations, it was self-supporting—(Hear, hear)—and it was the success it had met with which had necessitated the enlargement of the accommodation, and directed the attention of the promoters and the Committee to ask for this very moderate grant in aid to one of the most unostentatious but practical and moral movements which had yet been made in the colony. (Hear, hear.) There was a registry office attached to the Club for the benefit of the particular class for whom it was designed, which was availed of to a very considerable extent. The circumstance that a great deal of the money to found the institution was contributed by the bushmen themselves was a very striking fact, and he felt that the success of an institution like this would be a great benefit to the community, and in the long run save Government a great deal of expenditure in many of our public institutions. The object in establishing the institution was to a great extent a moral one —to give the men when they came to town an opportunity of lodging in a place where they could have respectable and innocent amusements, instead of making a wrong use of their time. He was sorry that the motion had not met with a warmer reception on the part of the Government.

"Mr. Hay would move an amendment, which would perhaps alter the views of the Government, to strike out 'on behalf of the Bushmen's Home,' and insert 'for the enlargement of the building now used as the Bushmen's Home.' There was no idea that the sum asked for should go towards the support of the institution, the intention of those frequenting it being he believed to contribute towards the support of their brother bushmen who were in indigent circumstances, and came to the Home looking out for work till they found it. He could have wished that the Home had been established in a more central position, the only fear he had for its permanency being its distance from the business part of the town. He considered it was in the wrong locality; but as the Superintendent ('William'), who had shown so much energy and devotion, and the Committee, who had given great attention to the institution, believed the present was a suitable locality, he deferred to their judgment so far as to agree to vote this £500; but he feared, if 'William's' supervision was taken away, for its permanency.

"The Commissioner of Crown Lands (Hon. A. Blyth) remarked that the hon. member's (Mr. Hay's) amendment altered the position of the motion very much indeed, and the objections, which he was sure the Committee must feel were very well founded, were to some extent met by it; but he could not help saying, speaking entirely on his own account, that he was afraid there was a very great evil abroad in the country—that of looking too much to the Government for assistance. (Cheers, and No.) With the exception of churches and chapels, and the schools connected with them, which they were not at all behind hand with, he thought they did not give as much as they ought. The Hospital was a charitable institution which certainly must engage the sympathy of any person who thought about the matter; but that simply £600 should be contributed towards it by the community, which comprised among its members many very wealthy individuals, and a large number of persons of great ease in monetary matters, was not creditable to them. Take another institution—the Benevolent and Strangers' Friend Society. Was £100 contributed towards that sufficient for the community? They were too much in the habit of looking at their giving in these matters as if they were not behind hand, but he thought they were very much. Were the proposition for a contribution towards the expenses of the Bushmen's Home he should stand out very strongly against it; but placed as it was by the amendment as a contribution towards the building, which was to be vested in trustees, and could not be diverted from the object for which the Club was instituted, it relieved his mind from a good deal of the objection which might be made against it.

"Mr. Murray accepted the amendment.

"Mr. Pearce supported the motion. He agreed with a great many remarks which had been made by the last speaker, the only doubt he had whether to support the motion being the class for whom assistance was sought. Whilst he admitted that the bushmen as a class should look to the Government for consideration, seeing that the pastoral lessees had been granted very valuable concessions, which led to a certain extent to the necessity for the Home, he doubted whether that class of the community (the lessees) should not have made provision for the bushmen without an appeal to that House. The allowing of fencing to be reckoned as an improvement had had a tendency to throw out of employment many bushmen, and as fencing continued this would be still more the case. As many of the men would be growing old, he hoped the Committee would consider the advisability of establishing in connection with the Club a Benefit Society as a provision for their old age. That would be a very valuable institution, and would relieve the revenue of the country of future calls, which he feared would otherwise be made upon it by the bushmen.

"Mr. Cavenagh should have liked the mover to have brought down the balance-sheet to show whether the institution was self-supporting or not. He had heard that it was, and therefore he was sorry that the matter had been brought before the House, although he should not oppose it, instead of the Committee making still greater endeavour to render it self-supporting.

"Mr. Murray said the only objection raised which had any weight was that the Bushmen's Club was not established in a proper part of the town. To some extent he admitted this, but it was altogether beyond the power of the Committee to get a Home established in a more suitable part of the town consistently with the means at their disposal. They had acquired the present building on very advantageous terms, and were putting up the buildings on the most economical principle. He was convinced that if it ever was required to be sold it would realize the full price paid for it. It was vested in permanent trustees, so that if ever it came to be sold the amount advanced by the Government would be at the disposal of the public for any other public purpose. He did not anticipate such a result, but believed the Home would increase. With respect to what had been said by the hon. member Mr. Cavenagh, the institution had been self-supporting except to the extent of £40 or £50, and after the erection of this new dormitory, which would afford accommodation for twenty-four more persons, he had no doubt next year it would be completely self-supporting. The hon. member Mr. Pearce was right in saying that the destitute were to some extent relieved by the Home. There had been seventy-eight cases in which bushmen had been relieved by it, who otherwise must have gone to the Asylum. He believed the Destitute Asylum and the Hospital would be relieved to a very large extent by the Club, for the habits of industry and sobriety inculcated there would prevent them going to those places for some time.

"Mr. Boucaut did not anticipate the Home would become a failure, and should give the hon. member for East Adelaide his warmest support, but it was the duty of the House to see that money voted from the public purse should not in the event of any possible failure of the institution fall into private hands. Such things had happened, and it was the duty of the Government to see that that possibility was guarded against. He would ask the hon. member to amend his motion further by adding 'such sum to be paid on the

Attorney-General being satisfied with the trusts declared in respect of the said Bushmen's Home.'

"Mr. Murray had no objection to the amendment.

"Mr. Duffield exceedingly regretted that the hon. member had brought forward this motion, as he thought there was spirit enough in the people to carry on the Bushmen's Home without appealing to the public treasury. When applied to he gave subscriptions according to his means, and he believed equally with other people; but if as soon as they had got all they could out of him and others in private subscriptions, the persons acting in the matter put their hands in the public purse, the faith of the public in subscribing to such institutions would be destroyed. In the form the matter would take with the last amendment, he was not sure the Bushmen's Home would not become a Government institution. Why should they not just as much support a common Labourers' Home, or a Carpenters' Home? The system was one which could not be consistently carried out in legislation, and he should oppose the motion.

"Mr. Coglin was surprised at the speech of the hon. member Mr. Duffield, after he had made an application and obtained a subsidy for a magnificent building within a quarter of a mile of his own house—the Gawler Institute. He was very much surprised that the hon. member, who he thought had a kind social good feeling to society and his fellow men, should have made such a speech. He hoped, after the very judicious amendment of the hon. member Mr. Boucaut, that the Government would support the motion. When a number of unfortunate men who came down, instead of going to various hotels and elsewhere, could have a good, moral, abstemious, and religious establishment superintended by a man like 'William'—he had never seen him, but he always read of good men and their works—the Government should give their aid, and he was sure the colonists would highly applaud their action.

"The motion for this grant to the Bushmen's Club was carried."

On the 13th October the following pleasing announcement was made in the *Evening Journal* :—

"BUSHMEN'S CLUB.—We are informed by 'William,' the Honorary Superintendent of the Club, that the Hon. T. Elder has promised the handsome donation of £100 to the funds. This is an example which may well be followed by other wealthy gentlemen interested in the welfare of the bushmen of South Australia."

It is presumed that this gift of Mr. Elder's was in lieu of his share of the piece of land formerly promised to the Committee, but in consequence of the conditions not being fulfilled by the other two persons interested in the land the matter fell through.

The following correspondence will speak for itself :—

"THE BUSHMEN'S HOME AND THE LABOUR OFFICES.
"TO THE EDITOR.

"Sir—Having an order for shearers, I could not get my complement, so I went to the Bushmen's Home, and enquired if there was any there to be had. I was told by the Superintendent there were none in the Home, when one man stepped up and said there were several shearers wanted work. I offered to engage them, but the Superintendent stated that it was not the rule to supply men for another labour office. May I ask if those men are to be kept idle because they belong to the Home?

"I am, Sir, &c.,
"R. GASON.

"Labour Office, Hindley-street, west."

"THE BUSHMEN'S CLUB AND THE LABOUR OFFICES.
"TO THE EDITOR.

"Sir— In reply to R. Gason's' letter about labour offices, &c., in this evening's *Express*, we respectfully beg that you will set the matter in its true light before the public.

"The case was as follows :—Gason called at the Club on the evening of the 10th instant, about 7 p.m. There were but six bushmen (all told) stopping at the Club that night. This being shearing season, the men are away at their work. Four of those were invalids, the other two were down in the city at the time. One of them, who is a drover, had but that day arrived from the bush; the other was not a shearer. We were present at the time Gason called and made his request. 'William' told him that he did not think there were any shearers at all in the Club just then, but as the inmates would most likely be altogether at breakfast on the following morning he would then ask, and if any were willing to undertake such work he would send them to Gason's office, and Gason left on this understanding.

"We may also add that 'William' did send one man named MacDonald to his office yesterday morning, thinking that, though no shearer, he might do for a knock-about hand. Gason's reasons for making such a statement about the Bushmen's Club, &c., is best known to himself.

"We are, Sir, &c.,
"THOMAS WARD.
"ARCHIBALD DUNCAN.
"'WILLIAM,' Superintendent of Club.
"October 12, 1871."

An allusion has formerly been made to a movement started in the sister colony of Western Australia to initiate a similar institution for the use of the bushmen of that colony, similar to the one established in South Australia. We clip the following short note on the subject from the *Adelaide Observer* of 14th October, and a few extracts from letters which have been published in the *Perth Magazine*, Western Australia:—

"BUSHMEN'S CLUB.—We see from the *Church of England Magazine*, a monthly publication issued at Perth, Western Australia, that Mr. E. H. Laurance, R.M., who acknowledges his indebtedness to 'William,' the Hon. Superintendent of the Adelaide Bushmen's Home, for documents, reports, rules, and useful information bearing upon the institutions, is, in a series of letters, urging upon the people of the adjoining colony the desirability of establishing a similar Home. The writer deals exhaustively with the subject, and the imitation of South Australia that he in this matter advises might well be thought of by the inhabitants of more prosperous provinces.—First voice from Western Australia."

"BUSHMEN'S HOME.

"TO THE EDITOR OF THE 'CHURCH OF ENGLAND MAGAZINE.'

"Sir—The subject of Bushmen's Homes is one to which my attention has been drawn during the past year, by witnessing the great disadvantages under which a working man labours when out of employment, or on a visit from the bush to the more settled parts of the colony. I therefore beg a small space in your pages to put before the public the want that exists in this colony in this respect, the outline of a scheme to meet the want, and a few particulars of the success which has attended the establishment of such an institution in South Australia. I do this in the hope that attention will be drawn to the subject, and that, among the many charitable and philanthropic objects which call for the sympathy and aid of Christians in this colony, the bushmen and other labourers may receive a share of sympathy in the temptations that surround them, and of assistance towards the amelioration of their physical, moral, and religious condition.

"It could hardly fail to strike one whose duty it becomes frequently to punish drunkenness and other lawlessness, that very little—might I say 'nothing?'—is done to give an opportunity to these casual visitors to our towns to avoid the temptations that await them. Shepherds, labourers, and other bushmen—either out of employment or on a holiday—have the strongest inducements to dissipate their earnings in drink; they have little alternative but to lodge at a public-house, or an even worse haunt—a low boarding-house. There are always 'chums' on the watch for them and their money, and it is a sadly frequent and notorious fact that large sums of money—£20, £30, £40, and even more—are speedily run through on such occasions. When the spree is over (with, too often, a climax of imprisonment), these men return to their work worse in pocket, body, and soul, to repeat the process at intervals.

"The law punishes them for drunkenness, but cannot directly reward them for sobriety; the public-house decks itself with meretricious attractions for their enticements, and boon companions eagerly welcome them, while no counter attraction exists. Society condemns them as degraded, improvident, hardened rioters, and 'passes by on the other side,' like the Pharisee of old. What have we ever done as a community, or as individuals, to stretch out a rescuing hand?

"It is true that for the residents in the towns, Working Men's Associations and Mechanics' Institutes afford opportunity of improvement, and a means of spending leisure hours profitably; but these agencies cannot be expected to reach the class to which I allude—the occasional visitors to towns—and would be insufficient to meet their need, even if the men would use them.

"Let any one seriously ask himself what a bushman is to do when he comes into town—where is he to go—with whom is he to associate—what amusements and enjoyments is he to obtain? Is it not almost inevitable that he will go to the haunts where alone he finds a welcome—a flaring bar or the secret slum? That he will associate with those who give him a hearty greeting? That he will enter into vicious enjoyments and amusements since no virtuous pleasures are offered to him? And that loss of money, health, and self-respect must be the end? How can he help it? Should we be likely to do otherwise were we placed in his position? Unless restrained by strong feelings of piety, he must follow the multitude, because no effort is made to lead him to better things.

"I am not so sanguine as to suppose a Bushmen's Home would draw away even a majority from the mode of life I have sketched; but on the other hand I cannot doubt that there are men among them who would gladly avail themselves of an escape, which should be made pleasant and profitable to them in every respect, and who would rather save their money, liberty, and their health, if opportunity were afforded them. The fact with which we ought to reproach ourselves is, that they have hardly any alternative but to be vicious.

"In calling attention to the desirability of Bushmen's Homes, it must not be overlooked that the benefits designed to arise from them are not confined to those who would use them as inmates; the squatter, farmer, and mechanic are in reality benefited by whatever contributes to the steadiness, the sobriety, and the vigour of the labourers they employ ; you cannot improve the condition of the one without conducing to the welfare of the other. Nor is it necessary for me here to point out how society at large is advantaged by the prosperity and respectability of the working man. Employers and employed should unite in recognising and helping a project tending to their mutual advantage.

"The idea is no novelty. Sailors' Homes, with similar objects to those I have indicated, exist in a large number of British ports ; great success has marked their efforts ; the English sailor knows that he has a comfortable home at each port where these friendly institutions are in operation ; and in very many cases their existence keeps him from a course of sin. Abundant testimony to their usefulness has been given by public writers and speakers, by officers of the highest rank in the navy, and by numbers of the grateful participators in their benefits.

"Unquestionably there are many difficulties in the way of the establishment of a Home ; the money, the proper superintendence, the enlisting of the interest of the men themselves in the project, are matters which may not easily be attained ; but if we are convinced that the institution is a desideratum, and would be calculated to raise the tone of the labouring classes, the difficulties are not insuperable. Trusting in your next number to give a sketch of the kind of Home that is required, I now leave the subject to the earnest consideration of your readers, and am, Sir,
"Your obedient servant,
"E. H. Laurance, Resident Magistrate,
"August, 1871." "Greenough, W.A.

Letter II. from Western Australia.
"TO THE EDITOR OF THE 'CHURCH OF ENGLAND MAGAZINE.'

"Sir—I propose in this letter to give an outline of an institution such as would meet the want to which I called attention last month. In doing so, I wish to acknowledge that I am indebted for many useful hints to the rules of the South Australian Club before alluded to.

"It is a matter of great importance to the success of such an institution, to enlist the sympathy and co-operation of the class for whom it is designed, by giving them a share in its management. I should like to see many of the elements of a Club introduced into its administration; that the Committee of Management should be elected by the members, and that fixed annual meetings should be held, which would give the members an opportunity of bringing forward any alterations they might desire in the rules or conduct of the Home.

"The main objects will be to secure board and lodging for working men at moderate rates; to provide for them means of healthful and innocent recreation and moral improvement; to act as a Bank of Deposit, where they can leave their savings to be invested, or otherwise taken care of; and to supply a general agency at which they can enquire for work, transact business, and receive other assistance.

"It will, I think, be readily admitted that such an institution must be conducted on temperance principles. If intoxicating liquors were once introduced on the premises, it would be difficult to prevent over-indulgence in them. Equally, of course, it would be absolutely necessary to exclude any man who was the worse for liquor. Innocuous beverages should be sold at the Home to its inmates.

"By using the term 'bushmen' I do not contemplate confining the use of the institution to those who work far away from the settled parts of the colony. The title was suggested by the special wants of that class, but in the towns probably other working men would be the most numerous members.

"The title 'Home' expresses the light in which its members should regard it, that whenever they come into the town or locality where the Home exists, they may look upon it as their regular place of abode. And there is no reason why it should be used by travellers only; there might be permanent lodgers.

"Membership should be obtained by an annual subscription of—say ten shillings. The advantages of membership should be the supply of board and lodging at a lower rate than non-members, the possession of a vote in the election of officers, and the use of the deposit and agency branch.

"The Home should provide board and lodging for non-members at moderate rates.

"Strict rules as to cleanliness, sobriety, regular hours for meals, and submission to the Superintendent in matters of order, would have to be drawn up, but this is not the place to suggest all the details. A paid Superintendent, upon whom thorough dependence could be placed, is a primary requisite; a married man, whose wife could act as a housekeeper, would be most suitable.

"The smallest accommodation that would do to start with would comprise a room for meals, reading-room, store-room, kitchen, two rooms for the Superintendent, and a dormitory, which might be divided by partitions, and should contain not less than six beds. There are many other apartments which suggest themselves as desirable, and of course the sleeping accommodation would have to depend on the demand, but the above might suffice at first.

"The reading-room should be furnished with papers and periodicals, writing materials, chess and other games, and in course of time a library. This room might be made available to non-members by the payment of a small subscription, so that men with homes of their own could make use of it, with advantage to the funds of the Home, and no additional expense.

"The Superintendent should be under the control of the Committee of Management, and receive directions from them as to the conducting of the Home. His authority should be recognised and supported by the members. It would be his duty to receive the deposits of money, to take charge of clothing and other property of members that they might desire to leave at the Home, to afford them assistance when possible by receiving and forwarding letters for them, and giving information as to situations, &c.

"From the above it will be seen that the first outlay will comprise the procuring and fitting up of a house, and the pay of a Superintendent and a female servant. It may be hoped that the Home would become self-supporting after a time, by means of members' subscriptions and a small margin of profit on the victualling; but it would certainly need considerable external aid at first. The Superintendent must be a man of intelligence and respectability, and at all times ready for his duties, but he might combine other occupation with them. If he were a mechanic he could work at his trade, and, receiving board and lodging at the Home, he need not be otherwise very highly remunerated. In country places, where expenses would be greater and patronage less regular, the institution should have land attached to it, to be farmed for the benefit of the Home, or by the Superintendent for his maintenance.

"The foregoing is an outline of a Home for working men on the most economical scale practicable. I have spoken on this subject to several bushmen, sandalwood cutters, and others, some of whom are now in the habit of running through their earnings in the manner related in my last letter. When the folly of their course is pointed out to them, they readily admit it, but naturally reply that they have no other amusements, and no place but the public-house to go to. They profess that they would gladly avail themselves of a Home; they see what a difference it would make in their comfort and their pockets; they allow that the greater part of their money goes for the gratification of their greedy associates, and that in every sense they are spending 'money for that which is not bread.' At Dongarra (Irwin) this state of things is painfully prevalent; bush labourers congregate more there than at the Greenough, and there is more money afloat; the amount that finds its way into the public-house is sadly large. I wish I could see the way to start a Home there.

"I must not make any further demand on your space this month, but will endeavour to supply your next number with a brief account of the establishment and progress of the Club in Adelaide, gathered from newspapers and other documents kindly forwarded to me by the Superintendent.

"I am, Sir,
"Yours faithfully,
"E. H. LAURANCE.

"September, 1871."

Extract from the Third Letter from Western Australia.

"TO THE EDITOR OF THE 'CHURCH OF ENGLAND MAGAZINE.'

"Sir—I have now to give you a few interesting and encouraging particulars regarding the Bushmen's Club in Adelaide, collected from circulars and newspapers furnished to me by 'William,' the Superintendent.

"In January, 1869, a committee, collected together by J. H. Angas, Esq., and 'William,' presided over by the Hon. T. Elder, M.L.C., was formed, and a prospectus was issued and widely circulated. This prospectus gave an outline of what it was proposed to do, and called upon the bushmen themselves to give it their support. In addition a well-known bush missionary (who goes by the name of 'William' and by that name alone) went round to the various stations, addressing the bushmen at each place on the subject, and giving them full information as to the objects and plans proposed.

"And here, and indeed throughout the undertaking, the devoted services of this Christian man form a prominent feature, and were of exceeding benefit to the scheme. 'William' had previously been among the bushmen, and by his earnest addresses and evident interest in their welfare, had won their confidence. With his more direct efforts to benefit their souls he combined a care for their moral and physical improvement, and went about it in the name of Christ and with the blessing of God. We may lack the help of such a 'William,' but let us hope that many, imbued with his spirit, will give such hearty co-operation as may be in their power.

"Another circumstance in favour of South Australia is its larger population and better means of travelling; the railway renders Adelaide much more a rendezvous and resort for bushmen out of work or on a holiday than any town in this colony can at present be. At first it was intended to establish the Home at the Burra, but the advantages of the capital soon caused Adelaide to be chosen in preference.

"The movement was, naturally, not unopposed; there were many who had an interest in keeping things as they were, and getting the earnings of the men into the public-house; there were some bushmen who opposed it as they would have fought against any good work; and there were others who were persuaded by the above that it was a plan to interfere with their wages and their freedom. But there seems to have been a large number who gladly hailed the project, and readily came forward to patronise it. As the self-governing nature of the institution became better understood, the false objections gave way. With the prospectuses circulars were issued requesting subscriptions, and many of these were returned with promises of contributions.

"In December, 1869, a large meeting was held, the Mayor of Adelaide in the chair, and Bishop Short being among the speakers. At that time £646 had been received, and it was mentioned, as a satisfactory proof of the interest taken by the bushmen themselves, that 1,067 persons on stations had contributed. At this meeting it was resolved to start the Club.

"Among the papers sent to me is a printed statement of the constitution of the Club and its rules and regulations. The Board of Management consists of three persons annually elected by the members; the Superintendent is appointed by them. There are also three Trustees. The yearly payment for membership is five shillings. The rules specify the charges for board and lodging and the hours for meals, and provide for the orderly conduct of the Club in other respects.

"Up to June a building was rented at £110 per annum. The success of the institution being then such as to give fair prospect of its permanency, it was resolved to purchase the property hitherto rented. The price was £1,000, of which about £500 was available. By donations of £100 each from Messrs. G. F. and J. H. Angas, and a loan of £500 for twelve months without interest from the former, the purchase was effected, and necessary additions were made. 'William' had also guaranteed his gratuitous services for two years, and the Club is in a most favourable position. The current expenses are met by the regular income. Besides the regular amusements—such as chess, draughts, &c., provided in the reading-room, special recreations in the way of lectures, debates, singing, &c., are contemplated. On Sundays the Superintendent holds services in the reading-room for those who cannot or will not go to church; and Sunday is observed with every mark of respect in the management of the Club. The food is unexceptionable, and plenty of refreshment is available during the day, but intoxicating drinks are prohibited; so is gambling and profane language.

"Such is the Bushmen's Club in Adelaide, and surely it affords encouragement to those who desire to establish similar institutions.

"I have entered at some length into its statistics, because I think they will be interesting to your readers, and will prove that the idea is not impracticable even in Western Australia. The documents in my possession contain further details which I shall be glad to communicate to any one who wishes for them.

"I have sent to England appeals on this subject, and hope to get promises of aid which may warrant the formation of a definite plan. But the people of this colony ought hardly to require extraneous help, and when it is considered how large a sum is spent by the working men in drink, it is clear there are sources from which money might be profitably drawn.

"In concluding these letters, I trust the suggestions will bear fruit in a hearty effort to do something for a class much tempted and much neglected, and I feel satisfied that the bushmen themselves will not be backward in co-operating when the proposal is put before them in a clear and definite shape.

"I am, Sir,
"Yours faithfully,
"E. H. LAURANCE, Resident Magistrate.
"Greenough Flats, Sept. 13, 1871."

The following pleasing communication has been taken from the *Express's* Parliamentary report of October 18, 1871:—

"Among the Messages from the Governor (borne by Mr. Morris, A.D.C.), there is one informing the House, in reply to Address No. 10, that he had caused the sum of £500 to be placed on the Estimates for 1872 for the purpose of supplementing contributions for the enlargement of the building now used as the Bushmen's Home."

A meeting of the Board was summoned for November 2nd, but in consequence of urgent business affairs a quorum was not obtained.

On the 23rd November the following appeared in the *Express*:—

"We had occasion a short time ago to chronicle the pleasing fact that the Hon. T. Elder, M.L.C., had generously promised £100 to aid in supplementing the Government grant of £500 lately voted (conditionally) by Parliament to the Bushmen's Club. We have now to mention that Captain W. W. Hughes has also promised £100 for the same purpose. 'William' begs to acknowledge, through our columns, with thanks, the receipt, through Mr. N. Blyth, of £5 from W. H. Charnock, Esq. As there is £500 to be raised by private subscriptions, in order to obtain the promised grant of a like sum, it is much to be desired that the stockholders and flockmasters, and friends to the bushmen's cause generally, will not be backward to assist in making up the required amount. The Club is about to sustain a great loss in the wise counsel and valuable help of Mr. N. Blyth, who retires from the Board of Management, after his second year's gratuitous services, through press of other engagements. Messrs. C. B. Young and H. Giles have, however, kindly consented to act again with another gentleman who will be nominated in place of Mr. Blyth at the annual general meeting to be held shortly. As these gentlemen have had experience in the working of the Club, and prosperity has hitherto crowned their efforts, they are better able to understand the various details of the institution than strangers, and it is felt that the interests of the entire class of bushmen and their Club could not, in its present transitory stage, be placed in better hands. Mr. J. H. Angas has expressed a wish to consider the bushmen's picnic this year as his own treat to them, and will relieve the management from expense on that score. This is a thoughtful and a gracious act on Mr. Angas's part, as it would be unseemly—not to say impolitic—to give a picnic while the Club was wanting funds. It is hoped that all true bushmen in town, whether inmates or not of the institution, and their friends will rally round the Club and join their fellow-bushmen on the appointed day, and make the picnic and the meeting—both to be held on the same day — a complete success."

On December 1 the meeting of the Board of Management was held. There were present Messrs. C. B. Young (chair) and H. Giles.

Bills, vouchers, &c., were called over and found correct. The Hon. Superintendent suggested the desirability of fitting up the dormitory and laying on gas; also the propriety of making some arrangements about sending destitute sick bushmen to the hospital (as hitherto he had been much indebted to private friends for their assistance—especially Messrs. G. F. and J. H. Angas, James Smith, and Dr. Mayo); also that it would be well to follow up the Hon. Captain Hart's suggestion respecting the free labour-office for the city, and that the best way to compass this matter would be to hire an office in town connected with the institution.

Total receipts for the month October, £118. Total receipts for the month November, £125 10s. Total number of tickets issued to date, 627.

The Hon. Superintendent reported that in November he sent a short advertisement to the *Mount Gambier Standard*, calling attention to the fact that an acting agent had been sent through the South-Eastern portion of the colony to collect subscriptions for the Club in Adelaide. That on the 14th November the new dormitory was passed as finished by the architect; that the gas had been laid on, and the fencing nearly completed. That the auditors should be warned that the accounts of the Club would be closed on the 9th December next. That he had written to Mr. J. H. Angas, asking him to preside at the annual meeting to be held on the 22nd of the next month : Mr. Angas not only consented to do so, but wished the picnic this year to be considered his own treat to the men. That Mr. W. H. Charnock had presented £5 to the Club through N. Blyth, Esq. That Mr. S. Davenport had agreed to serve on the Board of Management in place of N. Blyth, Esq., who retires through press of business. That Mr. Boothby had been supplied with the names of the office-bearers of the Club for his directory.

It was resolved by the Board that their next meeting should take place on December 15, to make arrangements for the general meeting.

The following is the notice of the picnic that was held on the day of the annual general meeting :—

"Bushmen's Picnic.

"On the day of the Annual General Meeting—to be held Friday, December 22—a trip to the Bay and supper on return home have been decided upon.

"The party will leave the Club-home, Whitmore-Square, at 8.45 a.m. punctually.

"Provisions, music, and amusements will be provided.

"Bushmen (who are not inmates of the Club) and their friends in town who wish to go with the party, are respectfully invited, and will please send their names, or apply to the Hon. Superintendent on or before the 20th instant, for a free pass for that purpose.

"There will be no charge.

"The meeting will be held (D.V.) in the evening (on the return of the excursionists), at 7 p.m.

"J. H. Angas, Esq., J.P., has again kindly consented to preside.

"'William,' Superintendent, &c.

"Adelaide, Dec. 4, 1871."

Here follows the report of the Bushmen's Club annual picnic and meeting :—

The members of the Bushmen's Club and their friends on Friday, December 22, enjoyed themselves in real good earnest. At a very early hour a number of flags in front of the Club-house gave indication of festivity, and shortly after 8 o'clock visitors began to assemble. Men of bronzed cheek and stalwart frame, who no doubt had long lived in the more retired parts of the colony, seemed to have come to do honour to the promoters of the Club. The invitation to them was a generous and noble one, and they responded in such a way as to show their appreciation of things done in this style. For more than half an hour before starting the band sent forth its enlivening strains, and laughter and pleasant joke passed freely round. Every one seemed happy and free from those influences that so frequently mar enjoyment and turn real pleasure aside. Shortly after 9 o'clock busses from Hill & Co.'s establishment drove up in front of the Club, the 'Leviathan' taking the lead, drawn by six beautiful bays. All being ready, away the party started amidst cheers and music, with banners and gay ribbons floating on the breeze, and after visiting the *Register* and *Advertiser* offices, and the York Hotel, they drove off merrily to the Bay. At the newspaper offices they cheered in acknowledgment of a friendly press, and at the York in honour of Mr. J. H. Angas, M.P., who had so generously provided them with the treat. The excursionists returned to the Club shortly after 6 o'clock, and after partaking of refreshment,

THE ANNUAL MEETING

of the members was held in the dining-room. There were between fifty and sixty bushmen present, and Mr. J. H. Angas, M.P., presided, and in opening the proceedings said in accordance with the advertisements in the daily papers they that evening were about to hold the second annual meeting of the Club. The business of the meeting was principally to lay before them a report of the proceedings of the Club during the past year. It was now three years since a meeting of gentlemen interested in bushmen decided upon the establishment of a Bushmen's Home, and two years ago a large public meeting was held to advance the interests of the undertaking. Since then the Home had been opened, and great progress had been made, it having been necessary to provide additional accommodation. He felt very much encouraged to find that the institution had been so well patronised, and that it had been so very highly spoken of by all the men who had taken up their quarters in the Home. The demand for accommodation had increased, and the report would give a very interesting account of their operations. He hoped that they would go on as encouragingly in the coming year as in the one which had so nearly drawn to a close. Before calling upon Mr. H. Giles to read the report, he mentioned that Mr. Neville Blyth had signified his inability to act upon the Board of Management, and he was sure they would all regret such inability. There was, however, another gentleman — Mr. S. Davenport — who had signified his willingness to occupy the position. It would be for the meeting to elect the Board of Management for the ensuing year. With the exception of Mr. N. Blyth, the whole of the other gentlemen were willing again to fill their positions on the Board, which they had occupied with so much credit to themselves and advantage to the Club. (Applause.) He then called upon

Mr. H. Giles, a member of the Board of Management, to read the annual report as follows :—

"Your Board of Management are highly gratified in being able to lay before you a very cheering report of the progress of the institution during the second year of its existence, and cannot fail to recognise the goodness of God in granting such a measure of success to the undertaking, and congratulate you and all the members of the Bushmen's Club, not only on account of its steadily growing prosperity, but also its increasing popularity among the persons most interested in its establishment.

"We are of opinion that it will be generally conceded by the members and their subscribing friends that there has been much real good work done, and that the labour and expenditure bestowed have, by the favour of Divine Providence, produced their legitimate results.

"At the last annual meeting your Board strongly recommended cordial co-operation among the bushmen and their friends to secure a freehold property for the Club. This we are happy to say has been done in the following manner :— Negotiations were opened with Mr. James Hosking (who held a right of purchase for the property of Sir C. Cooper), and arrangements were made with him to buy the large dwelling-house, a cottage, and outhouses, with sufficient land for the present purposes of the Club, for the sum of £1,000, cash on a given day. £500 was all the available funds in the hands of the Board, but upon stating the matter fully to George Fife Angas, Esq., he very generously placed at the disposal of the Trustees (upon their promissory-note) the sum of £500, without interest for twelve months, to relieve the Club from the dilemma, and thus enabled them to complete the purchase of the property ; and to this gracious act of Mr. Angas, and the liberal donations of the worthy chairman (Mr. J. H. Angas) and the bushmen themselves, may be mainly attributed the present favourable condition of the institution. It at once relieved the management from the heavy rental of £110 annually, which was clogging their movements, and enabled them to make sundry other much needed improvements and alterations. The £500 thus borrowed from Mr. Angas ought to be returned at the end of the twelvemonth, which expires in July next.

"Several applications having been made, it became necessary that more sleeping accommodation should be provided, to meet the increasing demand for room ; but until the freehold was secured the Board were not prepared to take action for supplying this great need ; so soon, however, as the deeds were handed over, a meeting of the Trustees and Board of Management was held in August last, when plans of a dormitory were examined, and that of Mr. James Cumming, architect, adopted ; but it was considered prudent to postpone further action until £400 could be raised.

"On September 5 another meeting was held, the matter being pressing, and it was resolved to erect the whole or half of the proposed addition, the Board undertaking to act as a Building Committee, being guided in their decision by the sum received. In a very short time, through the liberality of Messrs. Angas, Elder, Hughes, and a few other friends, the Board determined to add the dormitory (complete) to the western portion of the premises. Mr. Farr's tender for building—£440—being accepted, a good substantial stone building was soon raised. Its dimensions are—length, 56 feet ; breadth, 25 feet ; height, 13 feet to wallplate ; it is light, airy, well ventilated, is a credit to the architect and builder, and an ornament to the city ; it contains 20 separate sleeping apartments ; the walls are of Glen Osmond stone, with cement dressings ; the roof of galvanized iron. The foundation-stone was formally laid by D. Murray, Esq., M.P., on the 23rd September last, Mr. C. B. Young being present. The building was passed as finished and occupied on November 14. So far as these rooms go, each inmate will be enabled to get a plainly furnished separate sleeping apartment (with capacious lavatory attached), and if he so chooses can keep his own key whilst in town. The new building, by giving more space, adds very much to the comfort of the inmates, and there is already a cry-out for more rooms of the same description. A larger dining-room will soon be urgently required. On the suggestion of Mr. J. H. Angas, on 5th September last a petition was drawn up by Mr. Young to the Parliament, and presented by Mr. Glyde, M.P., asking for a supplementary grant of £500 to aid the promoters; and in October His Excellency sent a message to the House, that he had caused that sum to be placed on the Estimates for 1872 for enlargement of the building. It is to be hoped that this sum (when received) will place the Club in a still better position, and enable it to free itself from all encumbrances.

"A policy of insurance has been executed in the Imperial Office on the building for the sum of £800, and the furniture has also been insured for £300 in the Marine Office.

"There have been 355 tickets of membership issued during the last twelve months; the number reported last year was 285. These, added together, make a total of 640 issued since the opening of the Club in May, 1870. There are now good on the books 357. As might have been reasonably expected, many of the first year's members have failed to renew their tickets, the causes being deaths, marriages, departure to other colonies, want of opportunity, &c. On the other hand many new members are joining the Club.

"Last year it was reported that complete accommodation was provided for twenty-four persons. We are in a position to state that provision is now made to accommodate nearly double that number, there being forty-seven beds (including servants') made up in the Home and new dormitory, &c., combined, and ready for use in case of emergency.

"In the labour-department very little business has been done beyond making employers acquainted with the fact that there is a labour-office connected with the institution. This, no doubt, is to be accounted for in the following manner:— There are very few single men hired for the stations in the city. Large numbers of men travel the country at all seasons of the year in search of employment, and any vacancy that may occur upon a run is generally filled up from their ranks.

"During the debate on the Government grant in the House, allusion was made by Captain Hart to the desirability of establishing a free labour-office in connection with the Bushmen's Club, similar to the Shipping Master's office in the Seamen's Home. The Board suggest that when the Club is further advanced it may be desirable to rent an office suitable for the work in a good business portion of the city, and work it in connection with this Club. But this is a subject for further consideration after the matter has been well ventilated, and its necessity fully ascertained.

"The postal department in connection with the Club, and especially the plan adopted of advertising all unclaimed letters monthly, has proved a very great boon, and supplied a want long felt among the migrating bushmen, they having by this means sort of head-quarters where their letters, &c., can be addressed to them, thus enabling many of them to communicate with their friends, which they have been unable to do in some instances for many years before, having no settled abode.

"A large number of letters, papers, book parcels, &c., have passed through the Club to their destination (or retained, as desired); and, in instances where the parties are not found, they have been returned to the General Post Office after having been kept a reasonable time.

"Respecting the Savings branch, the following account will best speak for itself:—The total amount of property deposited by bushmen with the Hon. Superintendent for safe keeping during the past year (1871), in cheques, drafts, pass-books, cash, &c., amounted to the large sum of £4,900 0s. 5d. There was drawn out by instalments £3,865 19s. 2d., leaving £1,034 1s. 3d. still in custody. The following comparative statement will better show the state of affairs :—
1871—deposited, £4,900 0s. 5d.; repaid, £3,865 19s. 2d.; property left on hand, £1,034 1s. 3d. 1870—deposited, £1,372 16s. 2½d.; repaid, £1,213 17s. 8½d.; property left on hand, £159 4s. 6d. Increase, 1871—deposited, £3,527 4s. 2½d.; repaid, £2,652 1s. 5½d.; property left on hand,

£874 16s. 9d. Total since opening of the Club—deposited, £6,272 16s. 7½d. ; repaid, £4,079 16s. 10½d. ; property left on hand, £1,193 5s. 9d.

"Add to this the chests, swags, parcels of clothes, &c., of fifty different persons at present scattered throughout the colony to their work, and it must be admitted that these facts speak volumes in favour of the institution, showing the trust and confidence reposed in it by the men. It is a crucial test from which there can be no appeal. If the Club were not appreciated by the bushmen (as a rule), it is not reasonable that they would entrust their hard earnings in this manner. If the promoters continue steadily to show a firm front, prejudice and opposition will hide their heads and eventually die out.

"There are now belonging to the library 191 volumes. The number of books has been doubled since last year's report. There have also been some periodicals and files of papers added. We would avail ourselves of this opportunity to thank the kind friends who have so generously presented books, newspapers, and periodicals. They have been indeed both instructive and interesting, and very acceptable.

"The total number of weekly boarders during the past year was 361 ; casual boarders, about 500 ; travelling bushmen relieved, 35. The highest number of inmates at one time in the Club, 33.

"There have been several cases of death in the Hospital of bushmen belonging to the Club. This is to be accounted for in the following manner :—In most cases they remain too long in the bush when diseased without medical help, consequently the disease gets past remedy before the patient gets to town. Two only have left any property at the Club ; one named Kelly left £14 16s., and being entirely friendless this amount was paid over to the Curator of Intestate Estates ; the other, A. Anderson (a married man), his money and effects were sent to his wife and family. In each case a proper receipt was taken. Two others have been sent to the Lunatic Asylum ; one named Thos. Johnstone (*alias* Editor) was sent through the Hospital, and has since died, the other by doctor's certificate. We would here suggest the advisability of making arrangements with the authorities for provision in the Hospital for destitute sick bushmen when they come to town. Hitherto their admission has been obtained through the benevolence of ticket-holders. The Messrs. Angas have generously sent tickets and orders to 'William' for this and other medical purposes; but we would be glad to see a claim upon the Hospital, either by paying an annual sum to that institution, or otherwise.

"Many circulars and subscription-lists have been sent to the stations during the past year, and an agent was also sent to the various sheds during the shearing season to obtain subscriptions, with small results. The amounts received have been advertised monthly.

"There is still prejudice existing among some bushmen, and false reports made by captious individuals; so much so, that bushmen appear now to disregard anything that may be said about the institution, and content themselves by paying the Club a visit and trying it for themselves.

"On the first establishment of the Club at Whitmore-square, it was supposed by many that there would be a difficulty about the distance from the business part of the city. This idea is fast losing ground among the members of the Club. They find that, after a healthy invigorating walk of five or seven minutes, they can be in the bustle and turmoil of the city, and when tired of it they can retreat to the quietude of their present comfortable home.

"It is right on this fitting occasion to remember the painstaking preliminary Committee, and heartily to acknowledge our thanks to them all as the means, under God, of establishing this useful institution. It must be very gratifying to them to find their undaunted perseverance crowned with success; and we may hope that, through the Divine blessing, the Bushmen's Club of South Australia will yet extend its influence and usefulness to the neighbouring colonies, especially now the experiment has been fairly—and so far successfully—tried here.

"Though the Club is in such a favourable progressive state, the friends of the cause must not relax their efforts, for there remain many improvements to make, and much work to be done.

"We cannot conclude this report without bearing testimony to the valuable services rendered to this institution by the press generally, and we trust that kindly feelings may ever exist between this free, enlightened, and powerful friend and the Bushmen's Club.

"In conclusion, we suggest that it is desirable for the better working of the establishment, that the accompanying new rules, &c., should meet with the approbation of this meeting, and be hereafter incorporated with those already in existence.

"The following is a summary of the most important movements made and improvements done on the property during the last year:—The property for the Club has been purchased, a new dormitory built, fitted up, and furnished. The accommodation has been increased from sufficient for twenty-four up to forty-seven. Three sides of the property has been newly fenced. The drainage has been re-arranged and improved. The garden and walks are now undergoing a like process. Painting, whitewashing, &c., where necessary, done. A new Flavel's kitchener has been put up at a cost of over £20, and other minor affairs too numerous to particularise in a document of this kind.

"The statement of receipts and expenditure, amongst other items, showed a balance in hand to December, 1870, of £564 18s. 9d.; received for board and lodging, £685 9s. 3d.; subscriptions, donations, tickets, &c., £607 13s. 2d.; loan from Mr. G. F. Angas, £500, free of interest; overdraft at Bank, £231 1s. 5d.; interest, £27 19s. 5d. The expenditure embraced house expenses, £952 16s.; building, £449 2s. 11d.; purchase of premises, £1,000; fees returned by the Board of Management, £27 13s. 1d.; printing and stationery, £67 7s. 2d.; law charges, &c., £16 3s. 5d.; cash in hand, £45 4s. 11d. The balance-sheet showed—land and buildings, £1,600; donation from Mr. W. W. Hughes, £100; furniture, £309. The liabilities represented — overdraft at Bank, £231 1s. 5d.; accounts due, £45 6s. 1d.; loan from Mr. Angas, £500. Credit balance, £1,232 12s. 6d."

The Chairman said they had heard the report read, and he was sure it must be satisfactory to every member of the Club. (Applause.) He felt highly gratified at hearing of such encouraging results, and he trusted that the bushmen would not allow the Club to stand still, but that every member would do his utmost for the advancement of its interests. They had heard what had been done, and he hoped in their intercourse with bushmen they would try to make known the good the Club has effected. The promoters did not wish to puff up the Club, but were desirous of proving it to be an advantage to bushmen. He thought the fact that during the current year nearly £5,000 had been entrusted to the care of their excellent Superintendent, 'William,'—(cheers)—for depositing in the Savings Bank, spoke volumes for the institution. He really never thought that in two years they would have such a large sum of money brought to the Club for safe custody by bushmen visiting Adelaide. The Club was vested in three Trustees, and was brought under the Real Property Act, and could not be devoted to any other purpose but that of a Bushmen's Club, so that all the members would participate in all the investments that were made and in the results that would accrue from an establishment of its character. He believed that in Victoria a similar undertaking was being initiated, although he thought South Australia was the only one of the colonies which had in operation a Bushmen's Club. By the zealous efforts of "William" much information had been circulated, but nothing further had been done in the other colonies beyond receiving it, although he believed that at Bendigo a Bushmen's Club was about to be started. (Applause.) He trusted that by the experience they would gain through the South Australian Club they would be materially benefited, and that their institution might be largely patronised by the class for whom it was intended.

Mr. D. Murray moved—"That the very satisfactory report and financial statement now read be adopted and published, for the information of absent members and friends of the bushmen's cause, under the direction of the Board of Management." After the very valuable report they had heard, he thought they would feel that it was quite unnecessary for him to occupy much of their time with remarks. He believed they would all admit that the Club was in a most flourishing state, and their financial position could only lead them to rejoice in the success of the work. (Applause.) One thing that tended to make the Club popular was the comfort to be found in it. He had had considerable experience in travelling in the colony, and in contrasting some of the hotels and boarding-houses with the comfort and convenience found in the Club in the various departments; he could not but feel that every bushman that visited the Club would prefer to cast his lot amongst them, rather than go elsewhere. . He considered that the Club was appreciated very highly by the bushmen—(hear, hear)—and he believed when its benefits became more known it would receive more patronage. The Club was a credit to the members, and an ornament to the city. He was deeply gratified to find the necessity for an extension in the premises, and he thought they should have a larger dining-room. The new dormitories appeared to be perfect—being airy, clean, light, and comfortable. The first necessity for comfort was good sleeping accommodation, and he thought it would be better, if they contemplated extending the premises, to provide more dormitories, rather than a dining-hall. The Savings Bank in connection with the Club augured well, and the number of tickets (355) which had been issued was a proof of its usefulness, and he had no doubt that those bushmen who had not yet gone into the Club would feel the necessity of visiting it. Referring to the promised grant-in-aid of £500 from the Government, he said it would be given conditionally upon a similar amount being raised by the Club. He was glad to say that about half the required amount had been raised, and he had no doubt the other half would be made up shortly. He trusted that at the end of next year the Club would have all assets and no liabilities. (Applause.) He suggested that in future they should have an account of the amount received from the boarders as against the household disbursements for the day, so that they might see if the Club paid for itself. He thought the Club was paying its expenses, and that it would not require the aid of subscriptions. (Applause.)

Mr. C. Sabine seconded the motion with great pleasure, as it afforded him immense gratification to see the results of the labours of the Committee and their own exertions, as shown by the balance-sheet laid before them. He concurred with Mr. Murray that it would be more satisfactory if the balance between the receipts for boarders and the current household expenses were shown. The receipts at present appeared to be £770, and the expenditure for provisions, rent, wages, &c., £952. He thought there was cause for gratification at the small difference, and he believed next year, when the Club would have no rent to pay, that it would be a great success. He was glad there was likely to be a labour-office in connection with the Club in a more central portion of the city, as it would be a material help and convenience to bushmen and employers. He was glad also that Parliament was likely to give a grant of £500. It showed that bushmen were not going to be despised, but that they were likely to occupy a higher position in the social scale. He was pleased that their chairman had been returned to Parliament, and in the re-arrangement of the electoral districts he hoped that they would send into Parliament such men as would be able to advance their interests. (Applause.)

The motion was carried unanimously.

The Rev. James Lyall moved—"That the success which has attended the operations of the Bushmen's Club in the past demand from this meeting an expression of devout thanks to God, and lays a double obligation upon the bushmen and their friends to further the enterprise, not only in South Australia, but in all the sister colonies." He expressed his thorough interest in the welfare of the Club, and said he was present at the time when the undertaking was initiated, and he had been delighted from time to time to hear of its success and prosperity. He felt extremely gratified at the decided success of the institution, notwithstanding the many prejudices which had been awakened from every quarter. These, however, had been overcome, and the Club's success afforded encouragement for the establishment of similar institutions in this or the other colonies. He thought they should render their thanks to God for their success, and that it was a most suitable sentiment to give expression to at the close of such a day. He had long felt an interest in bushmen, and had often wished that the ministers in the city could get away more frequently to speak to them in the bush. When younger, he had preached to them with the greatest pleasure. They had achieved good results, and he was sure better things could not be done than that they should try to bring others to share in the benefits which he felt they so largely appreciated. (Cheers.)

Mr. H. Hussey seconded the motion, remarking that it contained sentiments that he approved, and which he was glad had been embodied in a resolution. They were called upon to thank God, and he thought that each bushman should remember that the undertaking was initiated by a man who had great faith in God, and that unless he had had faith it would not have been a success. With the co-operation of " William" he had been inspired to do a little, whilst others had done much, and " William" had abundantly proved the force of the sentiment, " Faith laughs at impossibilities and says it *must* be done." He trusted that God's blessing might still attend the labours of those connected with the Club, which he believed would be a lasting benefit to bushmen and to the colony.

The motion having been carried, a series of rules for the better government of the institution were discussed *seriatim* and adopted.

Mr. Thomas Knowles, one of the bushmen, moved— " That the thanks of the bushmen generally, and of the members of this Club particularly, are hereby presented to the Trustees—Messrs. J. H. Angas, D. Murray, and W. K. Thomas; to the Board of Management—Messrs. N. Blyth, C. B. Young, and H. Giles; to the Auditors—Messrs. D. Robin and C. Birks; and to the generous donors—Messrs. G. F. Angas, T. Elder, W. W. Hughes, and many other kind friends, for their unremitting exertions and practical sympathy with this movement on the bushmen's behalf; and that the following gentlemen now nominated be appointed as a Board of Management for the ensuing year:—Messrs. S. Davenport, C. B. Young, and H. Giles."

Mr. Charles Lewis, also one of the members, seconded the motion, which was carried without a dissentient.

Mr. D. Murray acknowledged the vote of thanks on behalf of the trustees, although he said their duties had been uncommonly easy, whilst he was sure their thanks were well deserving to those who had carried on the work. (Cheers.) The trustees felt a deep interest in the Club, and it had been their desire to carry out their functions so as to advance its success. (Applause.)

Mr. C. B. Young also returned thanks on behalf of the Board of Management. His duties on the Board had always been of a pleasurable character, because everything from the first had gone on so smoothly. They had been aided by gentlemen of ample means, whilst they had received liberal support from the public and the Parliament. He was also gratified at the success they had met with, and he was sure it must be pleasing to the office-bearers. There was one thing he should like to see provided, and that was a distribution in the bush of a better class of books. He knew the majority of bushmen were fond of reading, but he regretted that the principal class of literature in circulation was not of a desirable character. He was sure a different class of literature would be greatly appreciated by bushmen, but he did not know whether the Club could take the matter in hand. He hardly thought so, but he believed they could secure a travelling agent, who might have a circulating library, or could supply books at a little above cost price. The Trustees had worked harmoniously together, and he was sure they deserved more credit than Mr. Murray would have them believe.

The Honorary Superintendent "William" then read the following address :—

"Mr. Chairman and Gentlemen—There are one or two matters connected with the best interests of the bushmen which, with your kind permission, I will bring before this meeting. The first, and, I may venture to say, the most important, is the necessity of initiating or organising some kind of Benefit Society in connection with this institution, and raising a fund for the purpose of pensioning—if I may use the term—old and worn-out bushmen, in this way inducing them while young to provide for their declining years, and also for relieving cases of sickness or distress. For my own part, I cannot see that the Club, as a Club, will ever be complete without some such arrangement, and the question now is how to accomplish this object. Its desirability all must, I think, admit; but we have to look, in the second place, to its practicability.

"Several plans have passed in review before my own mind, but none yet sufficiently simple and workable. If the bushmen were a stationary class, the matter would be easy enough to settle; but anyone acquainted with the restless, migratory propensities of bushmen must see that there are apparent insurmountable difficulties to grapple with. Still I have a plan to suggest to this meeting, or rather, I would say, an outline to give, which may tend to ventilate the subject, and may call forth remarks or expressions of opinion from other persons better acquainted with such matters. If it only does this, I shall feel thankful. Now for the plan, such as it is.

"It appears to me that admission into the Society should be by fee according to age (on a graduated scale), and an annual payment afterwards of (say) from £2 to £5 per annum. This might be paid monthly or weekly, or for any number of years in advance, if desired; but whichever it might be, payment should be very strictly enforced upon pain of forfeiture of all former payments or benefit from the Society; only those who paid to its funds should be entitled to its benefits, and no payment should be made to a member until he has been a full year on the books. No one should be admitted (to begin with) in a sickly condition or of known bad character. It might be prudent to open the books of such a society when the names and fees of, say one hundred, were obtained, and it should be brought under the Friendly Societies' Act.

"I would gladly lend my energies to bring about any such a consummation as this, and should feel thankful to any of the secretaries of the different Friendly Societies for further information or advice on this important subject. I may now add that, when time permits, I am engaged in compiling a history of this Bushmen's Club from its very beginning, and intend (D.V.) to publish it when ready—which will be some little time yet—and will give the profits, should there be any, to assist in forming this Benefit Society.

"The next matter is a kind of land speculation. It occurred to me a short time ago that it would be advantageous to the Club could a piece of frontage on Gilbert-street be secured. It would give us a right-of-way southwards, and prevent others from building outhouses, &c., in front and close to the present premises. Should it be found necessary in the course of years to build a new homestead, it would be wise, I think, to have (if possible) sufficient ground on the south of the present building on which to erect it, for the progress of the Club should not be stopped while another building was being put up in the place of the present one. Why should not a new building be erected to face the south, which would be far preferable to facing the hot winds of the north? I merely mention this because a piece of land of any required size can now be purchased at £1 15s. per foot, and it will be too late to 'shut the stable door when the horse is gone.' If a frontage of 80 or 90 feet cannot be obtained, perhaps a right-of-way of 12 or 15 may be. I believe it will enhance the value of the Club property should it ever become necessary to dispose of it. One other subject, and then I have done. We only meet once a year, and God only knows whether we shall meet together again. Time is short, and we must work while it is called day. It has often come under my knowledge that married bush people when they come to town after living in the bush, or when about to change situations, labour under many disadvantages if they have to stop in town for any length of time. They are compelled, if they have no friends to shelter them, to either hire a house or rooms, and furnish it, or stop at an expensive hotel or boarding-house; and this soon swallows up their small savings, and many with their families (should times be dull) become destitute. I should like to see a nest (a row) of small cottages built round the premises—separate from the single men's, of course—and plainly furnished by the Club, which might be rented from the institution for any length of time, and the occupiers might board themselves in any way they liked. This would be, I believe, a great boon to many of the married bush people, and give them a decided interest in the general prosperity of the Club. I would also suggest that when more room is provided, any parents having boys from twelve years old and upwards, able to wash and take care of themselves, might entrust them to the Club to be boarded and schooled at the city schools at a low charge of, say 8s. or 10s. per week."

"William" then proposed a vote of thanks to the Chairman, which was seconded by Mr. H. Giles, and carried with three cheers.

The Chairman, in acknowledging the compliment, expressed his warmest sympathies with bushmen and their Club, referred to the noble character of the institution and the vast benefit that was likely to result from its influence, and spoke in the highest terms of the zeal and indefatigable energy of "William," who declined to labour in the good work otherwise than gratuitously.

The proceedings then terminated.

The following is a copy of the additional new rules, referred to in the annual report, added to those already in existence at the Club:—

To the Constitution clause 3, Rules and Regulations, was added the following, viz. :—

"Every proposition for altering the Rules, &c., must be in writing, and be signed by at least ten members of twelve months' standing, and must be delivered to the Superintendent two calendar months before the day on which the next annual meeting is to be held. It must be immediately copied by him and exhibited in a conspicuous place inside the Clubhouse. Such proposition (if carried) at the annual meeting shall be incorporated with the rules, &c., of the Club."

To Schedule A of the Rules and Regulations was added:—

"17. When a person has entered his name as a boarder his charges for board, &c., will go on, unless he gives proper notice to the Superintendent that he is going away. After a bushman's effects have been given in charge to the Club, they cannot be removed from the premises without permission from the Superintendent.

"18. Should any inmate on quitting the Club leave any property on the premises without specially giving it in charge to the Superintendent, the Board of Management cannot be responsible for its safe custody.

"19. If a boarder leaves the Club in debt, having property, it will be sold after the expiration of three months unless a satisfactory communication be received from him.

"20. Bushmen are strongly recommended to lodge in the custody of the Superintendent any money or articles of value, and not to leave such things in their rooms.

"21. For the better carrying out the Rules of the institution, and for the sake of the servants, the inmates are expected to be punctual for meals.

"22. Strangers cannot be allowed upon the premises without the sanction of the Superintendent; but inmates will be allowed to have their friends to visit and take meals with them, for which extra meals they will be charged the usual rate.

"23. Should the property of any inmate be missing, he is requested to inform the Superintendent of same without delay, that proper enquiry may be made.

"24. All payments or deposits will be made to the Superintendent, who is the only authorised person for receiving them.

"25. The Superintendent promptly replies to all enquiries respecting absent bushmen that may be made by friends or relatives, and takes charge of all letters addressed to his care, advertising all unclaimed letters lying at the Club, monthly or quarterly as needful."

The following article is from the *Advertiser*, December 26, 1871 :—

"One of the most important and interesting gatherings which have been held during the period of Christmastide was that of the Bushmen's Club, a full report of which we have presented to our readers.

"The first practical effort made to form an institution of this kind originated from a suggestion thrown out in this paper a few years ago. The most sanguine friends of the movement, however, could hardly at that time have anticipated such a successful result. It was well known that unfortunate bushmen in their periodical visits to Adelaide generally got into the hands of designing knaves and brazen prostitutes, who destroyed their health, robbed them of their hard-earned wages, and then when they were 'cleaned out' —as the phrase was—turned them into the streets. A few weeks' dissipation, during which they were plundered on all hands, sufficed to 'melt their cheques,' and, broken down in health and penniless in purse, they had again to return to the bush, 'sadder,' though in many cases not 'wiser men.'

"It was supposed, therefore, that a Home in town which would afford to bushmen the comforts of a respectable establishment at a moderate expense, and where they would be free from the temptations which ordinarily surrounded them in their periodical visits to Adelaide, if once established and its usefulness made known, would receive the support of the men themselves. Happily the matter was taken up from the first by the right sort of men. Gentlemen interested in pastoral pursuits gave both their money and their time to set the thing a-going. But we need hardly inform our readers that the great success of the Club is owing in a large measure to 'William,' the Hon. Superintendent, who first of all travelled over the most of the squatting districts, and personally pointed out to bushmen the practical advantages of the proposed institution, and then with noble generosity and self-denial offered his own services to the committee to start the Club in Adelaide. All the friends of the institution know how much it has been indebted for its success to the unwearied diligence and ceaseless zeal of this one man. In his previous unpaid missionary labours amongst the bushmen, 'William' had won their confidence, and they knew that any objects which he recommended for their benefit would be worthy of their support. (Here follows a copy of financial statement as from annual meeting.) Much as has been accomplished by the Club already, the indefatigable Hon. Superintendent has other schemes of usefulness in connection with it which he desires to introduce as soon as convenient. He wants a Benefit Society for the support of old bushmen when they are past work—a capital suggestion, which we hope to see taken up warmly by the men themselves. He also suggests that provision should be made in connection with the Home for the wives and children of bushmen. 'William' says—'I should like to see a nest, or row, of small cottages built round the premises—separate from the single men, of course—and plainly furnished by the Club, and let them be rented from the institution for any length of time, and let them (bushmen's families) board themselves in any way they like. This would be, I believe, a great boon to many of the married bush people, and give them a decided interest in the general prosperity of the Club. I would also suggest that when more room is provided, any parents having boys from twelve years old and upwards, able to wash and take care of themselves, might entrust them to the Club to be boarded and schooled at the city schools at a low charge of, say 8s. or 10s. per week.'

"We congratulate the bushmen on the decided success of their Club, and hope it will go on yet more prosperously, developing within itself fresh means of usefulness."

The next Board meeting was held on January 4, 1872. Present—Messrs. C. B. Young (chair) and H. Giles.

Bills and vouchers were called over and found correct.

Hon. Superintendent reported that sundry improvements and alterations had been made during the past month. That he had conferred with Mr. J. H. Angas about the piece of land fronting Gilbert-street; he (Mr. Angas) suggested that the matter should be brought before the Board of Management; this was done. That certain necessary alterations, suggested by Mr. Angas, were made in the trust-deed, and then returned to Mr. Scott (solicitor). Mr. W. Storrie presented the Club with *Chambers' Journal*, bound and complete for ten years. Received a letter from the Town Clerk, kindly granting permission to erect a sign-board on the corporation plantation (which is situated in front of the Club premises), provided the Trustees remove it when requested. That several large donations have been received during the past month, from Mr. F. J. Beck (L. L. & G. Insurance Company), £5; T. G. Waterhouse, Esq. (per Alexander Hay), £21; Henry Scott, 15 guineas donation, and a promise of an annual subscription of £5; H. T. Richmond, of Mount Brown, £20; Gavin D. Young, Esq., £10; F. H. Dutton, Esq., annually £5.

Total receipts from all sources, £104 10s.

The following short notice appeared in the *Evening Journal* of January 13, 1872:—

"BRANCH BUSHMEN'S CLUBS.—Mr. J. Riddoch, M.P., has offered £100 towards the establishment in a central part of the South-Eastern district of a branch of the Adelaide Club for bushmen. Other influential residents have also promised to assist."

The usual monthly meeting was held on February 3, 1872. Present—Messrs. H. Giles (chair) and C. B. Young.

The Hon. Superintendent reported that the Trustees recommended the partition in the dining-room to be removed; also the re-arrangement of the sanitary condition of the premises.

Total receipts from all sources, £191 10s.

Total number of tickets issued, 674.

It was resolved—That the advisability of the purchase of a piece of land fronting on Gilbert-street be left for the decision of the Trustees. That the Hon. Superintendent obtain a light for the front of the premises.

The following Circular, signed by the Board of Management, was sent to gentlemen likely to befriend bushmen:—

"Adelaide, February 7, 1872.

"Sir—The Board of Management of the Bushmen's Club have the honour of bringing before your notice the present position of that institution, with a view of seeking your assistance in completing its permanent establishment on a safe basis.

"Considering the depressed state of the colony at the time the Club was started, it met with a liberal amount of support, but the sum then subscribed—about £1,500—although enough to commence operations on a sufficiently large scale to give the experiment a fair trial, was not adequate to its permanent and efficient establishment when its success and usefulness were fully confirmed.

"The friends of the institution will be glad to learn that it is not from want of success that further funds are required, but that the usefulness of the Club demands an extension of its benefits and increased accommodation.

"The public benefits of the Club have recently been brought before Parliament, and a vote of £500 obtained to supplement private contributions. £200 have been generously contributed by two gentlemen, and a further sum of £300 is required. The Board confidently reckon on the ready assistance of the public in raising so small a sum towards so good a cause.

"The promoters of the institution, not being willing to delay the benefits of the Club until funds could be obtained to erect a large and expensive building, rented and have subsequently purchased the premises formerly occupied by Sir Charles Cooper, in Whitmore-square. The increasing demand for accommodation rendered it necessary that at least twenty bedrooms should be added, and a very neat and commodious dormitory has just been completed, with every convenience, for the sum of £480.

"That great benefits have been conferred on the class for whom it was intended by the establishment of the Home, is unquestionable; and that it has been appreciated, is proved by the number of persons who have availed themselves of it, and the fact that in so short a time it has become almost if not quite self-supporting.

"The friends of all benevolent institutions may reasonably hope that gratitude for returning prosperity may be evidenced by increased liberality on the part of all classes in support of all that is useful and good, and the promoters of the Bushmen's Club appeal with confidence to the public, and especially to those connected with the squatting interest, for the assistance they require.

"If you are disposed to contribute, we would ask the favour of your filling up the enclosed form with the amount you are willing to subscribe, and return it to the Honorary Superintendent, Whitmore-square, Adelaide.

"Neville Blyth,
"Henry Giles,
"C. B. Young,
} Board of Management.

(Form enclosed with above as following.)

"I enclose the sum of £ : : being my donation towards supplementing the conditional Government grant to the Bushmen's Club.

      "Name........................
      "Address... ...."

On the 9th of February, 1872, the following press telegram was received in Adelaide :—

"A meeting at Hamilton (Victoria) has resolved to form a Bushmen's Home, also an association for the prevention of stock stealing."

The usual monthly meeting came off on March 1. There were present—Messrs. Davenport (chair), H. Giles, C. B. Young; also Trustees, Messrs. D. Murray and W. K. Thomas.

Bills and vouchers were called over and found correct.

The Hon. Superintendent reported that the Trustees had purchased the said piece of land fronting on Gilbert-street for £233. That sundry improvements had been effected in the rooms of the Club. That the following gentlemen have responded to the circular sent out by the Board of Management for raising funds:—Messrs. C. B. Fisher, £2 2s.; E. W. Pitts, £1 1s.; Mr. J. C. Hawker, through H. Scott, £25; Messrs. J. McT. Gibson, £2 2s.; Anstey & Giles, £10 10s. The Hon. Superintendent "William" laid before the Board a scheme for the establishing a Benefit Society in connection with the Club, and a labour-office in town.

It was agreed to have the proposal circulated amongst the Trustees and members of the Board, and then brought forward for consideration at a future meeting.

The trust-deed, as modified by the Government, affecting the Constitution and Rules, was considered and approved— two of the Trustees, viz., Messrs. D. Murray and W. K. Thomas, being present and concurring.

Amount of receipts for past month, £122 6s. 1d.

Total number of tickets issued to date, 696.

Bearing upon the labour question, we clip the following from the *Adelaide Post* of October 6, 1871 :—

"The establishing of a Government labour-office has been lately advocated, with a view of profitably distributing whatever surplus labour there may be in the large towns over the whole colony. Naturally new arrivals cling to the metropolis, and frequently get rid of their last shilling before they discover the necessity of looking for employment. At present their only resort is the private labour-office, where the information as to the labour requirements of the country is naturally very limited. The establishing of a central Government office, well advised as to country labour necessities, and with the machinery at command for drafting applicants for work to any spot where it is to be found, has been urged strongly, and will no doubt find favour with the Government."

At the following monthly meeting (held April 3, 1872) there were present Messrs. S. Davenport (chair), H. Giles, and C. B. Young.

Accounts, &c., were found correct.

"William," the Hon. Superintendent, reported that sundry improvements had been effected; these were approved of by the Board. That Mr. W. Fowler had presented a donation of £5, and the National Bank £10.

Total receipts for the past month, £118 5s.

Total number of tickets issued to date, 707.

The alteration in the Constitution and Rules of the Bushmen's Club above alluded to, are as follows :—

Clause 3 to be read, "1, 2, 3, 5 of Rules and Regulations may be altered from time to time," &c., &c.

Clause 12, instead of "shall be held in the third week in December," should read "should be held about the third week in December," &c., &c.

Alterations suggested by Government.—The old clause 16 is abrogated.

New clause 16 reads thus—

"Failing which the Trustees shall be at liberty to sell and

dispose of all property belonging to the Club, and the proceeds to arise from such sale shall be applied in manner following, that is to say, in the first place all and every sum of money which shall have been advanced by Her Majesty's Government of South Australia, in aid of the said Club, shall be refunded to said Government, and the balance or remainder of the said moneys, to arise from such sale, shall be devoted to a fund for the benefit of sick," &c.

The following clauses have been added:—

"Clause 17.—A book to be called the Record-Book shall be kept, in which shall be entered the resolutions of the members present at every meeting, and all entries in such book signed by the chairman for the time being shall be conclusive evidence of the facts therein stated and of such meeting being duly convened.

"Clause 18.—It shall be lawful for a majority of members present at a meeting to be called by the Trustees for that purpose, and of which said meeting thirty days' previous notice shall be given as hereinafter mentioned, that is to say, such notice shall be inserted four times in each of the following newspapers published in Adelaide, that is to say, the *South Australian Register*, the *Adelaide Observer*, the *South Australian Advertiser*, and the *South Australian Weekly Chronicle*, and at which said meeting not less than twenty of the members for the time being on the roll of the said Club shall be present, to come to a resolution for the sale, mortgage, or leasing of the said piece of land or any part thereof at or for such price or sum for such term of years not exceeding fourteen years in possession, and at such rental, and upon, under, and subject to such terms and conditions as they shall determine. And the Trustees for the time being shall at all times carry out and fulfil, as far as in them lies, such resolution or resolutions as shall be come to or passed at such meeting.

"Clause 19.—It shall be lawful for a majority of members present at a meeting to be called by the Trustees for that purpose in the manner directed in the last preceding rule, and at which said last-mentioned meeting not less than twenty of the members for the time being on the roll of the said Club shall be present, to come to such resolution as they may think fit for the purchase of other land whereon to erect a branch Home in other parts of the said province, whensoever and so often as they shall deem it advantageous or proper for the said Club so to do, or for the removal of the said Home to some other part of the said province, in which last-mentioned case the said land and hereditaments hereinbefore described shall be sold, and the proceeds to arise from such sale shall be applied in or towards the purchase of other land and the erection thereon of a Bushmen's Home, and the said last-mentioned premises when so purchased as aforesaid shall be held by the Trustees for the time being of the said Club upon and for the like trusts and purposes as are herein set forth and declared."

BENEFIT SOCIETY.

Improvidence is one of the most conspicuous weaknesses of bushmen and does much to aggravate the ills to which, as a class, they are peculiarly subject. It is, therefore, a great good to place facilities in their way to make provision against human infirmities and bad times. Consequently at a meeting of bushmen, specially held for the purpose, it was unanimously considered desirable to establish a Fund in connection with the institution for the mutual benefit of the members. The following is the scheme proposed :—

"OBJECTS.

"The objects of the society would be as follows, viz. :—

"1st. To raise a fund (by entrance fees, by a regular annual payment, by donations, and by interest on capital) for insuring to men of good character medical assistance and pecuniary relief in time of old age and sickness, and for assisting members when travelling in search of employment, or in distressed circumstances.

"2nd. The name of the society should be 'The Bushmen's Mutual Benefit Society,' or abbreviated by the initials B.M.B.S.

"3rd. That this society should carry on its business on the premises known as the Bushmen's Club, situated in Whitmore-square, and should consist of an unlimited number of male members of any religious persuasion, of good moral character, free from disease, at fourteen and not above forty-five years of age. All candidates should produce a certificate of health from the society's doctor (if any), if not, from such duly qualified medical practitioner as may be satisfactory to the society.

"4th. That the Trustees of the Bushmen's Club should also be the Trustees of the B.M.B.S.

"5th. That the affairs of this society should be managed by the Trustees and by the Board of Management (for time being), assisted by the Superintendent and Secretary of the Bushmen's Club. The Superintendent and Secretary at all meetings should call over the names of the officers and members, and duly note the absentees, announce the receipts and disbursements, and in all respects keep good accounts and minutes of proceedings of the meeting; he should receive the notices of the sick members and lay them before the Board of Management, should be responsible for all sums of money that may from time time be paid into his hands by any person on account of the society; he should receive and pay all moneys on account of the Society. The Bank of the society should be the Bank of   in which he should deposit all sums of money to the credit of the society, in the names of the Trustees; he should have custody of all goods belonging to the society; he should receive all parcels, letters, and other correspondence on account of the society; he should answer all communications subject to the approval of the Trustees or Board of Management, and attend to the general business of the society; he should (if required) give security pursuant to Local Act No. 22 of 1852, intituled 'An Act to regulate Friendly Societies;' should prepare the annual returns (should the society be brought under said Act), and transmit them to the Governor-in-Chief as required by said Act, and he should give security for the money and property entrusted to his care pursuant to the said Act.

"6th. That the annual general meeting of the members of this society should be held about the 30th June in each year, to receive report of Trustees, statement of Secretary and Treasurer's account, appoint Auditors, and to elect

Officers of the society, and to transact any other important business.

"7th. That the Board of Management at their regular monthly meeting should have power to examine any books or papers connected with the society, hear and determine appeals, and transact the general business of said society.

"SCALE OF ENTRANCE FEES INTO THE SOCIETY.

"The cause of failure in the infancy of clubs is the general insufficiency of sums at interest and the scale of entrance fees; this scheme is designed to provide against this contingency.

"Males only, from 14 years old to 17 inclusive, £1
"   18   "   20   2
"   21   "   25   4
"   26   "   30   6
"   31   "   35   12
"   36   "   40   20
"   41   "   45   30

"The higher sums may be paid by instalments.

"N.B.—The annual payment not under £3, which must be paid in advance either weekly, monthly, or quarterly, &c.

"Note.—The average duration of life is calculated to be about thirty-two years.

"MEMBER'S PRIVILEGE.

"No person should receive benefit until the entire amount of entrance-fees of (   ) members, according to age, is paid up and invested.

"OLD AGE.

"It is suggested that the following allowance (as far as the funds will permit) be made, viz.:—An allowance of 16s. per week outside the Club, or a home for the remainder of their days (when incapacitated from work) at the Bushmen's Club, with an allowance of 6d. per diem, provided they give up the outside allowance of 16s.

"SICKNESS.

"Any member who has been admitted twelve calendar months, and who is not suspended for being in arrears, if he become sick and incapable of following any employment, if such incapacity is not occasioned by immoral conduct, he should receive from the society the following allowance for sick-pay, viz., outside the Club :—

"For the first four months of illness £1 per week.
"   second   "   15s.   "
"   third and in continuance 10s.   "

"The society should have power to regulate the rate of sick payments, according to the state of the funds.

"A member requiring assistance from the sick fund should produce a certificate from a legal medical practitioner, and he should be paid according to scale, and he should periodically give such proof of his inability to labour as the society may require. No member should be allowed to declare off the funds without a medical certificate. In any case where a surgeon recommends intoxicating liquors as medicine, such medicines must be labelled and furnished by the apothecary as other drugs.

"Any member in the receipt of the funds of the society, and found to be imposing thereon by stating himself to be sick and incapable of following his employment or usual avocation or calling, when he is able or actually doing so, or found gaming, or guilty of any gross misconduct, should for the first offence refund two weeks' sick pay, and for the second offence be expelled and forfeit all benefits in the said society.

"It should be optional with a member at any time whilst on sick pay to give up his outside pay and go into the Club to live, or to obtain a ticket for the Hospital (from the society) if preferred.

"Provided, that if the society grant him a bed in the Hospital (by free ticket), he should not receive the *full allowance* for a sick member, but a portion only, such portion to be hereafter decided upon.

"If a member choose rather to reside at the Club and obtain free medical attendance (from Club doctor) whilst there, he should pay a proportionate amount for his board, according to his weekly allowance as per scale.

" Should a member prefer other medical treatment to that provided by the society, and to board and lodge himself in the city or with friends elsewhere, he should pay his own private doctor, and receive the regular weekly allowance as per scale.

" No member (or other person) to claim moneys of the society if their sickness (or distress) is caused through drunkenness. No person should be admitted as a member of this society in a sickly condition, or of known bad character, or over forty-five years of age; and no person, unless a member, should participate in the benefits of the society. The expenses of interment of all members who have been good on the books of the society twelve calendar months, should be defrayed out of the general fund, such expense not to exceed   ; but no payments should be made from this fund for funerals until certificates have been received by the secretary from applicants as follows :—

" This is to certify that   [aged   a member of the B.M.B.S. died at   and was interred at by   The expenses of the interment amounted to £   :   :   .

                    " Signature ....
                    " Name ....
                    " Profession ....
                    " Residence...........................

" Witnessed by a legal medical practitioner, or minister, or two householders. Vouchers for payment must be presented at the same time.

" DISTRESS.

" The best thing (probably) will be to provide for a member's temporary want, and get him employment so soon as possible. A careful guard must be set over this department to prevent imposition.

" APPLICATION OF FUNDS.

" All moneys received on account of entrance fees, annual subscriptions, donations, and interest on capital, should be called the General Fund, and be applied in carrying out the objects of the society and in paying the expenses of management, according to the rules of the society. The Board should have power to make grants from the above-named fund for benevolent purposes; and so much of the funds of the society as may not be wanted for immediate use, or to meet the usual accruing liabilities, should be invested in any way the Trustees and Board of Management may decide to be most conducive to the best interests of the society. The Trustees and Board of Management should have power to establish a fund for the relief of widows and orphans of deceased members.

"Note 1.—As it must necessarily be some time before a young society can superannuate its old members (unless a very large number come in at the start), perhaps the best way to get over this difficulty would be, that every member of the society should be a member also of the Bushmen's Club, though it does not necessarily follow that every member of the Club must be a member of the society; and what assistance is rendered to aged persons may (if thought advisable) be given, in the first instance, out of any B.C. funds that may be to spare, provided that the applicant shall have been good on the books a given time (say a year).

"ADMISSION.

"All candidates requiring admission into the society should communicate (enclosing a deposit of five shillings) with the secretary, who would issue a printed form to be filled up. When this is approved by the Board, he should be informed of the fact, and upon paying the balance of the entrance fee—according to age—sign the rules, and comply with all the requisitions of the society; he should be enrolled as a member and receive his certificate as such, but should present himself once at one of the meetings at the Club-house before the expiration of his first twelve months' entry on the books. If the candidate be rejected, his deposit-money should be returned, less expenses. The forms for admission should contain columns, viz., date, name, age (last birthday), present place of abode, occupation, name of station last employed upon, nationality, whether married or single, if member of Bushmen's Club or any other society, and signature of medical officer by whom examined.

"The society should keep a registration-book in which those particulars should be entered, and when a member changes his place of abode, he should notify the same to the secretary, otherwise all communications should be sent to the last address, notified to the secretary, and be deemed duly forwarded.

"Every member should pay his member's-fees weekly (when practicable), and any one owing thirteen weeks' fees, and not making payment within that time, should be suspended and forfeit all benefits of the society for twelve months; and if he owes six months' fees, he should cease to be a member, but the society should have power to re-admit him (on payment of all money owing by him) as a new member.

"FORM OF CERTIFICATE.

"This is to certify that   of
aged   was duly enrolled a member of the
'Bushmen's Mutual Benefit Society,' Adelaide, the
day of   187 .
        As witness our hands,

.... ⎫
.... ⎬ Board of Management.
.... ⎭
..................Sec.

"EXPULSION OF BAD CHARACTERS.

"If any disputes arise between the members of the society, it should be referred to the Board of Management, and if not settled by them, it might be referred to a joint meeting of the Trustees and Board of Management; failing a settlement by them, it should be referred to the annual general meeting, their decision to be final.

"All complaints, or appeals, must be specified in writing, and a copy of the charge (if any) forwarded to the party accused, so as to afford reasonable time for his defence. No appeal should be received unless forwarded one month previous to the meeting at which it is to be heard, or within one month of the decision appealed against.

"Any candidate for admission making a false statement to any of the questions required to be answered by him, with a view to obtain admission into the society, should, on proof thereof, be immediately expelled.

"Before any member should be expelled, the following rule shall be observed :—The secretary shall lay the case before the Board of Management at their usual monthly meeting, after which the member charged with the offence should be furnished with a copy of the charge a reasonable time (say one month) before the time appointed for hearing; and every member having committed an offence, who shall go out of the way, or not appear when called upon to answer as to his conduct, shall be proceeded against as if present, but his expulsion may be appealed against as provided for in cases of dispute.

"Note.—The first thing to be done in establishing this society, is to have the report of a competent actuary, showing the average or established *laws of call* on the funds. Such actuary would have to consider the peculiar habits of life of bushmen, and this consideration would make any European fact vary, and he should be careful to leave the margin on the right side. A better idea could then be formed of the allowance to be made to widows and orphans."

The next monthly meeting was held on May 2, 1872. There were present—Messrs. H. Giles and C. B. Young (in the chair).

Minutes of previous meeting read and confirmed.

The Hon. Superintendent, "William," reported that a gentleman of Warcowie had presented a donation of £5 to the Club funds. That Captain Finniss had presented Chambers' Cyclopædia, four large volumes, worth £30; and that Mr. John Lindsay had given eight volumes *Westminster Review* and twenty-nine volumes of *McMillan's Magazine*, to the Club Library. That a lady of Mount Gambier had written to him with a view to promote the establishment of a similar institution at that place. That the property on the Gilbert-street side had been fenced in with a good six-feet lapped and strapped fence at a cost of over £20, and that the property was very much improved thereby. That twenty-five pairs of blankets had been obtained, and the gas fittings completed. The horse belonging to the Club, which had been taken care of by a gentleman living near Wellington, was got home during the past month, and appeared fit for work again. He ("William"), therefore, suggested to the Board the desirability of sending round an agent to sell and renew the members' tickets, to collect subscriptions and information about the Benefit Society, to prepare the way for the History of the Bushmen's Club among the men, and introduce the business of the Bush Book Association. He further reported that J. H. Angas, Esq., had made application to the Chief Secretary for the payment of the £500 grant; and that so soon as all the accounts were ledgered up to date, it would be necessary to take steps to raise another wing to the building.

It was resolved by the Board that this business be done.

Total amount of receipts for the past month, £78 5s.

Total number of tickets issued to date, 729.

The following article is taken from the *Register* of May 18, 1872 :—

"THE BUSHMEN'S CLUB.

"This useful institution has now been in existence for rather more than two years, and it is with pleasure we record the success it has achieved and the prosperity it continues to enjoy. The fact that 700 members have been enrolled since the Club was started is sufficient proof of its popularity with bushmen; and the generally large number of inmates shows that the institution really is appreciated as a home by the class it is intended to benefit. The liberal act of the Government in granting the Club the sum of £500 is highly commendable. It will enable the Directors to extend their operations, and probably to carry out needed improvements in connection with the buildings. Already 'William,' the Superintendent, is again pressed for room. The dining-room has had to be enlarged by taking in the smoking-room; but what is much wanted is a new building, similar to that recently erected as a dormitory, to include dining and smoking-rooms, which would allow the present rooms used for those purposes to be turned into bedrooms. The piece of land behind the Club, with a frontage in Gilbert-street, has at length been secured, at a cost of £233. This is a valuable addition to the property, and it will add considerably to the convenience of the place. If it could be done, the erection of a row of small cottages upon this frontage, to be let furnished to married bushmen, would be a great advantage. At present the Home affords no accommodation of this sort; and, as many married men are subscribers, it is only right that some provision should be made for them, so that when they visit town with their families they may not be compelled to lodge in expensive apartments, or to furnish rooms for the time of their stay.

"It is felt that the institution has by no means reached the limit of its usefulness, and hopes are entertained of gradually extending its operations until much shall have been effected which now can only be desired. One proposal is that the Home should board lads of fourteen years and upwards at a low rate, so as to admit of their being sent in from the bush for education in town. Such an arrangement, if it were carried out, would so evidently be productive of much good that nothing need to be said in its favour.

"Another proposal of the Superintendent is to institute a Benefit Society in connection with the Home, the objects of which would be to raise funds by entrance-fees, annual payments, donations, and interest on capital, for providing members in times of sickness with medical assistance and pecuniary relief, and in times of old age or incapacity for further work, with a permanent weekly sum or a home at the Club. There would also be the object of helping distressed members by relieving their temporary wants, and endeavouring to get them employment through the Bushmen's Club labour-office, the head-quarters of which 'William' hopes yet to see in the centre of the business part of the city. The Superintendent has prepared the prospectus of such a society, more, however, in the hope of receiving hints from those versed in these matters than with the desire for its immediate adoption. The principal features of the scheme are that the entrance-fees should vary from £1 to £45, according to the age of the person entering, fourteen being the lowest, and fifty the highest age taken; the annual subscription to be not under £3. These payments, 'William' believes, would secure to the member £1 per week for the first four months of illness, 15s. for the second four months, and 10s. for the third four, which sum would be continued if necessary. In the case of old age or incapacity for work the allowance would be 16s. per week, or a home in the Club and 6d. per diem. There are other details in the scheme, but these will suffice to show its general bearing. The establishment upon a good basis of a society with these objects, which bushmen might be induced to join, is a most desirable thing. We heartily hope that the scheme may be carried through, and be well supported by the class it would specially provide for. The foundation of a library to circulate in the bush is another measure contemplated. An influential committee of gentlemen have issued a circular calling upon those connected with the squatting interests to help in this work by giving subscriptions for the purchase of necessary books. The movement would afterwards be made self-supporting. The circulation in the bush of literature of a healthy kind is much needed. As it is, the books supplied on the stations by hawkers and others are for the most part novels of the most sensational kind. It is to be hoped, therefore, that the appeal made in order to starting a Bush Book Society will be extensively responded to.

"The whole of the Club property is now properly vested in trustees, to be held for all time for the Club purposes. An alteration became necessary in the deed before the Government grant could be received, providing that in the event of the institution falling through, and the property being sold, all moneys received from the Government shall be returned. Other clauses have also been added, providing for the keeping of a record-book, and giving power to the majority of the members at a properly convened meeting to direct the trustees to mortgage or sell the property, or to secure land in other parts for the establishment of branch Bushmen's Homes. But, as the promised 'History of the first Bushmen's Club established in Australia' is nearly completed, our readers will have the opportunity of gaining fuller particulars upon all these points than can be given here. In the meantime we hope the Home will continue to be extensively used by the bushmen of South Australia, and well supported by the public of the colony generally."

The following are the *Advertiser's* remarks upon the same subject, dated May 20, 1872 :—

"Amongst the most useful and successful of the benevolent institutions of the city must be classed the Bushmen's Home; for under the earnest and indefatigable superintendence of 'William,' the Home has attained a position of prosperity and apparent stability which the most sanguine of its promoters could hardly have anticipated. Several hundreds of bushmen have enrolled themselves as members of the Club, and from time to time the increasing demands for accommodation at the Home have necessitated the extension of the premises in Whitmore-square.

"The Superintendent has supplied us with some interesting information respecting this institution. We learn from him that only two years have elapsed since the Home was formally inaugurated by His Excellency the Governor, and since then its history has been one of progress. Since the last annual meeting extra dining-room accommodation has been afforded, but the accommodation is still found to be insufficient. It is suggested as an advisable improvement that a new dining-hall should be erected, and the room at present used for that purpose converted into temporary sleeping apartments and smoking rooms. The Gilbert-street frontage adjoining the Home has been purchased through the kind assistance of Messrs. J. H. Angas, M.P., and D. Murray, at a cost of £233, and this has necessarily enhanced the value of the property. The property has been formally vested in trustees, but before the trust-deed could be settled a modification of the Constitution was made necessary, to meet the reasonable representations of the Government, from whom a grant of £500 has been recently obtained. The principal alteration had reference to the winding up of the affairs of the Club, should circumstances arise which might necessitate the closing of the Home. In prospect of so untoward and, we hope, improbable an event, it is provided that if, after due notice has been given of the position of the Club, it shall be found impossible to re-organise the institution, the Trustees shall have power to sell the property and appropriate the proceeds—first, to repay all sums of money which may from time to time have been advanced by the Government; and second, to set apart the balance, if any, towards a fund for sick and distressed bushmen. Other alterations have been made to the effect that by resolution of a meeting of members, duly convened, the property may be sold, mortgaged, or leased ; that, at a meeting also duly convened, the trustees may be empowered to purchase land and erect a branch Home wherever it may be advantageous to do so ; or if considered desirable, they may sell the present property and apply the proceeds to the purchase of land and the erection of a Bushmen's Club elsewhere in the colony for like trusts and purposes as the present Home.

"Useful as the institution has been, we are pleased to learn that its sphere of usefulness is likely to be still farther extended. Hitherto the advantages of the Club have been offered to or accepted by adult bush labourers only; but a valuable suggestion has been made, and one which it is hoped will be carried to a successful issue, that lads from the bush, from fourteen years of age and upwards, should be admitted to the Home as boarders at a reduced rate, while being educated at the city schools. The education of children in the bush is a matter of so much importance, and yet attended with so much difficulty, that we hail this proposal with pleasure, and trust that the suggestion may not only be adopted, but be carried out with great benefit.

"We have also been shown a draft constitution of a projected Benefit Society in connection with the Club. It is proposed by this society to afford assistance to members when in sickness or distress, by a weekly payment of money, by board, lodging, and medical attendance at the Club, by admission to the Hospital, or by other means of relief. The establishment of a Bushmen's Labour Office in connection with the Home is also projected.

"Respecting the inmates, the Superintendent speaks very highly of their general demeanor and conduct. He expresses regret that there are still a number of bushmen who, through ignorance of the Home and its arrangements, avoid it, and prefer other less advantageous places of residence in the city, and he earnestly appeals to them to share the comforts which the Home affords. 'William' refers to the departure for Europe of Mr. David Murray, one of the trustees, who has evinced generous friendship and practical sympathy with the objects of the Home, and says he will carry with him the best wishes of the bushmen of South Australia, who are indebted to him so greatly. We hope the Home may become increasingly useful and increasingly prosperous, and that the new projects to which we have referred may be carried out with the same energy and success as have marked the brief history of the Club itself."

The following is a copy of correspondence respecting the Government grant to the Club, from the Chief Secretary to J. H. Angas, Esq., and also that gentleman's answer to the same :—

"Chief Secretary's Office,
"Adelaide, May 27, 1872.
" Sir—I am directed by the Chief Secretary to acknowledge the receipt of your letter of the 27th inst., applying on behalf of the Bushmen's Home for payment of the amount voted by the Legislature in aid of that institution, and in reply to draw your attention to the following extract from Address of the House of Assembly, No. 10 of 1871, having reference to this matter, for the purpose of supplementing contributions for the enlargement of the building now used as the Bushmen's Home, such sum to be paid on the Attorney-General being satisfied with the trusts in respect of the said Bushmen's Home, and to request you to be good enough to state whether such conditions have been complied with.
"I have the the honour to be, Sir,
"Your obedient servant,
"J. BOOTHBY, Under Secretary.
"J. H. Angas, Esq., M.P., Adelaide."

"Adelaide Club, May 30, 1872.
"The Honourable the Chief Secretary.
"Sir—I have the honour to acknowledge yours of the 27th inst., and in reply beg to state that the late Attorney-General (Mr. Boucaut) perused the trust-deed of the Bushmen's Club, and made some suggestions, which were adopted in accordance with his request. Messrs. Scott & Bakewell, solicitors to the Club, prepared the document. They will be

happy to furnish any further information which may be required.

"I have the honour to remain, Sir,
"Your obedient servant,
"J. H. ANGAS."

The following is a letter written by Mr. Angas to "William," Hon. Superintendent of the Bushmen's Club :—

"Adelaide Club, June 10, 1872.
"Hon. Secretary Bushmen's Club.

"Dear Sir—Will you have the goodness to inform the Board of Management that the grant of £500, voted by Parliament in aid of the Bushmen's Club, will, I expect, be payable this month.

"Also that I have had a conversation with Mr. Angas (my father) concerning the debt of £500 due to him from the Club. I informed him that the Club could pay off the debt, but I also stated that it was desirable to add a new wing to the building, whereupon he at once offered to lend the money for another year without interest. I would recommend the Board of Management to take these matters into immediate consideration, and to get plans of additions and alterations as soon as possible.

"Yours truly,
"J. H. ANGAS."

The following, copied from the *Evening Journal* of June 11, 1872, will no doubt be read with pleasure by many a lover of such institutions as our Bushmen's Home :—

"BUSHMEN'S HOME IN SYDNEY.

"On May 31 a meeting was held in the Central Police Court to inaugurate a Bushmen's Home. Captain Scott, M.P., presided, and there attended the Rev. A. W. Webb, Captain Evans, Messrs. T. Dawson, W. D. Meares, W. T. Pinhey, S. H. Lewis, H. B. Lee, De Beaker, Boran, Smart, and Lovett.

"Mr. T. Dawson proposed, and Captain Evans seconded—'That it is desirable that a Bushmen's Home be established in Sydney for the benefit of shepherds, stockmen, gold diggers, drovers, and others.'

"Carried.

"Mr. Lee moved, Mr. Smart seconding—'That a committee be appointed, consisting of the gentlemen present, with power to add to their number; that Captain Scott be chairman, and that three form a quorum.'

"Mr. Webb stated his inability to act, and his name was therefore omitted from the resolution as adopted. Mr. Smart was appointed Secretary, Captain Evans Treasurer. Subscription-lists were opened, and a sub-committee was appointed to prepare rules. The general committee decided upon holding fortnightly meetings."

The *Sydney Morning Herald* of Monday, June 3, 1872, has the following on this subject, which gives us much pleasure of inserting here, and shows what proceedings have been taken also at Sydney to inaugurate a Bushmen's Club in that city:—

"BUSHMEN'S HOME.

"In accordance with an advertisement (inserted by Captain Scott, P.M.) which appeared on Friday, convening a meeting for the purpose of taking into consideration the desirability of establishing a Bushmen's Home in Sydney, the following gentlemen attended:—Messrs. Evans, T. Dawson, W. D. Meares, W. T. Pinhey, S. H. Lewis, H. B. Lee, De Beaker, Boran, Smart, Lovett, Rev. A. W. Webb, and Capt. Scott.

"After some conversation respecting the object of the meeting, in the success of which all appeared to be deeply interested, it was proposed and carried—'That it is desirable that a Bushmen's Home should be established in Sydney.'

"It was afterwards proposed and carried that the gentlemen then present should form themselves into a committee, with power to add to their number, to carry out the objects of the meeting—Captain Scott being appointed chairman, and Messrs. Scott, Dawson, and Evans a sub-committee to frame and prepare rules and regulations to be submitted to the committee at a meeting to be held a fortnight hence, at 4 o'clock p.m., at the Central Police Office, for their approval; Mr. T. Walter Smart consenting to act as honorary Secretary, and Captain Evans as honorary Treasurer. The objects of this institution were fully explained and enlarged upon by the various gentlemen present, all of whom could personally attest to the great necessity which exists for its formation, as scenes witnessed by them occur daily and nightly in the streets, in the parks, at the Police Courts, in paddocks, in fact, everywhere, of persons lying about in a deplorable state of drunkenness or destitution.

"The object of establishing a Bushmen's Home is not a charitable one in a pecuniary sense, but one to provide bushmen, shepherds, stockmen, bullock drivers, diggers, &c., with a temporary home, where, for a small sum paid weekly, they will obtain wholesome food, clean beds, and good advice as to the investment of their savings, and in obtaining, through a registry-office established on the premises, speedy and respectable employment, without any extra charge, every inducement being held out to them to become strict teetotallers. Doubtless in course of time branch institutions similar to this Sydney one will be established at all the principal towns in New South Wales—Bathurst, Mudgee, Orange, Yass, New England, Maitland, &c.

"The only thing the committee solicit is, by subscription, to collect sufficient means to purchase beds and clothing, furniture, crockeryware, kitchen utensils, all of the humblest description, and to pay three months' rent, after which the institution will be a self-supporting one.

"The amount required will be about £150. Each member of the committee will receive subscriptions."

BUSHMEN'S HOME ON THE MURRUMBIDGEE.

While quoting from the *Adelaide Observer* a recent article respecting the marked success which has attended the establishment of a Bushmen's Club in South Australia, the *Hay Standard* of June 6 strongly urges the desirability of a similar institution being founded in the Upper River District. The paper mentioned contends that in the Darling, Lachlan, and Murrumbidgee country there is ample scope for such a Home, and pleads that the benefits it would confer should be secured. The special temptations and trials of bush life are also dwelt upon as reasons why action should be taken, and that early.

The Club in Adelaide.

A special meeting of the Trustees and Board of Management was held on June 12, 1872. Present—Messrs. C. B. Young (chair), H. Giles, and W. K. Thomas representing the Trustees.

It was resolved that Mr. Cumming be requested to prepare working plans and estimate, immediately with a view to the building of the eastern wing. A special meeting to be called on the 14th to consider estimate, &c.

On the 14th the said special meeting was held, the plans submitted by Mr. Cumming were approved, and it was considered desirable to complete the building as soon as there were any funds available for the purpose. Mr. H. Giles was requested to ascertain whether money could be legally borrowed on the Club property.

The next monthly meeting of the Board was held July 2, 1872. Present—Messrs. S. Davenport (chair), H. Giles, and C. B. Young.

Mr. Giles reported that no answer had been received to his enquiries respecting a loan on the Club property.

Vouchers and accounts examined and found correct.

Receipts for past month, £71 10s.

Number of tickets issued, 739.

Superintendent reported that Messrs. W. A. E. West and J. H. Angas had called during the month, and the former gentleman had given a donation of £3 to the bushmen's funds. Also that he had turned all spare land into a kitchen garden. That during the past month he had forwarded documents, &c., to three different places—two Victoria, one Sydney—containing sufficient information and instructions to enable the applicants to establish and work Homes for bushmen, thus making five movements in all on foot in the different colonies. Mr. Angas, sen., having generously permitted the £500 loan to continue for a further twelve months, the chairman was requested to thank him on behalf of the Committee.

The Committee concurred in the desirability of the following advertisement to the public for aid in raising £250, the deficiency delaying the erection of the required wing :—

"Bushmen's Club.

"It being found necessary to increase the accommodation at this institution by the addition of another wing to the existing building, which will cost about £500,

"The Committee will provide £250 if a like amount be raised by the friends of the institution.

"Donations will be thankfully received by 'William,' Hon. Superintendent, Whitmore-square, Adelaide."

The following short notice calling attention to the advertisement, appeared in the *Chronicle*, July 6, 1872 :—

"It will be seen by an advertisement that subscriptions are invited in aid of the Bushmen's Club, it being proposed to add another wing to the present building. That increased accommodation is again required, shows that the institution is being more and more appreciated."

"On the 13th July, 1872, the following article from a kindly hand appeared in the *Border Watch*, bearing upon the Home movement :—

"THE BUSHMEN'S CLUB MOVEMENT.
"*Communicated by M. C.*

"A very pleasing effect is said to be produced by viewing a snowy landscape through rose-coloured glass. The chilling expanse of snow and inhospitable fields, the frozen streams and bare trees, are all transformed by the soft warm haze that would fain heat the beholder to the belief that the dreariness of winter has been exchanged for the balmy charms of summer. But the delusion is as short-lived as it is harmless, the brightly tinted glass is soon laid aside, and the scene around is coldly prosaic as before. We are all, however, familiar with looking at matters *rose de couleur* in cases where the process is neither unhurtful nor transitory. One of the instances in which this is persistently done by well-meaning people is with reference to the social and intellectual advancement of our nation during the present era of its existence.

"Commercial enterprise, and munificent alms deeds are salient features of our modern civilization, and out of these facts an eminently comfortable and charming theory is frequently constructed as to our superiority in every conceivable point over past ages and peoples. Each charitable project, and every missionary enterprise is scanned with rose-coloured spectacles till, through their illusive glow, such marvellous statistics are compiled that we are almost hoaxed into believing we have attained to the millenium without knowing it. We are, most of us, a trifle sick of hearing that our morals and machinery are unrivalled in the universe; that British integrity and British calico are unimpeachable, and that we may defy creation in the matter of subscription-lists and Brummagem wares. Granted that there is a substratum of truth in all these highly-coloured assertions, still we have daily evidence around us that notwithstanding our vaunted liberality and widely-spread charities, our benevolent institutions and Bible societies, there is a large and ever-increasing number of our fellow-creatures whose whole lives and surroundings are a terrible protest against the snug complacency with which we eternally compliment ourselves, upon our moral and social condition as compared with other periods. We cannot shut our eyes to the fact that insobriety and impurity, poverty and squalor, and inhuman vices claim an appalling per centage in our midst. It is well to have glowing reports of missionary labours in the South Sea and Pacific Ocean, imposing statistics from religious tract societies, and a satisfactory import and export report; yet these hardly constitute a sufficient cause for pæans of national laudation, while our legislators refuse to grapple with the cankering evil of drunkenness for fear of diminishing the revenue, of offending this interest, or lessening the profits of the other.

"It may be rather pleasant thus to look at the darker phases of life around us through the incense which we burn at the shrine of our supposed moral elevation, but it is not the mode by which the social evils and difficulties that in one form or other perplex all states can be abolished or lessened. One of ours, as a community and colony, is undoubtedly the anomalous and unsatisfactory condition of a large section of our working people who are known among us as bushmen. While the increasing influx of population and its inevitable consequences have, in a measure, changed the whole aspect of colonial life during the past few years, the peculiar disadvantages under which this class labours remain still unaltered. The typical bushman now, as then, is a wandering nondescript workman; now here, now there—shearing, reaping, fencing, road making, tramping it in search of employment—doing anything that comes in his way, and not at all disinclined to do nothing. He is usually, politically speaking, of somewhat advanced views, with very fixed ideas as to individual rights, and the vaguest regarding theology. Erratic in his movements, irregular in his habits, the things that he can be counted upon for with least fear of disappointment is, not to miss a spree when the opportunity offers itself, nor turn a cold shoulder to a 'mate' in distress. Living at times a monotonous and isolated life, his recreations limited to a pack of greasy cards, and the singing of songs not strictly evangelical; his intellectual resources comprised in a sensational novel, and the relating of 'yarns' of doubtful veracity, and still more doubtful morality. Then a periodical visit to a township, where that summary process known as 'knocking down a cheque' is forthwith commenced, till the hardly-earned wages of months is dissipated in a few days' orgies, and before the poor deluded man has realized what he is about, he finds himself one morning, with an awfully muddled head and unsteady hand, lifting his 'swag' (if haply he has one left) to tramp it once more, perhaps haunted by the terrors of *delirium tremens;* perhaps to stray away and never be heard of more, till some chance traveller in a dim gully or shadowy range comes upon the ghastly remains of what was once a human being. There is a coroner's inquest, and then it is all over—the wretched misspent life that no one misses or regrets, save perhaps a sorrowing mother beyond the Pacific, who waits and fears through the long years till hope is dead.

"The story is extremely common-place, and altogether lacks the *sensationalism* which threatens to become an essential ingredient in every tale and grievance that would effectually commend itself to sympathy and redress. But the tragedy of a wrecked life and a godless death is, notwithstanding, infinitely more awful, more unspeakably sad, than any a sympathetic audience ever sighed or shuddered at in the brilliant light of a magnificent theatre. The adventures of a hero, after the Guy Livingstone type—clever, handsome, and reckless, with a decided penchant for violating the seventh commandment—may be more exciting, more picturesque, but they are hardly of such vital importance to us, as Christians and fellow-creatures, as the tale that is so legibly read in the bloated haggard faces and unsteady gait of the wretched, misguided men, who are permitted by the laws of our country to be stupified and beggared by water beer, raised to double strength by *nux vomica* and *cocculus indicus;* by a minimum of pure spirit, seasoned with white vitriol and oil of cinnamon and cayenne, by courtesy called gin, and such stuff, and then turned adrift to wander whither they will. Homeless, penniless, and friendless, tempted and despairing, God help them! We pass them by at our street corners and on our highways, terribly in need of a little sympathy and help, which, though we are so humane and benevolent, they somehow seldom receive.

"But even when those who have time and inclination to proffer both come to the fore, the grave problem arises— which is the most effectual way in which this may be accomplished? Those who have given most time and thought to the subject have come to the conclusion that the best and most practicable mode of doing this is by establishing bushmen's clubs in the centres of population throughout the colony. The movement was for some time under discussion in Adelaide, the result being that a Bushmen's Club has been successfully organized, and is now in capital working order therein.

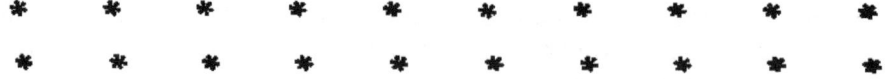

But it must be borne in mind that all movements which aim at the uprooting of long-existing abuses must inevitably meet with much opposition and misrepresentation; and though the scheme was long under discussion, it is but two years since the Club was fairly started. It was formally opened in May, 1870, by His Excellency and the late lamented Lady Edith Fergusson. Her Ladyship, as is well-known, took a warm interest in the movement, and with touching thoughtfulness alluded to it even in her dying hours as one which she deeply desired to be placed on an assured footing. Not for her noble birth, nor her exalted rank, should we deem that wish a sacred trust, but for the pure unselfish benevolence, and the tender womanly heart that prompted it. She has passed away to her reward, leaving behind her the memorial of a life of charity and good deeds, and the most fitting tribute we could pay to her memory would be to take up this movement, so noble in its aims and so practical in its designs, until in every bush township a *bonâ fide* Bushmen's Home or Club is established, to subvert and replace the order of things which has so long and disastrously prevailed.

"No one who candidly considers the question will fail to be convinced that these institutions are calculated to effect more towards accomplishing this end than any other agency that could be employed. Mechanics' institutes, and moral essays, cheap tracts, and temperance lectures are very good in their way; but no one who is not deeply affected by the infirmity of looking through coloured glass will venture to affirm that any or all of them can exercise a permanent or salutary effect on men whose only resort, when they leave the solitudes of the bush, are the public-house and the wine-shop. We see the fruits of this state of things daily around us, and all who seriously consider the matter must deplore it deeply. But we have the remedy partly in our own hands. With the results and experience of the Club in Adelaide before us, we have only to be really in earnest to make a united effort in order to establish a similar institution in Mount Gambier. Situated as we are in the centre of an extensive agricultural and pastoral district, there can be no question that a Bushmen's Club, properly organized, and efficiently conducted, would be liberally patronised, and in a short time self-supporting.

"The great thing is to set the movement on foot, and if only those who are interested in the moral welfare of this long-neglected class, and those who have time and influence at their disposal, would heartily co-operate in the matter, this might soon be effected. In the present state of affairs amongst us, commodious premises could be secured at a moderate rental, to give the scheme a fair trial, and test the practicability of permanently establishing such an institution in our midst. The handsome subscription of £100 is already guaranteed by a gentleman in the district towards this object, and we could always rely upon receiving a Government grant on the same conditions as it was advanced to the Adelaide Club; so that the expenses attached to the undertaking need not wholly scare us from taking it in hand."

On August 1, 1872, the Board met again for their usual monthly work. There were present—Messrs. C. B. Young (chair) and H. Giles.

Minutes of previous meeting were read and confirmed. Vouchers called over and found correct.

The Superintendent urged the necessity of providing more room. He reported that Mr. Wm. Watson had been appointed and sent to the bush as travelling agent during the shearing season. That an application should be made to the City Council about finishing up the watertable and forming the road in front of the premises. That it would be necessary to pass a resolution at the next annual meeting to enable the Trustees to mortgage the property if necessary, as per clause 18 of Constitution of Club.

A letter was read from G. F. Angas, Esq., informing the Trustees that the £500 loan would remain without interest till July 13, 1873, when the promissory-note would be presented at the Bank of Australasia for payment.

A deposit-receipt for £52 10s. was presented, being a donation from Mr. Price Maurice, per J. H. Angas, Esq.

Receipts for the month, £74 10s.

Number of tickets issued, 749.

"William" was directed to call on Mr. J. H. Angas to discuss the raising of funds for immediately commencing the new wing.

The following short articles, commenting upon the prospects

of the Club, are clipped from the *Evening Journal* and *Express* of August 2, 1872 :—

From *Evening Journal* :—

"It will probably be remembered that a generous friend of the Bushmen's Club lent £500 to the Trustees without interest for twelve months to assist it, and we now learn that he has renewed the loan on the same liberal terms for another year. 'William,' the Hon. Superintendent, also informs us that Mr. Price Maurice, through his agent, Mr. C. Sabine, has supplemented to the extent of 50 guineas the subscriptions that were collected on his runs to aid the establishment. This donation will go to the Building Fund, and the gift will be particularly acceptable and timely, because the Committee recently offered to provide £250 towards the cost of erecting a much-needed wing to the building on condition that the bushmen and their friends raised a similar sum. As the institution is calculated to do much good, well-wishers will be encouraged to support the enterprise cordially. It is regarded as certain that the accommodation which the Club can at present afford will be insufficient for the number of visitors to the city, who, after shearing is over, will, it may reasonably be presumed, desire to benefit by the advantages of the Home. Under these circumstances, it seems absolutely necessary that no time should be lost in providing the required funds, so that the needed additions may be erected some time before the end of the year. There is ample cause already for congratulating the supporters of the Club upon its success. When more space is provided, however, and the Mutual Benefit Fund has been fully inaugurated, even greater prosperity may safely be expected. The place is now useful, commodious, and comfortable, but it will be possible to extend the benefits conferrable when greater space is at the disposal of the officers. Honour is unquestionably due to the promoters and warm supporters of the movement for ameliorating the condition of bushmen. The anniversary of the Club is being looked forward to with interest, and preparations are already being made to celebrate it worthily. Some of the present and past inmates have suggested that as a great distance has to be travelled by many of the men who attend, the proceedings, instead of being restricted to the annual picnic and meeting, should be extended over a week. Probably when the treasury is fuller and the institution has become stronger, the Board will consider these and other suggestions bearing upon the fitting commemoration of the institution's start. It was at a late meeting of the Bush Book Association decided to ask the Board of Management to take charge of this affair, and the Committee have accepted the responsibility, regarding this undertaking as properly a branch of the general work. The dissemination on outlying stations of wholesome literature must be considered as a most important project. We learn that the scheme for founding a Bushmen's Benefit Society has advanced some stages, but is not yet matured. It is, however, receiving due consideration, and it is supposed that apparent difficulties will vanish."

From the *Express*:—

"Our readers will probably remember that a generous wealthy friend of the bushmen lent the sum of £500 (without interest) for twelve months for the advancement of the Bushmen's Club. It is with great pleasure that we now record the fact that the same gentleman has placed the same sum at the disposal of the Trustees for another year on the same understanding. The Hon. Superintendent also informs us that Mr. Price Maurice, through Mr. C. Sabine, has supplemented the subscriptions raised for the Club upon his runs by his employés to the amount of £52 10s., which sum is to go to the Building Fund. This timely gift of Mr. Maurice is very acceptable, particularly as the Committee have but recently offered to provide £250 towards building a much-needed wing to the present premises, if the bushmen and their friends raise a like sum. As the institution is calculated to do much good in the future, it is hoped that the friends of the movement will not be backward in raising the required amount. It is considered certain that there will not be sufficient room in the present premises (under present circumstances) for the number of inmates that may reasonably be expected to avail themselves of the advantages of the Club at the latter part of the year, after shearing, so that there is no time to be lost if the proposed extension is to benefit the institution this year. We heartily congratulate the bushmen and their good friends upon the success of the

Club so far; and we may safely venture to predict that when the new wing is added, and the mutual benefit fund set in motion, this institution bids fair to become one of the most useful, commodious, and comfortable establishments in the colony. All honour to the Messrs. Angas and other kind and generous friends who have so nobly come forward to mark out a new era for bushmen, by helping them, in this social manner, to help themselves. We hear that some of the men are already preparing for a grand gathering at their usual annual picnic and meeting. Some of them suggest that as this celebration takes place only once a year, and they have so far to travel, the holiday ought to last a week, but the desirableness for workmen who have to earn their living by the labour of their hands travelling long distances for the sake of a week's amusement is open to question. At a recent meeting of the Bush Book Association, it was resolved to apply to the Board of Management of the Club to take this matter also into their hands, and work it (if practicable) in connection with the institution. This the Committee have kindly consented to do, feeling that the development of this branch of usefulness rightly belongs to the Club; therefore all communications (in future) upon this subject must be addressed to the Hon. Superintendent 'William.' The scheme for the proposed Benefit Society has advanced a few stages, but more time is needed to mature the project, as it requires grave thought and consideration."

The following note appeared in the *Express's* notice to correspondents the same date:—

"SUBSCRIBER.—We have enquired into the matter referred to in your letter. The sum of £500 was voted for 1871 in the enlargement of the premises known as the Bushmen's Club, but there is no subsidy towards its maintenance. The engagement of servants is very properly vested in the Hon. Superintendent, who is responsible to the Board of Management. If any cause of complaint exists, it should be referred to the Board. Some of the servants now in the Bushmen's Club have been there a couple of years, and are highly spoken of by the Superintendent, although others have been changed after only short periods of service. The Club is as much a private institution as any other establishment (and there are many of them) to which a special vote of public money may have been granted, and an appeal to the Board of Managers is the proper course to be pursued by any one having grounds of complaint."

On August 6, 1872, it was decided to publish the History of the Club, and as a preliminary step the following advertisement was inserted in the leading daily papers :—

"It is contemplated to publish the History of the First Bushmen's Home in the colonies, provided a sufficient number of subscribers can be obtained. The work will contain about 300 closely-printed pages of highly interesting information respecting the rise and progress of this useful institution. It will be illustrated with views of the present premises and design of future erections, with a preface by the compiler, a copy of last balance-sheet, and other miscellaneous matter appended. Orders to be sent in immediately for copies of the first edition to 'William,' Hon. Superintendent of Club, Adelaide. As the profits arising from the sale of this work will be devoted to the interests of the Club, the prices will be as follows:—Stiff covers, 4s. 6d. ; Cloth, 5s. 6d. ; by post, 6d. added.

"A list of subscribers will be published with the work."

The *Advertiser* commented thereon thus :—

"We have pleasure in drawing attention to an advertisement elsewhere, announcing that a 'History of the Adelaide Bushmen's Home'—the first Bushmen's Home in the colonies—will shortly be printed, if sufficient encouragement is given by the public. It is proposed to devote the proceeds to the building fund of the Home. Doubtless many bushmen and others of the general public will be glad to subscribe to a work containing the history of an institution which has proved so very successful as the Bushmen's Home in this city. Full particulars respecting the book are given in the advertisement. We learn that the Committee of the Bushmen's Home have decided to add an eastern wing to the present building forthwith. This extra accommodation is required, and it is intended to carry it out at once in order to have it ready for the use of the men after shearing. The proposed additions comprise a dining-hall and smoking-room."

The following is from the *Register* :—

"THE BUSHMEN'S HOME.—In Tuesday's *Register* it was notified that 'William,' the Honorary Superintendent of the Bushmen's Club, Whitmore-square, intends compiling and publishing a volume of 300 pages, giving a complete history of this, the first such Home established in the Australias. The work is to contain interesting information regarding the rise and progress of the movement that so auspiciously resulted in the successful establishment of the present institution, and the interest will be heightened by views being presented of the premises now occupied, with the projected additions. Financial and statistical details will form a part of the production. In our business columns, as already mentioned, the intended publication has been described; but we may remark that in all probability many bushmen will be glad to possess such a record as the self-denying worker may be expected to send from the printing press. With his usual liberality, 'William' intends giving, in addition to his own labour, any pecuniary proceeds of the venture for the benefit of the establishment which has occupied so much of his time and energy. The class whose interests have been unselfishly promoted owe him a debt of gratitude, which it may reasonably be presumed they will not be slow to acknowledge in a way that will gratify the Superintendent, to wit, by immediately ordering a large number of subscription copies of his forthcoming book."

It being suggested to the Superintendent that some friends would assist the work forward by advertising therein, the following notice was issued August 8, 1872 :—

"HISTORY OF THE BUSHMEN'S CLUB.

"Special notice to tradesmen, &c., desirous of advertising among bush people and others.

"Any person forwarding (immediately) to 'William,' Hon. Superintendent (21s.) one guinea, will be entitled to a copy of the work (when printed), and two inches space for an approved advertisement in the first edition.

"N.B.—The profits arising from the sale of the books will be devoted to the interests of the institution."

On the 22nd August a friend in disguise undertook to enlighten the City councillors as to the state of the roads, &c., about the Club premises by sending the following letter to the *Register* :—

"TO THE EDITOR.

"Sir—As a citizen I venture to ask whether the councillors for Grey Ward know of the existence of the Bushmen's Club. Are they aware that for a praiseworthy purpose an outlay of about £2,000 has already been made; that a further sum of £500 is about to be expended in erections; and that up to the present moment the place is almost unapproachable? Do they know that the reserve in front of the main buildings is made a mud-heap, and that bushmen approaching the institution at night are in danger of being smothered? I think that the Club is deserving of more generous treatment, and hope that the councillors for Grey Ward will confer with each other as to what should be done. This neglect has an appearance that should be immediately remedied.

"I am, Sir, &c.,

"CITIZEN."

On August 12, 1872, a joint meeting of Trustees and Board of Management was held at Mr. Cumming's (architect) office, to decide on tender for building the eastern wing. Present—Messrs. C. B. Young, H. Giles, and W. K. Thomas, representing the Trustees.

"William" reported that, agreeably to the suggestion thrown out at the last meeting, he had called on Mr. J. H. Angas for counsel and advice respecting the raising of the £250, to enable the Board to proceed with the new addition. That gentleman kindly consented to lend the sum (£250) for building, without interest, for twelve months, on a joint promissory-note of the Trustees and Board of Management whenever the money was wanted. This gracious act of Mr. J. H. Angas enabling the Committee to commence the work, it was agreed that Mr. Farr's tender be accepted for £540, and that the matter of drainage be left to Mr. Cumming. And the first stone of the new eastern wing was laid (without ceremony) on August 26, 1872.

The Superintendent reported also that he had received a note from Mr. J. H. Angas, stating that his father was willing to give the £500 due to him to the Club next July, provided a like sum was raised by the friends of the institution by that date next year, 1873. That considerable work had been done during past month in pulling down old building, clearing away rubbish, and preparing for masons, &c. That Mr. H. A. Short called during the month and presented the Club with a copy of the *Australasian* for one year.

The following are the Press comments on the movements lately made, &c. :—

From the *Evening Journal*, August 30, 1872—

"The great importance of the pastoral interests of South Australia and their close connection with the welfare of the colony are subjects which all can appreciate. While sensible of the extent to which the success and value of our pastoral pursuits have arisen from the intelligence, energy, and enterprise of the squatters, it would be unfair not to take into account the important part bushmen have played in the growth of that branch of industry into a source of national advantage. They have supplied the labour, without which the capital and enterprise of the squatter would have been of little avail. Although the present system of managing runs leads to less manual help being required than was formerly the case, still there are some thousands of men employed in the colony in the various necessary departments of stationwork.

"Any movement to promote the welfare of the bushman should therefore have the sympathy and co-operation of the public. It is on this account that we have given considerable prominence in our columns to the affairs of the Bushmen's Club. We are especially glad that from the commencement of that valuable institution we have had to record its uninterrupted progress and prosperity. The Club has fully answered the expectations of the promoters in affording a home to bushmen visiting town. Hundreds have been glad to avail themselves of its comfortable accommodation, and so escape the temptations attending lodging at public-houses, or more questionable places. The Savings Bank connected with the Club has also been extensively used. The general agency the Home has afforded for transacting all kinds of bushmen's business has been valued to an equal extent. Some idea of the appreciation in which the Club is held will be gained from the fact that since its formation seven hundred and sixty-four members have been enrolled. Of these about four hundred remain good on the books. An estimate can also be formed of the large extent to which deposits of savings have taken place when it is stated that during the same time the Hon. Superintendent has repaid the men fully £10,000.

"The institution has been liberally helped by several friends, who from the first have never flagged in their interest and assistance. We have pleasure in calling attention to a very liberal offer recently made to the Trustees by Mr. G. F. Angas, proofs of whose generosity the colony is constantly witnessing. To enable the Trustees to purchase the freehold which is now used for Club purposes, Mr. Angas kindly lent the sum of £500 free of interest. Last month the loan was renewed for another year upon the same terms. But Mr. Angas now offers to give the Club that amount, conditionally upon other friends of the institution contributing a similar sum. Immediately on £500 being raised the promissory-note now held from the Trustees will be given back to them. We earnestly hope that it is only necessary for this liberal offer to be made public for the needful sum to be raised which will secure the carrying out of Mr. Angas's offer. The help will come very opportunely. The accommodation afforded in the present buildings, notwithstanding the recent additions, has become too limited to meet the growing wants of the Club. It has therefore been decided to build another wing similar to that erected last year. Already the walls are rapidly going up, and the addition when finished will provide a large dining-room and an adjoining smoking-room. The partition dividing these chambers will be removable, so as to give the extra advantage of a large room, available at any time for social gatherings.

"We strongly urge upon squatters and all who are

interested in the Club the desirableness of an effort being at once made to secure the gift we have referred to. The life of a bushman is one of considerable monotony and solitude. It is no wonder that the temptations of public-house life, to which in the past their holidays inevitably exposed them, have been extensively yielded to. The Home provides a beneficial check to the social excesses by which as a class they have been too much characterised. Already has its influence for good been widely exercised. The addition to its funds which this gift will make will place the institution in a most healthy financial position. The sum required to be raised is not a large one. A slight exercise of generosity on the part of those of our wealthy colonists who are more or less directly interested in pastoral pursuits will at once meet the case. We therefore hope that the Honorary Superintendent will soon be able to announce that the necessary £500 has been subscribed, and that the Club will consequently receive the benefit of Mr. Angas's liberality."

From the *Advertiser*, August 30, 1872—

"This very excellent institution has been so much appreciated that it is again found necessary to enlarge it, and with a view to doing that an appeal is now being made, not simply to those directly interested—the bushmen—but also to their employers, and to the public generally, who are asked to assist in rendering an institution that has proved itself such an advantage in the past, a still greater source of good. We understand that Mr. G. F. Angas, J.P., with characteristic liberality, has renewed for the second year a loan of £500 free of interest; and Mr. Angas is prepared to do still more. He offers, conditionally upon a like amount being raised, to make the Trustees a present of the loan; and it is to take advantage of this very generous offer that the present appeal is being made. We may point out that the institution is not solely a boon to the bushmen, but it is also an advantage to the proprietors of runs, and to the commercial public of Adelaide, amongst the latter of whom a considerable sum of money is annually spent."

The following short notices taken from the *Evening Journal*, September 3, 1872, respecting the formation and progress of

Bushmen's Homes in the sister colonies, will, without doubt, be read with great interest :—

"THE SYDNEY BUSHMEN'S HOME.—A public meeting was lately held in furtherance of the project of establishing a Bushmen's Home for New South Wales. Captain Scott, Police Magistrate, presided. Captain Evans, the Treasurer, reported that he had received £121 9s. 10d., which sum stood in the books of the Savings Bank, besides promised contributions. He had no doubt that another £100 would without difficulty be collected. It was resolved, on the motion of Mr. Meares, seconded by Captain Evans, that under these favourable circumstances it is expedient that a Bushmen's Home should be at once commenced. A Sub-Committee was then appointed, consisting of Captain Scott, Chairman ; Captain Evans, Treasurer ; Mr. J. W. Smart, Secretary ; Mr. W. D. Meares and Mr. Lavers, to select premises suitable, purchase furniture and other requisites, and report to the General Committee. The Chairman was authorised to request the Governor to become patron."

"BUSHMEN'S HOMES.—The example set by Adelaide in successfully founding the first public Home for bushmen in Australasia is now being worthily followed by Victoria and New South Wales. The latest example of this in the adjoining province is the projected erection at Hamilton, in the Western District, of a two-storey brick structure, with accommodation for about thirty, or even at times forty, inmates, irrespective of the Superintendent and his family. The ground floor will contain sitting and bed-rooms for the Manager, large dining-room and kitchen, the whole of the upper floor being the dormitory. The cost is expected to be about £500."

In consequence of the severe illness of the Hon. Superintendent, the next meeting of the Board of Management for general business was not held until November 4, 1872. Present—Messrs. H. Giles (chair) and C. B. Young.

Vouchers called over and found correct.

Total receipts for the past two months, £137 15s.

Total number of tickets issued to date, 838.

It was resolved by the Board that the annual general meeting be held December 20, 1872, and the following advertisement was published:—

"NOTICE TO BUSHMEN.

"The annual general meeting of the Club will be held (D.V.) at the Club-house on Friday, 20th December, 1872, at 7 p.m., for general business. Persons holding proxies (intended to have effect) are requested to send them to 'William,' Hon. Superintendent, before that date. Further particulars hereafter.

"By order of Board of Management,

"'WILLIAM,'

"Hon. Superintendent Bushmen's Club."

On the 3rd December the next meeting of the Board took place. There were present—Messrs. C. B. Young (chair) and H. Giles, when the usual monthly business was transacted.

Total receipts for November were £127 15s.

Total number of tickets issued, 865.

The greatest number of boarders ever attained at the Club was reached during this month—52.

The Superintendent reported that he was compelled to take possession of the new dining hall in consequence of so many boarders coming in. That he had provided twelve more beds, furniture, &c., and placed them in the late dining-room, which makes a nice light airy bed-room. That it would be necessary for him to give notice of the annual picnic and formal opening of the dining hall. That J. H. Angas, Esq., M.P., had kindly promised £10 towards the picnic. That the Club accounts would, with the Board's permission, be closed as usual on the 9th December, and the report and balance-sheet made out; and that a special meeting of the Board be called during the month to examine and pass same, also to make final preparations for annual general meeting to be held on the 20th inst.

To inform absent members and friends of the different movements on foot at this season, it was thought necessary to insert the following advertisement:—

"Important Notice to Bushmen.

"bushmen's picnic.

"On the day of the annual general meeting, to be held on Friday, December 20, 1872, a trip to Henley Beach and supper on return home, have been decided upon. The party will leave the Club Home, Whitmore-square, at 8.45 a.m. punctually.

"Provisions, music, and amusements will be provided.

"Bushmen (who are not inmates of the Club) and friends of members, who wish to join the party, are respectfully invited, and will please send their names, or apply to the Hon. Superintendent, on or before the 19th instant, for a free pass for that purpose.

"There will be no charge.

"On the return of the excursionists, about 6 p.m., J. H. Angas, Esq., M.P., will formally open the new dining hall, and has again kindly consented to preside (after supper) at the annual meeting. The day's recreation will terminate with a philharmonic concert, commencing about 8 p.m.

"'William,'
"Hon. Superintendent Bushmen's Club.

"Adelaide, December 5, 1872.

"Now, bushmen, rally round your Club, and make the entertainment a great success."

The following article bearing upon this subject appeared in the *Evening Journal* of December 6, 1872 :—

"The Bushmen's Club.—We understand that the new dining hall in connection with the Bushmen's Club is to be formally opened on Friday, the 20th inst. A request, signed by a large number of bushmen, has been forwarded to Mr. J. H. Angas, M.P., asking him to perform this duty, and we hear that not only has he consented, but will preside at the annual meeting. An advertisement elsewhere gives full particulars of the day's proceedings, and we see that the annual picnic is to take place at Henley Beach. Not only are the members themselves expected to lead in the day's enjoyment, but their friends are invited, and each will be furnished with a free ticket on applying to the Superintendent of the Club. By way of contributing towards the expenses, Mr. Angas has, with his accustomed liberality, promised £10, and no doubt as a large number of men are at the Club, the enjoyment of this festive day will surpass anything of the past; music, a variety of amusements, and refreshments of the best kind being provided. We also hear that all the members of the Board of Management have consented to serve again if re-elected. Messrs. H. Giles and C. B. Young, having generously kept at their post from the commencement of the Club, have made themselves well acquainted with its working, and are, as well as the Trustees, deserving of the best thanks of all who feel an interest in this institution. The proceedings will terminate with a philharmonic concert."

A special meeting of the Board was called for the 17th December, at which the report and balance-sheet was examined and passed for the annual meeting.

On December 20, 1872, the following notices appeared in the evening papers:—

Evening Journal—

"THE BUSHMEN'S PICNIC.—On Friday, at about 9 a.m. three large omnibuses, filled with bushmen, started, accompanied by a brass band, from the Club-house in Whitmore-square, under a good display of bunting, their destination being the seashore at Henley Beach, where the bushmen and their friends have arranged to spend the day. On their way they drove past the *Register* and *Observer* offices, and there gave three hearty cheers for Mr. W. K. Thomas, one of the Trustees of the Club; after which they proceeded on their journey, nothing daunted by a pelting shower which was falling at the time. The picnicers intend returning in time for this evening's proceedings at their institution."

"BUSHMEN'S CLUB.—The annual meeting of this useful institution will be held under the presidency of Mr. J. H. Angas, M.P., this evening. Arrangements have also been made for an excursion to the sea beach during the day, and for a concert in the evening."

Express and Telegraph—

"The bushmen's picnic is being held to-day at Henley Beach. Upwards of sixty bushmen and their friends started from the Home about 9 o'clock in three coaches supplied by Hill, Mills, & Co. The leading one, containing the Concordia Band and the banner bearing the inscription "United Bushmen's Club," was drawn by six horses. After proceeding along several streets, receiving as they passed the hearty cheers of the citizens, who turned out *en masse*, they drew up at the *Advertiser* office, and gave three hearty cheers; and then drove on to the *Register*, where a similar compliment was paid. Having returned to the Home to pick up any stragglers, the party proceeded on their way with every intention to enjoy themselves, in spite of the threatening state of the weather."

The following reports of the day's transactions, clipped from the evening papers of December 21, 1872, will, as a wind-up to this compilation, be acceptable to the general reader:—

From the *Evening Journal*—

"THE BUSHMEN'S CLUB.

"THE PICNIC.

"Friday, December 20, was a red-letter day to the bushmen of South Australia at present staying in Adelaide. At about 9 a.m. three large and well-filled omnibuses, started, accompanied by the Concordia Brass Band, from the Clubhouse in Whitmore-square, under a good display of bunting, their destination being the seashore at Glenelg, where the bushmen and their friends spent the day. On their way they drove past the *Register* and *Observer* offices, and there gave three hearty cheers for Mr. W. K. Thomas, one of the Trustees of the Club; they visited the *Advertiser* office and gave cheers there also, after which they proceeded on their journey, nothing daunted by a pelting shower which was falling at the time. At Glenelg a very pleasant day was spent in games of quoits, football, and other sports. A tent, which they took with them, was erected, and in this a good supply of refreshments was provided. The greatest harmony prevailed, and the men, necessarily having somewhat kindred tastes, enjoyed to the fullest extent the company of each other. At about 4 p.m. they started on the return journey under the joyous strains of music, and arrived at the Clubhouse at about 5 o'clock.

"OPENING OF THE DINING HALL.

"The appearance of the Club and grounds presents a marked difference to that of last year, and is vastly improved. A new wing is now added, and the garden has been laid out in beds, and shows signs of care and cultivation. The place was gaily decorated with flags, internally as well as externally. It is pleasant to observe that careful provision is made for the bushman's true and often in his loneliness his only friend —his dog. Neat little houses are erected, and kept remarkably clean, and in them we noticed several canine tenants.

"On the return of the party from the sea-side, the opening of the new dining hall took place. The ceremony was performed by

"Mr. J. H. Angas, M.P., who said that it afforded him much pleasure to meet them that afternoon, more particularly as he understood they had had a very enjoyable day for the picnic. The object of assembling was to formally open that new wing to the building, which had been erected in consequence of the accommodation being insufficient for the number of men who had joined the institution. They had been obliged to build according to their resources—to cut the garment according to the cloth—and had they had sufficient funds they would have erected a new building entirely. They were, however, compelled to put it up by degrees, and they had built these two wings with a view of carrying out the design, a drawing of which was exhibited in the library. He was pleased to find that the number of members had considerably increased, and he hoped it would continue to do so, in order that they might ultimately be able to complete the building, and erect the centre portion in accordance with the design. The building just completed formed the eastern wing of the general plan, and comprised a dining-room 40 by 25 feet, and a smoking-room 25 by 16 feet, separated by a movable partition, so that the whole could be thrown into one hall, when required, measuring 65 by 25 feet, and having a height of 18 feet. Ample provision was made for ventilation, both by the windows and the roof. When the friends of the institution were in a position to warrant the erection of the central building, it was intended to convert the east wing into a dormitory in the same manner as the west wing, which was completed last year, and with which it corresponded in exterior. The style of the building was Italian, and was constructed of hard bluestone, with dressings of cement. The contract was taken at £540 by Mr. Farr, who carried out the work under the direction of Mr. James Cumming, as architect. He had examined the plans originally prepared, and he could assure them that the Trustees had made such alterations as to insure the best arrangement for carrying out the design. He had seen the works several times while in course of construction, and he believed them to be finished in a very satisfactory manner. The object they had in view was not only to provide a dining and smoking-room, but when the partition was removed it would form an excellent lecture hall and a room in which they could hold their periodical meetings, soirees, and entertainments. The settlers often had such meetings in the country, and he did not see why they should not enjoy similar social gatherings at their Club. Knowing that many among them were men of intelligence and well able to contribute to the enjoyment of their companions, he trusted that these periodical meetings would be held. There were no men, he thought, who could not in some measure benefit their fellow-creatures; and if they only made good use of the talents and opportunities with which Providence had blessed them, they could not fail to exert a beneficial influence upon those associated with them. The Club could not be considered a decided success until it was a self-supporting institution, and he hoped they would do what they could according to their several abilities to promote its well being. He then formally declared the hall open.

"The company having given three cheers for Mr. Angas sat down to dinner, an excellent spread having been provided.

"THE ANNUAL MEETING was afterwards held. There was a large attendance of bushmen and others. The President (Mr. J. H. Angas, M.P.) occupied the chair, and there were also present Messrs. J. M. Solomon, M.P., W. K. Thomas, J.P., R. L. Coward, and other friends of the institution.

"The President said that this was, as they were aware, the third anniversary of the Bushmen's Club. As there was to be a concert at 8 o'clock the proceedings must necessarily be very brief, therefore he should not trouble them with many remarks. If it had not been that they were straitened for time he should have indulged in a few remarks to them as bushmen, but he trusted that he should have another opportunity of doing so. There were several gentlemen who had received invitations. He had received a letter from Mr. James Smith regretting his inability to be present as he was unwell, but he sent his thanks for the invitation, hoped they might have a good gathering, and that the institution would meet with continued and increased success. He also had a letter from Mr. David Fowler, who would have been glad to have attended, had not circumstances prevented. The principal matters mentioned in the programme were the report of the proceedings during the last year and the financial statement. He would now call upon 'William,' the Superintendent, to read the report, which would give them full information as to what had been done.

"The Superintendent then read the report of the Board of Management for the year ending 9th December, 1872, as follows:—

"Mr. Chairman and Members of the Bushmen's Club—Your Board of Management are highly gratified on this occasion to meet you, and render an account of their transactions during the third year of the establishment of this increasingly-popular institution, and take this opportunity first of all to acknowledge the goodness of Almighty God in prospering the work, for without His favour nothing good, strong, or durable is accomplished. Secondly, to congratulate you, Mr. Chairman, the members, and all the friends of bushmen, not only on account of the Club's continuance, but its steadily-growing usefulness to the class of men it is more especially intended to benefit, as the following particulars will show.

"It will be necessary, to get a clear idea of the work done in the past twelvemonth, to draw a slight sketch of transactions during the first and second years of the Club's existence.

"You will probably remember that in the beginning of 1870 the present premises were rented from Mr. Jas. Hosking, for £110 per annum, and that it was strongly recommended by the Board (at the first annual meeting) that measures should be taken to secure the freehold to save that £110. In 1871 negotiations were opened with Mr. Hosking, which resulted in the purchase of sufficient land and buildings for present purposes for the sum of £1,000 cash down on a given day. It will also be remembered that George Fife Angas, Esq., came to the fore, and (as the Committee had not so large a sum available) lent £500 without interest for twelve months; that to this timely generous act on the part of Mr. Angas, sen., the liberal donations of our worthy Chairman, and the subscriptions of the bushmen themselves, together with the efficient services of the Hon. Superintendent 'William,' must be attributed the security and present favourable condition of the Club. It will be remembered that, on account of more sleeping accommodation being required, it was resolved to add a new wing to the building, and on the 23rd September, 1871, the foundation-stone of a dormitory was formally laid by D. Murray, Esq., M.P. The building was finished and opened for use on the 14th November following.

"It was suggested by the Board at last annual meeting that a large dining-room would soon be needed to meet the pressing need for space. Shortly after this it was proposed by Mr. Angas to draw up a petition to Parliament. This was prepared by C. B. Young, Esq., and duly presented by Messrs. D. Murray and L. Glyde, asking for a supplementary grant of £500, which sum was placed on the Estimates for 1872. The same gentleman also recommended that a frontage on Gilbert-street be secured to the Club.

"Your Board are now in a position to state that the Government grant of £500 was duly received, but conditionally :—1st. That a like sum of £500 be raised by private subscriptions. 2nd. That, in the event of the undertaking proving a failure, the money borrowed from Her Majesty's Government be returned.

"To meet the first requirement the bulk of the subscriptions were soon raised, the following gentlemen generously giving each the handsome sum of £100 :—Messrs. G. F. Angas, J. H. Angas, T. Elder, and Captain W. W. Hughes ; the balance was made up by the bushmen and their friends.

"A frontage on Gilbert-street (before alluded to) of 148 feet was secured to the Club in February last for the sum of £233. Messrs. J. H. Angas, Hon. Thos. Elder, and D. Murray undertook the responsibility in this case, there being no funds to spare ; and these gentlemen, together with Messrs. Anstey & Giles, W. Duffield, and H. B. Hughes, eventually made it a present to the Club.

"On the 13th July last notice was received from Mr. Angas, sen., stating that in accordance with the request of the Trustees he had agreed to allow the promissory-note for £500 that day due to stand over for another year—again without interest. But the kindness of Mr. Angas was not to rest here ; he did more than that, for on the 28th August last the Hon. Superintendent received a note from our respected Chairman, stating that on £500 being raised by subscriptions for the Building Fund of the Club, his father would give back to the Trustees the promissory-note due to him in July, 1873. In consequence of this a fund has been opened, called the Angas Contingent Fund, and it is now urged upon the bushmen and the friends of the bushmen to make a strong effort to obtain this noble gift of Mr. Angas's.

"Again, it has recently been found necessary to increase the accommodation by the addition of a second wing to the building, which will cost between £500 and £600, and on the 2nd July your Board offered to provide £250 out of the current funds if the other part was raised by the friends of the institution. As the matter was very pressing and it was considered desirable that the building should be ready for use after shearing time, application was made to Mr. J. H. Angas again, who considerately offered to advance £250, without interest, for one year, to meet the wishes of the Board, and by his so doing it enabled the Board to commence building at once, and the fine dining-hall we are now assembled in is the result of that act of kindness.

"A policy of insurance has been executed on the building for the sum of £800, another on the furniture and fittings for £300. Last meeting it was reported that accommodation was provided for forty-seven persons; we can now state that the Home is prepared to receive sixty persons without overcrowding, the large room lately used for dining purposes having been converted into a dormitory containing twelve beds.

"There have been 234 tickets of membership issued during the past year. The total number reported last meeting was 640; these added together make a total of 876 tickets issued since the opening of the Club in May, 1870. There are now 271 good on the list, and though there is a falling off in the number of members there is a considerable increase in the number of boarders. This decrease of members is attributed to various causes. A great number of bushmen have left the colony; many fail to renew their tickets for want of opportunity; prejudice, marriages, and deaths have their influence also. It appears that there has been so much said *pro* and *con.* about the institution that the men disregard anything that may now be urged, and content themselves by paying the Club a visit and trying it for themselves.

"Very little business has been done in the labour department. This is to be accounted for by the facts that none but bush labour is obtained at the Club Office, and the vacancies on the runs being generally filled by persons seeking employment in the country.

"The suggestion of Captain Hart respecting a free general labour office for the whole of the colony, similar to the Shipping-Master's Office in the Seamen's Homes, to be opened and worked in connection with this establishment, has not been carried out, your Board being of opinion that the institution has not yet sufficiently advanced to undertake the work.

"The Club Post-Office has been kept pretty busy during the year, and has greatly benefited the bush people. A very large number of letters, papers, book-parcels, &c., have been passed on to their destination.

"The library has slowly but steadily increased to 227 volumes. There have been some periodicals and files of papers added. We gladly return thanks to Messrs. Storrie for their valuable gift of 'Chambers's Journal' complete for ten years; also for a gift of four large volumes of 'Chambers's Explanatory Dictionary,' valued at 30 guineas, presented by Mr. Finniss; to Mr. H. A. Short and other kind and considerate friends, for papers, periodicals, &c. They afford much interest and instruction to bushmen—a class proverbial for reading.

"The number of weekly boarders admitted during the year was 580; casual, about 620; travelling bushmen relieved, 69; showing an increase on last year's report of 217 weekly boarders, 120 casual boarders, 34 travellers, &c., relieved. The highest number of inmates at one time in the institution, 52; last year's report gives 33.

"In the savings department there have been large sums in cash received and paid back in instalments, and a number of cheques, drafts, Savings Bank pass-books, &c., have been left in the Superintendent's custody. It should be observed here that the moneys deposited for safe keeping are liable to withdrawal at any time. The Club derives no profit from the transaction, but confers great benefit on the bushmen by securing their means for them and by paying it back in small sums as required.

"There are also the chests, swags, bags, parcels of clothing, &c., of over eighty different bushmen left in store, while the owners of same are away in the country at their work. These facts undoubtedly prove the need, usefulness, and increasing popularity of the institution among the men.

"A workable scheme for a Benefit Fund has not yet been found, though it is not lost sight of, and it is considered at present prudent not to risk the character or integrity of the Club on any mere speculation. Should any practicable plan be forthcoming it will be adopted by your Board. The same rules which guide other Friendly Societies are impracticable for bushmen generally.

"There have been four cases of death in the Hospital of men belonging to the Club during the past year, and the sum of £8 4s. with a silver watch was handed over to the

Curator of Intestate Estates, and a proper receipt obtained for the same.

"Several tickets have been given away for medical attendance, supplied chiefly through the Messrs. Angas. In a short time arrangements may be made to supply the great want of medical attendance for sick bushmen in town from the Club itself.

"On this occasion it is our pleasant duty to recognise the services of all those who in any way contributed so liberally, and were instrumental under God in establishing this useful institution. The efforts put forth have not failed to elicit praises and to stir up the energies of the friends of bushmen in all the principal sister colonies. It must be very gratifying to them all to find that their labours have been appreciated in the right way. It is further hoped that the bushmen and the friends of the institution will not relax their efforts, and will endeavour to make the Club not only useful, but permanent and self-supporting—bearing in mind that there yet remain many useful and important branches to shoot forth.

"In drawing this report to a close we desire to bear testimony to the invaluable services rendered to this institution by the Editors of the *Register, Advertiser*, and Press generally.

"In conclusion, it may be remarked that the promised history of this, the first Bushmen's Club in the colonies (compiled by 'William'), is now in the press, and will (D.V.) be published some time in the beginning of the coming year; and as the profits arising therefrom are to be devoted to the benefit of the institution, a very large circulation is anticipated."

"The financial statement was read, and showed:—Assets—Land and premises, £2,022 9s. 3d.; furniture and fittings, £499 4s. 6d.; cash in hand at date, £51 10s. 3d.—total assets, £2,573 4s. Liabilities—Loan due to Mr. G. F. Angas, £500; overdraft at Bank of Australasia at date, £147 12s. 6d.—total liabilities, £647 12s. 6d. Excess of assets over liabilities, £1,925 11s. 6d. In reference to Mr. Angas's loan of £500, it was stated that it was lent without interest, and on the understanding that if an equal amount should be raised by July 5, 1873, it should form part of the estate of the Club.

"Mr. R. L. Coward moved—'That the very satisfactory report and financial statement now read be adopted and published for the information of absent members and friends; and that the measure of success which has attended this establishment demands from this meeting an expression of devout thanks to God, and lays a greater obligation upon all concerned in its prosperity.'

"Mr. J. M. Solomon, M.P., seconded in an able speech, and the motion was carried.

"Mr. James Joyce moved, and Mr. Charles Lewis seconded, and it was resolved—"That the thanks of the bushmen generally, and of the members of the Club particularly, are hereby tendered to the Trustees—Messrs. J. H. Angas, D. Murray, and W. K. Thomas; to the Board of Management —Messrs. S. Davenport, H. Giles, and C. B. Young; to Messrs. G. F. Angas, J. H. Angas, Hon. T. Elder, Captain W. W. Hughes, Messrs. H. B. Hughes, D. & W. Murray, and other kind and considerate friends, for their practical sympathy and support; and that the following gentlemen now nominated—Messrs. H. Giles, C. B. Young, and R. A. Tarlton —be appointed as a Board of Management for the ensuing year.'

"Thanks to the Chairman and the Honorary Superintendent closed the meeting.

"THE CONCERT.

"It must have been with feelings akin to those of triumph that 'William' and the other zealous friends of the institution saw how liberally patronised their efforts were by the public in that department of their labours in which the public might be expected to participate. Before the business meeting was fairly closed, ladies and gentlemen began to assemble in the large dining hall in anticipation of the evening's concert. Before it commenced the room was full, and a little later it became quite crowded, several of the *elite* graciously adding their welcome presence to the entertainment. Great praise is due to the ladies and gentlemen who so unostentatiously and benevolently gave their services as performers; and we are sure that they felt amply rewarded when at the close of the evening sixty powerful lungs vigorously testified to the appreciation as many hardy bushmen had of the efforts which had been so successfully made to entertain them.

"Mr. J. H. Angas, with a few appropriate observations, introduced the performers. After an overture had been well played by Herr Ivison, Mr. J. C. Hawker sang 'The Englishman,' and as he sang, the tones struck familiarly on the ear of one of the sons of the bush, who, taking up the refrain from the middle of the room, where he was sitting, astonished the crowded assembly by joining lustily in the song. Herr Fischer then sang 'The Death of Nelson' in a key about a third lower than that in which Braham has written it with excellent expression, and elicited warm applause, as indeed did all the performers. Mrs. Proctor sang 'The Last Rose of Summer,' Miss Vaughan sang 'The Dashing White Sergeant,' Dr. R. Peel sang 'Molly Bawn,' Mr. Burrell sang 'When other Lips,' Mr. Jagoe sang the 'Friar of Orders Grey,' Mr. Bell sang in several duets and part songs, and Mr. Oughton took the bass in two unaccompanied quartettes. Messrs. Watson and Peacock sang in character two comic songs—'Married to a Mermaid' and 'The Cork Leg' respectively. Several other duets made up a capital programme, which it is no flattery to say was gone through exceedingly well from beginning to end. If we were called upon to particularize we should mention as being highly entertaining the duet between Mrs. Proctor and Dr. Peel called 'The Lovers' Quarrel.' It is a little musical drama in itself, and it was certainly very cleverly performed, and met with an encore. The recitation 'Monsieur Tonson' is familiar to everybody; but we think that no one who heard it recited at the Bushmen's Club on Friday evening by Mr. Fred. Whitington ever heard it better delivered. The entertainment was a great treat, and such as bushmen rarely have the opportunity of enjoying.

"The National Anthem was then sung, and Mr. Solomon, M.P., called for three cheers for the Chairman, which were immediately given. The company then dispersed."

From the *Express and Telegraph*—
"The Bushmen's Club.
"ANNIVERSARY CELEBRATION.

"The members of the Bushmen's Club, Whitmore-square, celebrated their third anniversary on Friday, December 20, by a picnic on the Glenelg Beach. Upwards of sixty bushmen and their friends started from the Home about 9 o'clock in three coaches supplied by John Hill & Co. The leading one, containing the Concordia Band and the banner bearing the inscription " United Bushmen's Club," was drawn by six horses. After proceeding along several streets, receiving as they passed the hearty cheers of the citizens, who turned out *en masse*, they drew up at the *Advertiser* office, and gave three hearty cheers; and then drove on to the *Register*, where a similar compliment was paid. Having returned to the Home to pick up any stragglers, the party proceeded on their way with every intention to enjoy themselves, in spite of the threatening state of the weather. Arrived at the scene of the day's festivities a variety of games, comprising cricket, football, quoits, &c., were indulged in, and the weather having cleared up, and being delightfully fine, thorough enjoyment and harmony characterised the proceedings. About 5 o'clock the party returned to the Club, where the men assembled in the newly-erected eastern wing of the premises.

"OPENING OF DINING HALL.

"Mr. J. H. Angas, M.P., addressing the men, said it afforded him much pleasure to meet them that afternoon, more particularly as he understood they had had a very enjoyable day at the picnic. The object of assembling them was to formally open that new wing to the building, which had been erected in consequence of the accommodation being insufficient for the number of men who had joined the institution. They had been obliged to build according to their resources—to cut their garment according to their cloth; but had they had sufficient funds, they would like to have erected a new building entirely. They were, however, compelled to put it up by degrees, and they had built the two wings with a view to carrying out the design exhibited in the library. He was pleased to find the number of members had considerably increased, and he hoped it would continue to do so in order that they might ultimately be able to complete the building, and erect the centre portion in accordance with the design. He then mentioned that the building just completed formed the eastern wing of the general plan, and comprised a dining-room 40 x 25, and a smoking-room 25 x 16, which were separated by a movable partition, so that the whole could be thrown into one hall when required, measuring 56 x 25 feet, and having a height of 18 feet. Ample provision was made for ventilation, both by the windows and the roof. When the funds of the institution were in a position to warrant the erection of the central building it was intended to convert the eastern wing into a dormitory in the same manner as the western wing which was erected last year, and with which it corresponded in its exterior. The style of the building was Italian, and was carried out in hard bluestone with dressings of cement. The contract was taken at £540 by Mr. C. Farr, who had executed the work under the direction of the architect (Mr. James Cumming). He had examined the plans, and he could assure them the Trustees had made the best arrangements for carrying out the detail. He had seen the works several times during their construction, and he believed them to be completed in a satisfactory manner. The object they had in view was not only to provide a dining and a smoking-room, but when the partition was removed it would form an excellent lecture room, in which they could hold periodical meetings, readings, and entertainments. The settlers often had these meetings when in the country, and he did not see why they should not hold such social gatherings at their club. Knowing that many among them were men of intelligence and well able to contribute to the enjoyment of their companions, he trusted these periodical meetings would be inaugurated. There were no men he thought who could not in some measure benefit their fellows, and if they only made a proper use of the talents and opportunities with which Providence had blessed them, they could not fail to exert an influence for good upon those associated with them. He hoped they would do what they could, according to their several abilities, for the welfare of the institution. He then formally declared the hall to be open.

"Cheers having been given for Mr. Angas, the company sat down to an excellent supper.

"ANNUAL MEETING.

"At 7 o'clock the annual meeting of the members was held in the large hall opened that evening. The whole of the bushmen resident in the Club were present, and took a deep interest in the proceedings. Mr. J. H. Angas, M.P., presided. In opening the meeting, he remarked that that was the third anniversary of the Bushmen's Club. As, however, there was to be a concert at 8 o'clock, and the proceedings must be brief, he should not trouble them with many remarks, although he should like to have indulged in a few words regarding the bushmen and their interests, but he trusted he should have another opportunity of addressing them. There were several gentlemen who had received invitations to be present that evening, but he regretted to say some of them were unable to attend. Mr. James Smith had sent a note regretting his inability to be present, expressing his thanks to the bushmen for their kind invitation, and hoping they would have a successful gathering, that the institution might meet with continued and increased success. Mr. D. Fowler also wrote, regretting that he could not be there, and expressing his hearty sympathy with the institution. The principal matter to be brought under their notice was the report and financial statement, which he would ask 'William,' the Hon. Superintendent, to read.

"'William' then read the report, as published in to-day's *Advertiser* and *Chronicle*.

"Mr. R. L. Coward moved—'That the very satisfactory report and financial statement now read be adopted and published for the information of absent members and friends, and that the measure of success which has attended the establishment demands from this meeting an expression of devout thanks to God, and lays a greater obligation upon all concerned in its prosperity.' He said it was not expected of him to make many remarks, seeing that the time was so far gone, and they were all in expectation of spending a pleasant evening. He could not, however, help saying a few words respecting the report, in the part referring to the *pros* and *cons*, which had been expressed in the bush with regard to the Club. Therefore, he had come down from the bush as a bushman—not as a shepherd or a stockholder, but as a bushman—to know what kind of an establishment the Bushmen's Club was; and he could say with the Queen of Sheba, 'Not half has been told.' He was sure in no part of the colony was there such a place. He had taken up his abode for several days in the Club, and he had found in it everything a bushman could desire. They ought to be proud in possessing such an institution; and he trusted every one of them would endeavour to do all in his power to further its success. (Applause).

"The Chairman, in asking Mr. J. M. Solomon, M.P., to second the resolution, remarked that that gentleman, when Mayor of this city, was one of those who had taken a lively interest in inaugurating this movement, and he was pleased to welcome him in their midst. (Cheers.)

"Mr. Solomon, in seconding the resolution, said the Chairman had been pleased to refer to him as one of the first who had taken an active interest in the formation of the Bushmen's Club. He certainly did not anticipate that in three years it would have made the rapid strides it had. They must not forget the indefatigable exertions of 'William,' seconded by the princely gifts and labours of Mr. G. F. Angas and his son, the Chairman; and there must be a pride that South Australia stood first in the efforts she had made in this matter, and that the other colonies, which were considered much more important, were following in her footsteps. He need not remind them that that evening they and a number of lady and gentlemen friends had attended, not so much to listen to speechifying as to celebrate the success of the Club. He should therefore curtail the remarks he might otherwise have indulged in. Their Club had made such rapid strides as had characterised no sailors' home, or institution having kindred objects, in any of the other colonies; and therefore he thought South Australia might be justly proud of the position she occupied in this movement. It had had an effect which he was sure had been noticed by all in their city, for they now no longer saw their bushmen going through the streets having no one to care for them. They saw that men with their hard-earnings were not led away into scenes of vice as they were at one time. Therefore he considered upon that ground alone the institution should be encouraged by every one, and more particularly by the Government. He wished the Club every prosperity. (Applause).

"The resolution was carried *nem. con.*

"Mr. James Joyce then moved—'That the thanks of the bushmen generally, and of the members of the Club particularly, are hereby tendered to the Trustees—Messrs. J. H. Angas, M.P., D. Murray, and W. K. Thomas; to the Board of Management—Messrs. S. Davenport, H. Giles, and C. B. Young; to Messrs. G. F. Angas, J. H. Angas, M.P., Hon. T. Elder, Captain W. W. Hughes, and Messrs. H. B. Hughes and D. & W. Murray, and other kind and considerate friends, for their practical sympathy and support; and that the following gentlemen now nominated—Messrs. H. Giles, C. B. Young, and R. A. Tarlton—be appointed as a Board of Management for the ensuing year.' He thought there was no man present who did not feel it his bounden and grateful duty to record his thanks to the gentlemen he had mentioned in the resolution. (Hear, hear.)

"Mr. Chas. Lewis seconded the resolution.

"Mr. Solomon, in submitting the resolution, remarked, with reference to the Chairman, that he was sure the vote of thanks was not one-tenth part of what he and his family deserved for the interest they had taken in the Club. (Applause).

"The resolution was then carried unanimously.

"The Chairman explained that a change had been made in the Board of Management, Mr. Tarlton being appointed in the place of Mr. Davenport, in consequence of the latter gentleman's business engagements preventing his regular attendance at the Board meetings.

"Mr. A. S. Stewart then proposed, and 'William' seconded, a vote of thanks to the Chairman, which was carried with three cheers, and 'one more.'

"The Chairman returned thanks for the hearty vote of thanks they had accorded him. He was very pleased to be with them that evening, especially as the report was one that must have satisfied them all. He trusted every year they might see an increased number of men in the Club, for he was sure it met all the requirements of bushmen. As he had said before, he hoped it would not only be used as an eating and sleeping establishment, but that lectures, entertainments and such like meetings, which tended to elevate them in the social scale, might be instituted; for he was satisfied they had friends of valuable attainments who would assist them on such occasions. He impressed upon them, however, that whilst so much was being done by their friends on their behalf, they must not forget that a great deal of the success depended upon their own efforts and individual support. They had two wings to their building, and he hoped they would soon be able to fly. (Laughter.) They now wanted the body. (Laughter.) He held in his hand a photograph of the Bushmen's Home which had been established in Castlereagh-street, Sydney, by Captain Scott's exertions, after obtaining papers and information from 'William.' Judging from the photograph, the building was not so good as that of the South Australian Bushmen's Home; but he trusted it would be of great benefit to those for whom it was organised, and that by the establishment of such institutions throughout the colonies, bushmen might be morally, socially, and pecuniarily benefited. (Applause.)

"Upon the motion of Mr. John Bryan, seconded by Mr. Wm. Patterson, three hearty cheers were then given for 'William.'

"The Chairman said 'William's' services had been rendered cheerfully, and without remuneration, in season and out of season. His motives were pure and honest, and he hoped he he might reap his reward in a higher world. (Cheers.)

"THE ENTERTAINMENT

was very largely attended by the members, and lady and gentleman friends of the institution. Mr. J. H. Angas presided, and in opening the proceedings said he certainly did not think twelve months ago he should have witnessed such a scene as was presented in the hall that evening. He was sure they need not say that their bushmen were neglected, after what they saw. It showed the members of the Club had the sympathy of the people of Adelaide and surrounding districts. The ladies and gentlemen who were to entertain them had voluntarily offered their valuable services for their gratification, and he knew they would highly appreciate their kindness. The programme was then proceeded with, and was of a high-class character, comprising choice songs, duets, quartettes, and recitations, the ladies and gentlemen taking part in the entertainment being Mrs. Proctor, Miss Vaughan, Herr Fischer, Dr. Peel, and Messrs. J. C. Hawker, G. F. Bell, G. Oughton, W. H. Burrell, L. Jagoe, and F. Whitington. The entertainment was a most enjoyable termination to the day's festivities. Mr. W. K. Thomas, in moving a vote of thanks to the ladies and gentlemen who had so generously assisted, said he thought a more excellent entertainment could not have been provided. He suggested to those who had the control of the institution that the entertainment which had been so well inaugurated should be the precursor of many more. (Hear, hear.) He thought if once a month such entertainments could be arranged the bushmen and their friends would appreciate the efforts made in that direction. A vote of thanks having been accorded to the Chairman, the proceedings terminated with the singing of the National Anthem."

On the 25th December, 1872, a leading article appeared in the *Register*, commenting on the progress of the Club thus:—

"Of all the philanthropic movements started in the city, none has been attended with more genuine prosperity than the Bushmen's Club. The history of this institution, as detailed at the annual meeting held last week, is full of interest, and of instruction too. The gentlemen who originally took the matter in hand were wise enough not to attempt too much at first. They saw that bushmen coming to town required a place of resort which would combine as far as possible the comforts and enjoyments of a home with perfect freedom of individual action, and this want they have been gradually supplying. Had they determined upon collecting four or five thousand pounds before beginning to carry out their design, the probability is that they would not by this time have made a single step in advance. As it is, the success attained during the day of small things has stimulated private liberality, and has induced the Parliament to make a special grant for building purposes. It is exceedingly gratifying to read of the progress that is being regularly made by the establishment. Every year it is increasing in popularity, and every year the amount of accommodation provided is being extended. At first an old building was rented at an annual cost of £110. An advantageous offer for its purchase was made and accepted, and the money, thanks to the timely aid of Mr. G. F. Angas, was paid down. In its then state the edifice was not capable of providing sleeping room for more than two or three dozen inmates—a much smaller number than it was thought desirable to make provision for. The Board of Management, after feeling their way, gave orders for the erection of a new wing, which was completed in the course of a couple of months, the opening ceremony taking place in November last. The next step was to purchase a frontage to Gilbert-street; then to build a new dining-hall; then to erect a second wing; and now it is contemplated, although this addition may not be carried out for some time to come, to have a large central edifice connecting the wings. For all these improvements money, either in the way of loan without interest or actual gift, has been readily forthcoming—the only assistance received from the State being the aforesaid grant of £500. The Club, besides being well supported by bushmen, has secured the sympathy and substantial support of wealthy men, such as Messrs. G. F. and J. H. Angas, T. Elder, W. W. Hughes, D. Murray, H. B. Hughes, Anstey & Giles, and W. Duffield. A more deserving channel for the liberality of well-to-do colonists it would be difficult to find, and it is pleasing to observe that they have fittingly responded to the calls made upon them. The Home, we are told, will now readily accommodate sixty inmates. It is furnished with a library and various other accessories, which must materially contribute to the satisfaction with which bushmen can take up their quarters there. It is moreover well and inexpensively conducted, and it is no unworthy boast that it still holds the lead amongst the bushmen's homes of Australia, not only in respect to the date of its organization, but also in reference to the efficiency of its management. The disinterested efforts of the Superintendent to make it a real home for the class in which he feels so deep an interest are beyond all praise. To this may be chiefly attributed the unqualified success which the institution has met with. We commend the course taken in building up the Bushmen's Club as an example that may well be followed by all having in view the promotion of movements of a philanthropic nature. The lesson it teaches, and teaches most impressively, is that the most should be made of moderate means."

The compiler feels that he cannot conclude his work in a better manner than with the few following remarks, viz. :—

The protection afforded to morals and character in this institution can hardly be overstated, and this is accomplished by a measure of control and by regulations which are felt a burden only by the disorderly and the dissolute.

This experiment (for so it must be called) has so far been eminently successful, and there is reason to believe that the improving influence of Clubs, such as these, will act upon the other lodging-houses for the good of the working classes generally.

The object in publishing this work is particularly to call the attention of those who may be in circumstances to establish such institutions to the pecuniary means which are required, and to the facilities which are afforded by the experience already gained in the management.

It has already been shown that with a small capital (less than £1,000) the first Club for bushmen in the Australias has been set up, which in less than three years has become worth over £2,000.

It will be well to add, for the guidance of any patriotic persons who may have it in view to set up Clubs (or other institutions of a similar nature) on a *smaller* scale, that *small Clubs* can hardly be made self-supporting, unless the Committee and Superintendent can give their time gratuitously to give them a good start at the commencement.

ADELAIDE BUSHMEN'S CLUB.

Balance Sheet for the Year ending December 9th, 1872.

Assets.

December 9, 1872.

	£	s.	d.
To Land and Premises— Amount expended on and estimated value at this date	2,022	9	3
" Furniture and Fittings— Amount expended for to this date, less 10 per cent. estimated depreciation for wear and tear	499	4	6
" Cash— Balance in hand at this date	51	10	3
	£2,573	4	0

Liabilities.

June 9, 1872.

	£	s.	d.
By G. F. Angas, Esq.— Loan due by Club, without interest. This amount will form part of the assets should an equal amount be collected before July 5, 1873	500	0	0
" Bank of Australasia— Overdraft at this date	147	12	6
	647	12	6
" Stock Account— Excess of assets over liabilities	1,925	11	6
	£2,573	4	0

Adelaide, December 9, 1872.   Thos. Pope, Accountant.

MISCELLANEOUS EXTRACTS.

The following articles, letters, &c. (which will no doubt be deeply interesting to bush people), are collected from various sources, but chiefly from that truly valuable newspaper, *The Australasian*, and introduced here for perusal. The following, however, is taken from the *South Australian Advertiser*:—

"BOOKS FOR BUSHMEN.

"A meeting was held in Mr. Henry Scott's office in Adelaide on Thursday, March 14, 1872, for the purpose of organising some plan for the systematic circulation of books of a suitable character amongst persons employed in the bush. Mr. C. B. Young, as convener of the meeting, was called to the chair. Letters were received from several gentlemen, who were unable to attend, promising their support to the movement, and one from the Honorary Superintendent of the Bushmen's Club, offering to render any assistance in his power, and enclosing £1 from a 'Bushman' in aid of the funds.

"The Chairman said, it was not so much with a view of getting his own ideas on the subject carried out, as of obtaining the opinions of others perhaps better qualified than himself to suggest the most suitable means of supplying a known want, and putting within the reach of the bush people books of an improving and instructive character in place of the trashy novels which were at present almost the only books they were able to obtain. He would, however, submit his own scheme, with a view of its being improved upon by others.

"1st. A central depôt would be required in Adelaide; probably arrangements might be made for having it at the Bushmen's Club.

"2nd. Depôts would be established in each of the outside townships, which would involve no expense, as the books could be left for sale with respectable storekeepers.

"3rd. Each head station would be a local depôt for circulating books on the run where the owners chose to avail themselves of the movement.

"4th. It would be desirable, if possible, to have a travelling agent to supply the places the other arrangement could not conveniently apply to; but, as this might be too costly, possibly a few respectable hawkers might be found, who would undertake the sale of the books. There were three difficulties to encounter in starting such an undertaking— funds, selection, and distribution. With regard to the first, he did not wish to see a society formed with anything like an annual begging-list. The persons for whose benefit the contemplated society would be formed were able and, he believed, quite willing to pay for the advantages they would receive. There must, however, be a fund to start with for the purchase of books. He would be contented to see the thing started with a capital of £250, if more could not be obtained, and would propose an annual subscription of from two to five guineas from the stations, according to the number of persons employed. Probably the proprietors would, in most cases, be willing to contribute one-half, and the men the other. There must be a committee of management, and a special committee for selecting books, which would not be a very easy task. The books would be passed on from station to station, or exchanged every six months, or oftener, if necessary.

"Mr. H. Scott said that, though the meeting was not a very large one, and might be considered of a preliminary character, it would be as well to take the initiative in the matter by passing such resolutions as would lead to the commencement of a society for the contemplated purpose. He would therefore move the first resolution — 'That it is desirable that steps be taken to supply suitable books to persons employed in the bush.'

Mr. F. Stokes would second the resolution. He believed it would be a very beneficial movement. There were very many persons in the bush fond of reading, and great difficulty experienced in getting readable books. It would be advisable, however, that the books supplied should not be of too dry a character; there should be a variety suited to all tastes, and works of fiction of a wholesome character, as well as those of a more solid description should be supplied. If such an observation would not be out of place, he hoped that something would be done in the way of educating the children in the bush. They were now much neglected, and it was as important to teach them to read as to supply books. He thought the difficulty of passing the books from station to station might be overcome by grouping the runs—four or five of the adjacent stations arranging to exchange at fixed periods, and then getting fresh supplies from the central depôt.

"Carried.

"Mr. J. A. Fergusson would move—'That, in accordance with the former resolution, an association be formed to carry out the proposed object.'

"Mr. C. Sabine thought the capital mentioned, £250, would be very small and insufficient; it would not purchase more than a thousand volumes at most, which would not go far to the extensive circulation proposed. There would also be a difficulty in exchanging the books from station to station, as there might be fifty men on one station and ten on another, the books that had supplied the fifty men for six months could not be read by the ten men in the same time. He would second the resolution.

"Carried.

"Mr. Thomas Giles proposed—'That a committee be formed, consisting of the gentlemen present, and others whose names might be suggested by the meeting.' He thought it desirable that the co-operation of as many persons interested in pastoral pursuits as possible should be obtained. It was very much a matter for the squatters themselves, though some organization was necessary to carry it into effect. He supposed it was not intended that the operations should be confined to the North, and it would be well to seek the assistance of settlers in the South-East, Port Lincoln, and Yorke's Peninsula districts as well. He did not think there would be so much difficulty about exchanging the books; it was easy enough to send a box of books on to the next station. Some trustworthy person on each station would have to take charge of the books, and be responsible for them; probably where there was a storekeeper he would undertake the charge.

"Mr. Smeaton would second the resolution. He did not imagine that such an extensive scheme was contemplated. He thought that the idea would be to get books and periodicals gratuitously from any persons willing to contribute them. There were many persons who, when they had read a book or magazine, would give it to such a society as was contemplated. From this source he thought a considerable supply might be obtained; and, if not sufficient to carry out the object, it would at any rate be a great help.

"The resolutions were all carried *nem. con.*, and the names of a number of gentlemen were suggested to be written to asking their co-operation."—*Advertiser*, March 18, 1872.

Referring to the above subject, the following article is also taken from the columns of the same paper of March 18th, 1872:—

"For some years past considerable interest has been taken by persons connected with pastoral pursuits, and by the public generally, in the social condition of that class of the community commonly designated 'bushmen,' and several schemes for their benefit have been at various times suggested. Out of this desire to do something for a class so far removed from the common comforts and blessings of civilized life sprang the Bushmen's Home, an institution which was launched in the face of much prejudice and great misgivings. The persons for whom this Home was intended being principally those engaged in pastoral labour, it was felt that the chief duty of providing for their wants devolved upon those who profited by their toil—namely, the squatters, and it was feared that the squatters would rather discourage than help forward the movement. However, in this the lessees were unfairly judged, as many of them have come forward liberally, and, indeed, the most generous supporters of the

Home rank amongst the sheepfarmers and stockholders of the colony. Another difficulty arose in the minds of the bushmen themselves, who thought that the idea was a squatter's own idea, and the intention that of reducing wages, or in some way interfering with the freedom of the men. This prejudice has vanished, or is fast vanishing away, and numbers of bushmen can themselves attest the advantages of the Home or Club, and are ready to prove that, whilst it confers all the benefits promised, it is entirely free from all the objections which were urged against it. Another movement for the advantage of bushmen is now on foot; we refer to the project of establishing a Circulating Bushmen's Library, as shadowed forth in the report of a meeting held a few days since in the city of Adelaide. That meeting was but of an incipient character; but the names of the gentlemen who convened and attended it are security that they mean to do something.

"It must be understood, in starting, that this is not an appeal to general public charity. The bushmen, to a great extent, have the means of supplying their own wants; but, though they have the means, they have not the opportunity. Removed by considerable distances from the centres of population, they are dependent for their reading upon whatever literature travelling hawkers may see fit to carry about, and to a large extent this is of a very trashy description. The idea of the gentlemen who have now taken up the matter is, that a good library should be established, comprising works to suit all tastes, selected by a competent committee, the books to be located in various central spots, whence they could be conveyed in boxes to head stations and other suitable places for distribution amongst the men, and then to be forwarded on somewhere else—a perpetual circulation being thus kept up. There are far more reading men in the bush than would be imagined by persons who merely judge of bushmen by the shaggy appearance of the more conspicuous members of the fraternity in the streets of Adelaide and other towns; and we believe they would not only willingly, but gladly contribute to the establishment of a library which they could justly claim as their own. Mr. C. B. Young, by whom the meeting was called together, very properly deprecated 'an annual begging-list,' and proclaimed his belief that the parties for whom he pleaded were both able and willing to pay for the advantages which would be secured to them. In the same spirit of self-reliance Mr. Thomas Giles said 'it was a question very much for the squatters themselves'—that is, so far as the bushmen required help; and we cannot too highly commend this recognition of the maxim that 'property has its duties as well as its rights.' Still, whilst maintaining that the bushmen themselves should, by their own contributions, make the library their own, and whilst agreeing with Mr. Giles that the bushmen, so far as they may really require extrinsic help, should receive it from the lessees of the Crown, there is no reason why other classes of the community should not aid in the first establishment of the enterprise. Funds will be wanted, and it must be remembered that books will need to be frequently renewed, as they will not last so long in the huts of bushmen and out in the scrub as they would in city dwellings.

"There is just one thing absolutely necessary to the success of the enterprise—namely, that the bushmen be not allowed to suppose that they are going to be drilled and schooled into a particular class of reading. Of course it is not intended to limit their choice, nor to put restraints on their intellectual tastes; but whilst there is no such intention there may arise the suspicion, and steps should be taken to anticipate it. In appealing to bushmen to patronise and support their own library, they should be invited to *nominate books for selection*, and printed forms should be supplied to them, upon which they might inscribe the titles of books they would like to read. All works so nominated by the bushmen should receive special consideration by the Committee of Selection, as nothing would more powerfully convince him that the library really belonged to himself and his mates than to find that he could name a work and have it added to the library; and, to facilitate choice, a catalogue of good and useful works should be freely distributed. Much more might be said on this subject, but we forbear. The idea is a good one, and we hope the result will be the circulation of a sound and healthy literature throughout our outlying districts."

The following shows the first practical effort made towards this object :—

South Australian Bush Book Society.

Committee :—J. H. Angas, Esq., M.P., Neville Blyth, Esq., J.P., S. Davenport, Esq., J.P., Hon. Thos. Elder, M.L.C., J. A. Fergusson, Esq., Thomas Giles, Esq., J.P., Henry Giles, Esq., J. A. Hartley, Esq., George Main, Esq., Henry Scott, Esq., J.P., F. W. Stokes, Esq., J.P., T. D. Smeaton, Esq., J.P., Clement Sabine, Esq., H. H. Turton, Esq., J.P., C. B. Young, Esq.

[Circular.]

"Sir—At a meeting held in Mr. Henry Scott's office, in Adelaide, for the purpose of forming a society for the circulation in the bush of suitable books and periodicals, it was resolved to apply to gentlemen connected with the squatting interest, and others who might be likely to aid in the contemplated work, for their assistance in forming a fund for the purchase of books and for such other help in carrying out the undertaking as it may be in their power to give.

"It is proposed to have a central depôt in Adelaide, and as soon as practicable branches at the various outside townships, and to arrange a system of distribution and circulation among the stations.

"It is intended to make the society self-supporting, and not to seek aid from those not immediately interested in the matter, *except in establishing a fund for the purchase of a stock of books in the first instance.*

"The substitution of books of a healthy tone in place of those now mostly in circulation in the bush being a matter of national importance, the committee think that they may fairly seek aid from all classes in commencing the work; but, when once started, they will look to the readers themselves for the means of continuing the supply.

"In being asked to contribute towards this object, you are requested to do so without special reference to any particular district or station, but with a view to the general good; nor can the committee bind themselves to supply any particular locality from the circumstance of their having received donations from it, although they will make every exertion to accommodate those who show a willingness to help in the work.

"Your early reply, and a remittance of any sum you are willing to contribute, will oblige, in order that the work may be commenced at once.

"I have the honour to be, Sir,
"Your obedient servant,

"Hon. Sec. *pro. tem.*"

In the month of July, 1872, the Hon. Superintendent of the Bushmen's Club was requested to report to the Board of Management that a resolution was passed at the last meeting of the Bush Book Association to apply to the Committee of the Club to take the matter in hand, and blend its affairs with those of the Club.

The following note bearing upon this subject is taken from the Minute Book, August 1, 1872 :—

"A proposal was submitted from the Committee of the Bushmen's Book Association to hand over the donations promised (to the Association) to the Bushmen's Club for the purposes contemplated by the Book Association. The proposal was agreed to by the Board of Management."

"HARD DRINKING AS A HABIT AMONG BUSHMEN.
"TO THE EDITOR OF THE 'AUSTRALASIAN.'

"Sir—I was struck by some remarks in your journal the other day, occurring, I think, in an extract from some other paper, on the prevalence of hard drinking as a habit among bushmen, taking that term to denote the ordinary hands employed by squatters. The writer went on to say that they were and felt, as a class, isolated—no community of feeling between them and their employers, no interest taken in them; couldn't something be done? and so on.

"I agree thoroughly with the writer, that the habit to which he alludes is a great evil; that it is well-nigh invariable among the lower classes of bush labourers. I have always felt great sympathy with these *enfans perdus*, who, as it were, perish in the breach, and over whose corpses the march of civilization passes onward. I have aided them with advice, and occasionally with more substantial assistance; but such aid has nearly always been inoperative. I therefore fear that we must search for the causes of this evil, so universal, so incurable, in the lower strata of our common nature.

"Want of education, want of recreation, and generally what we commonly call 'dulness,' are the chief predisposing causes of drinking in the bush. Not that the first of these disabilities obtains among bush labourers invariably. Many shepherds and ordinary workmen are comparatively highly educated, having fallen from higher positions. They subscribe for newspapers, they buy books, yet they have contracted the fatal habit, and in their intervals of leisure are among the most hopeless drunkards. The rank and file are uneducated; their general barrenness of mind, their periods (often protracted) of toilsome monotony, or monotony without labour, lead to an uneasy, depressing, half conscious sense of dulness, which alcohol in excess certainly relieves for the time, with what certain though delayed injury to mind and body let physicians and philantbropists decide.

"It must also be borne in mind that we are dealing with Anglo-Saxons and Anglo-Celts by birth or descent, and thus descended from those northern races which have always been notorious for hard work and hard drinking. It would seem to be a rule that all classes of men who lead irregular lives, lives in which there are irregular allotments of labour—danger, privation, and repose—are given to hard drinking. Sailors, lumber-men, navvies, hunters, and savages all come under this category.

"When I admit that the practice is all but invariable among all classes of bush labourers, I except the younger men. Many of these—our best and highest class of labour at certain seasons—are the sons of small farmers in the more populous districts. Many of them are freeholders themselves. They are sober, hard working, and generally economical. They have a settled purpose for which to labour and to save, and are neither reckless or desperate like their older comrades. 'The old hands,' as they are often called, know themselves but too well, and in law they are slaves, in fact *adscripti glebæ*. They know from years of experience that the next public-house is the mælstrom into which they must be swept—that inevitable hell from which they will emerge penniless to face another year's work, another year's loneliness, as the case may be.

"All this is very 'sad, bad, and mad,' as Mr. Browning hath it ; but still I do not see that squatters and managers are open to any of the blame which your writer evidently hints that they deserve. On most of the stations—particularly the larger ones—the men are comfortably housed and very well fed ; their wages afford them many small luxuries; newspapers and books are lent to them ; and they are encouraged and advised to save their money. More than this is not done, and I contend that more cannot be done. If sick, they are cared for ; and in most of the larger bush towns there are excellent hospitals, where they are taken in for long periods, and provided with lodging and medical treatment gratuitously. These hospitals are largely supported by the subscriptions of squatters, though the men contribute fairly also. Again, I ask, what more can be done?

" We cannot, by way of diminishing the feeling of isolation, ask the station hands to dinner, Professor Kingsley notwithstanding. Nor can we permit them the unrestricted run of our kitchens. Paterfamilias in London demurs to indiscriminate hospitality to Policeman X, or the man-at-arms of the period, from prudential reasons. The same reasons govern us.

" I have sketchily thrown together some of the facts and ideas bearing on this important subject. I have alluded to the causes as they have presented themselves to me after many years' experience and some thought on the subject. But the remedy I cannot say that I have discovered with any show of certainty. More education, more recreation—were these procurable, something might be gained from the enemy. It may be, that with a more concentrated population, habits more domestic, and dispositions more open to gentleness, gaiety, and harmless excitement may be developed among our workmen. But, I fear me, that for many years the great army of 'roving men' that must tend and shear the flocks of Australia Deserta will be Arabs in everything but temperance.

"Yours, &c.,
"ISHMAEL."

"THE BUSHMAN.
"TO THE EDITOR OF THE 'AUSTRALASIAN.'

"Instant her circling wand the goddess waves,
To hogs transforms them, and the sty receives."

" Sir—I have read 'Ishmael's' letter with much attention, and, with your permission, will endeavour to point out how the class of bushmen might be ameliorated without asking them to dinner. Had I not carried my swag, and looked for work in New Zealand, Queensland, New South Wales, and Victoria, I should not have the experience, or have gained the knowledge, and perhaps, I may add, the private history of families that I possess. In the first place I would suggest to squatters to improve the accommodation they give to their working men. Many a station hut is filthy in the extreme. Never listen to men who yarn about their fellow-workmen, but dismiss on the spot the tale-bearer. The practice of jacketing makes incalculable mischief. I know by experience that gentlemen squatters do not yarn concerning their men's merit, but others who are not gentlemen do, and to a large extent. Permit no grog on the station. Have a weekly service, and create debating classes on large stations, and show that you are interested in the welfare of your men. All squatters know that when men are comfortable they will remain, and not want a change, except perhaps a visit to Melbourne or the nearest township yearly, and then will return again to work, and work all the better for their trip (after the first few days). In the townships those unlicensed public-houses called boarding-houses should be closely watched. The keepers of these houses and the keepers of some of the lower class of public-houses are the leeches who suck the life-blood of the bushman, and fatten like dung-flies on his cheque. The liquor supplied by these worthies is not often in the state supplied by the brewer or the spirit merchant. They simply sell poison flavoured to taste like brandy, gin, &c. The maddening effects of these drinks tend to fill our lunatic asylums, and occasionally offer a victim to the scaffold. Until a law is enforced for the punishment of the sale of adulterated spirits, and sly grog shops abolished, the bushman will be the victim of these people. Above all, in large townships, and even in Melbourne, create homes for men out of employment on the principle of sailors' homes, with a registry attached. The establishment of these places would pay well, and the further they are built from the public-house the better.

"I write from experience about boarding-houses in the bush.

"A CARTHUSIAN."

"OUR BUSH POPULATION.

"TO THE EDITOR OF THE 'AUSTRALASIAN.'

"Sir—Your correspondent "Ishmael," in your issue of September 19, does something towards keeping alive attention to the present unsatisfactory state of our bush labouring population. With nearly all his facts I am quite willing to coincide. With his wishes for the formation among them of 'more domestic habits, and of dispositions more open to gentleness, gaiety, and harmless excitement,' I also heartily concur; but from his conclusion that a little more education and recreation are all we can do to mend matters, I most emphatically dissent.

"My hopes are not so Utopian as to anticipate that by any possible alteration of the system of treating our bush hands we will convert them as a class from roving, dissipated, discontented drudges, to frugal, reputable, and cheerful assistants; but I do hope that by gradual alteration of that system we may improve the position of some of them to such an extent as to induce emulation among the rest.

"I am not one of those who would lay all the blame of the men's present mode of life at the doors of the squatters and managers. They themselves are victims of the present situation. A few of them make spasmodic efforts to correct it; but, like 'Ishmael,' soon relapse into the can't-be-helped cry, and resign themselves to await the arrival of a *Deus ex machina*. I think, however, your correspondent must have been connected with some exceptionally philanthropic settlers to find such attention as he speaks of bestowed on the men. I am pretty well acquainted with the working of more than a hundred stations in Victoria and New South Wales, and I do not know half-a-dozen where such attentions are the rule. The undisputed facts, however, are, that our bushmen (as a class) take no interest in their employer or their employment, that unless 'dogged' they neglect their work, that dissipation and vagabondism act among them as recruiting sergeants for the hospitals, the gaols, and the paupers' graveyards, and that the few married men among them are by their mode of life contributing a rising generation whose future is beset with danger and uncounteracted temptation.

"Anxiety to evoke the opinions of others, and not any dogmatic belief in my own nostrums, lead me to offer a few suggestions for the amelioration of this state of affairs. The first is, that until we can get our patients sufficiently long settled with us to be operated upon (if you like the word), we cannot expect by any fugitive treatment to correct a chronic disease. To a good man there is no such anchor as home, and no home is so dear as one made by their own hands. Most stations are erected on the portion of the run most likely to repay a little cultivation, whether in garden or paddock, and most settlers hold by purchase a section or two round their houses. Let them get over that grasping feeling which grudges a patch of earth to another, and on favourable places round their homestead mark out ten or twenty-acre blocks, and sell or give long leases of these to the best and steadiest men they can find. Every hour's labour that these men bestow on their plots is another bond between them and the place. Every shilling that they expend on improvements is a shilling kept back from publican's poison.

"The squatter will certainly be poorer by the grass of six or ten sheep, but his work will be done for him by a man having an interest to do it well. Mutual forbearance and kindly feeling will in time convert eye-service into heart-service; the comfort of the three or four men settled round the home station will be an inducement to the others to acquire a similar position, and a standing protest against the wretchedness of the 'wallaby track.' In a few families so formed, one of the mothers may be able to give rudimentary education to the children of the others; another may help her husband's earnings by keeping for sale a few pounds' worth of the small store and knicknacks not usually found in a station store; another might keep a sort of boarding-house for the single men and casual labourers, of which more anon.

"Next, let us see if the squatter can do anything to induce habits of forethought and economy among the men. At present they know that a junk of meat and a bit of damper will be ready for them at a certain time without any care of their own, and that, however wasteful, they will never be hungry. They see no money and never use it. Their cheque comes to them in a lump, and they abuse it. The very accumulation of their pay is often an inducement to them to give warning, or to 'work for the sack,' so that they may handle the representative of their earnings. To meet this, I believe the boldest innovation is required, a little troublesome perhaps at first, but perfectly feasible. Make the men their own bankers and their own providers. Discontinue payment by rations entirely. Add the equivalent to the current wages, and pay them as far as practicable every week. Allow them to organise their own messes, or to board with a married fellow-workman, as they may prefer. As soon as possible get rid of station storekeeping and all store accounts, and let the men learn by their stomachs, the most powerful of all reasoners, that if they are not themselves thrifty they will be hungry. At the same time let it be the rule that travellers shall not be gratuitously fed, and that loafers and sturdy beggars must betake themselves elsewhere. I feel convinced that these alterations would, in the course of twelve months, shut up half of the public-houses in the country, and that the houses so shut would be those kept by the least respectable of the publican fraternity. The dissipated among the men will be the least careful for some time. Their food and clothes will cost them more, and if inclined to drink, they will have less money to spend, and after spending it all, they will be taught by hunger to be more careful next time. The objectors to this will come out with the stereotyped bugbear of these men then killing sheep, firing the grass, and robbing huts. Of course, some of them will. Was there ever any good unaccompanied by some evil? Surely the improvement, however gradual, of the bulk of our men, to say nothing of the actual saving of £100 to £500 a year for rations now extorted by loafers and drunkards for the sole benefit of publicans, is some equivalent for the exercise of a little extra vigilance in the protection of our own property. Every criminal caught in these acts should be rigorously prosecuted, and every insolvent loafer made practically acquainted with the working of the Vagrant Act and the discipline of the gaol.

"Another matter that is within the power of settlers is, by improving the accommodation provided for the men, to civilise their tastes, to make them fond of the comfort accompanying lengthened permanent employment, and to make it contrast more favourably with the tramp consequent on dismissal. Sooth to say, the contrast at present is not great. Food is extorted often in greater quantities than necessary. An eight or ten mile saunter in fine weather is no great hardship, and on three hundred nights out of the three hundred and sixty-five a camp-fire in the open air is infinitely preferable to a sheepskin in a bug-infested, stinking, leaky, smoky men's hut.

"Some nice critic will feel shocked at such a description. Depend upon it he has never been on the 'wallaby track.' I have. On 'Ishmael's' model stations books and newspapers are provided for the huts. I am glad to hear it, but think it would be better to encourage the men to combine to procure them for themselves. In a majority of the huts I am acquainted with, it would be hard to find a place light enough to read them in without joining the circle of card players; and such a place found, it would require considerable powers of abstraction to understand them amid the foul language and 'cute dodges that are occupying the attention of the other lodgers.

"So far I have only tried to show that we can help ourselves. But there are some other possibly remedial measures that are in the province of the Government. The first of these is the system of licensing public-houses. Let a higher standard of house and householders be insisted on, increase the license-fee, and make an annual certificate from the police, endorsed by the local bench, an absolute necessity for the issue of a renewal of license. Let the opening of unnecessary houses be opposed as tending to substitute two or three badly kept dens of rowdiness for one well-to-do and welcome inn. Make it one of the penalties of the Publicans' Act, that after a certain number of complaints a policeman be quartered in the house, and let the clauses against supplying drink to men already drunk be strictly enforced.

"There are other ways in which Government might help powerfully, though less directly; but to them I shall barely allude. The settlement of the men is an important question, but the settlement of the masters is no less so. While the master holds under a tenure so uncertain as the present land law, self-interest is all-powerful in compelling him to get all he can out of his station in the four or five or ten years that are assured to him, if such a term can be used where his whole run might be free selected between breakfast and dinner. Did the masters see a prospect of a portion of their runs, however small, forming a home for themselves and descendants, they would think more of the servants they were destined to spend their lives with. With most of them the present idea is—after me the deluge.

"Again, Government might secure the chance to the working man of getting a patch of land in the neighbourhood of his work, independent of the will of an occasional selfish owner. It might set apart a section here and there as an endowment for future schools. It might enact a compulsory school and hospital rate; or it might carry on public works in the districts that contribute so large a part of the revenues now devoured by the metropolitan maw. It might promise to do all this, and a great deal more, but will it do anything? Lord Macaulay once said—'If, then, there be an end to which Government is bound to attain, if there are two ways only of attaining it, if one of these ways is by elevating the moral and intellectual character of the people, and the other way is by inflicting pain, who can doubt which way every

Government ought to take?' Nobody; but I have very little doubt of our colonial Governments finding a third way—that is, drawing their salaries regularly, and doing nothing unless compelled. My hopes for the improvement of the condition of our fellow-bushmen lie not in Government, but in the neighbourly feeling of thoughtful and conscientious masters.

"Yours, &c.,

"VIDETTE."

"BUSH TRAVELLERS.

"TO THE EDITOR OF THE 'AUSTRALASIAN.'

"Sir—If you have room for the accompanying perhaps you will insert it. As long as squatters make a practice of hiring men in the bush, they must feed travellers, or ought to do so; and from my practical experience I can believe a shy man would come off badly, travelling in winter, subsisting on a diurnal ration of one pound of flour, seldom meat, and often without tea.

"The 'Peripatetic' is too hard, much, on the swagsman. How many in this colony are there who have carried their swags and looked for a job, and now may be seen in affluence? Were they loafers? *Ex uno disce omnes* is exploded long ago. Every one knows that there are loafers in the bush as well as in town, but it is too hard to say that all men who say they are looking for work should be treated as loafers.

"Knife-and-fork stations are few and far between, a pint of flour and a little tea and sugar being given on most stations, but no meat; when meat is given, then the tea and sugar are withheld. The fat wether days are gone. A little more than a year ago I worked with a survey party, and saw plenty of men who lamented that the good old days had passed, and that on the best station in the west (for travellers) seven pints of flour was the allowance for travellers, even if there were twenty.

"Before concluding, I believe there are some few stations open for travellers, and a hearty welcome afforded. A very good anecdote is told of one western squatter, when asked to join others in starving travellers, who replied, 'Be Jasus, if

I don't feed them, Biddy will.' I have laid my swag away and settled, but I do not like to see men abused because there are many bad in the crowd.

"Yours, &c.,
"CARTHUSIAN."

"BUSH TRAVELLERS.

"TO THE EDITOR OF THE 'AUSTRALASIAN.'

"Sir—I am glad to see that attention has been drawn to the vexed question of bush travellers, better known as 'swagsmen.' The letters of your correspondents 'Vidette' and 'Carthusian' serve to indicate the difference of opinion as to how these men should be treated; while the first would resolutely decline to feed travellers, the latter contends that squatters 'must or ought to feed them, at any rate so long as they make a practice of hiring men in the bush.'

"In answer to this last I will speak for myself, and I dare say many others, that I would most willingly forego the advantage of labour brought in this fashion to one's door, because for every man engaged, I have a penalty of fifty other men imposed on me whom I don't want, but who, nevertheless, all expect to be fed at my expense. I am quite sure most settlers would willingly travel a considerable distance to engage the men, could any plan be carried out to establish bush homes or depôts. The subject is one of considerable moment to this young country, and merits the attention of legislators, as well as of the more immediately interested settlers. I notice that one of your leading articles in the last issue is devoted to the subject of immigration, and there we are told that there is room for any number of people out here; and surely no sane person will dispute that this country is capable of supporting a far larger population; but then we must deal with things as they are, and to pour an additional number of working men in upon us at present would, I think, but add to the grievance complained of. Very few will deny that many of those who have been wandering in search of employment are men both able and willing to work. It is no use blinking the question by summing them up as a parcel of loafers; this answers no good purpose, and will never help us out of the difficulty. I have had occasion to hire several men during the past few months; they were all glad to get employment, and, excepting one or two, proved themselves steady workers. Nor does the dearth of employment arise from the excessive rate of wages. I don't think many will be found to say that the price of unskilled labour is too high with us, and I've mostly remarked that the men most ready to cut down wages are the last to take advantage of the reduction by employing more labour.

"The causes of this surplus of bone and sinew have been ably traced in one of your leading articles. Gold digging entailed its good and evil; but I think our Government has much to answer for in the present unsatisfactory condition of the poor man. Stopping supplies, and thereby causing a cessation of public works, has helped to keep the poor still poorer, and made many a poor fellow carry a swag for the first time. Shearing and washing will occupy a good many for a time, and the harvest will require an extra number of hands, but when that is over, a similar state of things will recur, and the same bands of men be seen roving about. This is not encouraging, and I wish I could say how to meet the difficulty. Of course, if men were prudent and saved their money, the slack time could be tided over better; but this they won't do, and indeed it is hard to blame them for going to the public-house. In most cases they have no place else to go; once there they become the prey of veritable bloodsuckers, for, as a rule, the class of men who keep public-houses in the bush are most unfit to be licensed; magistrates or police have scarcely any power over them. If by any means homes could be established here and there throughout the country, a most important step would be gained; but how to accomplish this is the question, whether by private enterprise or Government assistance. I think the settlers should do it themselves; eventually, I believe, they would be self-supporting. I have trespassed enough on your space, and humbly offer these remarks for your consideration.

"AN OLD SETTLER.

"P.S.—I may add that at the present time, in the midst of shearing, an unusual number of men are moving about in quest of work. One reason is that water being scarce, very few settlers are washing. While reprobating the poltroonery of feeding loafers 'for fear of being burned out,' I think a better motive might prompt settlers at such a time in giving those who are now travelling something to eat."

"SWAGMEN.

"TO THE EDITOR OF THE 'AUSTRALASIAN.'

"Sir—Permit me to say, with reference to a letter on 'swagmen' in your last issue, that it may be found practicable for shire councils and road boards to afford employment to those who are really anxious for it in slack seasons. Overseers and other appliances might be provided, and such work as clearing, draining, and forming of roads held over to slack seasons. In such circumstances the present demoralising system of indiscriminate feeding of swagmen might cease, as a fair day's wages could be had for a day's work. Corporate bodies can, I believe, undertake work in sections, not exceeding £100 each, by means of day labour. As matters stand at present, these bodies are often competing for labour at thriving seasons, and are not able to afford employment when it is most wanted. I could mention various instances in which road works have been satisfactorily carried out by day labour at less than half the sums demanded by contractors.

"I am, &c.,

"A SQUATTER."

"STATION HUTS.

"TO THE EDITOR OF THE 'AUSTRALASIAN.'

"Sir—Now that our squatters are at rest as to the disposal of the public lands, now that the paralysing cloud of uncertainty is cleared away from their horizon, is it not time that many of them turned their thoughts to the state of the dwelling-places on their stations for their men, properly called 'huts'? Sheepwashes, yards, woolsheds, fences, dams, wells, &c., are being attended to; shall we not ask that these huts be also improved?

"No one at all familiar with the up-country station huts can for a moment question the need of improvement. The need is urgent. The cry of the working men on stations is loud and bitter for better accommodation.

"The Legislature enjoins its officers (the police or other functionaries) to examine the factory, the workshop, and the lodgings of the innkeeper. I must say that it is high time that some such power of inspection be granted for the huts of our stations. No words may exaggerate the wretchedness of some of these station huts.

"Let me draw the picture of one in which a family of five are now living, on a station which brings in many thousands a year to an owner, without mortgage or debt of any sort. It is a hut 12 x 16, made of logs, the walls seven feet high, the floor like the road for dust (it was in summer when I saw it last), while in winter, of course, there is mud. The window is a pane of glass, the door some rough battens between which you may put your finger, the chimney tumbling down. In this place the woman must wash and cook, and the family must sleep and eat. The roof is of bark, letting the daylight in, while the logs are so rotten that they absorb the rain, and keep everything damp the winter through.

"Near by is a square hole some few feet deep, into which in winter is drained the surface water, and with it goes the droppings of the goats, the hens, and the dogs. This is their summer beverage, so thick that they must strain it through muslin, and then so bad that a thirsty man in February can hardly put his lips to it. Such, I assure you, Sir, is no overdrawn picture of some of our bush huts in which young colonists are born, cradled, and brought up.

"A 'men's hut' at a home station is the home of the bullock-driver, the ploughman, the boundary-rider, the carpenter, and of the other men—from one to forty—who may be employed on the station. If there are any men at all working throughout the year, the men's hut is their abode.

"I am glad to say that there is an improvement in these men's huts, but they are as yet miserable places for the most part for the home of regular hands on a station. They are too often filthy in the extreme. The usual habit is to hang the sheep for the day's supper nigh the breakfast table; men's huts are often thus like butcher shops on a small scale. Too often the hut has no divisions; the men eat, sleep, and drink all in the one apartment, while the cook has his work to do at the fire-place in the same room.

"There is a want of light in winter and ventilation in summer, or possibly there is too much of both, for the roof may leak, and the shrunken logs may never be filled in.

"I want to see whitewash in these huts, and soap, and windows, and a sleeping-room, and an eating-room, and a safe. Indeed, I want the decencies of civilisation to be observed. I want no master or manager to be able to say, 'I have not been in my men's huts for a year.' I want movable benches, so that men may not need to sit on buckets turned up when they draw to the fire in winter.

"You have before heard of the shearing huts. These are used only for the short season of shearing. I pity the decent and respectable in these places. Where perhaps thirty to a hundred men assemble, you must calculate on a few foul-mouthed, abominable characters, whose every sentence is embellished with an oath.

"I think that there should certainly be a sort of choice left where the number exceeds thirty or so, and that there should be two huts or more, so that the more moral might perhaps escape the misery of having their ears polluted with obscenity, their Sunday night's rest broken in on by gaming and such-like profligacy. I think it is cruel to our young men to force them to associate with such men as are invariably found at the woolsheds.

"I do not ask for well-built, well-fitted huts to be used for such a short season, but I do say that there ought not to be that excessive over-crowding so common, where men are compelled to sleep among the bales in the shed, or anywhere to the danger of health of body or health of morals.

"Indeed, Sir, I hope to see our station men more cared for, and I feel sure that they will learn in time on their part to care for their masters; at present there is nothing but discontent in the master's office with the master against his men, and in the hut with men against the master.

round their skins, so tight that the cord is sunk into the flesh. They are continually asking for medicine, of which castor oil is their favourite. It is wonderful to see with what gusto they drink it, and how they smack their lips afterwards. They are generous to the very last morsel, and are otherwise willing to assist, as they say, 'white fellow.' I have heard it asserted that the blacks have no idea of a future state. Nothing is more erroneous; they have a perfect belief in future rewards and punishments. 'Buckin boree' (the white devil) will take them down to his hole and eat them, if they do wrong; while 'Deoe' (God) will take them to his everlasting rest if they act right. They also believe that their doctor and law-giver can bring rain when he likes. He is a great man with them, and presides over the ceremony of what is erroneously called 'making young men'; but which is in reality a sort of making of Freemasons. Their lodges are well laid out, in length from east to west, in breadth from north to south. Their emblematic devices are carved on trees. The candidate is met by a guide who conducts him to the lodge, and after initiation a front tooth is knocked out. No white man, as I am told, was ever yet permitted to see this ceremony. The black race is fast disappearing, even on the Paroo, our habits and customs not seeming to agree with them; and they are often badly treated even for the most trivial offence, and sometimes horsewhipped when they don't deserve it."

"AN ADVENTURE IN THE SCRUB.
*   *   *   *

"I had occasion to travel from the Black Swamp to Mount Drummond, on the sea coast. The road (called so by courtesy, though really only a rough bush track) avoided the scrub, and ran round the base of the Marble Ranges, following slightly the coast line. This, though a pleasanter way, was a much longer one than might be found, and as my business was urgent, I determined to scrub it. By leaving the road at a spring called the Fountain, a straight line could be struck through a gap in the Marble Ranges, and Mount Drummond reached at a saving of twenty miles.

Though the distance was much shortened by taking this route, few ever travelled it, in consequence of the scarcity of water and the necessity for each one to strike out his own track. A friend, knowing my hurry, advised me to try it, and gave me the necessary directions for finding the watering places, three of which lay between the Fountain and Mount Drummond. I therefore rolled up my swag and started on my journey.

"My first day's march brought me to the Fountain—not an inn, be it remembered, replete with all creature comforts, but a spring—and such a spring. I merged from the scrub on the evening of my hot day's march upon one of the most lovely spots I ever beheld. In the distance to the north lay the Marble Ranges, the waving woods that covered its slopes glittering in the rays of the declining sun; to the west a dense forest extended to the coast; and to the east and north-east a vast sea of scrub reposed, bounded to the view by the horizon alone. The gem of the scene lay, however, close before me, like an oasis in the desert. In the centre of a small patch of grass, most refreshingly green, was a very small lake, glittering like a diamond in a setting of emeralds. A shea-oak or two, with their beautiful drooping foliage, stood on its banks, and an ancient gum, which, though its head was still verdant, seemed tottering to its fall, reigned monarch of the place. The margin of the pool was fringed with bulrushes, out of which, on my approach, two or three ducks rose with a whir and flew sulkily away. Near the trees was situated the spring which gave the name to the locality. From among the stones, and spouting up to the height of several inches, gushed forth a spring of the purest, coolest, most translucent water. Mournfully musical was the refrain which it sang, and which seemed to be echoed from the rushes around us. The night-forewarning breezes swept in gentle gales among their stems, or rippled the still surface of the waters, as if invisible fairy footsteps were tripping lightly and gaily over the lake. To add life to the scene, a few wild pigeons were either drinking on the margin of the pool, or mournfully cooing in the branches of the gumtree. After quenching my thirst by repeated draughts from the fountain head, I made a fire, and from flour which I had with me made some cakes. After I had satisfied my hunger, I gathered a quantity of dry boughs, with the leaves still upon them, and laid them down as a mattrass, upon which I spread my blanket. To ward off the night-wind, I broke down some green boughs, and placed them scientifically between my bed and the wind. Then I sat down to read a page or two from a book which I always carried with me.

"The calm still night, the gentle sighing of the wind in the featherly foliage of the shea-oaks, the rustling of the reeds, the mourning of the pigeons, and the distant howl of the Australian jackall, exercised a saddening influence upon my mind, and made me feel alone in the world. But as I read a portion of the 23rd Psalm, 'The Lord is my Shepherd,' I felt that His sleepless eye saw me there as I sat, sad and solitary by my little watchfire, and that the hand of His providence was there; and so, confiding in Him, I lay down, and slept calmly and peacefully. I awoke with the first dawn of day, and having indulged in a good wash, made my breakfast, and long ere the sun had risen had started on my way.

"I have already stated that my friend had directed me to cross the saddle between the north block and the Marble Ranges. I should have said that was the direction he ought to have given me; instead, he directed me outside the block altogether, thus placing me in a position of considerable danger. The first day's march was unattended by any particular circumstance. The day was hot, certainly, and the heat was increased by reflection from the hard earth or white sand I had to traverse. Still, it was to be borne, and I manfully struggled on in expectation of a cooling drink when night should find me camped at the next spring. As the day drew to a close, I began to look about anxiously for the accustomed signs of water. None, however, were to be seen. The scrubby rises looked parched and barren; not a forest tree was near, nor a bird to be seen, save where high up in the air an eagle winged his circling flight, perhaps regarding me with wonder, or following my track with the pleasant anticipation of supping off my carcase. I listened in vain for that sure token of the close proximity of water—the sudden whir of a startled pigeon, and mile after mile I travelled, every moment growing more anxious. Hope struggled against the constantly recurring thought that I was off the track, and I fully expected to see at the foot of each rise I crossed the welcome spring. But the night drew on. The sun set amidst coppery clouds, betokening a hot day for the morrow. The stars came twinkling through the heated haze, and the stillness of night settled on everything. Stillness, I said! yes, the stillness of an Australian summer's night, when the locusts make the woods re-echo with their continuous chirping singing note, and when the grasshoppers and crickets, having slept through the heat, burst forth into a mad revelry of noise, at the ascension of cloud-enveloped night to her starry throne. Fearing that in the dark night I might possibly pass the locality of the spring, I determined with a heavy heart to camp; so without lighting a fire I unrolled my bedding, and threw my wearied limbs down until the first dawn of morning should enable me to proceed on my way. When I again started all was quiet. At first the air was cool, but as the sun approached nearer and nearer the horizon, it grew hotter; and when at last he jumped with his fiery face into view, the heat grew oppressive at once. The prospect around me was dreary. Nothing but scrub as far as the eye could reach, save occasional patches of heath, which looked ready to take fire from the lightest spark. Here and there at long intervals a few stunted forest-oaks lifted themselves above the smaller shrubbery, but only to make the scene more solitary by their isolated appearance. But few signs of life were about. Now and then a lizard would run briskly away on my approach, or a snake would cross my path—nothing else was to be seen. I did not observe a single bird, save my companion of the night before, who had taken up his lodgings in the boughs of a dead gum, and who had soared into the air when I commenced my march, and went circling on his way along the track I was pursuing. I looked upon this as a bad omen. It seemed to me as if this bird, seeing my mistake, concluded my certain death and the luxurious repast for him that was to follow. On I marched, still preserving the course given me, the heat increasing as the day advanced. Over the tops of the scrub the warm air dashed in undulating vibrations, and that deceit of the desert—the mirage—spread its barmecide waters occasionally before my path. Towards evening two or three crows flew high over my head in the direction I was steering, and a few dry-looking birds were startled away at my approach. These signs revived me a little. I concluded that water could not be very distant, and that the crows were hastening their way thither. My senses must by this time have become much confused, otherwise I should not have considered such small birds as signs of water. Such birds as those I saw exist upon dew, or upon moist roots gathered from the ground. But so it was; each time a bird flew out, I fancied water near, and much precious time was lost in searching. Sadly wiser at last I pressed forward, determined to let nothing stop me or turn me aside, as I knew that two days more at the furthest would find me on the coast, and then water was certain. As night set in, with tired limbs, parched throat, and glazing eyes, I entered upon a little gully or further depression, between two small hills. At the bottom of this depression stood three weird shea-oaks, and my eye was struck by something hanging from the branches of one of them, which to my imagination, and in accordance with my desires, appeared to be a signal hung out by some former bushman that water was there. To add to the justness of this conclusion, the gully I was traversing formed itself into a little creek, dry, it was true, where I was, but indicating, as I thought, water lower down. So I hastened my steps, and just as the twilight was darkening into night, I entered upon a little patch of naturally clear ground covered with grass, in the centre of which stood the three shea-oaks around the bed of a dry waterhole, into which the creek entered and where it stopped. But though the dry hole first attracted my attention, it did not absorb it. A noise on my left attracted me, and looking in the direction I saw the gaunt form of a wild dog with glistening eyes and his red skin stretched tightly over his bones, which were painfully apparent. He was gnawing ravenously at something, which, upon scaring him away, I found to be bones—human bones. The truth flashed upon me at once. This poor man had strayed from the track, had found this waterhole, and had found it dry. Unable to travel further, and with the faint hope that somebody would see it, he had hung a portion of his blanket upon a branch in order to attract attention—but in vain. Here now lay all that remained of him—a few bleached bones, gnawed and regnawed by wild dogs, a few particles of dress, and an old quart pot. My heart sickened at the sight, and I laid me down to rest, not knowing but that I might have to keep him company until the last trumpet should summon our dust together, and call us from our lonely retreat into the presence of the Infinite Creator. Such were my thoughts as I lay on my blankets gazing at the stars, which seemed to twinkle so serenely high up above the heavens, and again the words of that psalm came to my mind, 'He shall lead me beside the still waters.' Ah! what visions those words 'still waters' conjured up. I slumbered but uneasily, continually being awakened by the sound of bubbling waters only to be reminded by my parched throat of the 'baseless fabric' they were built upon. The wild dog whom I had startled from his scanty meal kept prowling about, and I had great difficulty in preserving my boots, swag, straps, and provisions from his purloining inclinations. Indeed, on the impulse of the moment, I threw him a piece of damper, when I saw him glaring at me from behind a bush, but the shot scared him away, and I saw him no more. Stiff and unrested I arose with the dawn, and after giving a parting glance at the remains of my unknown bedfellow, started on my last day's tramp. I felt that I could not hold out for more than the day, and I experienced a gloomy satisfaction at knowing that I should have at least one companion in the scrub, that my bones would not be so far from other men's bones. The day was oppressively hot, fearfully so, though a thin mist over the sky prevented the sun's rays beating so powerfully as the day before. Still, the heat was dreadful; every now and then the mirage would open out before me, when the country would appear like one vast lake dotted with islands. So deceptive was the appearance, and so muddled was I with the heat, that I would walk, as it seemed to me, up to my ancles in water, and the delusion would not vanish until I stooped to drink. The day's march was much the same as the previous one, only the pangs were much more intensified. My skin blistered and my tongue swelled until it was too large for my mouth, and protruded between my teeth. A viscid spittle, which I could not discharge, glued my lips together, almost suffocating me, and every attempt to swallow gave intense pain. High above me soared the noble eagle, and trotting behind, with hanging tongue, drooping tail, and panting sides, came the wild dog of the night before. When he came too close, I turned and charged, at which he would run a short distance, only to return again on my track as soon as I resumed my march. The eagle from above sometimes swooped down, and once so closely as to brush me with his wing. As the day wore on my stength lessened, and I staggered along followed by my two companions. As the shades of evening drew on, a slight breeze arose. Oh! how cooling it was to my fevered brow, and how it nerved me for a last trial. I staggered on, my eyes bent upon the ground, and my mind thoroughly bewildered. Suddenly a whirring sound from close to my feet aroused me, and looking up I saw a pigeon fly before me, and lodge upon a little plot of grass, so green and lovely. Then my ears seemed to be suddenly unstopped, and I could hear the cooing of pigeons and the sweet twitting of birds among the branches of a copse of shea-oaks, into which I had unconscientiously strayed. Hastening my steps, I was on the margin of a little basin in the limestone rock, and in another minute was laving my swollen tongue with the water, while my heart was welling up in thankfulness to God for His sparing mercy. Reinvigorated by frequent draughts, and afterwards by a meal of Johnny-cakes, I was enabled to drive away my unwelcome companions, and after a night's refreshing sleep, to proceed on my way. Early next morning I reached the station I was bound for, and concluded one of the most trying passages in my life."

DICK'S MATE.

You ask who's the sick man, Mister ? why, that is my old mate, Jack;
'Tis two year ago come shearin' he'd a fall as hurt his back.
Ye see we was after cattle, an' his horse it warn't half broke,
It rared and kem down a cropper on the roots of an old scrub oak,
An' Jack, the poor dear ole fellow, when we went ter raise him, then
Said ' Let me lie still here, mates, for I never shall ride again.'
And that were the truth, sir, surely, for ever since that there time
Quite helpless he has been lyin' up in that ole hut of mine.
Most of them wanted ter send him to the hospital ; but no,
I sed as I meant ter keep him, and I wouldn't let him go.
So I got the Boss ter order some cushions an' things from town ;
And Jack shan't want for nothin', not while Dick hev got a crown.
'Twould hev bin mean if I hedn't stood to him in his sore need,
For, but thanks to old Jack only, I'd hev given the crows a feed.
As it was 'twere a close shave rather, an' believe me when I say
If it warn't for my poor mate yonder, I'd not hev bin here to-day.
How that was, I see you'd ask me: I will tell you then the tale,
How he from a death once saved me, that would make the boldest quail.
But at that time I am certain you wouldn't ever have found
A stronger chap than Jack Joiner in all the wide country round—
A real fine, great, handsome feller, no more like that poor wreck there,
Propped up in the pillers yonder, than a bandicoot's like a bear ;
An' he everywhere was reckoned the ringer of all the sheds,
From Moolna on to Mooranga, and right to the Reedy Beds.
Well, me and him was a making from the Mulga Billabong,
For the shearin' here at Moolna, an' the tramp was dry and long ;
So we started on our journey by the back track through the scrub,
We had one canteen of water, an' a tidy store of grub.
We made the well by the guandongs, the place we had meant to stop,
Next day soon after dinner time ; 'twas dry to the smallest drop !
So then there was nothing for us, but to push on while we could
For the tank on the track to Cooper's, where the old out-station stood ;
It would make our way much longer, by some thirteen mile, but then
We thought there was no help for it, so we started on again.
But I tell ye, sir, 'twas the worstest thing we ever could have tried,
For 'twas sundown when we reached it, an' the tank was choked an' dried.
As soon as I fairly saw it, all my brain seemed turning round,
An' I got quite sick an' dizzy, and fell senseless on the ground.
When I came back to my senses, Jack was holdin' up my head ;
The fool, like a girl, was crying, for he thought as I was dead.
When once more I tried to travel, I found that I couldn't stand,

An' again I should have fallen, but for my poor mate's strong hand.
I'd been ill before we started, an' the drouth hed done me up,
But I knew he could make to Moolna without another sup.
I wanted him to leave me, but do you think the chap 'ud start ;
He swore we was mates for the journey, an' that we wouldn't part ;
So he jest stooped down, and put me up on to his brawny back,
An' leaving our swags in the mallee, starts off on the station track.
An' I tell ye, sir, he bore me right on through that desert wild,
To within five miles of Moolna, like a mother her ailing child ;
Then at last his great strength failed him, an' he tottered to the
   ground,
And fell right there in the dray track, an' I couldn't bring him round.
So there we laid both together, right under the burning sun :
It seemed as our journey was ended, an' our tramp for ever done.
But Providence must have started Black Bill with the bullock dray,
Going out with the shepherd's rations, to travel along that way ;
An' there on the sand he found us, myself quite gone in the head,
An' Jack, in a faint with weariness, lying as though he was dead.
So that is the reason, Mister, why I sticks to my poor old mate,
For ye see 'twas him who saved me that day from my dreadful fate.

   *   *   *   *   *   *   *   *

A burden ? Oh ! bless ye no, sir, I've managed quite well till now ;
No, thank you. I don't take money, that cannot be done no how.

THE BUSHMAN'S LAMENT.

This wilderness and bush of ours
  Is but a lonely spot,
Where scentless bloom the dingy flowers,
  And wild birds warble not.
And, passing through the sylvan scene,
  The traveller finds no shade
From fiery suns his head to screen
  In forest, plain, or glade.

But feeble streams roll threads of brine
  Through pastures bleak and dry ;
No gurgling brooks, no silver streams
  Relieve the weary eye.
And if you lie upon the ground,
  Where wattles sometimes bloom,
Ten thousand ants will soon surround,
  To make one fret and fume.

And if you slumber in the woods
  That lie around salt lakes,
And listen to the stir of life
  As day on darkness breaks—
And hear the wond'rous melodies
  (Not soon will one forget)
That rise within these ancient woods
  When suns arise or set—

A melody of restlessness
  That brings the morning's woes,
The countless hum of blowflies' wings,
  The sting of mosquitoes.
The *blackbird's* voice is strangely rich :
  His never varied song
Is *Caw, Caw, Caw*, in croaking notes,
  That last the whole day long.

But chief among them is the sound,
  So weird-like, deep and clear,
The magpie daily hurls around
  Upon the morning air.
And crawling melancholy forth
  From sheepskins, half asleep,
The shepherd lights his morning pipe,
  And follows spoony sheep.

Yes, tuneful birds and scented flowers
  Are few and far between ;
And pleasant sights and happy hours
  Can here be never seen.
Among the sombre old gum trees
  A swagsman came along,
And speaking forth such words as these
  He sang this doleful song.

William Kyffin Thomas, Printer, Grenfell-street, Adelaide.

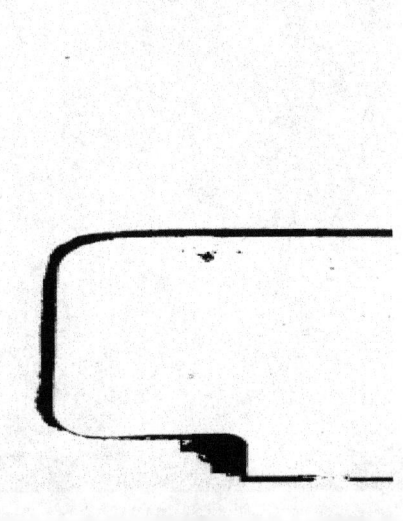

Check Out More Titles From HardPress Classics Series In this collection we are offering thousands of classic and hard to find books. This series spans a vast array of subjects – so you are bound to find something of interest to enjoy reading and learning about.

Subjects:
Architecture
Art
Biography & Autobiography
Body, Mind &Spirit
Children & Young Adult
Dramas
Education
Fiction
History
Language Arts & Disciplines
Law
Literary Collections
Music
Poetry
Psychology
Science
…and many more.

Visit us at www.hardpress.net

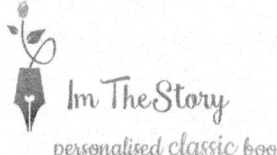

Im TheStory
personalised classic books

"Beautiful gift.. lovely finish.
My Niece loves it, so precious!"

Helen R Brumfieldon

★★★★★

UNIQUE GIFT

FOR KIDS, PARTNERS AND FRIENDS

Timeless books such as:

Alice in Wonderland • The Jungle Book • The Wonderful Wizard of Oz
Peter and Wendy • Robin Hood • The Prince and The Pauper
The Railway Children • Treasure Island • A Christmas Carol

Romeo and Juliet • Dracula

Visit
Im TheStory.com
and order yours today!

CPSIA information can be obtained
at www.ICGtesting.com
Printed in the USA
BVHW081808220819
556561BV00019B/4241/P